4th Celtic Language Technology Workshop (CLTW 4)

Held at LREC 2022

Marseille, France
20 - 25 June 2022

Editors:

Theodorus Fransen
William Lamb
Delyth Prys

ISBN: 978-1-7138-6114-0

Printed from e-media with permission by:

Curran Associates, Inc.
57 Morehouse Lane
Red Hook, NY 12571

Some format issues inherent in the e-media version may also appear in this print version.

Association for Computational Linguistics
209 N. Eighth Street
Stroudsburg, Pennsylvania 18360

Phone: 1-570-476-8006
Fax: 1-570-476-0860

acl@aclweb.org

Additional copies of this publication are available from:

Curran Associates, Inc.
57 Morehouse Lane
Red Hook, NY 12571 USA
Phone: 845-758-0400
Fax: 845-758-2633
Email: curran@proceedings.com
Web: www.proceedings.com

LREC 2022 Workshop
Language Resources and Evaluation Conference
20-25 June 2022

4th Celtic Language Technology Workshop
(CLTW 4)

PROCEEDINGS

Editors:
Theodorus Fransen, William Lamb and Delyth Prys

Proceedings of the 4th Celtic Language Technology Workshop at LREC 2022 (CLTW 4)

Edited by:
Theodorus Fransen, William Lamb and Delyth Prys

EAN: 9791095546733

For more information:
European Language Resources Association (ELRA)
9 rue des Cordelières
75013, Paris
France
http://www.elra.info
Email: lrec@elda.org

Preface

These proceedings include the programme and papers presented at the 4th Celtic Language Technology Workshop (CLTW 4), co-located with the Language Resources and Evaluation Conference (LREC) in Marseille, June 2022.

In Classical times, Celtic languages were found across a wide swathe of modern Eurasia. Today, they are spoken in regions of the UK, France and Ireland, as well as in emigrant communities in Argentina and Canada. The modern languages are: Breton, Cornish, Irish, Manx, Scottish Gaelic and Welsh. Although the hereditary communities of these languages are small compared to those of most other European languages, they continue to have a vibrant presence in their traditional areas as well as in urban centres. While Irish is the only Celtic language that has official EU language status (since 2007), Welsh, Gaelic and Manx have co-official status. Breton and Cornish also have some limited status in their home regions. That said, all Celtic languages face the same issue in lacking natural language processing (NLP) resources to ensure continued technology support in the digital era.

Until recently, the Celtic languages lagged behind in the areas of NLP and applied language technology. Consequently, research and resource provision for this language group was poor. In recent years, however, some Celtic languages have been able to benefit from improved provisions for under-resourced languages in academia and the tech industry. Some now also have dedicated research teams working on language and speech processing technologies and related resources. The CLTW community and workshop, inaugurated at COLING (Dublin) in 2014, provides a forum to help connect these researchers and their associates to one another, to disseminate cutting-edge work and to raise the profile of Celtic language technology, more generally.

The accepted papers cover an extremely wide range of topics, including: computer-assisted language learning (CLL); automatic speech recognition (ASR), handwriting recognition; speech synthesis; syntactic parsing; part-of-speech tagging; NLP with mediaeval languages and coreference resolution.

We thank our invited speaker, Prof Kevin Scannell of Saint Louis University. We also thank our authors and presenters for their hard work, and workshop attendees for their participation. We are also very grateful to our programme committee for reviewing and providing invaluable feedback on the work published.

The CLTW 4 Workshop Organisers

Dr Theodorus Fransen, National University of Ireland, Galway
Prof William Lamb, The University of Edinburgh
Prof Delyth Prys, Bangor University

Organisers

Theodorus Fransen, National University of Ireland, Galway
William Lamb, The University of Edinburgh
Delyth Prys, Bangor University

Programme Committee

Beatrice Alex, The University of Edinburgh
Colin Batchelor, Royal Society of Chemistry
Ann Foret, Université Rennes 1
John Judge, ADAPT, Dublin City University
Teresa Lynn, Dublin City University
Mark McConville, University of Glasgow
John P. McCrae, National University of Ireland, Galway
Marieke Meelen, University of Cambridge
Ailbhe Ní Chasaide, Trinity College Dublin
Neasa Ní Chiaráin, Trinity College Dublin
Brian Ó Raghallaigh, Fiontar, Dublin City University
Thierry Poibeau, Laboratoire Lattice, CNRS, École Normale Supérieure, Sorbonne Nouvelle
Kevin Scannell, Saint Louis University
Elaine Uí Dhonnchadha, Trinity College Dublin
Monica Ward, Dublin City University
Pauline Welby, Laboratoire Parole et Langage, CNRS, Aix Marseille Université
David Willis, University of Oxford

Additional Reviewers

Adrian Doyle, National University of Ireland, Galway

Invited Speaker

Kevin Scannell, Saint Louis University

Table of Contents

Conference Programme

Monday, June 20, 2022

09:00–09:10 *Welcome*
CLTW organisers

09:10–09:50 *Keynote*
Prof Kevin Scannell, Saint Louis University

09:50–10:15 Oral Session 1

09:50–10:15 *Multilingual Abstract Meaning Representation for Celtic Languages*
Johannes Heinecke and Anastasia Shimorina

10:15–11:00 Coffee Break / Poster Session

10:15–11:00 *Diachronic Parsing of Pre-Standard Irish*
Kevin Scannell

10:15–11:00 *Creation of an Evaluation Corpus and Baseline Evaluation Scores for Welsh Text Summarisation*
Mahmoud El-Haj, Ignatius Ezeani, Jonathan Morris and Dawn Knight

10:15–11:00 *CLILSTORE.EU - A Multilingual online CLIL platform*
Caoimhín Ó Dónaill

10:15–11:00 *Evaluation of Three Welsh Language POS Taggers*
Gruffudd Prys and Gareth Watkins

10:15–11:00 *Iterated Dependencies in a Breton treebank and implications for a Categorial Dependency Grammar*
Annie Foret, Denis Béchet and Valérie Bellynck

10:15–11:00 *Automatic Speech Recognition for Irish: the ABAIR-ÉIST System*
Liam Lonergan, Mengjie Qian, Harald Berthelsen, Andy Murphy, Christoph Wendler, Neasa Ní Chiaráin, Christer Gobl and Ailbhe Ní Chasaide

10:15–11:00 *Development and Evaluation of Speech Recognition for the Welsh Language*
Dewi Jones

Monday, June 20, 2022 (continued)

10:15–11:00 *Handwriting recognition for Scottish Gaelic*
William Lamb, Beatrice Alex and Mark Sinclair

10:15–11:00 *Celtic CALL: strengthening the vital role of education for language transmission*
Neasa Ní Chiaráin, Madeleine Comtois, Oisín Nolan, Neimhin Robinson-Gunning, John Sloan, Harald Berthelsen and Ailbhe Ní Chasaide

10:15–11:00 *Cipher – Faoi Gheasa: A Game-with-a-Purpose for Irish*
Elaine Uí Dhonnchadha, Monica Ward and Liang Xu

10:15–11:00 *Towards Coreference Resolution for Early Irish*
Mark Darling, Marieke Meelen and David Willis

10:15–11:00 *Use of Transformer-Based Models for Word-Level Transliteration of the Book of the Dean of Lismore*
Edward Gow-Smith, Mark McConville, William Gillies, Jade Scott and Roibeard Ó Maolalaigh

10:15–11:00 *Introducing the National Corpus of Irish Project*
Mícheál Ó Meachair, Úna Bhreathnach and Gearóid Ó Cleircín

11:05–11:55 Oral Session 2

11:05–11:30 *BU-TTS: An Open-Source, Bilingual Welsh-English, Text-to-Speech Corpus*
Stephen Russell, Dewi Jones and Delyth Prys

11:30–11:55 *Developing Automatic Speech Recognition for Scottish Gaelic*
Lucy Evans, William Lamb, Mark Sinclair and Beatrice Alex

Monday, June 20, 2022 (continued)

11:55–13:00 Oral Session 3

11:55–12:20 *Handwritten Text Recognition (HTR) for Irish-Language Folklore*
Brian Ó Raghallaigh, Andrea Palandri and Críostóir Mac Cárthaigh

12:20–12:45 *AAC don Ghaeilge: the Prototype Development of Speech-Generating Assistive Technology for Irish*
Emily Barnes, Oisín Morrin, Ailbhe Ní Chasaide, Julia Cummins, Harald Berthelsen, Andy Murphy, Muireann Nic Corcráin, Claire O'Neill, Christer Gobl and Neasa Ní Chiaráin

12:45–13:00 *Valedictory Session*
CLTW organisers

Proceedings of the CLTW 4 @ LREC2022, pages 1–6
Marseille, 20-25 June 2022

Multilingual Abstract Meaning Representation for Celtic Languages

Johannes Heinecke, Anastasia Shimorina
Orange Innovation
22300 Lannion, France
{johannes.heinecke,anastasia.shimorina}@orange.com

Abstract

Deep Semantic Parsing into Abstract Meaning Representation (AMR) graphs has reached a high quality with neural-based seq2seq approaches. However, the training corpus for AMR is only available for English. Several approaches to process other languages exist, but only for high resource languages. We present an approach to create a multilingual text-to-AMR model for three Celtic languages, Welsh (P-Celtic) and the closely related Irish and Scottish-Gaelic (Q-Celtic). The main success of this approach are underlying multilingual transformers like mT5. We finally show that machine translated test corpora unfairly improve the AMR evaluation for about 1 or 2 points (depending on the language).

Keywords: AMR, multilingual, low-resource languages, Celtic languages, Welsh

1. Introduction

Abstract Meaning Representation (AMR) is a representation language designed to provide data for natural language understanding, generation, and translation. It implements a simplified, standard neo-Davidsonian semantics (Davidson, 1967; Higginbotham, 1985); its formal origins are in unification systems (Kay, 1979) and other works in the 1980s and 90s. AMR has been formalised by Banarescu et al. (2013), and its motivation is to uniform and organize various semantic annotations like named entities, coreferences, word sense disambiguation, semantic relations, discourse connectives, temporal entities, etc. For verbal predicates, AMR makes extensive use of PropBank framesets as concepts where available (Kingsbury and Palmer, 2002; Palmer et al., 2005). If a concept is not defined in PropBank, English lemmas are used instead. AMR is heavily grounded onto English and is expressively not an interlingua of any kind, even though research work with AMR on languages other than English exists.

AMR graphs are directed, acyclic graphs where nodes are instances or concepts, and edges are relations. An example of an AMR graph is given in Figure 1. Currently AMR does not annotate number, tense or modality, in contrast to UMR (Van Gysel et al., 2021), which proposes to extend AMR in this sense.

Other formalisms to describe the semantics of sentences or texts are, for instance, Discourse Representation Theory (Kamp and Reyle, 1993; Kamp et al., 2011, DRT) and its derivates (Economical DRT, Segmented DRT), Universal Networking Language (Uchida et al., 1996, UNL, http://www.unlweb.net/unlweb/), Universal Conceptual Cognitive Annotation (Abend and Rappoport, 2013, UCCA), or Groningen Meaning Bank (Bos et al., 2017, GMB). However currently AMR seems to be the formalism with the largest interest[1].

```
(h / have-org-role-91                  # instance relation
   :ARG0 (c / city                     # edge relation
      :name (n / name
         :op1 "Cardiff"))              # attribute relation
   :ARG1 (c2 / country
      :name (n2 / name
         :op1 "Wales"))
   :ARG2 (c3 / capital))
```

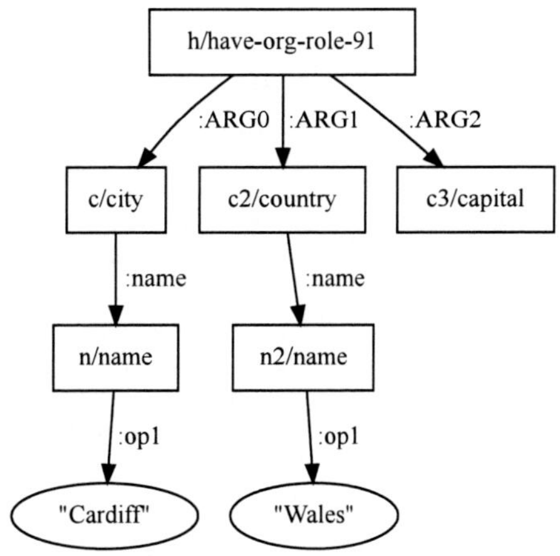

Figure 1: AMR graph (PENMAN format on top, graphical version below) for "Cardiff is the Welsh capital"; the red "/" is an *instance relation* which defines that a variable is an instance of a concept, in blue the *edge relations* which link instances and in green the *attribute relations* which link constants as strings or numbers to an instance. *have-org-role-91* is one out of a short list of special concepts which do not originate in PropBank, but are defined for AMR. Note that in the graphical version instance relations are not explicitely shown with an arrow and a label like $c \xrightarrow{:is\text{-}a} city$ but with a simple "/": *c / city*.

[1]For AMR in comparison to other formalisms see https://github.com/nschneid/amr-tutorial/raw/master/slides/AMR-TUTORIAL-FULL.pdf, pp. 115-121

The main AMR corpora of annotated data are available at Linguistic Data Consortium (LDC) for English[2]:

- LDC2020T02: LDC general release AMR 3.0 (2020), with 59,255 sentences;
- LDC2017T10: LDC general release AMR 2.0 (2017), with 39,260 sentences.

The sentences of the test corpus of AMR 2.0 were translated by human translators into four languages (LDC2020T07: AMR 2.0, four translations of AMR 2.0 test set into Italian, Spanish, German, Chinese, 1371 sentences per language).
However no translations are officially available for any of the Celtic languages. So we prepared translations into Welsh and Irish for the entire corpus (train/dev/test) using the Google Machine Translation (MT) API and had the 1371 sentences of the Welsh test corpus manually corrected and validated by a native speaker of Welsh[3]. Please note that in any case, the AMR graphs in the corpora do not change, "translation of the AMR corpus" means that the only the sentences themselves are translated into another language.
The remainder of this paper describes related work in multilingual parsing into AMR (Section 2) and our experiments (Section 3) on three Celtic languages: Welsh, Irish, and Scottish Gaelic.

2. Related Work

Although AMR had been conceived primarily for English, recently the interest to parse languages other than English into AMR has greatly increased. The approaches vary, and the results come close to the state-of-the-art results obtained for English AMR parsing. However, due to the absence of test data, all multilingual work is concentrated on the four languages for which human translated AMR test corpora exist, Chinese, German, Italian and Spanish; of which three are Indo-European languages, and Italian and Spanish are even more closely related Romance languages.
Currently Spring[4] (Bevilacqua et al., 2021) and X-AMR[5] (Cai et al., 2021), have the best results for English and the latter also for the four languages for which manual translations exist (cf. Table 1). Both Spring and X-AMR modify the AMR structures ("`<n> concept`" notation for variables instead of "`n / concept`" to distinguish variables from constants, since the former do not have semantics), optimize the AMR linearisation and add AMR relations to the underlying mBART tokenizer. Uhrig et al. (2021) chose to simply translate non-English sentences into English before calling an AMR parser (AMRlib[6]). Other approaches have been presented earlier by Damonte and Cohen (2018) (AMREager, using a transition-based parser) and by Blloshmi et al. (2020) (XL-AMR[7], a cross-lingual AMR parser which disposes of word aligners, i.e., word-to-word and word-to-node).

	de	it	es	zh
Damonte and Cohen (2018)	39.0	43.0	42.0	35.0
Blloshmi et al. (2020)	53.0	58.1	58.0	43.1
Uhrig et al. (2021)	67.6	72.3	70.7	59.1
Cai et al. (2021)	**73.1**	**75.4**	**75.9**	**61.9**

Table 1: Smatch scores for multilingual AMR parsing. Best scores in bold. All approaches are based on AMR 2.0

The performance of AMR parsers is evaluated by the *smatch score* which expresses the maximal score over all possible edge alignments (Cai and Knight, 2013)[8]:

$$P = \frac{\#\text{edges}_{\text{correct}}}{\#\text{edges}_{\text{gold}}} \quad R = \frac{\#\text{edges}_{\text{correct}}}{\#\text{edges}_{\text{system}}}$$

$$\text{smatch score (F1)} = \frac{2 \times \#\text{edges}_{\text{correct}}}{\#\text{edges}_{\text{gold}} + \#\text{edges}_{\text{system}}}$$

To calculate the smatch score, the optimal alignment of a gold AMR graph with a predicted AMR graph is to be found, which is a non-trivial task (Cai and Knight, 2013). Different runs of the evaluation can therefore produce slightly different results.

3. Experiments

3.1. General Multilingual Approach

Our approach to multilingual (and Celtic) AMR parsing draws from some of the approaches described in Section 2. As a parser we used a modified version of AMRlib[9], since the code for X-AMR (Cai et al., 2021) was not yet available in late 2021. The baseline was the original AMRlib with its model trained using the AMR 3.0 English corpus and T5 (Raffel et al., 2020) – a large pretrained language model. Expectedly all languages but English have very bad results (cf. first line of Table 2). In order to process other languages than English we first replaced the original T5 language model by the multilingual mT5[10] (Xue et al., 2021), retrained and tested the 4 human translated test corpora (LDC2020T07) on this mT5-based model (Table 2, 2nd line). This replacement shows gains in scores for all languages. In a next step we translated the train and development corpora into Chinese (zh), German (de), Italian (it) and Spanish (es) with MarianMT (Junczys-Dowmunt et al., 2018) and tested again on the 4 human translated test corpora. This time we observed a

[2] Other corpora are available at https://amr.isi.edu/download.html

[3] A great thank you to Delyth Prys, University of Bangor. Diolch yn fawr iawn i'r athro Delyth Prys, Canolfan Bedwyr, Prifysgol Cymru am ei help amhrisiadwy.

[4] https://github.com/SapienzaNLP/spring

[5] https://github.com/jcyk/XAMR

[6] https://github.com/bjascob/amrlib

[7] https://github.com/SapienzaNLP/xl-amr

[8] https://github.com/snowblink14/smatch

[9] https://github.com/bjascob/amrlib

[10] `google/mt5-base` model at HuggingFace.

large increase in Smatch score (Table 2, 3rd line). We then concatenated the English and the translated corpus for each language (both, for training and validation) and tested on the manually translated test sentences. Apart from Chinese we could not observe significant improvements (Table 2, lower four lines). These figures are very close to the SOTA results shown in Table 1. Please note that the evaluations in Table 1 is based on AMR 2.0, while our experiments are based on AMR 3.0. It is reported that AMR 3.0 results are in general slightly lower than AMR 2.0 (Bevilacqua et al., 2021).

trans-	training			test data		
former	data	en	de	es	it	zh
T5	en	81.1	56.5	49.7	45.8	10.7
mT5	en	**81.7**	58.9	62.4	59.7	54.9
mT5	*de/es/it/zh*		**71.1**	**74.4**	73.3	60.2
mT5	en + de	81.2	71.0			
mT5	en + es	81.5		74.3		
mT5	en + it	81.6			**73.9**	
mT5	en + zh	81.5				**61.1**

Table 2: Results (smatch scores) for training with English and translated corpora (MarianMT for train/dev, human translators for test), best scores in bold. *de/es/it/zh* means that the train and development corpora are in the same language as the test corpus. All training corpora are from AMR 3.0.

3.2. Celtic Languages

In this Section we describe our experiments for three Celtic languages: Welsh (cy), Irish (ga) and Scottish Gaelic (gd). Whereas the former is a P-Celtic language, the latter two are closely related Q-Celtic languages. Welsh has about 500,000 native speakers in Wales; Irish, even though the national language of Ireland, and Scottish Gaelic have much less native speakers. Except very young children all native speakers of these three languages are bilingual with English. All Celtic languages are under-resourced languages[11]. For written text, the Welsh Wikipedia, Welsh language press, official language production (Welsh Parliament[12]) provide text corpora of usable size, however linguistically annotated resources are quite limited. It is important to note that Welsh and Irish are amongst the 100 languages used to train mT5, whereas Scottish Gaelic is not included (neither are Breton, Manx and Cornish).
In order to obtain Welsh and Irish training and validation corpora, we used the Google Machine Translation API (the MarianMT models for Welsh[13] did not produce usable results). For Scottish Gaelic we only translated the test corpus. The next steps are identical to the experiments done for the four languages in Section 3.1. Again, we used models trained (on mT5) using the English training corpus, the Welsh/Irish corpus and the concatenated English and Welsh/Irish corpus (cf. Table 3).

trans-	training		test data	
former	data	cy	ga	gd
mT5	en	44.7	44.2	41.7
mT5	cy	73.4	39.9	36.2
mT5	en + cy	**74.3**	40.1	35.3
mT5	ga	39.7	**72.4**	**47.7**
mT5	en + ga	40.0	72.1	47.1

Table 3: Smatch scores for Celtic languages on models trained on English, Welsh, English and Welsh, Irish or English and Irish; best scores in bold.

At least for Welsh, the model trained on the combined data English and Welsh still improves the results, for Irish and Scottish Gaelic no improvement detectable. Using an Irish or Scottish Gaelic test corpus on a model trained on Welsh does not work (as was expected), whereas Scottish Gaelic improves slightly if a model trained on Irish is used (instead of English).
A simple error analysis showed that attribute relations (cf. Figure 1) in contrast to instance and edge relations are less likely to be incorrect. This means that named entities with different labels in other languages are nevertheless correctly rendered using the English label: The sentence *Mae Llundain yn brifddinas Lloegr* ("London is the capital of England") is parsed into the a graph, using the correct English labels "London" and "England" (cf. 2).

```
(h / have-org-role-91
    :ARG0 (c / city
        :name (n / name
            :op1 "London"))
    :ARG1 (c2 / country
        :name (n2 / name
            :op1 "England"))
    :ARG2 (c3 / capital))
```

Figure 2: AMR graph for *Mae Llundain yn brifddinas Lloegr* ("London is the capital of England")

The prediction of edge relations causes the drop in smatch score for all languages, including (the non-translated) English (cf. Table 4[14]).

3.3. The Effect of Machine Translation vs. Human Translation

Until now we have not yet addressed a weak point: for Welsh the entire corpus is machine-translated, includ-

[11] The Universal Dependency project (https://universaldependecies.org) provides treebanks for 5 Celtic languages, however their sizes are comparatively small.

[12] Cf. also the National Corpus of Contemporary Welsh (https://corcencc.org/), which provides a valuable source of written Welsh.

[13] https://huggingface.co/Helsinki-NLP/opus-mt-en-cy

[14] calculated using `smatch.py` (https://github.com/snowblink14/smatch)

lang.	relation type attribute	 instance	 edge	global smatch score
en	90.5	87.2	73.7	81.7
de	86.5	71.9	68.7	71.0
es	84.1	77.4	71.7	74.3
it	85.3	75.9	71.6	73.9
zh	71.5	63.6	60.3	61.1
cy	83.5	76.7	71.7	74.3
ga	85.7	75.1	68.5	72.1
(gd	69.5	42.1	50.2	47.1)

Table 4: Global smatch scores and smatch scores for different relation types. Test corpora used were the human translations for Chinese, German, Italian and Spanish and machine translations (Google) for Welsh, Irish and Scottish Gaelic. Training was done using mT5 on the concatenated corpus (AMR 3.0) of English and the language concerned (except for Scottish Gaelic, where English and Irish was used instead).

ing the test corpus, whereas for Chinese, German, Italian and Spanish at least the test corpora were translated by human translators. Even though machine translation produces impressive results, it is not always perfect, especially for under-resourced languages like the Celtic languages. Our question is therefore: are the results (for Welsh AMR parsing, Table 3, third line) only as good as they are because the translation is bad and resembles more the source language (English) than proper Welsh? To test our hypothesis, we had the Welsh translation of the test corpus corrected and validated by native Welsh speakers. In parallel, we translated the test corpus from English into the four languages for which human translations exist (de, es, it, zh). For that, we used two MT systems: Google's MT API and MarianMT. We then parsed the translations and evaluated the result.

	de	*es*	*it*	*zh*	*cy*
human tr.	71.0	74.3	73.9	61.1	74.2
MarianMT	**74.8**	**76.2**	75.2	**68.5**	n/a
Google MT	74.0	76.1	**75.6**	68.2	**74.3**
mean diff.	3.40	1.85	1.5	7.25	0.1

Table 5: Comparison of smatch scores with translations (AMR models trained on English + *language*). Welsh was translated with Google MT only because MarianMT did not work well for this language.

Table 5 shows that the machine translated test corpora get a higher smatch score than the human translated ones. This confirms our hypothesis that translations using MT give higher scores due to their possibly greater similarity to English than human translations.
The difference in smatch score between the used MT systems is neglectable, even though for several MT metrics the Google MT API achieves higher values than MarianMT (table 6[15]). Table 6 also shows that there is an inverse correlation between the quality of the translation (with respect to the human translation) and the smatch score of the AMR evaluation: the better the MT evaluation with respect to the human translation, the worse the AMR smatch score. E.g., for German and Spanish all MT metrics show the preference to Google, meaning that its translations are closer to the human references, and Table 5 shows that the parsing of Google translations had a lower smatch score. The AMR parsing of human translations results in a even lower smatch score.

metric	*MT*	*de*	*es*	*it*	*zh*	*cy*
BLEU	M	43.11	59.70	49.82	33.89	n/a
	G	**50.70**	**65.29**	**53.16**	**43.84**	91.89
TER	M	45.12	26.87	36.05	**149.52**	n/a
	G	**38.70**	**22.67**	**32.70**	190.34	5.41
BERTsc.	M	73.77	84.24	78.17	63.20	n/a
	G	**78.31**	**86.31**	**81.10**	**70.51**	98.60
chrF++	M	66.98	78.33	71.55	n/a	n/a
	G	**71.43**	**81.57**	**73.68**	30.10	95.52
BARTsc.	M	-5.53	-5.31	-5.57	-6.92	n/a
	G	**-5.31**	**-5.13**	**-5.44**	**-6.53**	-4.21
	hum.	-3.47	-3.69	-3.65	-3.84	-3.65
=	M	7.5%	11.5%	6.9%	1.8%	n/a
	G	**9.9%**	**13.2%**	**8.1%**	**3.8%**	66.0%
LD (av.)	M	49.07	26.69	35.6	22.62	n/a
	G	**42.74**	**22.99**	**33.08**	**19.36**	12.58
LD (med)	M	39.0	20.0	29.0	18.0	n/a
	G	**35.0**	**18.0**	**27.0**	**15.0**	9.0

Table 6: Comparison of the machine translated test corpora (M: MarianMT, G: Google) with the human translated version, best score for each metric in bold. The BLEU score for the translation of Chinese has been calculated using the *zh*-tokenizer provided by sacreBLEU. Since MarianMT does not output any tokenization for Chinese, the character-based chrF++ metric is not applicable. For BARTscore we added a value for comparing two identical files (human translation: hum.) which is not 0, to have a base value to judge the other BARTscore values better. "=" indicates the percentage of sentences where MT and human translations are identical, "LD" is the average and mean Levenshtein-Damerau distance (Levenshtein, 1966). For TER and Levenshtein 0 is the best score; for BARTscore 0 is the best theoretical value too, but in reality even identical sentences have BARTscores below 0. All other metrics have 100 as best score.

Note that for Welsh, the difference between the human translation and the machine translation is minimal

[15] We use the following tools to calculate the MT metrics: BERTScore (Zhang et al., 2020): https://github.com/Tiiiger/bert_score, BLEU (Papineni et al., 2002; Post, 2018) and TER (Snover et al., 2006): https://github.com/mjpost/sacrebleu, BARTScore (Yuan et al., 2021): https://github.com/neulab/BARTScore and chrF++ (Popović, 2017): https://github.com/m-popovic/chrF

(BLEU 91.89). This may be due to the fact that the Welsh human translated test corpus had been in fact translated from English with MT and then manually corrected and not translated from scratch by a human translator. This is confirmed by the very good values for Welsh in Table 6, and the fact that in 66% of the Welsh sentences, MT and human correction do not differ at all.

4. Conclusion and Perspectives

We showed in this paper that thanks to machine translation and the fact that Welsh and Irish are present in modern multilingual pretrained language models like mT5, it is sufficient to train a model for an AMR parser which produced state-of-the-art results, comparable to AMR parsers for Spanish, Italian, German. A manual correction of the training corpora might improve these figures slightly, however, correcting up to 60,000 machine translated Welsh and Irish sentences would require many resources and is probably not necessary any more. This approach is not restricted to Welsh or Celtic languages. As long as the AMR training corpus can be (machine) translated into any language which in turn is also supported by the underlying language model (mT5), our approach should work for any language.

Even though AMR has been presented in 2013 (Banarescu et al., 2013), due to the lack of tools able to parse (English) sentences into AMR graphs, AMR was not used largely in NLP until recently, with the implementation of Seq2Seq transformer-based tools. The quality obtained with these tools opens the path to many downstream applications based on a more formalized semantics like, multilingual information extraction, question-answering on knowledge bases etc., as the increasing number of papers around AMR shows[16].

5. Acknowledgements

We would like to thank Professor Delyth Prys from Canolfan Bedwyr, University of Bangor for her help in validating and, when necessary, correcting the Welsh translations of AMR's test corpus.

6. Bibliographical References

Abend, O. and Rappoport, A. (2013). Universal Conceptual Cognitive Annotation (UCCA). In *51th Annual Meeting of the Association for Computational Linguistics*, pages 228–238, Sofia, Bulgaria. Association for Computational Linguistics.

Banarescu, L., Bonial, C., Cai, S., Georgescu, M., Griffitt, K., Hermjakob, U., Knight, K., Koehn, P., Palmer, M., and Schneider, N. (2013). Abstract Meaning Representation for Sembanking. In *Proceedings of the 7th Linguistic Annotation Workshop and Interoperability with Discourse*, pages 178–186, Sofia, Bulgaria. ACL.

[16]https://nert-nlp.github.io/AMR-Bibliography/

Bevilacqua, M., Blloshmi, R., and Navigli, R. (2021). One SPRING to Rule Them Both: Symmetric AMR Semantic Parsing and Generation without a Complex Pipeline. In *Proceedings of the AAAI Conference on Artificial Intelligence*, pages 12564–12573.

Blloshmi, R., Tripodi, R., and Navigli, R. (2020). XL-AMR: Enabling Cross-Lingual AMR Parsing with Transfer Learning Techniques. In *EMNLP*, page 2487–2500, Online. Association for Computational Linguistics.

Bos, J., Basile, V., Evang, K., Venhuizen, N., and Johannes, B. (2017). The Groningen Meaning Bank. In Nancy Ide et al., editors, *Handbook of Linguistic Annotation*, page 463–496. Springer, Berlin.

Cai, S. and Knight, K. (2013). Smatch: an Evaluation Metric for Semantic Feature Structures. In *ACL*, page 748–752, Sofia, Bulgaria. Association for Computational Linguistics.

Cai, D., Li, X., Chun-Sing Ho, J., Bing, L., and Lam, W. (2021). Multilingual AMR Parsing with Noisy Knowledge Distillation. In *Findings of the Association for Computational Linguistics: EMNLP 2021*, pages 2778–2789, Punta Cana, Dominican Republic. Association for Computational Linguistics.

Damonte, M. and Cohen, S. B. (2018). Cross-lingual Abstract Meaning Representation Parsing. In *NAACL: Human Language Technologies*, pages 1146–1155, New Orleans, Lousiana, USA. Association for Computational Linguistics.

Davidson, D. (1967). The Logical Form of Action Sentences. In Nicholas Rescher, editor, *The Logic of Decision and Action*, pages 81–95. University of Pittsburgh Press, Pittsburg.

Higginbotham, J. (1985). On semantics. *Linguistic inquiry*, 16(4):547–593.

Junczys-Dowmunt, M., Grundkiewicz, R., Dwojak, T., Hoang, H., Heafield, K., Neckermann, T., Seide, F., Germann, U., Fikri Aji, A., Bogoychev, N., Martins, A. F. T., and Birch, A. (2018). Marian: Fast neural machine translation in C++. In *Proceedings of ACL 2018, System Demonstrations*, pages 116–121, Melbourne, Australia, July. Association for Computational Linguistics.

Kamp, H. and Reyle, U. (1993). *From Discourse to Logic. Introduction to Modeltheoretic Semantics of Natural Language, Formal Logic and Discourse Representation Theory*. Studies in Linguistics and Philosophy 42. Kluwer, Dordrecht.

Kamp, H., Genabith, J. v., and Reyler, U. (2011). Discourse Representation Theory. In Dov M. Gabbay et al., editors, *Handbook of Philosophical Logic. Vol 15*. Springer, Heidelberg.

Kay, M. (1979). Functional grammar. *Annual Meeting of the Berkeley Linguistics Society*, 5:142–158.

Kingsbury, P. and Palmer, M. (2002). From TreeBank to PropBank. In *LREC*, Las Palmas, Canary Islands, Spain. European Language Resources Association.

Levenshtein, V. I. (1966). Binary codes capable of

correction deletions, insertions and reversals. *Soviet Physics Doklady*, 10(8):707–710.

Palmer, M., Gildea, D., and Kingsbury, P. (2005). The Proposition Bank: An Annotated Corpus of Semantic Roles. *Computational Linguistics*, 31(1):71–106.

Papineni, K., Roukos, S., Ward, T., and Zhu, W.-J. (2002). BLEU: a Method for Automatic Evaluation of Machine Translation. In *Proceedings of the 40th Annual Meeting of the Association for Computational Linguistics*, pages 311–318, Philadelphia, PA, USA. Association for Computational Linguistics.

Popović, M. (2017). chrF++: Words Helping Character n-grams. In *Proceedings of the Conference on Machine Translation*, pages 612–618, Copenhagen, Denmark. Association for Computational Linguistics.

Post, M. (2018). A Call for Clarity in Reporting BLEU Scores. In *Proceedings of the Third Conference on Machine Translation*, pages 186–191, Belgium, Brussels. Association for Computational Linguistics.

Raffel, C., Shazeer, N., Lee, K., Narang, S., Matena, M., Zhou, Y., Li, W., and J., L. P. (2020). Exploring the Limits of Transfer Learning with a Unified Text-to-Text Transformer. *Journal of Machine Learning Research*, 21:1–67.

Snover, M., Dorr, B., Schwartz, R., Micciulla, L., and Makhoul, J. (2006). A Study of Translation Edit Rate with Targeted Human Annotation. In *Proceedings of association for machine translation in the Americas*, pages 223–231.

Uchida, H., Zhu, M., and Della Senta, T. (1996). UNL: Universal Networking Language. An electronic language for communication, understanding and collaboration. Technical report, Institude of Advanced Studies, United Nations University (IAS/UNU).

Uhrig, S., Rezepka García, Y., Opits, J., and Frank, A. (2021). Translate, then Parse! A strong baseline for Cross-Lingual AMR Parsing. In *Proceedings of the 17th International Conference on Parsing Technologies and the IWPT 2021 Shared Task on Parsing into Enhanced Universal Dependencies*, pages 58–64, Online. Association for Computational Linguistics.

Van Gysel, J. E. L., Vigus, M., Chun, J., Lai, K., Moeller, S., Yao, J., O'Gorman, T., Cowell, A., Croft, W., Huang, C., Hajič, J., Martin, J. H., Oepen, S., Palmer, M., Pustejovsky, J., Vallejos, R., and Xue, N. (2021). Designing a Uniform Meaning Representation for Natural Language Processing. *Künstliche Intelligenz*, 35:343–360.

Xue, L., Constant, N., Kale, M., Al-Rfou, R., Siddhant, A., Barua, A., and Raffel, C. (2021). mT5: A Massively Multilingual Pre-trained Text-to-Text Transformer. In *Conference of the North American Chapter of the Association for Computational Linguistics*, pages 483–498. Association for Computational Linguistics.

Yuan, W., Neubig, G., and Liu, P. (2021). BARTScore: Evaluating Generated Text as Text Generation. https://arxiv.org/abs/2106.11520.

Zhang, T., Kishore, V., Wu, F., Weinberger, K. Q., and Artzi, Y. (2020). BERTScore: Evaluating Text Generation with BERT. In *International Conference on Learning Representations*.

Proceedings of the CLTW 4 @ LREC2022, pages 7–13
Marseille, 20-25 June 2022

Diachronic Parsing of Pre-Standard Irish

Kevin P. Scannell
Department of Computer Science
Saint Louis University
St. Louis, Missouri, USA 63103
kscanne@gmail.com

Abstract

Irish underwent a major spelling standardization in the 1940's and 1950's, and as a result it can be challenging to apply language technologies designed for the modern language to older, "pre-standard" texts. Lemmatization, tagging, and parsing of these pre-standard texts play an important role in a number of applications, including the lexicographical work on *Foclóir Stairiúil na Gaeilge*, a historical dictionary of Irish covering the period from 1600 to the present. We have two main goals in this paper. First, we introduce a small benchmark corpus containing just over 3800 tokens, annotated according to the Universal Dependencies guidelines and covering a range of dialects and time periods since 1600. Second, we establish baselines for lemmatization, tagging, and dependency parsing on this corpus by experimenting with a variety of machine learning approaches.

Keywords: parsing, part-of-speech tagging, diachronic treebank, Irish, lexicography

1. Introduction

Irish is relatively well-resourced in terms of language technologies for grammatical analysis, including a rule-based part-of-speech tagger (Uí Dhonnchadha and van Genabith, 2006) and a dependency parser (Lynn, 2016) that both achieve high levels of accuracy. Older texts present a problem for these resources, however, in part because of a significant spelling reform that was undertaken in the 1940's and 1950's with the introduction of an official standard for the written language, *An Caighdeán Oifigiúil* (Rannóg an Aistriúcháin, 1945). The standard resulted in an orthography that was both simpler (e.g. *déidheannaighe* becomes *déanaí*) and more consistent (e.g. *Meirceá, Meiricea, Aimeirice, Meirioca, . . .* and so on all become *Meiriceá*), and has been embraced widely by the Irish-speaking community. In addition to the challenges presented by this orthographic discontinuity, older texts exhibit a number of grammatical features that have all but disappeared in the modern language, e.g. various synthetic verb forms, wide use of the nominal dative case, etc. The language technologies that exist for the modern language are unable to handle these phenomena in a reliable way.

Lemmatization, tagging, and parsing of these pre-standard texts are all of tremendous importance. First and foremost, these are important enabling technologies for lexicography. There are two significant lexicographical projects underway in Ireland at present: the Royal Irish Academy's historical dictionary of Irish covering the period from 1600 to the present[1], and new general-purpose monolingual and bilingual dictionaries funded by Foras na Gaeilge[2]. Both projects make use of large corpora that include millions of words of pre-standard text. Effective searching of these corpora for lexicographical purposes is impossible without, at minimum, indexing them by standardized lemmas and parts of speech.

Grammatical analysis of older texts has other potential applications, for example as an aid to historians or linguistic scholars who are engaging with Early Modern Irish source texts, a challenging task even for those with a fluent command of modern Irish. The Léaṁ project[3] was established with precisely this audience in mind; the project website provides a grammar and glossaries for Early Modern Irish, as well as several carefully annotated texts to help scholars learn the nuances of the language. At present, these texts are produced through time-consuming manual annotation; with suitable language technologies tailored to this time period, additional texts could be prepared much more quickly.

Currently, there are no resources for *direct* tagging or parsing of pre-standard texts. Instead, the general strategy has been to start with a best-effort automatic standardization (Scannell, 2014), and then to make use of modern taggers and parsers. Good results have been obtained with this approach, although there are some inherent limitations. First, given the absence of tools for direct analysis of the source texts, the standardizer must do its job without part-of-speech tags or other linguistic annotations. Instead, it relies only on "shallow" techniques: a set of rule-based spelling changes, a large lexicon of pre-standard/standard word mappings, and a language model on the target (modern Irish) side. Second, the standardization task generally becomes more difficult for older texts, and errors introduced by the standardizer, along with the frequent occurrence of out-of-vocabulary words, negatively impact the quality of tagging and parsing. Third, by definition, this approach is unable to handle grammatical phenomena that do not

[1] See https://www.ria.ie/research-projects/focloir-stairiuil-na-gaeilge

[2] See https://www.focloir.ie/

[3] See https://léamh.org/about-the-project/

occur in the modern language.
The goal of this paper is two-fold. First, we present a new reference corpus of pre-standard texts published between 1602 and 1936, representing various time periods and dialects, and annotated according to the Universal Dependencies (UD) guidelines (Nivre et al., 2016). Second, we experiment with a number of tagging and parsing models and evaluate them on this reference corpus, establishing baseline scores for lemmatization, part-of-speech tagging, and dependency parsing on pre-standard Irish.

2. Related Work

Text analysis tools for standard Irish

As noted above, modern Irish is relatively well-resourced among minority languages in terms of language technology. There is an rule-based part-of-speech tagger and lemmatizer going back to Elaine Uí Dhonnchadha's Ph.D. thesis in the early 2000s (Uí Dhonnchadha and van Genabith, 2006; Uí Dhonnchadha, 2008). Teresa Lynn produced a large dependency treebank for Irish (Lynn et al., 2021) as part of her Ph.D. work (Lynn, 2016), and has used that to train dependency parsers that achieve very good results on a range of domains and text types (Lynn et al., 2012; Lynn et al., 2014; Lynn and Foster, 2016; Barry et al., 2021). The present author has developed a standardization tool (Scannell, 2014) that grew out of earlier work on spelling and grammar correction, and which plays an important role in this research.

Old and Middle Irish

Although outside of the scope of this paper, it is worth mentioning some important work on grammatical analysis for Old and Middle Irish, given that Early Modern Irish texts exhibit linguistic phenomena that survive from these older varieties. In the future it might be desirable to unify some of these efforts to produce diachronic corpora ranging from the earliest Old Irish texts to the modern Irish of present-day speakers.
Plain text corpora for Old and Middle Irish exist in abundance[4], and there are even some annotated corpora, including the Parsed Old and Middle Irish Corpus (Lash, 2014) and the St. Gall Priscian Glosses (Bauer et al., 2018), the latter having been converted into Universal Dependencies format by Adrian Doyle, although with part-of-speech tags and morphological features only.[5]
Tools for lemmatization, tagging, and parsing of Old and Middle Irish are still at an early stage of development, although there has been significant progress in recent years; see (Dereza, 2016; Dereza, 2019; Doyle et al., 2019; Doyle et al., 2018; Fransen, 2020).

Parsed corpora in other languages

Finally, we would like to situate this work among others that involve the development of treebanks, taggers, and parsers for historical language varieties, and the interesting linguistic work on diachronic syntax enabled by these efforts (Eckhoff et al., 2020).
In addition to the work on Old and Middle Irish cited above, we are aware of constituency or dependency treebanks for Medieval French (Prévost and Stein, 2013), Middle and Early-modern English (Kroch, 2020), Old High German (Petrova et al., 2009), and historical varieties of Portuguese (Galves, 2018), Icelandic (Wallenberg et al., 2011), Basque (Estarrona et al., 2020), and Russian (Berdičevskis and Eckhoff, 2020).

3. Datasets

Motivation

As noted above, our strategy for analyzing pre-standard Irish texts has traditionally been to pass them through the standardizer and then use tools designed for the modern language. Tagged corpora created with this approach have been used in lexicographical projects, and have been incorporated into the search functionality on the `corpas.ria.ie` site.
Evaluations of the individual components in this pipeline have been performed and reported in the literature. See (Uí Dhonnchadha et al., 2014) and (Scannell, 2014) for the standardizer, (Uí Dhonnchadha and van Genabith, 2006) for the lemmatizer and tagger, and (Lynn et al., 2012; Lynn and Foster, 2016; Barry et al., 2021) for the dependency parser. Nevertheless, *no formal evaluation of the effectiveness of the full pipeline has been performed on pre-standard texts*, and so we have no objective measure of how well it is working, and no way to decide if modifications to the process result in significant improvements.
Our primary aim is therefore to put this research on a more solid foundation by establishing an annotated test corpus consisting of texts from the period 1600 to 1936, annotated according to the Universal Dependencies guidelines. The resulting treebank (Scannell, 2022) is freely available for others to use in their own experiments on tagging and parsing of pre-standard Irish; our aim is to have it included in the 2.11 release of the Universal Dependencies treebanks.

The Texts

With limited time for manual annotation, we decided to keep the test corpus quite small, while at the same time endeavoring to include texts that represent a range of time periods and dialects.
The pre-standard texts published in the late 19th century and early 20th century (from roughly the founding of Conradh na Gaeilge in 1882 through the introduction of the Official Standard in the 1940's) are, generally speaking, much easier to process than older texts. Even though the orthography is still quite different from the

[4] See, for example, `https://celt.ucc.ie/`.
[5] See `https://github.com/UniversalDependencies/UD_Old_Irish-DipSGG/blob/dev/README.md`.

standardized orthography, there is much more consistency and the grammatical differences are relatively minor. We selected three texts from this period, one from each of the major dialects: *Deoraidheacht* by Pádraic Ó Conaire (Connacht Irish, first published in 1910), *Peig* by Peig Sayers (Munster Irish, first published in 1936), and *Scairt an Dúthchais*, a translation of Jack London's *Call of the Wild* by Niall Ó Domhnaill (Ulster Irish, first published in 1932).

We then selected three older and much more challenging texts to round out the corpus: *Foras Feasa ar Éirinn* by Seathrún Céitinn (1634), the 1602 translation of the Gospel of John by Uilliam Ó Domhnaill, and *Cín Lae Amhlaoibh*, a hand-written diary kept by Amhlaoibh Ó Súilleabháin between 1827 and 1835. This diary is perhaps the most challenging text for computational processing despite being written in the 19th century, because of the informal nature of the writing and tremendous variation in spelling.

All six source texts are included in the Royal Irish Academy's Historical Corpus of Irish (Dillon, 2017).

Annotation Guidelines

There are two existing Universal Dependencies treebanks for modern Irish that use the same annotation guidelines: the Irish Universal Dependencies Treebank (IUDT) (Lynn et al., 2021) and the TwittIrish treebank of Irish language tweets (Cassidy et al., 2021). Generally speaking, we followed these guidelines very closely; the details are provided on the Universal Dependencies website[6]. Here we will make note of a few consequences of this design choice that arose when annotating the pre-standard corpus, and a couple of ways that we diverged from the existing guidelines.

First, the modern Irish treebanks perform some gentle standardization in the lemmatization field. For example, a misspelling like *neamhspléach* is corrected in the lemma field to *neamhspleách*, and a pre-standard or dialect spelling like *thaisbeáint* is lemmatized to *taispeáint*. We followed this convention in the pre-standard treebank as well, but in our case it applies to a large proportion of the words in the corpus vs. the occasional misspelling or dialect spelling. We believe this is the correct design choice for the lexicographical applications we have in mind, where indexing by a standard spelling is sure to be useful. That said, this also makes the task of "lemmatization" much more difficult from a machine learning perspective, since the task now really amounts to *both* lemmatization and standardization, and there is no easy way for a machine learning algorithm to tease apart strictly morphological phenomena from changes that come from standardization of the lemma (e.g. when we lemmatize *inneosad* to *inis* vs. *innis*).

Nouns with explicit marking for the dative case are much more common in the pre-standard corpus than in modern Irish. The modern Irish treebanks only include the feature `Case=Dat` in the few set phrases where the noun has a distinct dative form in standard Irish, e.g.: *ar leith, i gcrích, in Éirinn, os cionn*, etc. We followed this convention in the pre-standard treebank, even though explicitly-marked datives are common enough that an argument could be made for annotating all nouns that appear in a dative context with `Case=Dat`, in much the same way that all genitives in the modern treebanks are annotated with the feature `Case=Gen`, even when the surface form agrees with the nominative (e.g. *uisce* in *acmhainní uisce*). We leave this point for future discussion with the other Irish treebank maintainers.

Some care was needed in dealing with noun genders, since some nouns have changed genders over time, and there is some variation across dialects as well. We reviewed all cases where internal evidence (usually an initial mutation) suggested that a noun might be of an unexpected gender, and determined whether these were actual variations or mere performance errors, the latter being exceedingly common in *Cín Lae Amhlaoibh*, e.g. *Do sheid* ***an gaoth*** *go ciuin* ..., or ... *an smolach,* ***an fuiseog****, agus gac einín bin eile*. Even the well-edited texts from the 20th century contain some examples like this; the first edition of Peig contains the phrase *Is beag* ***an beann*** *a bheadh agamsa* ..., where *beann* would normally be feminine and therefore lenited in this context (and indeed, later editions of the book "correct" this to *an bheann*). In cases like these, we referred to existing dictionaries as well as the wider corpus for evidence of gender variation of the given noun before deciding on the best annotation.

Tokenization was the one place where we diverged significantly from the annotation guidelines for modern Irish. The general UD guidelines allow for so-called "multiword tokens"; these are orthographic tokens that are decomposed into multiple words for the purpose of syntactic analysis (e.g. the French treebanks decompose the token *du* into two syntactic words, the preposition *de* and the determiner *le*). The modern Irish treebanks do not use multiword tokens at all. For the pre-standard treebank, we decided to make use of them in cases where a single token would be normally be written as two or more words in the modern orthography. For example, *ar anadhbhársain* is common in the 17th century Bible translations (usually corresponding to *therefore* in English translations), but would standardize to *ar an ábhar sin*. Here we would annotate *anadhbhársain* as a multiword token. As another example, in older texts it was common to fuse the verbal particle *do* with the verb: *dochuáidh, dorinne*, etc., whereas these would be written separately in the standard orthography.

There are further subtleties to take into account when annotating these multiword tokens. In the examples above, the decomposed words all appear explicitly as part of the surface token (*do* + *rinne*, etc.). When they

[6]See `https://universaldependencies.org/ga/index.html`.

do not appear explicitly in this way, we choose not to annotate as a multiword token. For example, the standardizer converts the synthetic verb form *thóigéubhtháoi* to *thógfaidh sibh* but this is treated as a single token in the treebank, with features `Number=Plur` and `Person=2`, the same way synthetic verbs in the modern language would be handled.

Building the treebank

The Irish standardizer outputs word-aligned standardizations; these alignments are critical in what follows, because our goal is to build the pre-standard treebank using *cross-lingual projection* via these word alignments (Yarowsky and Ngai, 2001).

Our six chosen books were run through the standardizer, and then the resulting standardized texts were annotated using a parser trained on the IUDT corpus (see §4.1 below for details), with the goal of projecting these annotations back to the original, pre-standard source. Across the six texts, 97.5% of tokens are aligned one-to-one with their standardizations, and in these cases the annotations were projected directly.

Of the remaining 2.5% of tokens, the majority involve one-to-many standardizations, of the type discussed in the previous subsection (*anadhbhársain*, *dorinne*, etc.). These are trivial to annotate given our decision to treat them as multiword tokens; the annotations on the individual standardized words are simply projected back to the individual source words comprising the multiword token.

The remaining cases involve many-to-one standardizations; these require a bit more care and some manual intervention. Typical examples include:

- *ana mhaith* (standard *an-mhaith*)
- *deagh Ghaedheal* (standard *dea-Ghael*)
- *ró naomhtha* (standard *rónaofa*)
- *cé 'r bh'* (standard *cérbh*)
- *dh'á rírìbh* (standard *dáiríre*)
- *le n'ár* (standard *lenár*)
- *ní fhuilim* (standard *nílim*)

The most common 700 of these many-to-one mappings were surveyed, and the correct annotation of the individual words was determined manually and stored in a database for the projecting parser to use. These rules include the part-of-speech tags for each token, an indication of the head of the phrase, and internal dependency relations so these can easily be incorporated into the annotation of the full sentence. In the remaining (rare) cases of many-to-one mappings, we default to assigning the part-of-speech tag `X` to each pre-standard token, and assign the root of the sentence as the head.

We call this process, starting with a pre-standard source text and ending with a valid CoNLL-U file, the *projecting parser*. We applied the projecting parser to each of our six texts, shuffled the sentences, and then split into training, development, and test sets. The test sets were chosen to be balanced across the six books, with 25 sentences taken from each, resulting in a treebank containing 150 sentences and 3804 tokens. This treebank was then manually corrected, resulting in the gold-standard corpus used in our evaluations below.

Treebank	Sentences	Tokens
IUDT train	4005	95881
IUDT test	454	10109
Silver train	11479	232771
Older test	75	1530
Oldest test	75	2274

Table 1: Summary of the treebanks used for training and testing of our parsing models.

4. Parsing Models

In this section, we will introduce the seven parsing models that we evaluated on the test set described in the previous section. All models were trained using version 1.2.1 of UDPipe (Straka and Straková, 2017) using the "swap" transition system. UDPipe also allows the incorporation of pre-trained `word2vec` word embeddings into the parsing models. We did this for each of the models below, using the skip-gram model, a window size of 10, and 50-dimensional word vectors (following the recommendations of the UDPipe maintainers). The details of the corpora that we used to train the word embeddings varied from model to model; these details are given in the subsections that follow.

Modern Irish parser

Our first baseline involved looking at the performance of the unmodified standard Irish parser on pre-standard texts, as a kind of "zero-shot" evaluation. For this, we trained a model using the IUDT training set distributed with version 2.9 of the Universal Dependencies treebanks. This corpus contains 95881 tokens across 4005 sentences. We incorporated pre-trained word vectors using `word2vec`, trained on a large web-crawled corpus of modern Irish containing about 127 million words. The results for this model are labeled "UD" in Table 2 below.

Projecting parser

This model is precisely the projecting parser described above in §3.4. In short, it involves standardizing a given input text, parsing the standardized text with the modern Irish parser, and then projecting those annotations back to the original text using the word alignments output by the standardizer. Again, most of the care is needed to handle the cases of many-to-one standardization. The results for this model are labeled "Projecting" in Table 2 below.

Silver parser

Since we do not yet have a gold treebank for pre-standard Irish beyond our small test set, the idea here was to take the output of the projecting parser on the training portion of our six chosen texts, and use those trees to train a new model with no post-editing (hence the name "silver"). In total, there were 232,771 tokens across 11479 sentences in this training set. The resulting model is our first parser trained to act directly on pre-standard Irish without making use of the standardizer as part of the parsing pipeline. We combined it with `word2vec` embeddings trained on a 30 million word subset of the Royal Irish Academy corpus (Dillon, 2017). The results for this model are labeled "Silver" in Table 2 below.

Bilingual model

We were interested in training a single model that would give good results on both standard and pre-standard Irish. With this in mind, we simply combined the IUDT training set with the silver training data from the previous model. Similarly, we trained `word2vec` embeddings on the union of the training corpora used for the previous two models. The results for this model are labeled "UD+100%" in Table 2 below.

Cross-lingual word embeddings

This is a small variation on the previous model, again with the aim of getting good results on both standard and pre-standard Irish. We used the same training set, but combined the monolingual word embeddings from the first two models (for standard and pre-standard Irish, respectively) into a single embedding using Facebook's MUSE (Lample et al., 2018). MUSE requires "seed" translations in order to build the cross-lingual representation; in our case these were taken from the bilingual lexicon used by the Irish standardizer. The results for this model are labeled "UD+100%+MUSE" in Table 2 below.

Balanced multilingual model

Since we are able to produce virtually unlimited amounts of silver training data, we worried that perhaps the size of the silver corpus would overwhelm the high-quality annotations from the gold IUDT data. We therefore recreated the bilingual model above, but using only 25% of the silver training corpus combined with the full IUDT training corpus. The results for this model are labeled "UD+25%" in Table 2 below.

Modern parser with enhanced lexicon

The syntactic differences between pre-standard and standard Irish are minimal; most of the problems arise from differences in morphology and orthography. We therefore wondered if a modern Irish parser could achieve good results on older texts if it were augmented with a tagged lexicon that provides reasonable coverage of pre-standard Irish. For this, we simply extracted the surface form, lemma, part-of-speech tag, and features for all of the tokens in the silver training corpus and used those as the lexicon with the modern Irish parser (our first model above). In this way we hoped to transfer a good bit of the lexical knowledge embedded in the standardizer to this model without introducing noisy dependency relations.

5. Results

The experimental results are presented in Table 2. Each of the seven models from the previous section was evaluated on three separate test sets. The first test set, corresponding to the columns labeled "Standard" in the table, is the official IUDT test set distributed with version 2.9 of the Universal Dependencies treebanks (Lynn et al., 2021); we included these results to give a sense of how well the models perform on standard Irish. The second test set, labeled "Older" in the table, consists of the 75 gold-standard sentences from the three 20th century texts discussed above (*Deoraidheacht*, *Peig*, and *Scairt an Dúthchais*). The third test set, labeled "Oldest" in the table, consists of the 75 gold-standard sentences from the three oldest and most challenging texts (*Foras Feasa ar Éirinn*, the 1602 Gospel of John, and *Cín Lae Amhlaoibh*).

The "POS" columns refer specifically to the Universal Dependencies ("UPOS") part-of-speech tags, and "Feat" refers to the UD morphological features. "UAS" and "LAS" are unlabeled and labeled attachment scores, respectively. All scores were computed using the evaluation script from the CoNLL 2017 Shared Task.

The first observation is that, as expected, the IUDT parser performs poorly on the pre-standard test sets, with the worst results on the oldest texts.

Next, we see that the projecting parser achieves the best results across the board for the two pre-standard test sets, although we believe some caution is required when interpreting these results. The Irish standardizer that drives the projecting parser has been under continuous development for almost 15 years, and many improvements have been made based on analysis of its output on various corpus texts, including the six comprising our test set. We expect that similar scores would be obtained on pre-standard texts from the same periods, but verifying this would require expanding the test sets to include a more diverse set of sources, ideally including some that were not available during development of the standardizer.

The results for the Silver parser are encouraging. They are only a few percentage points worse than the projecting parser, while not making direct use of the standardizer. We do note that its performance on the standard Irish test set is significantly worse than the IUDT model, which is unsurprising since it was trained only on pre-standard texts with noisy annotations.

This defect was fixed in the UD+100% model, which achieves scores comparable to the IUDT model on

Model	— Standard — Lem	POS	Feat	UAS	LAS	— Older — Lem	POS	Feat	UAS	LAS	— Oldest — Lem	POS	Feat	UAS	LAS
UD	95.8	94.4	82.1	81.8	74.5	80.8	85.2	74.4	77.6	67.4	63.8	72.3	56.4	61.2	46.8
Projecting	95.0	94.3	81.3	81.1	74.0	**97.9**	**96.4**	**89.8**	**84.8**	**77.3**	**89.4**	**89.7**	**77.5**	**73.0**	**63.1**
Silver	90.8	91.0	76.0	74.9	67.4	95.3	94.8	86.8	84.0	75.6	85.1	86.7	72.3	70.6	60.6
UD+100%	94.6	94.8	**83.9**	80.6	74.4	95.3	94.8	86.6	84.0	75.6	85.0	86.8	72.6	71.8	61.7
"+MUSE	94.6	94.8	**83.9**	**82.0**	**75.5**	95.3	94.8	86.6	84.4	76.4	85.0	86.8	72.6	71.8	61.4
UD+25%	95.3	94.7	83.4	81.8	75.0	92.2	93.3	84.2	81.4	72.9	80.0	83.9	68.5	70.4	58.7
UD+Lex	**95.9**	**94.9**	83.6	81.7	75.0	92.4	92.6	81.4	80.0	71.3	81.2	84.0	65.1	68.6	56.1

Table 2: F_1 scores for lemmatization, tagging, and parsing for each model across the three test sets.

standard Irish, and comparable to the Silver parser on the two pre-standard test sets. The next row shows that the addition of the MUSE cross-lingual word embeddings gives a sizable improvement to parsing accuracy on the standard and "older" test sets, while having no significant effect on the "oldest" test set.

As expected, the UD+25% model showed a small improvement in parsing on the standard test set over the UD+100% model, but this was hardly worth it given the steep decline on the two pre-standard test sets. It is clearly important to keep as much of the silver training data as possible to obtain satisfactory performance on these older texts. The results for the UD+Lex model were similar: slight improvements over the UD and UD+100% models on the standard test set, but a large drop-off on the other two, with scores even worse than UD+25%.

6. Conclusion

In this paper, we presented a new dataset for evaluating lemmatization, part-of-speech tagging, and dependency parsing of pre-standard Irish language texts. In addition, we performed a number of experiments to establish baseline scores for these tasks.

The results in Table 2 show clearly that a parser trained only on standard Irish performs poorly on pre-standard texts; this observation was the motivation behind this paper. The projecting parser gave very good results, but these may be slightly inflated given that the standardizer achieves very high performance on the six texts comprising the test set. The remaining models show that it is possible to achieve competitive results on both standard and pre-standard Irish without any gold training data, and without making use of the standardizer at all. This suggests that the most promising way forward will be to develop a large gold-standard treebank of pre-standard Irish, most likely by post-editing the output of the projecting parser. This treebank could then be combined with the IUDT training data and MUSE cross-lingual word embeddings to achieve high-quality lemmatization, tagging, and parsing on both standard and pre-standard texts with a single model.

7. Acknowledgements

I would like to acknowledge Teresa Lynn for her many years of work on the Irish treebank; without that resource, none of this research would have been possible. I am grateful to my students Sai Shreyas Bhavanasi and Jianjun Zhang at Saint Louis University for many discussions that helped me understand the mathematics behind cross-lingual word embeddings more deeply. This project originally arose out of conversations with Charlie Dillon at the Royal Irish Academy in early 2020 just before the COVID pandemic; my thanks to Charlie and the RIA for hosting me during that visit, and for inspiring this line of research.

8. Bibliographical References

Barry, J., Wagner, J., Cassidy, L., Cowap, A., Lynn, T., Walsh, A., Ó Meachair, M. J., and Foster, J. (2021). gaBERT – an Irish Language Model. *arXiv preprint arXiv:2107.12930.*

Berdičevskis, A. and Eckhoff, H. (2020). A Diachronic Treebank of Russian spanning more than a thousand years. In *Proceedings of the 12th Language Resources and Evaluation Conference*, pages 5251–5256.

Dereza, O. (2016). Building a dictionary-based lemmatizer for Old Irish. In *Actes de la conférence conjointe JEP-TALN-RECITAL*, volume 6, pages 12–17.

Dereza, O. (2019). Lemmatisation for under-resourced languages with sequence-to-sequence learning: A case of Early Irish. In *Proceedings of Third Workshop "Computational Linguistics and Language Science"*, volume 4, pages 113–124.

Doyle, A., McCrae, J. P., and Downey, C. (2018). Preservation of Original Orthography in the Construction of an Old Irish Corpus. *Sustaining Knowledge Diversity in the Digital Age*, pages 67–70.

Doyle, A., McCrae, J. P., and Downey, C. (2019). A Character-Level LSTM Network Model for Tokenizing the Old Irish text of the Würzburg Glosses on the Pauline Epistles. In *Proceedings of the Celtic Language Technology Workshop*, pages 70–79.

Eckhoff, H. M., Luraghi, S., and Passarotti, M. (2020). *Diachronic Treebanks for Historical Linguistics*, volume 113. John Benjamins Publishing Company, Amsterdam.

Estarrona, A., Etxeberria, I., Etxepare, R., Padilla-Moyano, M., and Soraluze, A. (2020). Dealing with dialectal variation in the construction of the Basque historical corpus. In *Proceedings of the 7th Workshop on NLP for Similar Languages, Varieties and Dialects*, pages 79–89.

Fransen, T. (2020). Automatic morphological analysis and interlinking of historical Irish cognate verb forms. In *Morphosyntactic Variation in Medieval Celtic Languages: Corpus-based approaches*, pages 49–83. De Gruyter Mouton.

Galves, C. (2018). The Tycho Brahe Corpus of Historical Portuguese: Methodology and results. *Linguistic Variation*, 18(1):49–73.

Lample, G., Conneau, A., Ranzato, M., Denoyer, L., and Jégou, H. (2018). Word translation without parallel data. In *International Conference on Learning Representations*.

Lynn, T. and Foster, J. (2016). Universal dependencies for Irish. In *Proceedings of the Second Celtic Language Technology Workshop*, pages 79–92.

Lynn, T., Çetinoğlu, Ö., Foster, J., Uí Dhonnchadha, E., Dras, M., and van Genabith, J. (2012). Irish treebanking and parsing: A preliminary evaluation. In *Proceedings of the Eighth International Conference on Language Resources and Evaluation (LREC'12)*, pages 1939–1946.

Lynn, T., Foster, J., Dras, M., and Tounsi, L. (2014). Cross-lingual transfer parsing for low-resourced languages: An Irish case study. In *Proceedings of the First Celtic Language Technology Workshop*, pages 41–49.

Lynn, T. (2016). *Irish Dependency Treebanking and Parsing*. Ph.D. thesis, Macquarie University and Dublin City University.

Nivre, J., De Marneffe, M.-C., et al. (2016). Universal Dependencies v1: A multilingual treebank collection. In *Proceedings of the Tenth International Conference on Language Resources and Evaluation (LREC'16)*, pages 1659–1666.

Petrova, S., Solf, M., Ritz, J., Chiarcos, C., and Zeldes, A. (2009). Building and Using a Richly Annotated Interlinear Diachronic Corpus: The Case of Old High German Tatian. *Trait. Autom. des Langues*, 50(2):47–71.

Rannóg an Aistriúcháin. (1945). *Litriú na Gaeilge. An caighdeán oifigiúil arna ullmhú ag Rannóig an Aistriúcháin d'Oifig Thithe an Oireachtais mar threorú do litriú na Gaeilge i ngnóthaí oifigiúla.* Oifig an tSoláthair, Baile Átha Cliath.

Scannell, K. (2014). Statistical models for text normalization and machine translation. In *Proceedings of the First Celtic Language Technology Workshop*, pages 33–40, Dublin, Ireland. Association for Computational Linguistics and Dublin City University.

Straka, M. and Straková, J. (2017). Tokenizing, POS tagging, lemmatizing and parsing UD 2.0 with UDPipe. In *Proceedings of the CoNLL 2017 Shared Task: Multilingual Parsing from Raw Text to Universal Dependencies*, pages 88–99.

Uí Dhonnchadha, E. and van Genabith, J. (2006). A Part-of-speech tagger for Irish using Finite-state Morphology and Constraint Grammar Disambiguation. In *Proceedings of LREC 2006*, pages 2241–2244.

Uí Dhonnchadha, E., Scannell, K., Ó hUiginn, R., Ní Mhearraí, E., Nic Mhaoláin, M., Ó Raghallaigh, B., Toner, G., Mac Mathúna, S., D'Auria, D., Ní Ghallchobhair, E., and O'Leary, N. (2014). Corpas na Gaeilge 1882–1926: Integrating Historical and Modern Irish Texts. In *LREC 2014 Workshop LRT4HDA: Language Resources and Technologies for Processing and Linking Historical Documents and Archives-Deploying Linked Open Data in Cultural Heritage, Reykjavik, Iceland, May, 2014*, pages 12–18.

Uí Dhonnchadha, E. (2008). *Part-of-speech tagging and partial parsing for Irish using finite-state transducers and constraint grammar*. Ph.D. thesis, Dublin City University.

Yarowsky, D. and Ngai, G. (2001). Inducing multilingual POS taggers and NP bracketers via robust projection across aligned corpora. In *Second Meeting of the North American Chapter of the Association for Computational Linguistics*.

9. Language Resource References

Bauer, Bernhard and Hofman, Rijcklof and Moran, Pádraic. (2018). *St. Gall Priscian Glosses*. stgallpriscian.ie, 2.0.

Cassidy, Lauren and Lynn, Teresa and Foster, Jennifer and McGuinness, Sarah. (2021). *The TwittIrish Universal Dependencies Treebank*. Universal Dependencies project, UD 2.9.

Dillon, Charles et al. (2017). *Corpas Stairiúil na Gaeilge 1600-1926*. Acadamh Ríoga na hÉireann.

Kroch, Anthony. (2020). *Penn Parsed Corpora of Historical English LDC2020T16*. Linguistic Data Consortium.

Lash, Elliott. (2014). *The Parsed Old and Middle Irish Corpus (POMIC)*. Dublin Institute for Advanced Studies, 0.1.

Lynn, Teresa and Foster, Jennifer and McGuinness, Sarah and Phelan, Jason and Scannell, Kevin and Walsh, Abigail. (2021). *The Irish Universal Dependencies Treebank (IUDT)*. Universal Dependencies project, UD 2.9.

Prévost, Sophie and Stein, Achim. (2013). *Syntactic Reference Corpus of Medieval French (SRCMF)*. ENS de Lyon/ILR Stuttgart, 0.92, ISLRN 899-492-963-833-3.

Scannell, Kevin P. (2022). *Universal Dependencies Treebank for Pre-Standard Irish*. Cadhan Aonair, 1.0.

Wallenberg, Joel C. and Ingason, Anton Karl and Sigurðsson, Einar Freyr and Rögnvaldsson, Eiríkur. (2011). *Icelandic Parsed Historical Corpus (IcePaHC)*. 0.9.

Proceedings of the CLTW 4 @ LREC2022 , pages 14–21
Marseille, 20-25 June 2022

Creation of an Evaluation Corpus and Baseline Evaluation Scores for Welsh Text Summarisation

Mahmoud El-Haj[1], Ignatius Ezeani[1], Jonathan Morris[2] and Dawn Knight[3]
[1]UCREL NLP Group, Lancaster University,
[2]School of Welsh, [3]School of English, Communication and Philosophy, Cardiff University
{m.el-haj, i.ezeani}@lancaster.ac.uk, {knightd5, morrisj17}@cardiff.ac.uk

Abstract

As part of the effort to increase the availability of Welsh digital technology, this paper introduces the first human vs metrics Welsh summarisation evaluation results and dataset, which we provide freely for research purposes to help advance the work on Welsh summarisation. The system summaries were created using an extractive graph-based Welsh summariser. The system summaries were evaluated by both human and a range of ROUGE metric variants (e.g. ROUGE 1, 2, L and SU4). The summaries and evaluation results will serve as benchmarks for the development of summarisers and evaluation metrics in other minority language contexts.

Keywords: summarisation, Welsh, evaluation, corpus, annotators

1. Introduction

Work on automatic text summarisation has a long history in Natural Language Processing (NLP). The majority of research on text summarisation was originally focused only on English, as a global lingua franca (Goldstein et al., 2000; Svore et al., 2007; Svore et al., 2007; Litvak and Last, 2008; El-Haj et al., 2011; El-Haj and Rayson, 2013). Recently this started to change with researchers shifting their focus towards a range of other language contexts, including French, Spanish, Hindi, Arabic, amongst others. Research community efforts such as the 'MultiLing' (Giannakopoulos et al., 2011) project and its associated workshop series, for example, are a noteworthy champion of developing text summarisation in a range of the world's 7000+ different languages. The MultiLing website[1] provides an open repository for summarisation tasks test/training data, model summaries, amongst others.

The development of the Adnodd Creu Crynodebau (ACC) project[2] contributes to both the development of summarisation tools in minority languages more generally and to the digital infrastructure of Welsh. Improving digital infrastructure for the Welsh language is a cornerstone of current Welsh Government policy designed to safeguard and promote the language[3]. Specifically, the Welsh Government's aim is to ensure that the Welsh language is at the heart of innovation in digital technology to enable the use of Welsh in all digital contexts (Welsh Government 2017: 71).

The development of an automatic summarisation tool contributes to this aim insofar as it will facilitate the preparation of summaries among professional content creators which can be made available online. From the user's perspective, ACC gives the reader agency to create easy-to-read summaries of long texts which enables the use of Welsh on the internet.
Table 1 shows a sample of a text in Welsh and a system summary that was generated using the Welsh Text Summary Creator (ACC) v.1.0[4] (Ezeani et al., 2022). The article in Table 1 can be found on Wikipedia both in Welsh[5] and English[6].

In this paper, we focus on the evaluation process of summaries created by ACC. Specifically, we compare the results of human evaluation with those produced using the ROUGE summarisation metric. Evaluating the output of summarisation tools using metrics such as ROUGE is a common practice in the field, but using this metric relies on comparison data. As ACC is the first summariser for Welsh, comparison data were not available and therefore human evaluation was needed. The evaluation metrics used were ROUGE-1, ROUGE-2, ROUGE-L and ROUGE-SU4. In addition, we provide results for human evaluation for summaries generated by our best performing summariser.

The remainder of the paper presents more context on the Welsh language and the development of the tool, before we turn to the methodology used to compare the human and ROUGE metrics and the results. The dataset and the code we used to create the summarisers are available on the Welsh Summarisation Project

[1]`http://multiling.iit.demokritos.gr`

[2]English translation from Welsh: "Welsh Summary Creator": `http://wp.lancs.ac.uk/acc/`

[3]Welsh Government: Cymraeg 2050 - A million Welsh speakers: `https://gov.wales/sites/default/files/publications/2018-12/cymraeg-2050-welsh-language-strategy.pdf`

[4]`https://share.streamlit.io/ucrel/welsh_summarizer/main/app/app.py`

[5]`https://cy.wikipedia.org/wiki/Yr_hawl_i_iechyd`

[6]`https://en.wikipedia.org/wiki/Right_to_health`

GitHub page[7].

Welsh text:
Mae Erthygl 25 o Ddatganiad Cyffredinol Hawliau Dynol 1948 y Cenhedloedd Unedig yn nodi: Mae gan bawb yr hawl i safon byw sy'n ddigonol ar gyfer iechyd a lles ei hun a'i deulu, gan gynnwys bwyd, dillad, tai a gofal meddygol a gwasanaethau cymdeithasol angenrheidiol. Mae'r Datganiad Cyffredinol yn cynnwys lletyaeth er mwyn diogelu person ac mae hefyd yn sôn yn arbennig am y gofal a roddir i'r rheini sydd mewn mamolaeth neu blentyndod. Ystyrir mai Datganiad Cyffredinol o Hawliau Dynol fel y datganiad rhyngwladol cyntaf o hawliau dynol sylfaenol. Dywedodd Uchel Gomisiynydd y Cenhedloedd Unedig dros Hawliau Dynol Navanethem Pillay fod y Datganiad Cyffredinol o Hawliau Dynol yn ymgorffori gweledigaeth sy'n gofyn am gymryd yr holl hawliau dynol - sifil, gwleidyddol, economaidd, cymdeithasol neu ddiwylliannol - fel cyfanwaith anwahanadwy ac organig, anwahanadwy a rhyngddibynnol.
System Summary:
Mae Erthygl 25 o Ddatganiad Cyffredinol Hawliau Dynol 1948 y Cenhedloedd Unedig yn nodi: Mae gan bawb yr hawl i safon byw sy'n ddigonol ar gyfer iechyd a lles ei hun a'i deulu, gan gynnwys bwyd, dillad, tai a gofal meddygol a gwasanaethau cymdeithasol angenrheidiol. Dywedodd Uchel Gomisiynydd y Cenhedloedd Unedig dros Hawliau Dynol Navanethem Pillay fod y Datganiad Cyffredinol o Hawliau Dynol.

Table 1: Example text with an automatically generated summary.

2. The Welsh Language

It is estimated that over a quarter (29.2%) of the population in Wales aged over 3 consider themselves to be Welsh speakers[8]. This estimate represents an increase in the proportion of the population who reported speaking Welsh at the (2011) census[9] and can be attributed, at least in part, to the ongoing attempts by Welsh Government and its stakeholders to safeguard the language and promote its use among the population (Carlin and Chríost, 2016).

Despite the promotion of Welsh in various domains, the use of Welsh language websites and e-services remains relatively low, despite the fact that numerous surveys suggest that Welsh speakers would like more opportunities to use the language, and that there has been extensive campaigning in order to gain language rights in the Welsh language context (Cunliffe et al., 2013). One reason for the relatively low take-up of Welsh-language options on websites is the assumption that the language used in such resources will be too complicated (Cunliffe et al., 2013).

Concerns around the complexity of public-facing Welsh language services and documents are not new. A series of guidelines on creating easy-to-read documents in Welsh are outlined in Cymraeg Clir (Arthur and Williams, 2019). Williams (1999) notes that the need for simplified versions of Welsh is arguably greater than for English in Wales considering (1) many Welsh public-facing documents are translated from English, (2) the standard varieties of Welsh are further removed from local dialects compared to English, and (3) newly-translated technical terms are more likely to be familiar to the reader. The principles outlined in Cymraeg Clir therefore include the use of shorter sentences, everyday words rather than specialised terminology, and a neutral (rather than formal) register (Williams, 1999).

Whilst the Welsh language is not necessarily more structurally complex than other languages for which automatic summarisation tools have been developed, there are sociolinguistic considerations which do need to be considered. In addition to the various dialects, there are differences in register between formal and informal varieties of Welsh, with informal registers formally found mainly in spoken Welsh now increasingly appearing also in written text. This has led to increased morphosyntactical and lexical differences between written varieties. As is shown below, this was considered when formulating guidance for those involved with the preparation of the human gold-standard summaries but does not necessarily mean that variation is not present in the dataset.

Our work will contribute to the digital infrastructure of the Welsh language. Given the introduction of Welsh Language Standards (Carlin and Chríost, 2016), which places requirements on public institutions to provide fully bilingual web content, and a concerted effort to both invest in Welsh language technologies and improve the way in which language choice is presented to the public, the development and evaluation of ACC will complement the suite of Welsh language technologies (e.g. Canolfan Bedwyr 2021[10]) for both content creators and Welsh readers. It is also envisaged that ACC will contribute to Welsh-medium education by allowing educators to create summaries for use in the

[7] https://github.com/Welsh-Summarization-Project

[8] https://gov.wales/welsh-language-data-annual-population-survey-july-2020-june-2021

[9] https://statswales.gov.wales/Catalogue/Welsh-Language/Census-Welsh-Language. The results of the 2021 Census are not yet released.

[10] Cysgliad: Help i ysgrifennu yn Gymraeg. Online: https://www.cysgliad.com/cy/

classroom as pedagogical tools. Summaries will also be of use to Welsh learners who will be able to focus on understanding the key information within a text.

3. Methods

Figure 1 shows the four key processes involved in the creation and evaluation of the Welsh summarisation dataset i.e. **a.** collection of the text data; **b.** creation of the reference (human) summaries; **c.** building summarisers and generating system summaries and **d.** evaluating the performance of the summarisation systems outputs on the reference summaries both using automatic metrics and human effort.

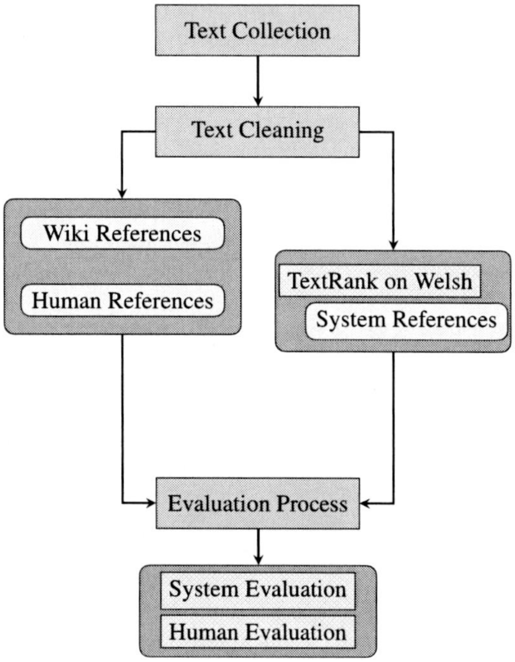

Figure 1: An overview of the process diagram

3.1. Text Collection

In order to be able to automatically evaluate the generated system summaries, we needed to first create reference human summaries (gold–standards). To do so we started by collecting 513 Wikipedia articles from the Welsh Wikipedia[11]. We then pre-processed the articles in order to extract the textual content. The data extraction applied a simple iterative process and implemented a Python script based on the WikipediaAPI[12] that takes a Wikipedia page; extracts key contents (article text, summary, category) and checks whether the article text contains a minimum number of tokens. At the end of this process. Figure 2 shows token counts of the 513 Wikipedia articles used for training of system summarisers as well as the average counts of the articles and the summaries. The majority of the articles (about 80%) contain between 500 and 2000 tokens. A total of 28 articles contain more than 5000 tokens. The extracted dataset contains a file for each Wikipedia page with the following structure and tags[13]:

```
<title>Article Title</title>
<text>Article Text</text>
<category>Article Categories</category>
```

The data files are also available in `plain text`, `.html`, `.csv` and `.json` file formats.

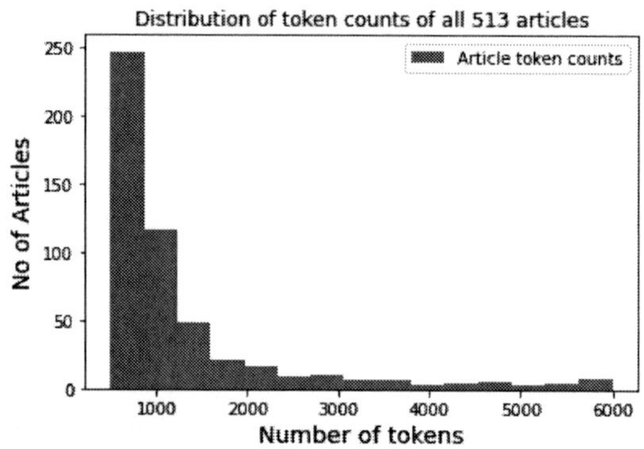

Figure 2: Distribution of tokens count

3.2. Reference Summaries Creation

In this work, two sources were used: a) the Wikipedia summaries extracted using the Wikipedia API[14] during the text collection stage and b) the summaries created by the human participants. A total of 19 undergraduate and postgraduate students from Cardiff University were recruited to create, summarise and evaluate the generated summaries, 13 of them were undertaking an undergraduate or postgraduate degree in Welsh, which involved previous training on creating summaries from complex texts. The remaining six students were undergraduate students on other degree programmes in Humanities and Social Sciences at Cardiff University and had completed their compulsory education at Welsh-medium or bilingual schools. Students were asked to complete a questionnaire prior to starting work, which elicited biographical information. Specifically, they were told that the aim of the task was to produce a simple summary for each of the Wikipedia articles (allocated to them) which contained the most important information. They were also asked to conform to the following principles:

[11]Welsh Wikipedia: `https://cy.wikipedia.org/wiki/Hafan` (Wicipedia)

[12]https://pypi.org/project/Wikipedia-API/

[13]The tags are there to help users find and extract part of the data they are interested in.

[14]Class WikipediaPage has property summary, which returns a description of a Wikipedia page `https://pypi.org/project/Wikipedia-API/`

- The length of each summary should be 230 - 250 words.
- The summary should be written in the author's own words and not be extracted (copy-pasted) from the Wikipedia article.
- The summary should not include any information that is not contained in the article
- Any reference to a living person in the article should be anonymised in the summary (to conform to the ethical requirements of each partner institution).
- All summaries should be proofread and checked using spell checker software (Cysill) prior to submission[15].

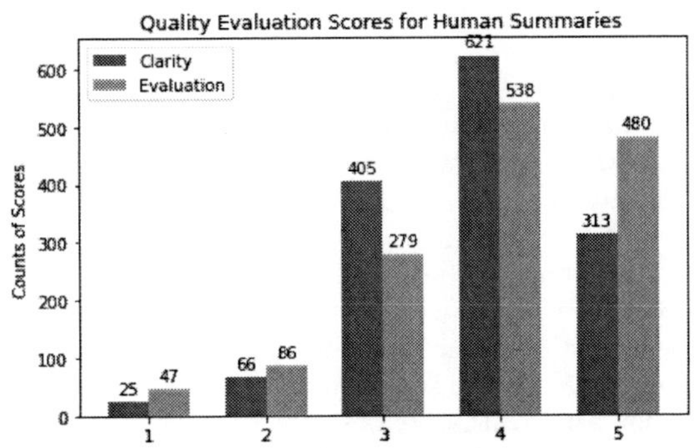

Figure 3: Distribution of the readability (clarity) and overall quality evaluation scores

Further instruction was given on the register to be used in the creation of summaries. Students were asked to broadly conform to the principles of Cymraeg Clir (Williams, 1999) and, in particular, avoid less common short forms of verbs and the passive mode, and use simple vocabulary where possible instead of specialised terms. In total the participants generated a number of 1,430 human summaries with an average of 3 summaries per article. In addition, three of the postgraduate students recruited were asked to evaluate the human summaries by giving a score between one and five.

Each summary was evaluated only once (by 1 participant) as the process here was to double check the summaries are according to the given instructions. Figure 3 shows the distribution of the readability (clarity) and overall quality evaluation scores for all the 1,430 currently available in the Welsh Summarisation Dataset. The mean and median scores for the human summaries were 4. The evaluators were instructed to fix common language errors (such as mutation errors and spelling mistakes) but not to correct syntax. All the participants were duly paid an approved legal wage for their work. Table 2 shows the marking criteria. The same criteria were later used when evaluating the system summaries.

[15]Cysill: www.cysgliad.com/cy/cysill

Score	Criteria
5	• Very clear expression and very readable style. • Very few language errors. • Relevant knowledge and a good understanding of the article; without significant gaps.
4	• Clear expression and legible style. • Small number of language errors. • Relevant knowledge and a good understanding of the article, with some gaps.
3	• Generally clear expression, and legible style. • Number of language errors. • The knowledge and understanding of the article is sufficient, although there are several omissions and several errors.
2	• Expression is generally clear but sometimes unclear. • Significant number of language errors. • The knowledge and understanding of the article is sufficient for an elementary summary, but there are a number of omissions and errors.
1	• Expression is often difficult to understand. Defective style. • Persistently serious language errors. • The information is inadequate for summary purposes. Obvious deficiencies in understanding the article.

Table 2: Criteria for the marking of summaries

3.3. Building Summariser Systems

The second phase of this summarisation project is to use the corpus dataset to inform the iterative development and evaluation of digital summarisation tools. The approaches used in this work is extraction-based summarisation. The successful extraction of content, when using summarisation tools/approaches, depends on the accuracy of automatic algorithms (which require training using hand-coded gold-standard datasets). As an under-resourced language with limited literature on

Welsh summarisation, applying summarisation techniques from the literature helps in having initial results that can be used to benchmark the performance of other summarisers on the Welsh language. In this project, we implemented and evaluated basic single-document extractive summarisation systems. That included the use of first-sentence-summary and a simple TF.IDF approach, but when evaluating the summaries using ROUGE we found that TextRank consistently outperformed the others systems when generating summaries of no longer than 250 words. In this paper we only focus on summaries generated using TextRank. The evaluation process took into consideration the human reference summaries as well as the Wikipedia summary (see Section 3.2). The summaries and their ROUGE evaluation results are explained in details in (Ezeani et al., 2022).

TextRank technique was introduced by Radev et al. (2004). This was the first graph-based automated text summarisation algorithm that is based on the simple application of the PageRank algorithm. PageRank is used by Google Search to rank web pages in their search engine results (Brin and Page, 1998). TextRank utilises this feature to identify the most important sentences in an article.

4. Evaluation Methodology

The performance evaluation of the system summarisers was carried out using variants of the ROUGE[16] metrics as well as human evaluators by scoring summaries generated by the best performing summariser (TextRank in our case (Erkan and Radev, 2004)). ROUGE measures the quality of the system generated summaries as compared with the reference summaries created or validated by humans (see Section 3.2). The current work uses the ROUGE variants that are commonly applied in literature: *ROUGE-N* (where N= 1 or 2) which considers N-gram text units i.e. unigrams and bigrams; *ROUGE-L* which measures the longest common sub-sequence in both system and reference summaries while maintaining the order of words; and *ROUGE-SU4* is an extended version of *ROUGE-S*[17] that includes unigrams. In this work we focus on ROUGE-1 as it was found to correlate particularly well with human judgement(Lin and Hovy, 2003).

Common implementations of ROUGE (Ganesan, 2018) typically produce three key metric scores precision, recall and F1-score as described below.

$$precision = \frac{count(overlapping\ units)}{count(system\ summary\ units)}$$

$$recall = \frac{count(overlapping\ units)}{count(reference\ summary\ units)}$$

$$f1 = (1+\beta^2) * \frac{recall * precision}{(\beta^2 * precision) + recall}$$

where the value of β is used to control the relative importance of *precision* and *recall*. Larger β values give more weight to *recall* while β values less than 1 give preference to *precision*. In the current work, β is set to 1 making it equivalent to the harmonic mean between *precision* and *recall*. The term '*units*' as used in the equation refers to either words or n-grams.

It is possible to achieve very high recall or precision scores if the system generates a lot more or fewer words than in the reference summary respectively. While we can mitigate that with F1 score to achieve a more reliable measure, we designed our evaluation scheme to investigate the effect of the summary sizes on the performance of the systems. We achieved this by varying the lengths of the system-reference summary pairs[18] during evaluation with `tokens = [50, 100, 150, 200, 250` and `None]` where `tokens` indicates the maximum tokens included in the summary and None signifies using the summary as it is. More details on the All reported scores are averages of the individual document scores over all the 513 Wikipedia documents used in the experiment.

In addition, we hired three undergraduate students at Cardiff University to perform the human evaluation of some of the summaries generated by TextRank[19]. In total 80[20] system summaries were evaluated with each summary being scored by each of the evaluators. The participants are two females and one male all aged 20 from Ceredigion, Denbighshire, and Gwynedd in Wales. All are native Welsh speakers. The evaluators followed the same scoring criteria shown in Table 2. In order to avoid bias, they were not told whether those are human or system summaries.

5. Results and Discussion

To measure the degree of agreement among the raters we asked the three annotators to blind score the 80 summaries generated by TextRank, all the summarised documents are articles collected from the Welsh Wikipedia as explained earlier (see Section 3.1). Each summary was scored by each of the annotators. To calculate inter-rater agreement we used Pearson Correlation Coefficient and Spearman's Rank Coefficient results, both coefficients were used in previous research to investigate the correlation between ROUGE metrics and hu-

[16]Recall-Oriented Understudy for Gisting Evaluation (Lin, 2004)

[17]Default *ROUGE-S* uses skip-gram co-occurrence which considers any pair of words in a sentence allowing for arbitrary gaps while maintaining the order.

[18]Note that the reference summaries have a length between 230 and 250 words as explained in Section 3.2. Therefore, studying a varying number of smaller lengths helps us in understanding the effect of summary size on the evaluation process.

[19]TextRank generated Welsh summaries of no longer than 250 words each.

[20]With only three evaluators, we were only able to manually evaluate 15% of the generated summaries. The summaries were chosen randomly.

man evaluations (Liu and Liu, 2008; Murray et al., 2005).

The correlation results in Table 3 show low agreements between the human evaluators[21], which is expected given that there is no ideal summary, especially that each evaluator would have personal perspectives and preferences on what to consider key information despite following the same guidelines (El-Haj et al., 2010; El-Haj et al., 2009). The table shows consistent correlations between Pearson and Spearman's, which shows that the evaluators did not agree most of the time, having said that the results are not suggesting zero relationship between the scores given by the human evaluators. Although this might sound negative in a way, we still believe the results are important to shed light on the complexity of the automatic summarisation task in general and in particular (e.g. Welsh text summarisation).

Evaluators	Pearson	Spearman's
E1 vs E2	0.170	0.161
E1 vs E3	0.325	0.355
E2 vs E3	0.327	0.233
R1 vs E1	0.154	0.168
R1 vs E2	0.007	0.117
R1 vs E3	0.014	0.201

Table 3: Inter-rater agreement scores (Pearson Correlation Coefficient and Spearman's Rank Coefficient). E: Evaluator; R: ROUGE-1.

In addition, we calculate the correlation between the human scores and ROUGE metrics, taking as a use case the results of ROUGE-1. As reported by (Lin and Hovy, 2003), ROUGE-1 was found to correlate particularly well with human judgement. The results in Table 3 show less correlation between ROUGE-1 (R1) and each of the human evaluators, especially when it comes to Pearson's linear relationship correlation, which seems to contradict to the findings reported by Lin and Hovy (2003). This disagreement could be due to the fact that the human evaluations originally run by the Document Understanding Conference (DUC)[22], was performed on news corpora and those are known to be shorter and less informative than Wikipedia articles. The correlation scores could also suggest that ROUGE may be less suited for summaries written in Welsh or languages other than English.

Table 4 shows the distribution of scores in terms of agreement/disagreement. This is shown between the human evaluators themselves as well as between them and ROUGE-1 scores. The results show low agreement between the given scores, again confirming with the correlation results from Table 3.

[21]Note that due to the notion of Pearson and Spearman's formulas, we observe scores > 0.0 despite the lack of agreement between Evaluator 1 and Evaluator 3.

[22]`https://duc.nist.gov/`

Evaluators	Agree	Disagree	%
E1 vs E2	4	76	5%
E1 vs E3	0	80	0%
E2 vs E3	34	46	43%
R1 vs E1	31	49	39%
R1 vs E2	7	73	9%
R1 vs E3	2	78	3%

Table 4: Scores agreement between the raters and ROUGE. E: Evaluator; R: ROUGE-1.

Table 5, shows the breakdown of the Likert Scale scores given by the human evaluators. In addition, we show the ROUGE-1 scores transformed into the same 1-5 Likert Scale for comparison purposes. As shown in the table, ROUGE-1 scores seem to alternate between a scale of 2 and 3, which is expected given the notion of ROUGE's similarity measure, which uses n-grams overlap. This would suggest that it will be difficult for a summary to have a score of zero and again, and given the lack of idealism in summarisation, would also mean that a score of 5 (total overlap) is near impossible since the human (reference/gold-standard) summaries were created using abstractive human summarisation method as explained in Section 3.2. It is also worth noting that the length of the generated summaries is no longer than 250 words but also not less than 10% of the original document, this is to avoid bias towards shorter summaries.

The results show that the human evaluators were more keen to give scores that are either 1 or > 3, which seems to be difficult to achieve using ROUGE. Figure 4 plots that distribution showing a somehow similar pattern between the second (E2) and third (E3) evaluators. On the other hand and given that the first evaluator (E1) scores are confined between 1 and 3, we can examine a pattern between those scores and the ones given by ROUGE-1 (R1).

Evaluators	1	2	3	4	5	Total
E1	38	29	13	0	0	80
E2	1	2	17	34	26	80
E3	0	2	5	33	40	80
R1	0	50	30	0	0	80

Table 5: Evaluation scores given by each of the raters and ROUGE. E: Evaluator; R1: ROUGE-1.

6. Conclusion and future work

This work shows the creation and evaluation of the first publicly available and freely accessible high-quality Welsh text summarisation dataset. Given that Welsh is considered low-resourced with regards to NLP, this dataset will enable further research works in Welsh automatic text summarisation systems as well as Welsh language technology in general. Overall, the development of the automated tools for Welsh

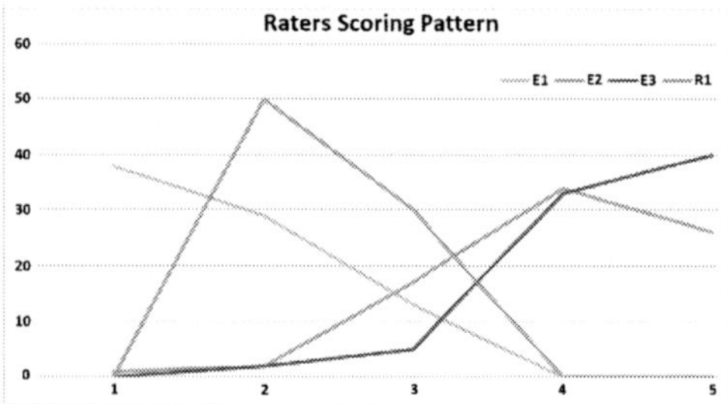

Figure 4: Evaluation (Likert) scores pattern for each of the human raters and ROUGE-1.

language and facilitate the work of those involved in document preparation, proof-reading, and (in certain circumstances) translation. In addition, providing a comparison between human and automatic evaluation results for Welsh summaries should help researchers in developing evaluation metrics that work for complex languages, where there is a less chance of overlapping n-grams between system and human summaries. The correlation results we got are consistent with correlation results in previous research applied on summaries written in English (Liu and Liu, 2008; Murray et al., 2005), which may suggest that the lack of correlation between ROUGE and human evaluations is consistent across different languages. Of course more research is required to fulfil this claim.

We are currently focusing on leveraging the existing state-of-the-art transformer based models for building and deploying Welsh text summariser model. The summarisation state of the art literature shows a great shift towards using deep learning to create extractive and abstractive supervised and unsupervised summarisers using deep learning models such as Convolutional Neural Network (CNN), Recurrent Neural Network (RNN), Long Short Term Memory (LSTM) and many others (Song et al., 2019; Zmandar et al., 2021a; Zmandar et al., 2021b; Magdum and Rathi, 2021).

In our future work we will examine the correlation between a larger set of system summaries generated using more complex and state-of-the-art summarisation methods as explained earlier and work on recruiting a large group of evaluators to try and match the previous effort by DUC conference.

7. Acknowledgements

This research was funded by the Welsh Government, under the Grant 'Welsh Automatic Text Summarisation'. We are grateful to Jason Evans, National Wikimedian at the National Library of Wales, for this initial advice.

8. Bibliographical References

Arthur, R. and Williams, H. T. (2019). The human geography of twitter: Quantifying regional identity and inter-region communication in england and wales. *PloS one*, 14(4):e0214466.

Brin, S. and Page, L. (1998). The anatomy of a large-scale hypertextual web search engine. *Computer networks and ISDN systems*, 30(1-7):107–117.

Carlin, P. and Chríost, D. M. G. (2016). A standard for language? policy, territory, and constitutionality in a devolving wales. In *Sociolinguistics in Wales*, pages 93–119. Springer.

Cunliffe, D., Morris, D., and Prys, C. (2013). Young bilinguals' language behaviour in social networking sites: The use of welsh on facebook. *Journal of Computer-Mediated Communication*, 18(3):339–361.

El-Haj, M. and Rayson, P. (2013). Using a keyness metric for single and multi document summarisation. In *Proceedings of the MultiLing 2013 Workshop on Multilingual Multi-document Summarization*, pages 64–71.

El-Haj, M., Kruschwitz, U., and Fox, C. (2009). Experimenting with automatic text summarisation for arabic. In *Language and Technology Conference*, pages 490–499. Springer.

El-Haj, M., Kruschwitz, U., and Fox, C. (2010). Using mechanical turk to create a corpus of arabic summaries.

El-Haj, M., Kruschwitz, U., and Fox, C. (2011). Multi-document arabic text summarisation. In *2011 3rd Computer Science and Electronic Engineering Conference (CEEC)*, pages 40–44. IEEE.

Erkan, G. and Radev, D. R. (2004). Lexrank: Graph-based lexical centrality as salience in text summarization. *Journal of artificial intelligence research*, 22:457–479.

Ignatius Ezeani, et al., editors. (2022). *Introducing the Welsh Text Summarisation Dataset and Baseline Systems*, Marseille, France, 20-25 June. The 13th Language Resources and Evaluation Conference, LREC 2022.

Ganesan, K. (2018). Rouge 2.0: Updated and improved measures for evaluation of summarization tasks.

Giannakopoulos, G., El-Haj, M., Favre, B., Litvak, M., Steinberger, J., and Varma, V. (2011). Tac 2011 multiling pilot overview.

Goldstein, J., Mittal, V. O., Carbonell, J. G., and Kantrowitz, M. (2000). Multi-document summarization by sentence extraction. In *NAACL-ANLP 2000 Workshop: Automatic Summarization*.

Lin, C.-Y. and Hovy, E. (2003). Automatic evaluation of summaries using n-gram co-occurrence statistics. In *Proceedings of the 2003 human language technology conference of the North American chapter of the association for computational linguistics*, pages 150–157.

Lin, C.-Y. (2004). Rouge: A package for automatic evaluation of summaries. In *Text summarization branches out*, pages 74–81.

Litvak, M. and Last, M. (2008). Graph-based keyword extraction for single-document summarization. In *Coling 2008: Proceedings of the workshop Multi-source Multilingual Information Extraction and Summarization*, pages 17–24.

Liu, F. and Liu, Y. (2008). Correlation between rouge and human evaluation of extractive meeting summaries. In *Proceedings of ACL-08: HLT, short papers*, pages 201–204.

Magdum, P. and Rathi, S. (2021). A survey on deep learning-based automatic text summarization models. In *Advances in Artificial Intelligence and Data Engineering*, pages 377–392. Springer.

Murray, G., Renals, S., Carletta, J., and Moore, J. (2005). Evaluating automatic summaries of meeting recordings.

Radev, D. R., Jing, H., Styś, M., and Tam, D. (2004). Centroid-based summarization of multiple documents. *Information Processing & Management*, 40(6):919–938.

Song, S., Huang, H., and Ruan, T. (2019). Abstractive text summarization using lstm-cnn based deep learning. *Multimedia Tools and Applications*, 78(1):857–875.

Svore, K., Vanderwende, L., and Burges, C. (2007). Enhancing single-document summarization by combining ranknet and third-party sources. In *Proceedings of the 2007 joint conference on empirical methods in natural language processing and computational natural language learning (EMNLP-CoNLL)*, pages 448–457.

Williams, C. (1999). *Cymraeg Clir: Canllawiau Iaith.* Bangor: Gwynedd Council, Welsh Language Board and Canolfan Bedwyr.

Zmandar, N., El-Haj, M., Rayson, P., Litvak, M., Giannakopoulos, G., Pittaras, N., et al. (2021a). The financial narrative summarisation shared task fns 2021. In *Proceedings of the 3rd Financial Narrative Processing Workshop*, pages 120–125.

Zmandar, N., Singh, A., El-Haj, M., and Rayson, P. (2021b). Joint abstractive and extractive method for long financial document summarization. In *Proceedings of the 3rd Financial Narrative Processing Workshop*, pages 99–105.

Proceedings of the CLTW 4 @ LREC2022, pages 22–29
Marseille, 20-25 June 2022

CLILSTORE.EU - A Multilingual Online CLIL Platform

Caoimhín Ó Dónaill
Ulster University
York Street, Belfast
c.odonaill@ulster.ac.uk

Abstract

CLILSTORE.EU is an open educational resource (OER) that was created by the Erasmus+ funded CLIL Open Online Learning (COOL) project which ran from 2018-2021. The project consortium included teaching practitioners from the primary, secondary, tertiary and vocational sectors who each brought their influence to bear on the design and functionality of the OER and subsequently evaluated its development within the learning contexts of their respective sectors. CLILSTORE.EU serves as both an authoring and sharing platform where multimedia learning materials can be created and accessed. Its name comprises the acronym CLIL, owing to its particular suitablity as a tool to support the Content and Language Integrated Learning methodology (Marsh, 2002). The main educational aims of the OER are to provide teachers with a relatively straightforward means of creating reusable, multimodal learning units that can be used within the classroom or via remote learning to underpin and scaffold the delivery of curricular content in any subject area, especially in contexts where learners are acquiring new knowledge through the medium of a second or additional language. The following account details recent development work on the OER's functionality and usability and presents case studies showing how it can benefit Celtic languages.

Keywords: CLIL, Multilingual, Irish, Scottish Gaelic, Manx, Celtic

1. Introduction

The COOL project (2018-2021) was designed to help language teachers and curricular subject teachers seeking to innovate in their teaching practices through the adoption and implementation of the Content and Language Integrated Learning (CLIL) methodology. The project's main objectives were focused on: (i) teachers' professional development needs in relation to gaining a working knowledge of the theoretical background to CLIL, and (ii) teachers' practical needs in relation to curricular delivery, materials' development and supporting learners (ii). The first objective was met by developing a certified MOOC *How to create lessons using Clilstore*,[1] which provides an introductory course in CLIL. The second objective was met by undertaking a significant redesign and updating of Clilstore, an online facility which had been previously developed by the TOOLS for CLIL Teachers project (2012-2014).[2] The original Clilstore facility[3] had proved popular with end users and by January 2018 it had attracted 2448 registered authors and the site had recorded in excess of 1.7 million visits. Indictors of Clilstore's impact on end users include the European Commission's selection of the TOOLS project as one of its 'Success Stories' and a 'Good Practice Example',[4] and Clilstore's inclusion in *The Handbook of Technology and Second Language Teaching and Learning* (Chapelle and Sauro, 2017).

Research carried out by members of the TOOLS project also established that teachers from a range of European countries who had received training in CLIL methodology and in the use of Clilstore to support the delivery of their curricula agreed that Clilstore was a "useful tool in order to create, publish and deliver learning materials that aid in conducting dual-focused teaching by supporting content learning as well as foreign language learning" (Gimeno Sanz, Ó Dónaill & Andersen, 2014). Clilstore was also found to be very effective in helping students within a higher education setting to acquire new vocabulary by benefitting from Clilstore's multimodal delivery of content, embedded extension activities and dictionary consultation facilites (Ó Dónaill, 2013).

1.1 Case for support

The case for support for the redesign and updating of Clilstore was based on a number of factors: (i) Although the original coding of Clilstore was still working as designed[5], the unique working version of the program and database were being hosted on a server in a remote area of Scotland, which meant that local power cuts could result in a loss of service and the program and database could have been lost entirely if the server had suffered physical damage. Therefore, the migration of the program and database to a cloud hosting service and the creation of an exportable version of the program would ensure future viabilty and development; (ii) the appearance of the user interface, although still practical and logical, had become dated by contemporary standards and it was not responsive for mobile devices; (iii) the program needed to be updated to faciltate the integration of Web3 technologies and HTML5 based learning applications; (iv) the original user experience was weighted towards the needs of teachers and a clear rationale existed for providing a separate, streamlined experience for both teachers and students; (v) given Clilstore's emphasis on encouraging and facilitating learners to perform dictionary consultations as they read through embedded texts, there was a clear imperative to develop this activity further by providing learners with a means of tracking and recording their dictionary consultations and noting meaningful definitions and translations in order to assist with vocabulary retention and recall. The development of a learner login system,

---

1 https://www.upvx.es/courses/course-v1:Filologiainglesa+clilstore+2021-01/about

2 http://languages.dk/tools/index.htm

3 Hosted at http://multidict.net

4 https://erasmus-plus.ec.europa.eu/projects/search/details/82d89d4e-e381-42ff-b72f-fc9a11f3c674

5 For a full technical description of how Clilstore and its related functions work, see Ó Donnaíle, 2014.

therefore, offered a means of further enhancing the learner experience by enabling registered learners to create personal vocabulary lists and glossaries for the language(s) and subjects they were learning and to develop learning games based on same; (vi) end users had expressed a desire for Clilstore to include a facilty for teachers to link with classes and individual learners via shareable portfolios; (vii) while it had been demonstrated that Clilstore could be used to support the creation and exploitation of learning units in a wide range of European languages and non-European languages such as Arabic, the user experience from authoring to navigation through the site was available in English only. This was problematic for learning contexts where English was neither the language of instruction nor the learners' target language.

2. Clilstore, Wordlink & Multidict

Users visiting CLILSTORE.EU[6] are met with a choice of three facilities:

- **Clilstore**, a repository of learning units where students can find content at their desired learner level on various topics, comprising texts where every word is linked to a choice of online dictionaries in the unit's language, and an authoring tool where teachers can create, store and organise multimedia learning units for use by students
- **Wordlink**, a tool which enables webpages to be automatically linked word-for-word to online dictionaries in a choice of languages. This scaffolds the reading of webpages for learners by allowing them to read texts until they meet words they don't know and to then easily perform dictionary consultations by clicking on the new word and seeing a definition or translation in a separate frame next to the webpage text.
- **Multidict**, a matrix of online dictionaries that facilitates easy switching between online dictionaries in many languages and the flexible pairing of languages for bilingual consultations.

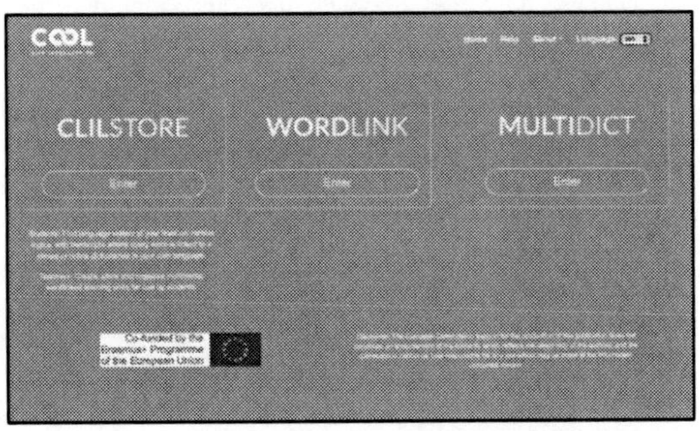

Figure 1: The CLILSTORE.EU homepage.

[6] https://clilstore.eu

A comprehensive practitioner guide to CLILSTORE.EU which details all of the learner and teacher focused functions is available to download (in English, Irish, Danish, Italian and Spanish).[7]

3. Key Developments

As stated in 1.1 above, the COOL project set out to develop a series of new features in order to make the OER more useful as a tool for promoting linguistic diversity within language and subject teaching and learning, to promote deep learning of vocabulary and subject knowledge and to facilitate reflective learning. The following sections provide a description of items iv-vii from the Case for support (1.1).

3.1 Streamlined user interfaces

Having entered Clilstore, visitors are now presented with a choice of proceeding with an experience optomized for (1) students or (2) teachers. Unregistered users can also access the registration facility (3) from this page.

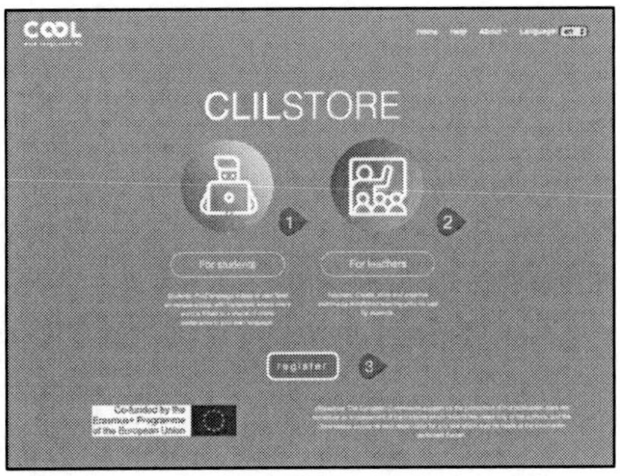

Figure 2: The Clilstore user gateway.

If the user selects the 'For students' pathway, they are taken to the following page, which features links to: (1) user profile (Options), the vocabulary builder and the portfolio tools; and (2) the learning units' search and filter facility.

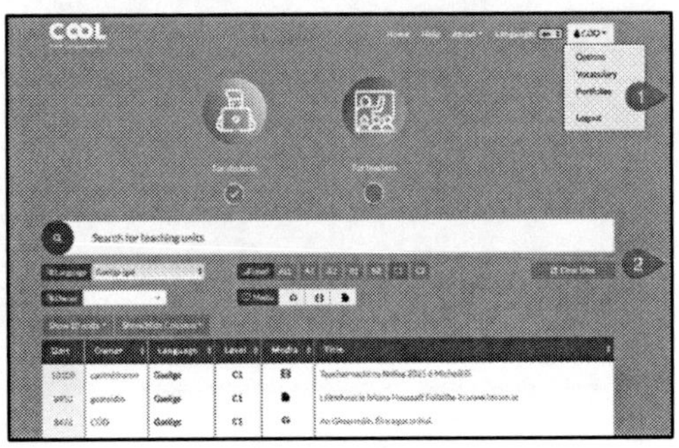

Figure 3: The student interface.

[7] https://riunet.upv.es/handle/10251/181708

If the user selects the 'For teachers' pathway, they are taken to the following page, which features links to: (1) user profile (Options), a list of the units they have authored (My units), a link to the authoring facility (Create a unit) and a link to the portfolio tool to view student portfolios that have been shared with them; (2) the learning units' search and filter facility; and (3) edit and delete options for units they have authored.

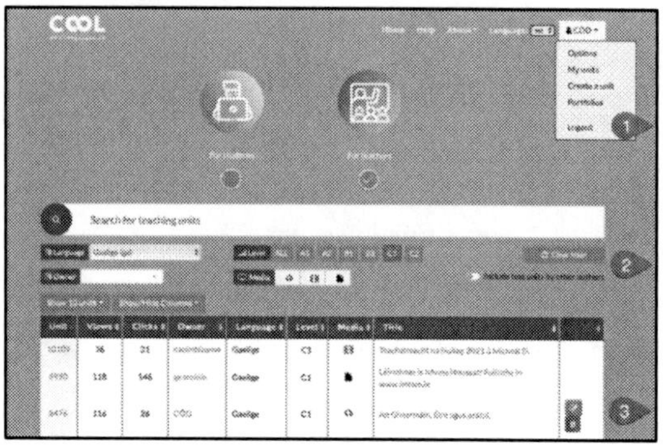

Figure 4: The teacher interface.

3.2 Vocabulary Builder

When accessed from the Student interface, the Vocabulary Builder provides the user with an editable list of the words they have looked up in Multidict as they have been working through their chosen learning units. The tool compiles a separate list for each language the user is learning (1). It provides options for exporting the lists for safekeeping or futher use outside of Clilstore, and for clearing existing lists (2). The user can easily create learning games based on their own lists, where they can hide the meanings and test their recall (Hide all), or decouple and randomize the words from their meanings in order to create a drag and drop exercise (Randomize). When viewing their vocabulary lists, users can click on the word to view it in Multidict again, or click on the unit number to view the word in the context where they encountered it again (4). The recording of dictionary consultations can be easily turned off if not required.

Figure 5: The Vocabulary Builder tool.

3.3 Portfolios

The portfolio tool was developed as a facility to help student users reflect upon and make a note of what they have learnt from using individual learning units or groups of learning units. The student user can use it for private reflection, or they can choose to share and unshare their portfolio with other registered users, e.g. their teacher(s).

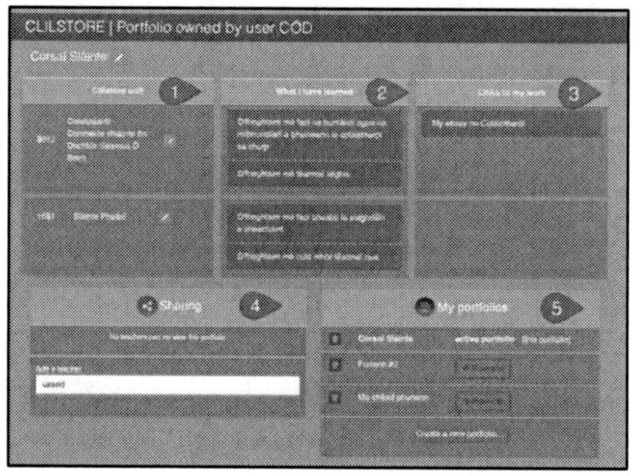

Figure 6: The Portfolio tool (Student view)

The portfolio layout has been designed to suit users of any age. The first step is for users to create and name a new portfolio. Once they have done this, they can start adding units to the portfolio (1), and then write short reflections on their experience of using the units (2). In immersion education contexts, this is a good opportunity for students to practice written composition in the target language. If the students have been tasked with creating a separate piece of work based on the Clilstore unit(s), e.g. an essay which they have written and saved in Google Docs, or a short video presentation which they have uploaded to YouTube, they can choose to share links to these via the portfolio (3). Portfolios can be easily shared with other registered users by entering their Clilstore user id (4) in the Sharing field. Finally, students can keep track of all their portfolios, change the order in which they appear and delete any portfolios which they no longer require (5).

To access the portfolios that have been shared with them, the teacher simply has to select Portfolios from the list of options in the Teacher interface (Figure 3, Item 1) and they will see a list of shared portfolios by Student Id.

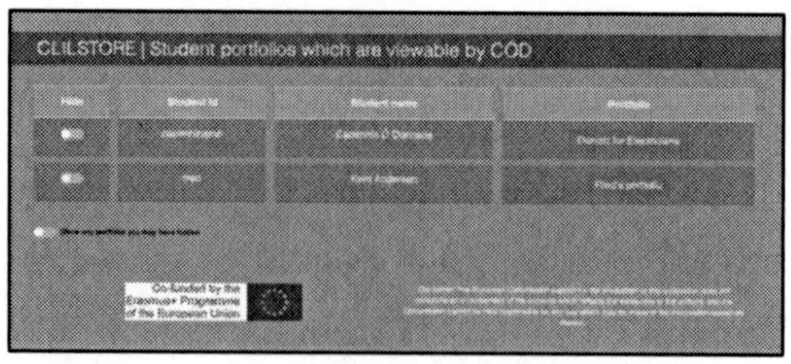

Figure 7: The Portfolio tool (Teacher view)

3.4 Internationalization

The internationalization of the Clilstore/Wordlink/ Multidict system, and full localization into 10+ languages has been a major successful outcome of the COOL project, and a very good example of international cooperation by both the project consortium and other members of the community of practice who kindly volunteered their time to localize the facilties into their own languages. The interface is currently available in: Breton, Irish, Scottish Gaelic, Danish, Serbo-Croatian, French, Italian, Portuguese, Spanish and English. Work is currently ongoing in a number of other languages and there is limitless scope to keep adding new interface languages. Previously, the resources were only available with an English interface, which meant that Romanian workers in Spain, for example, who were using Clilstore to help them acquire Spanish, would have had to struggle with an interface in a third language; or students using the resources in an Irish medium school would be forced to use English to navigate their way through the OER within a learning context where efforts are focused on limiting the use of English.

The internationalization of Clilstore/Wordlink/Multidict was facilitated by **Smotr**, an in-house system whose name is a portmanteau of '**SMO TR**anslation system' (SMO = Sabhal Mòr Ostaig, one of the COOL project partners and the home institution of the project's programmer, Caoimhín Ó Donnaíle). Smotr was initiated to provide a bilingual Gaeilge/Gàidhlig interface to An Sruth, a database of idioms and phrases hosted by SMO,[8] however, most of the Smotr system was developed in the COOL project, with the help of testing and feedback from the project partners and other users. Smotr is now used to provide internationalization for six facilities: Clilstore, Wordlink, Multidict, An Sruth, Bunadas, and Smotr itself.[9]

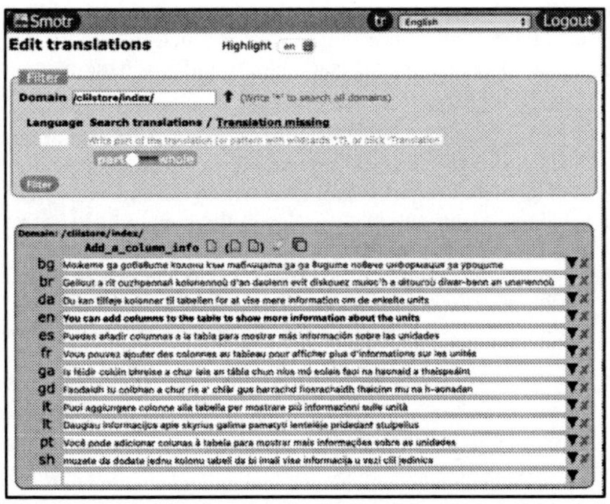

Figure 8: The SMOTR internationalization facility

Smotr comprises a number of innovations which are uncommon in internationalization/localization systems. The translated strings come real-time from a database. This makes it possible for users to switch languages on any page, without the need to return to the home page of the facility or to perform a restart. More importantly and unusually, it means that the human translators can see the result of their translation work instantly and in context, and can immediately see whether their translation is appropriate, or problemmatic in any way (e.g. too long compared to the original English language string).

In fact, when someone with translation rights is logged in, they see in the title-bar a 'tr' button which takes them instantly to the translation strings which are used by that page, with the ability to add or alter a local translation. Smotr is hosted at the multidict.net interface only, however, the localization is applied to both Multidict.net and CLILSTORE.EU in real time. If any strings on the webpage are not yet translated into the current interface language, they are shown on the page in a default language (usually English, but a sequence of default languages can be specified in the facility). They are shown preceded by a ¤ symbol, which lets the translator and users know that a translation is required. Making translations instantaneously available in a production system could be a security risk in a major system, but is not a problem on the scale we are working at. This approach makes the experience much more enjoyable for the human translators, in comparison with the usual method of working blindly through long lists of strings with little or no context.

Smotr is designed to enable the sharing of translations between pages and parts of a system, and even between different systems. This is done by each webpage specifying a 'translation domain' when it registers with Smotr. The unitinfo.php page in Clilstore, for example, registers itself with Smotr using the translation domain '/clilstore/unitinfo/'. When Smotr is asked to supply a translated string, it will look first for a translation from those labelled '/clilstore/unitinfo/', next it will try '/clilstore/' (translations common to the whole of Clilstore), and finally it will try the top-level translation domain '/'. This saves work for the translators. It means that a statistics page can be generated giving a real-time overview of the translation work which has been done and which still needs to be done.[10]

Translators can click on any cell in this table to be taken straight to a list of strings which still need to be translated in that translation domain.

Another feature of Smotr is that whenever it gets a request for a translated string, it records the page which made the request (and updates a count and timestamp). This means that translators can see which strings are being used by which pages, and if they change a translation, they can quickly check that their change is appropriate for all the pages where that translation is used.

Future development of Smotr will include adding a facility for the programmer to flag translations which need checking by human translator following some change they have made to the program. Two possible flag levels are

[8] https://www3.smo.uhi.ac.uk/teanga/sruth/?hl=en

[9] https://www3.smo.uhi.ac.uk/teanga/

[10] https://www3.smo.uhi.ac.uk/teanga/smotr/aireamhan.php

envisaged: 'still usable but needs checking' and 'not usable until checked and if necessary corrected'. The Smotr statistics page would consequently include a means of displaying where checks were required.

4. Celtic Language Case Studies

Learners of Less Widely Used and Taught Languages (LWUTLs) such as Irish, Scottish Gaelic and Manx have a much more limited choice of open access content available to them in comparison to the major European and World languages. The COOL project and its predecessor project TOOLS for CLIL Teachers, have included partners from Ireland and Scotland who have sought to ensure that Clilstore could cater for Irish and Scottish Gaelic in particular, and potentially other Celtic languages. The following case studies highlight three separate initiatives that were undertaken to highlight Clilstore's potential as a tool to assist teachers and learners of Celtic languages.

4.1 Case study 1: Irish language units

The principal motivation to create these materials was to facilitate autonomous learning for students within Higher Education study programmes, however, given that the materials are open source, they can cater for a wider group of users, e.g.: independent learners, adult learners within community education programmes and learners from secondary education. Content and Language Integrated Learning (CLIL) provides a methodological framework that establishes a productive relationship between teacher and learner, whereby the emphasis is on presenting content to learners and taking steps to enable them to make sense of it, and acquire receptive and productive competence in using the language in which the content is delivered. An important additional consideration in CLIL methodology is the need to focus on the cultural aspect of language use, and to assist learners in familiarising themselves with how the target language is used in context. Using authentic content generated by members of a speech community for the purpose of communicating with other members of that community can succeed in fulfilling the objectives of CLIL in a way that non-authentic materials can not, particularly regarding the cultural imperative.

The language attainment level for undergraduate, Bachelor of Arts programmes at Ulster University, and in Third Level Institutions throughout Ireland, is benchmarked to Level B2 on the Common European Framework of Reference for Languages (CEFR) (Council of Europe, 2001). In terms of listening competence, the CEFR sets out the following indicators at Level B2:

Can understand standard spoken language, live or broadcast, on both familiar and unfamiliar topics normally encountered in personal, social, academic or vocational life.

Can understand the main ideas of propositionally and linguistically complex speech on both concrete and abstract topics delivered in a standard dialect, including technical discussions in his/her field of specialisation. Can follow extended speech and complex lines of argument provided the topic is reasonably familiar, and the direction of the talk is sign-posted by explicit markers.

Basing learning units on authentic content has the advantage of enabling learners to use the language classroom or their personal learning space as a safe zone in which challenging material, in line with the above indicators, can be worked through with the assistance of available reference and practice materials.

Any attempt to try and create audio/audiovisual materials to expose students to the breadth of content implied by the above indicators would have considerable resource implications in terms of time alone. Furthermore, the opportunity to provide a dry run of real-world communication within the safe confines of a programme of study is potentially missed by using simulated materials created solely for the purpose of teaching and learning.

In light of this, Ulster University approached Raidió na Gaeltachta (RnaG), an Irish language radio station which forms part of Raidió Teilifís Éireann (RTÉ), Ireland's national public service media organisation, to request permission to use its archive of recordings as the basis for language learning units to be hosted on the Clilstore OER. Using recordings from this archive would of course guarantee authenticity, as the station exists principally to serve the needs of its listeners, L1 and L2 speakers of Irish seeking information and entertainment, and not specifically as a language learning resource. As most learners at undergraduate BA level and below desire to join this speech community and feel comfortable within it, it stands to reason that we should be using this type of archival material to model the language for learners within language study programmes.

RnaG's archive stretches back to when the station was established in 1972, it is the largest minority language archive in Europe (de Mórdha, 2019). Its content spans a wide array of topics including: news, current affairs, interviews with people from all walks of life, commentary on sporting events, folklore, song and music. It caters for an eclectic listenership with both scholarly and casual interests and serves an important function in documenting the life of a unique and rapidly changing speech community.

A key feature of the Clilstore OER is the ability for authors to curate the material selected for a language learning unit. The metadata fields provided within the authoring interface allow a unit author to: indicate the source of the material; provide a description of the content; provide a description of the language used in the embedded media (e.g. dialectal features, genre etc.); the duration of the clip; information about copyright staus; and indicate the optimal learner level of the unit based on the Common European Framework of Reference for Languages (2001). Text provided within these fields is discoverable by Google. This data is available to all users by clicking on the ■ icon within the unit itself (see Figure 9 below). This field also provides user analytical data which allows the author to see how their unit is being used. It provides a live record of the number of views and also the total number of words that have been clicked on within the unit. A list of the words that have been clicked on in order to look them up in Multidict is also provided. This allows a teacher, for example, to see which words are providing the greatest comprehension challenge for student users. From the Unit Info field, students can also choose to view a Google translated version of the embedded texts and also get a plain text version of the texts.

The process then of harvesting materials from an archive such this involves: the careful selection of content on the basis of its language learning potential and its thematic content; the preparation of verbatim transcripts; the curation of the material using the metadata form and the preparation of language learning exercises to extend and deepen the learning experience. The following url[11] provides a direct link to a sample unit based on authentic content from RnaG. It contains: (i) an audio recording streamed from the Soundcloud hosting provider; (ii) a verbatim transcript with spellings normalized to the standards of Foclóir Gaeilge-Béarla (Ó Dónaill, 1977) and all words hyperlinked to Multidict; and (iii) a linked comprehension exercise created using the online application LearningApps.org.[12] This is one of over 50 RnaG focused units that are available and discoverable from the CLILSTORE.EU unit index. The provision of exemplars such as this are also intended to inspire other authors to create materials in a similar vein using the CLILSTORE.EU author interface.

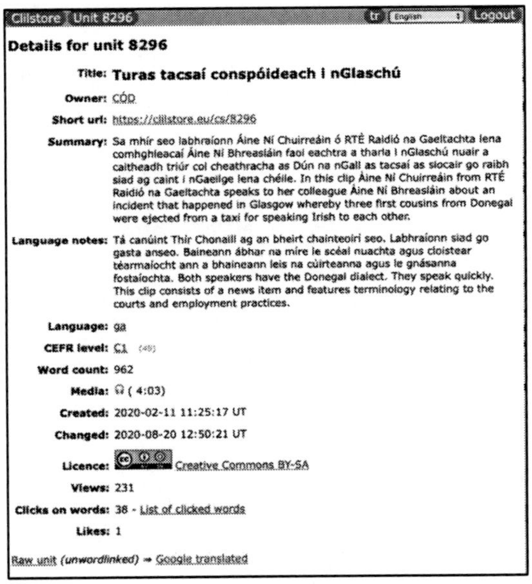

Figure 9: The Unit Info field

4.2 Case study 2: Manx language units

The Covid lockdown in 2020 brought with it something new and exciting for Manx, a series of advanced reading classes taught via Zoom by Chris Lewin, the foremost expert on the Manx language. This series was so successful, with class numbers averaging over 16, that it was followed six months later by another series of 10 classes, and then another, all supported by Culture Vannin. In all, a total of 60 hours of quality teaching. Chris made the class materials available via Dropbox: authentic Manx texts of historical and cultural importance from the 18th and 19th centuries in Word and PDF format, together with sound recordings he made in various sound formats.

Caoimhín Ó Donnaíle, the programmer from the COOL project, attended all the classes, and realizing that this was an ideal application for Clilstore, turned the soundfiles and texts into Clilstore units. Since these Clilstore units proved much more convenient than the Dropbox files, as well as having the huge advantage of instantaneous online dictionary lookup, they quickly became the main resource used in preparation work by the class students. Chris, the teacher, demonstrated during classes how to use Clilstore and how to use it look up words in the Manx dictionaries. Evidence that the class students really were using the Clilstore units, and using them for dictionary lookup, was provided by the fact that they would complain if the material was late in appearing in Clilstore, and also objected on one particular occasion when a unit was accidentally given the wrong language code so that dictionary lookup did not work.

The classes were attended by many Manx speakers in the Isle of Man itself, but also by many people outside the island who were more fluent in Irish or Scottish Gaelic than in Manx. For these speakers of other Gaelic languages, Clilstore really is an ideal resource for learning Manx. Nearly all Manx words are similar to words in Irish or Scottish Gaelic, but the Manx spelling system very often makes them unrecognizable. The sound files and the instantaneous dictionary lookup neatly overcome this problem.

For a very small language, Manx fortunately has excellent provision of online dictionaries, and all of these are available via Multidict. Fockleyreen is excellent and comprehensive. Craine is excellent and very legible. As well as these modern online dictionaries, the classic Manx dictionaries, Cregeen (1835) and Kelly (1866) have been scanned by the WebArchive, and since Multidict has a page-index to the 180 pages of Cregeen and to the 430 pages of Kelly, it can go instantaneously to the relevant page.

The 59 Clilstore units produced for these online Manx reading classes should prove to be an enduring resource. They contain a total of almost 5 hours of quality sound recordings, and 58 thousand words of authentic text. They represent a major teaching resource at advanced level for this small and threatened language.

The following urls[13] provide direct links to sample Manx (Gaelg) units based on the materials described above.

4.3 Case study 3: Scottish Gaelic language units

The CLILSTORE.EU unit index contains over 200 units for Scottish Gaelic (Gàidhlig). A large proportion of these were created by the Island Voices/Guthan nan Eilean

[11] https://clilstore.eu/cs/8296

[12] https://learningapps.org

[13] https://clilstore.eu/cs/8657 and https://clilstore.eu/cs/9800

project.[14] This material has a strong community emphasis, and focuses on capturing and curating samples of authentic speech, sourced almost exclusively in the Western Isles, the most highly concentrated Gaelic-speaking area in Scotland, according to the census figures. These units offer qualitative insights into real-life Gaelic interactions and focus on a range of thematic areas such as life outdoors, generations and enterprise. The collection also includes interviews with well known characters and raconteurs offering reflections and recounting anecdotes from their lives.

The following url[15] provides a link to one such example. At the time of writing, this unit had been viewed 3000+ times and 1200+ dictionary consultations had been performed by users.

The Guthan nan Eilean units offer a different perspective on how CLILSTORE.EU may be used as a tool for creating learning materials. Whereas the Irish and Manx case studies above focused on the adaptation of existing content and the steps taken to add value to it and repurpose it with the assistance of the CLILSTORE.EU technology, the Guthan nan Eilean units demonstrate the power of user generated content. In this scenario, the creation of learning units can follow a predetermined thematic area and the raw materials can be modified as they are being produced, if necessary. This highlights the OER's potential as a vehicle for ethnographic retrieval initiatives and a tool for promoting fragile minority language cultures alongside the more robust languages hosted on the platform.

5. Impact and Reach

The COOL project set out to build an active community of practice made up of language teachers and learners who would register with Clilstore, learn how to use the authoring tool and sharing functions, and create interactive, multimedia learning units in the project languages and many other languages besides.

By the end of the funded period of the project (September 2018 - December 2021) 9852 learning units in over 30 languages had been created covering approximately 40+ countries, incorporating the EEA, East Asia, the Americas and Australasia. The learning units (including test units) had generated over 4,516,385 views and over 807,901 dictionary consultations using the in-built Multidict feature had been performed within the units. This provides evidence of deep learning taking place with the help of the Clilstore units. Feedback received from end users during the project period allowed the team to debug errors and also to make programming adjustments to Clilstore's coding in order to streamline how the OER works and to meet the end users' needs.

The project website[16] has provided a key reference point for end users internationally. It contains supporting documents for end users e.g. promotional and training videos, project newsletters and curated selections of exemplary learning units that have been mapped to the 5Cs of CLIL (Content, Communication, Cognition, Competences and Community). These materials provide new users with valuable contextual information that enables them to evisage how Clilstore may be integrated into their classroom and institutional practice. During the project period (September 2019 - December 2021) there were 537,987 visitors to the project website. The annual number of visitors has varied from year to year during the project period; 2018 (First 3 months of the project, September - December) = 61,000 visitors; 2019 = 230,967 visitors; 2020 = 149,946 visitors; 2021 = 96,074 visitors. Each visitor consulted several pages.

6. Evaluation

During January-February 2021 a cross-section of educational practitioners who had registered with CLILSTORE was invited to complete a feedback survey focusing on a range of factors relating to the platform's functionality and the impact it had made to their professional practice. There were 61 responses with a sectoral breakdown of:

Secondary = 36%; HE = 28%; FE = 27%; Other (Primary, Community) = 9%

6.1 Uptake

70% of respondents reported that they had learned about the resource through direct engagement at training courses organised by the project team, with a further 8% and 8% respectively indicating that they learned of the resource at a conference, or from a friend.

6.2 Exploitation

In terms of exploiting the resource, 50% use it to create learning units for students, while 36% both employ existing units and create new units for their classes.

6.3 Uniqueness

41% of users reported they would not be able to replicate the functionality of Clilstore by using other software solutions, while also confirming that the learning outcomes of their students improved through their advocation of Clilstore.

6.4 Innovation

80% agreed the resource supports innovation, with 60% of respondents confirming that they had gained new ideas from using the resource, and 53% reporting they were able to promote independent learning for their students "in a way not previously possible".

6.5 Intercultural Awareness

64% of the users agreed that using Clilstore supports intercultural awareness. Open feedback responses further commended the resource e.g. *"[Clilstore] offers the opportunity to have a huge selection of subject matters of your interest"* and "*[Clilstore] has a lot of potential for increasing students' interaction with the target language independently*".

14 http://guthan.wordpress.com/about/

15 https://clilstore.eu/cs/4510

16 https://languages.dk

7. Conclusion

CLILSTORE.EU has been designed to empower teachers to create and publish multimedia learning units that facilitate the multimodal delivery of language content in a wide range of languages. The software makes it easy for learners using the units to look up unfamiliar words as they work through embedded texts rather than pass over them and to engage in activities that foster deep learning. Learning unit authors are free to incorporate their own selection of digital content and to continue to adapt and update their units as necessary. They can also now use the OER to promote reflective learning with their students.

For these reasons, CLILSTORE.EU should be viewed as an educational tool of the people, especially as it is completely free to use and it does not seek to exploit its end users in any way. The emphasis is on sharing and enabling the cross-fertilization of ideas between and within language and subject areas. In the context of the Celtic languages, it offers the potential to host and share materials according to a common format and to bring new life to culturally rich content that does not receive the exposure that it deserves. It can also provide a platform for ordinary community voices, thereby enabling others to learn from what they have to say and how they say it.

8. Acknowledgements

On behalf of the COOL project partners, I wish to record our gratitude to the European Commission for co-funding the development and dissemination of CLILSTORE.EU. I am grateful to the anonymous reviewers for their helpful comments on an earlier draft of this paper. I also wish to thank my colleague Caoimhín Ó Donnaíle for providing details on the Smotr internationalization system and the Manx case study.

9. Bibliographical References

Chapelle, C.A. and Sauro, S. (eds.) (2017). *The handbook of technology and second language teaching and learning.* New Jersey.

Council of Europe. (2001). *Common European Framework of Reference for Languages: Learning, teaching, assessment.* Cambridge University Press.

Cregeen, A. (1835) *A Dictionary of the Manks language, with corresponding words or explanations in English.* Douglas.

de Mórdha, D. (2019). *RTÉ Raidió na Gaeltachta agus cultúr phobal na Gaeltachta.* Unpublished PhD Thesis, University College Cork. URL https://cora.ucc.ie/handle/10468/8560 (accessed May 20, 2023).

Gimeno-Sanz, A., Ó Dónaill, C. & Andersen, K. (2014). Supporting content and language integrated learning through technology. In S. Jager, L. Bradley, E.J. Meima, & S. Thouësny (Eds), *CALL Design: Principles and Practice; Proceedings of the 2014 Eurocall Conference, Groningen, The Netherlands* (pp.107-112). Dublin: Research-Publishing.net.

Kelly, J. (1866). *Fockleyr Manninagh as Baarlagh.* Douglas.

Marsh, D. (2002). *CLIL/EMILE - the European dimension: actions, trends and foresight potential.* University of Jyväskylä.

Ó Dónaill, C. (2013). Multimedia-assisted content and language integrated learning. *Multimedia-Assisted Language Learning, 16-4*, 11-39.

Ó Dónaill, N. (ed.) (1977). Foclóir Gaeilge-Béarla. Baile Átha Cliath.

Ó Donnaíle, C. (2014). Tools facilitating better use of online dictionaries: Technical aspects of Multidict, Wordlink and Clilstore. In *Proceedings of the First Celtic Language Technology Workshop* (pp. 18-27). Association for Computational Linguistics.

Proceedings of the CLTW 4 @ LREC2022 , pages 30–39
Marseille, 20-25 June 2022

Evaluation of Three Welsh Language POS Taggers

Gruffudd Prys, Gareth Watkins
Bangor University,
Bangor, Wales,
{g.prys, g.watkins}@bangor.ac.uk

Abstract

In this paper we describe our quantitative and qualitative evaluation of three Welsh language Part of Speech (POS) taggers. Following an introductory section, we explore some of the issues which face POS taggers, discuss the state of the art in English language tagging, and describe the three Welsh language POS taggers that will be evaluated in this paper, namely WNLT2, CyTag and TagTeg. We then describe the challenges involved in evaluating POS taggers which make use of different tagsets, and introduce our mapping of the taggers' individual tagsets to an Intermediate Tagset used to facilitate their comparative evaluation. We introduce our benchmarking corpus as an important component of our methodology, before describing how the inconsistencies in text tokenization between the different taggers present an issue when undertaking such evaluations, and discuss the method used to overcome this complication. We proceed to illustrate how we annotated the benchmark corpus, then describe the scoring method used. We provide an in-depth analysis of the results followed by a summary of the work.

Keywords: POS Tagger, Welsh, Evaluation, Machine Learning

1. Introduction

POS tagging remains an important tool for modern methods of extracting information from data, and it is often used alongside the artificial intelligence techniques that currently claim the headlines. Due to the growing use of these methods, it is important to ensure that the POS taggers available to the Welsh language are of a high standard, that their strengths and weaknesses are known, and that they are proven to be fit for purpose.

However, creating a fair quantitative comparison between existing taggers is not a straightforward task due to their use of different tagsets and their reliance on differing methodologies (namely rule-based and statistical approaches) where the methods used to develop and evaluate the taggers are not directly comparable.

1.1. Impartiality

This paper summarizes an unpublished report on Welsh part-of-speech taggers that we were commissioned to write for the Welsh Government as one of the outputs of the Text, Speech and Translation Technologies for the Welsh Language project - the same project which also funded our work on the the TagTeg tagger. We therefore find ourselves evaluating taggers that include our own, and wish to make our interests clear. Whilst we have strived to be open and impartial in our evaluation, it is inevitable that TagTeg will fit closely with our ideal of how a tagger should behave as we could influence its design. To ensure a fair test of each of the three taggers, we have opted for a simple evaluation that treats different linguistic theoretical perspectives as equally valid, accepting tagging that is different from our preferred interpretation providing it has linguistic justification and is not clearly a mechanical error on the part of the tagger. We have also sought to justify our criticisms (especially in the more qualitative aspects of the evaluation), in an open and transparent way that allows the reader to draw their own conclusions.

2. Taggers

Accurate automatic tagging is not a simple task. As Hagerman (2012) notes in reference to English "Many of the most common used words have more than one possible usage, making their part-of-speech ambiguous". Automatically tagging Celtic languages such as Welsh is further challenged by complex morphological processes such as initial letter mutations which can lead to what Lamb and Danso (2014) call 'data sparsity', as well as an increase in ambiguous forms.

2.1. Accuracy of English Language Taggers

Over a decade ago, Manning (2011) reported that state-of-the-art English language taggers could achieve an accuracy of 97.3% at word level, and that such accuracy was comparable or even better than that of a human annotator. Figures reported by the Association for Computational Linguistics (2019) show that systems have not improved significantly since 2011 in terms of accuracy. It appears that rules based methods are currently less used than statistical methods, which 'have become the mainstream ones obtaining state-of-the-art performance' (Nguyen et al., 2016). Sadredini et al. (2018) appear to agree, in part, noting that 'Generally in NLP, and specifically in POS tagging, statistical and neural network (NN)-based approaches have been favored over rule-based approaches, because they have shown higher accuracy and the training is straightforward to automate'.

2.2. The Taggers Selected for Evaluation

Due to time constraints, our funder's interests, the complexities involved in evaluating taggers which are fundamentally different,[1] and the need to map multiple tagsets to a common interset (discussed in section 5 below), we limited our evaluation to a cross section of taggers recently developed within Welsh universities with public funding. Thus we describe the evaluation of the University of South Wales' Welsh Government funded WNLT2 tagger (Cunliffe et al., 2022), the CyTag tagger (Neale et al., 2018), produced as part of the Cardiff University-led AHRC and ESRC funded CorCenCC project (Knight et al., 2020), and Bangor University's TagTeg tagger (Prys et al., 2020), also funded by the Welsh Government. In the future we also hope to evaluate other taggers, such as the Cyslib tagger (Hicks, 2004; Jones et al., 2015) (part of the Welsh spell/grammar checker Cysill) and the Autoglosser 2 tagger (Donnelly, 2018).

2.3. WNLT2

WNLT (Welsh Natural Language Toolkit) predates the other taggers. The first version was developed by the University of South Wales Hypermedia Research Group between 2015 and 2016. A second version, WNLT2,[2] was developed in a follow-up project between 2016 and 2017. It uses the GATE (General Architecture for Text Engineering)[3] architecture originally developed by the University of Sheffield in 1995. WNLT2's tagging component is based on the Hepple tagger (Hepple, 2000), but with major modifications designed to enable it to categorise Welsh language input (Cunliffe et al., 2017).

A rules-based tagger, WNLT2's lexicon is based on a version of Eurfa (Donnelly, 2013) modified to use the Hepple tagset. However, WNLT2 only uses rules when trying to tag words not found in the lexicon. It does so based on their endings (e.g. by specifying that an unfamiliar word ending with ending with 'fa' is a feminine noun). Ambiguous wordforms appear to be given the same default POS in all contexts. For instance, in the lexicon 'mae' (English:it is) is listed as a verb. This is correct however 'mae' can also be a mutated form of the noun 'bae' (English:bay). The implication of this is that 'mae' will never be correctly tagged as a noun when it acts as such. The basis on which one possible tag is prioritized over another in the WNLT2 data is not clear, but the logical choice would have been to choose based on frequency. (Jurafsky and Martin, 2021) note that accuracy of up to 92% could be achieved with a similar approach in the case of English. When the tagger is unable to find a wordform in the lexicon, and when its rules are unable to determine the POS of the wordform, WNLT2 assigns its noun tag (NN) as default (a common tactic to improve the score a tagger is likely to get).

2.3.1. Ease of Use

The WNLT2 team developed a simple user interface for their tool, one which benefits novice users as it does not require them to learn how to use the more complex GATE architecture. However, tagging 1500 sentences using this simple interface proved very slow, even on powerful machines (CPU i7, 32Gb RAM). It was also necessary to turn to Mac computers for the purpose of the evaluation. We failed to get the program to work on Linux machines, and although it worked on Windows machines, it was restricted to using the Windows default encoding,[4] thus on Windows machines UTF-8 characters such as 'ŷ' and 'ŵ' were corrupted. We chose to ignore these UTF-8 problems for the evaluation, but the need for a Mac computer to make real use of the software is potentially problematic.

2.3.2. Reported Accuracy

WNLT2 authors reported an accuracy of 81% from the first version of WNLT on a gold corpus of 2221 tokens (Williams, 2017).

2.4. CyTag

CyTag[5] is another rule-based Welsh POS tagger. Neale et al. (2018) note that their "motivations for developing a bespoke solution for Welsh POS tagging are based on the requirements, aims and scope of the CorCenCC ... project", that is, CyTag was created to tag the corpus of contemporary Welsh that would form the main outcome of that project.

In common with WNLT2, CyTag uses a version of Eurfa for its core lexicon. CyTag is based on the VISL-CG3 library,[6] a software library for implementing constraint grammar (Karlsson, 1990), a technique used for tag disambiguation. It works by implementing rules handwritten by linguists to identify the syntactic context of a token and limit the number of possible interpretations for the token's tag accordingly. Thus, unlike WNLT, CyTag can select the appropriate tag for a POS-ambiguous wordform according to its syntactic context.However many rules are required to enable accurate disambiguation, and although rule-based taggers have historically produced good results, one of their disadvantages is that developing and maintaining these rules while avoiding conflict between them is specialized and often difficult work. In the case of CyTag, it appears that the rules do not always resolve some common cases where more than one tag corresponds to a single wordform. In the case of the wordform 'ceir', for example, the lexicon indicates that it can represent a verbal form of 'cael' (English:to have) or a plural

[1] I.E. rule based v statistical.

[2] Available free of charge under the LGPL3 license from https://sourceforge.net/projects/wnlt-project/

[3] See https://gate.ac.uk/

[4] Windows-1252

[5] Available for download under the GPL-3.0 license from https://github.com/CorCenCC/CyTag

[6] Available for download under the GPL-3.0 license from https://visl.sdu.dk/constraint_grammar.html

noun (English:cars), but the tagger does not successfully disambiguate between them, and at times suggests a preposition. In addition, there appears to be no provision for coping with common words missing from the program's lexicon. As a result, words that are not in its lexicon are tagged with the unk (unknown) tag.

2.4.1. Ease of Use

We were able to follow the instructions, download CyTag and install VISL-CG3 without issue. Users will need to be comfortable using the command line and Python to do so. Python is often used for doing NLP work and has a reputation for being relatively easy to learn. However, the documentation for VISL-CG3 starts with a prominent *Caveat Emptor* section, and users are instructed to download the latest nightly version rather than a proven release. The coding conventions and structure of CyTag seemed streamlined, but the lack of version information on the GitHub meant we could not ensure that the CyTag we tested was the same as that described by Neale et al. (2018) in 2018.

2.4.2. Reported Accuracy

An early version of CyTag was reported to have reached 93% accuracy when tagging with basic tags on a gold standard corpus of 611 tokens (Neale et al., 2018).[7]

2.5. TagTeg

TagTeg[8] is our statistical Welsh-language POS tagger, based on the tagger found in spaCy's[9] NLP library. spaCy offers several advantages. It provides clear and comprehensive documentation. It is a free and open source library that is actively developed and updated. The impressive results reported by the developers of spaCy (2022) are supported by academic and peer-reviewed experiments and comparisons such as Jiang et al. (2016) and Schmitt et al. (2019) which have shown that spaCy compares well with similar technology, being both fast (Choi et al., 2015; Schmitt et al., 2019) and accurate (Partalidou et al., 2019).
The way spaCy's tagger works is not based on rules set by the developer. Rather, it must be trained with a corpus of human annotated sentences. To this end, a corpus of Welsh language sentences was collected and annotated. Prodigy[10] and spaCy were used to facilitate the annotation. In order to further improve results, the tagger was also trained with a list of 76,000 individual words where each had only one possible interpretation in terms of their POS. These words were sourced from Bangor University's comprehensive lexicon (Prys et al., 2021), however their inclusion as single word training sentences should not be seen as adding a lexicon to the model but rather as a means of influencing the probabilities contained within the model.
The Universal Dependencies (UD) tagset was used to tag the sentences' tokens. This tagset is based on "an evolution of (universal) Stanford dependencies (de Marneffe et al., 2006, 2008, 2014), Google universal part-of-speech tags (Petrov et al., 2012), and the Interset interlingua for morphosyntactic tagsets (Zeman, 2008)." (Universal Dependencies, 2021a).

2.5.1. Ease of Use

As with CyTag, installing spaCy is a simple matter for anyone who is familiar with Python. Also as with CyTag, a non-technical user-friendly interface, such as that provided by WNLT2, is not currently available.

2.5.2. Reported Accuracy

An early model resulted in 91% accuracy when testing using a test corpus that was not part of the training data.[11]

3. Tagsets

One of the major challenges identified during evaluation was the taggers' use of different tagsets. WNLT2 uses a tagset of 27 tags based on the Hepple tagset, which itself closely matches the well-known Penn Treebank tagset (Gorrell et al., 2010). CyTag uses two tagsets, one 'basic', one 'enriched'. The basic tagset consists of 13 tags (14 if we count the unk tag), but maps to an enriched tagset of 145 categories for a more detailed description of the Welsh language's morphological features. The tagset follows Expert Advisory Group on Language Engineering Standards (EAGLES) to enable mapping to other languages through 'Intermediate Tags' (Leech and Wilson, 1996). As mentioned, TagTeg uses the UD tagset. This tagset is a relatively simple tagset containing 17 POS tags, and was designed to facilitate crosslingual tagging. UD also provides for a comprehensive list of morphological features as additional features.

3.1. Rules-Based Tagging and Statistical Tagging: Implications

In the case of rule-based taggers, the tagger is closely tied to the tagset used within the tagger's tag rules. Changing this tagset is no trivial task, and as will be discussed in the following paragraph, neither is mapping between tagsets. However, statistical taggers can be trained to use any tagset by feeding it a corpus of materials annotated using that tagset. In addition, by annotating corpora rather than developing grammar rules, alternative statistical taggers can be trained on

[7]Neale et al. (2018) also describe the content of this corpus. We believe this is the test set used: `https://github.com/CorCenCC/welsh_pos_sem_tagger/blob/master/data/cy_both_tagged.data`

[8]Available to download under the MIT licence from https://github.com/techiaith/model-tagiwr-spacy-cy

[9]See https://spacy.io/

[10]See https://prodi.gy/

[11]Available from https://github.com/techiaith/brawddegau-tagiedig

the same data.[12] This makes it possible to maintain lists such as those of the Association for Computational Linguistics (2019) which directly compare the accuracy of the different taggers trained on the same corpora and using the same tagsets.
However, as this evaluation consisted of two rule-based (non-trainable) taggers, and a total of three different tagsets that did not map directly to each other, evaluation based on a pattern similar to that used in ACL's 'State of the Art' list was not possible. Therefore, to enable a fair and valid comparison between taggers, it was necessary to develop an Intermediate Tagset as illustrated in Table 1. Direct mapping between the three tagsets was impossible. As can be seen in Table 1, Tagteg's ADJ tag can be represented by several tags in WNLT2: namely JJ, JR, JJS and PDT. However WNLT2's PDT tag can also be represented by TagTeg's DET tag. The inability to map one tagset to another directly is compounded when we attempt to map additional tagsets together. In order to overcome these difficulties, we adopted an approach of generalisation. We also decided to allow for multiple 'correct' answers within the gold corpus, so that individual taggers were not penalized incorrectly if the tag used was justified under the schema used by the tagger. This point is exemplified in section 6.1 below. The process resulted in a simplified tagset featuring basic tags to which the the three taggers' complex tags were mapped. By functioning as a bridge between the different tagsets, the Intermediate Tagset enables a comparison of the respective taggers' output. Such a technique has been used by others to facilitate the comparison of different NLP systems (see, for instance Jiang et al. (2016) and Schmitt et al. (2019)).

Intermediate tag	WNLT2 tag	CyTag tag	TagTeg tag
ADF	RB	Adf	ADV
ANS	JJ, JR, JJS, PDT	Ans	ADJ
ARDD	IN	Ar	ADP
ATALN	PN	Atd	PUNCT
BAN	DT, PDT	Ban, YFB	DET
BERF	VB, VBD VBDI, VBDP, VBF, VBI	B	AUX, VERB
CYS	CC	Cys	CCONJ, CONJ, SCONJ
EBYCH	INTJ	Ebych	INTJ
ENW	NN, NF, NNM, NNS	E	NOUN
GEIR	RP	U	PART
MISC	SC	Gw	SYM, X
PRIOD	NNP, NNPS	Ep	PROPN
RHAG	INT, PP	Rha	PRON
RHIF	CD	Rhi	NUM
?		unk	

Table 1: Mapping between tagsets.

4. The Benchmarking Corpus

In order to compare the accuracy of different taggers, we curated a corpus of 1,500 Welsh sentences drawn from a variety of different sources. This Benchmarking Corpus was specifically designed to include a broad representation of contemporary Welsh. The corpus contains a variety of registers and styles to reward taggers that are able to generalize and recognize less-standard forms and orthography in addition to the more literary and formal forms. The Benchmarking Corpus contains examples of transcribed Welsh from recordings of spoken Welsh that use standard informal written apostrophed forms e.g. 'cer'ed' (= cerdded, English:walk). The corpus also includes natural informal written Welsh from text messages and emails where there is less use of the apostrophes than found in 'standard' informal Welsh. Efforts were made to ensure that the sentences also included a variety of dialects and subject matter, and reference was made to the sample frameworks used by CEG (Ellis et al., 2001) and CorCenCC in doing so. The sentences featured a variety in terms of person and tense, and were of varied lengths. The corpus contains sentences from important sources such as Wikipedia, Coleg Cymraeg Cenedlaethol Cymru[13] materials and the CorCenCC and Siarad (Deuchar et al., 2009) corpora. The corpus is available for distribution under the CC-BY-SA license, as used and required by some of these constituent resources.

5. Tokenization

One of the other considerations that complicates the comparison of different taggers is that each tagger may tokenize differently Paroubek (2007), and the three taggers described in this paper each tokenize some texts differently. For instance URLs are tagged differently by all three taggers. Moreover WNLT 2 tokenize 'ar gyfer' (for) and 'er mwyn' (for the sake of) and other commonly used multi word prepositions as single tokens. However, this decision isolates 'ar gyfer' (for) from related forms such as 'ar ei gyfer' (for it/him), and is not followed by CyTag and TagTeg which choose to tokenize multi word prepositions as individual tokens. As a result, comparison between a sentence tagged by a tagger and the 'gold standard' sentence is not straightforward. To facilitate comparison, it was decided to limit the evaluation to identically tokenized sentences.

[12] For example, we understand that Dr Johannes Heinecke has already used the data annotated by us to train a UDPipe tagger.

[13] See https://www.colegcymraeg.ac.uk/

This gave us just over 500 sentences, which we deemed sufficient to give the taggers a fair and useful evaluation.

6. Gold Tagged Benchmarking Corpus

6.1. Annotation Method

The 500 sentence gold corpus was annotated or hand-tagged by an experienced researcher and verified by a senior researcher. In most cases, each token was annotated with one POS tag from the Intermediate set, as can be seen in Table 2. Where it was not possible to map the expected tagger-assigned tag to one specific Intermediate tag, more than one acceptable tag was considered permissible, as exemplified in Table 3. These were separated by a comma. Where it was not possible to map the expected tagger-assigned tag to one specific Intermediate tag, more than one acceptable tag was considered permissible, as exemplified in Table 3. These were separated by a comma.

Mae	Huw	yn	siarad	Cymraeg
BERF	PRIOD	GEIR	BERF	PRIOD

Table 2: Example tagged sentence (sentence literal translation: 'Be Huw is speak Welsh').

Beth	sydd	angen	ei	wneud
RHAG	BERF	ENW	BAN, RHAG	BERF

Table 3: Tagging with more than one tag (sentence literal translation: 'what is need it doing').

6.2. Dealing with Taggers that Offer More than One Possible Tag

While TagTeg and WNLT2 assign one tag per token, CyTag often offers a number of possible tags where the tagger failed to reach a specific conclusion. This is problematic when trying to determine the appropriate method for evaluating these taggers alongside each other. To a degree, the desired behaviour of a tagger depends upon its intended use. In some circumstances, it is arguably better to offer a choice of possible tags rather than risk suggesting the wrong tag. This is the case with the tagger used by Welsh spell/grammar checker Cysill, for example, where it is essential that the checker does not misinterpret the grammar of a text as this could lead it to recommend that the user amends a correct text. Nevertheless, most typical applications expect taggers to output an explicit and unambiguous output, and the inability to select one tag from amongst the number of possible tags should arguably be considered a shortcoming of the tagger. However, as the most appropriate behaviour is task-dependent, we decided to evaluate CyTag's output twice; once in a 'strict' manner, penalizing any ambiguous tagging as if it was an incorrect tag, and again in a 'generous' way by marking ambiguous tagging as correct (where the correct tag was included). By reporting both scores, we let the reader decide on the appropriate interpretation.

7. Scoring Method

We started by using the latest available versions of the three taggers to tokenize and tag the 1500 sentences found in the Benchmarking Corpus. From those 1500 sentences we selected 500 sentences where the tokenization was consistent between each tagger (see Section 5). Those 500 sentences were then manually annotated using the Intermediate Tagset to create the gold standard evaluation corpus. The tags assigned by each tagger were then mapped and converted to the corresponding tags in the Intermediate set. For example, each WNLT2 tag which corresponded to a noun, namely NN, NNF, NNM and NNS, was mapped to the ENW intermediate tag. In doing so, each sentence, along with its corresponding tags, was converted to a common structure in order to compare each of them in turn with the corresponding gold sentences and their associated tags, as can be seen in Table 4.

To facilitate the scoring, we created a benchmarking script that reads the output of each tagger in turn, and works its way through the sentences using these structures to compare the tagger's tags with the corresponding gold tags. The script records the correctly and incorrectly assigned tags and records which combination of token and tag was problematic for the tagger. This provided a score in the form of a percentage of the correct tags in a sentence, and allowed us to calculate a total for all text in the 500 sentence selection from the benchmarking corpus. It also provided an overview of the number of tagging errors and a list of all the tokens incorrectly tagged. To concentrate on a simple, clean cut comparison we avoided mention of precision, recall and F scores in our report.

In addition, we were able to create a complete report for each sentence, which shows every token in the sentence and displays the tag assigned originally by the tagger (following conversion to the relevant Intermediate tag), whether that tag was correct or not, and, where the assigned tag was incorrect, the correct or expected tag. We used that feature to ensure that we were not penalizing taggers whose interpretation was correct. Figure 1 shows a Scoring Report for one specific sentence.

8. Results

8.1. Accuracy of Tokens

The 500 sentences contained a total of 7,675 tokens. We believe that this total is sufficient to prevent the percentages we report being unduly affected by any minor evaluation errors. Table 5 provides an overview of the main results of the evaluation, displaying the number of tokens correctly tagged by each tagger and the percentage of the total that that number represents.

WNLT2	CyTag	TagTeg	Gold
[('Ynddi','ARDD'), ('mae','BERF'), ('20','RHIF'), ('o','ARDD'), ('ganeuon','ENW')]	[('Ynddi','ARDD'), ('mae','BERF'), ('20','RHIF'), ('o','ARDD'), ('ganeuon','ENW')]	[('Ynddi','ARDD'), ('mae','BERF'), ('20','RHIF'), ('o','ARDD'), ('ganeuon','ENW')]	[('Ynddi','ARDD'), ('mae','BERF'), ('20','RHIF'), ('o','ARDD'), ('ganeuon','ENW')]

Table 4: Common structure for evaluation (sentence literal translation: 'In it it is 20 of songs').

```
Token        WNLT2         Correct
----------   ------  ---   ---------
Gelwir       PRIOD   X     BERF
y            BAN     ✓
ffenest      ENW     ✓
hon          RHAG    ✓
yn           ARDD    X     GEIR
ddehonglydd  ENW     ✓
neu          CYS     ✓
gragen       ENW     ✓
(            ATALN   ✓
shell        ENW     X     MISC
)            ATALN   ✓
.            ATALN   ✓
```

Figure 1: Scoring Report.

Tagger	Number of Correct Tags	Token Accuracy (%)
WNLT2	5992/7675	78%
CyTag	6304/7675	82%
TagTeg	7029/7675	92%

Table 5: Main results of evaluation.

By running the evaluation twice, we calculated that CyTag's score of 82% would be 84% if we were to allow multiple tags. We feel that disallowing multiple tags is appropriate as neither WNLT2 nor TagTeg offer ambiguous results. However, as noted, we include the more generous figure here so that the reader can come to their own conclusions. TagTeg has benefited somewhat because the predicative 'yn' and the preverbal 'yn' have both been treated as particles within this evaluation, rather than being divided into two distinct categories. On the other hand, WNLT2 and CyTag have benefited from us allowing a verbnoun (such as 'canu/to sing') to be tagged as either a noun OR a verb. TagTeg however attempts to distinguish between the two uses and is penalised when it gets this wrong.

8.2. Sentence Level Accuracy

Manning (2011) questions measuring accuracy at the Token level when taggers routinely score in the high 90s, and suggests using sentence accuracy as an alternative benchmark. In table 6 we therefore provide an overview of sentence accuracy for each tagger. As Manning suggests, the results for the sentences give a better impression of the ability of taggers to correctly tag entire sentences or texts. This is important if the ultimate goal is for computers to correctly understand the information contained in textual data.

Tagger	Number of Sentences 100% Accurate	Sentence Accuracy (%)
WNLT2	41/500	8%
CyTag	48/500	10%
TagTeg	168/500	34%

Table 6: Sentence accuracy.

8.3. Analysis of Results

These results show that TagTeg is significantly more accurate than CyTag and WNLT2, the two rules-based taggers. This is despite the fact that TagTeg is currently trained on a relatively small collection of complete sentences. Although some of the differences between those scores are due to problems specific to CyTag and WNLT2, we believe this generally shows, contrary to Neale et al.'s suggestion (Neale et al., 2018), that statistical methods can be effective with a relatively small amount of data.

The difference between the method used to train TagTeg and that used, for example, by Lamb and Danso (2014), was that, as noted in section 2.5, the training sentences were 'reinforced' with one word tagged 'sentences' in the form of 76,000 inflected wordforms. The success of this method is welcome news for less resourced languages (which often have dictionary style resources that can be adapted to be used in a similar way). It suggests that collecting and tagging training sentences is an easier and less specialized task than the formulation of grammatical rules, especially when those rules begin to increase in complexity and start to conflict with other rules.

Despite these relatively high token-level scores, at the sentence level the results are significantly poorer. Table 5, where the highest score is 34%, shows that there is still much work to be done to improve taggers to a point where they can be considered completely reliable.

8.4. General Findings

Analyzing the data from a general perspective, we summarize our overall findings on the performance of the three taggers.

8.4.1. The Importance of recognizing English

English words occur frequently within contemporary Welsh texts, whether in the names of companies or organizations, in quotations, or when code switching occurs between Welsh and English. As a result, a useful modern tagger should be able to cope with English words. CyTag is able to identify English words if those are found within its lexicon of English words. WNLT2 lacks this ability completely. TagTeg is able to specify English forms as X (the UD tag for foreign words, among other things) but its ability to specifically label these forms as English could be further improved, as will be discussed in section 8.7.

8.4.2. Informal Welsh

Informal and dialectal Welsh is common on social media, as are misspellings. It is therefore important that a Welsh tagger can cope with the variety of non-standard language contained within such discourse. CyTag can correctly tag many of the most commonly used 'standard' forms of informal Welsh words, but informal vocabulary seems to be a problem for WNLT2. TagTeg now has a normalization component to deal with less standard language, but would also benefit from the inclusion of more spoken sentences in the training data so that there would be no need to include a normalization component in the pipeline to deal with informal forms appropriately.

8.4.3. Destructive Tokenization

One issue that can affect taggers is that of 'destructive tokenization'. This refers to the loss of information detailing the location of spaces and tabs etc. in the tagged output, which can make reproducing the original texts impossible if discarded or lost. Whilst WNLT and TagTeg keep a note of where the spaces were found within a sentence so that the original raw sentences can be reproduced after tokenization, this is not true of CyTag. This is also a problem with the version of the tagged CorCenCC corpus that was shared with us, and may be a significant problem for the future if plain text copies of the original corpus data were not retained.

8.5. Discussion of WNLT2 Results

Thanks to its use of the Eurfa lexicon and of rules to tag unknown words, WNLT2 can provide a tag for most words found in a text. However, its inability to disambiguate wordforms which may correspond to multiple POS tags is problematic. This means that it cannot attribute the correct tag to words when they occur in their alternative function, and users are not alerted to this when using the program. For example, it can assign only one tag to ambiguous words such as 'y' (English:the/that/which), 'yn' (English:is/in), 'i' (English:for/to/me) and 'a' (English:and/that/which). These wordforms make up circa 15% of the words in Welsh texts. As this issue affects such a large proportion of Welsh words, it has a significant impact on the accuracy of the tagger. It's worth noting, however, that Cunliffe et al. (2022) recognise the lack of disambiguation as an issue, noting "The current Tagger does not disambiguate such uses but it is possible to address such cases involving post-processing rules [..] or by developing generic rules via corpus training and machine learning." Moreover, "The WNLT provides the basis of an operational open-source, Part of Speech tagger that can be improved by future iterations." Thus, this open source tool is a starting point, ripe for further development.

8.6. Discussion of CyTag Results

As CyTag, like WNLT2, uses the Eurfa lexicon, it succeeds in tagging most of the Welsh words it encounters, but is less effective at identifying unknown words, tagging a number of words which would be assigned meaningful tags by WNLT2 and TagTeg, with the unk tag.

Importantly, CyTag is more sophisticated than WNLT2 in its ability to appropriately tag wordforms which may correspond to more than one tag. However, it does not always succeed in disambiguating between multiple possible tags as there are instances where CyTag outputs multiple tags for a token whereas WNLT2 and TagTeg consistently specify a single tag only. Furthermore, some obvious words are simply tagged incorrectly. For instance, it is difficult to understand why the verb 'ceir' (English:to have) is sometimes tagged as a preposition.

CyTag's main weakness is that the tagging rules of the version tested for this paper appear inconsistent in places. The most obvious example of this is that 'yn' and its shortened enclitic form ''n' are treated differently without obvious justification. Some pronouns are classified as both pronouns and determiners, whilst other similar pronouns are treated as pronouns only. These factors mean that the tagger has scored lower than it could. It should also be noted that CyTag was developed stage by stage using their test set. That is, the test set was also used to develop the tagger's grammar rules (Neale, 2022). Thus, the discrepancy can be attributed to the reported figure representing CyTag's performance on the test set rather than its typical performance on completely unseen texts.

8.7. Discussion of TagTeg Results

As a statistical tagger, TagTeg is not dependant on rules and a lexicon, but rather on annotated sentences. One of its main advantages is its ability to generalize from the training data and learn to tag unfamiliar words appropriately based on similar patterns of sentence placement and prefixes and endings. We believe this partly explains why TagTeg's accuracy is at least 10% higher than the other taggers evaluated here.

One of the issues with TagTeg is that it is difficult to identify a pattern to its errors. It will occasionally fail to appropriately tag a wordform that is otherwise routinely tagged correctly. For example, occasionally TagTeg will incorrectly tag proper nouns such as 'Sioned' even though it usually tags them correctly. Without many examples of 'Sioned' in the training data, it may be that the tagger's probabilistic model is influenced by the fact that -ed is a common verbal suffix.

We believe the addition of further training sentences including 'Sioned' and other proper nouns will improve this situation. Further examples should also solve TagTeg's issue where it should tag title tokens such as 'Hybu Cig Cymru' (English:Meat Promotion Wales) with the POS of the common word (eg VERB for 'Hybu' (English:Promotion)) as Universal Dependencies guidelines dictate (Universal Dependencies, 2021b), rather than PROPN.

Another current shortcoming is that it does not consistently identify some common dialectal forms such as 'chdi' (English:you) and 'isho' (English:want) as there are currently no examples of such forms in the training data. We intend to add additional dialectal sentences to the training data to address this.

Another issue that arises from analysing the TagTeg results is the manner in which it tags English words such as 'slow' when found within a Welsh sentence such as 'mynd yn slow iawn' (English:going very slowly) with Welsh POS tags, instead of the expected X tag. To err on the side of caution, we have penalized TagTeg here, but its interpretation is arguably correct under certain theoretical approaches, especially those favouring more descriptive analysis over prescriptivism and linguistic purism. Interestingly, however, TagTeg is very good at identifying chains of English words which combine to form a title, such as 'The Phantom of the Opera'. We believe that TagTeg has the potential to improve its ability to tag individual English words given additional training with appropriate data.

Overall, an accuracy of 92% meant that many of the TagTeg tagged sentences contained few, if any, mistakes. As a result, we believe that TagTeg represents a successful tagger with plenty of scope for improvement. Unlike the case with rule-based taggers, we believe that this improvement can be achieved relatively easily by identifying and annotating additional training sentences that target the current areas of weakness.

8.8. Further Work

As mentioned, this evaluation is not an exhaustive evaluation of all Welsh-Language taggers. In the future, we hope to expand our evaluation to include taggers such as UDPipe (based on Welsh Syntax Corpus data forthcoming by Dr Johannes Heinecke), the Cyslib tagger (historically used in Cysill), and Autoglosser 2, a rule based tagger which may improve on the results given by CyTag or WNLT.

9. Conclusions

In this work we have described three Welsh language POS taggers and introduced our tagger evaluation methodology. In order to be able to compare the performance of the three different Welsh POS taggers, their output was converted to a consistent general format so that they all display the same tag for nouns, verbs, adjectives and so on. Accuracy was scored by comparing the output of the three taggers when used on the same set of 500 sentences with corresponding annotations made by experienced linguists.

The results show a significant difference in accuracy between the TagTeg statistical tagger and the two rules-based taggers, with a 10% difference between TagTeg and the nearest tagger. This difference can be attributed to three factors, the first being the superiority of the statistical method over the rules-based method. Internationally, statistical methods have proven to be dominant over rule-based ones for many years. Cole et al. (1997) noted that statistical methods 'have been dominant since the early 1980s'. Brants (2000) too notes that statistical approaches 'yield better results'. More recently, it is telling that all of the taggers listed in ACL's regularly updated POS Tagging (State of the art) list are all statistical taggers. Some of the benefits of the statistical method include their ability to generalize and assign appropriate POS tags to unfamiliar words based on features such as their sentence placement, capitalization, prefixes and suffixes. This also means that they can better cope with the misspellings, dialectal forms and unfamiliar proper nouns that characterize real-life data. Moreover, it is easier to maintain and develop a statistical tagger than a rule-based tagger as writing and tagging training sentences is easier than trying to write rules that build on one another whilst also ensuring that the rules do not conflict with each other. The second reason is that CyTag has no method for guessing unfamiliar words, so words that aren't already in the tagger's vocabulary are tagged as unk. CyTag also tags some frequently occurring words incorrectly or inconsistently. Thirdly, WNLT2 does not attempt to disambiguate wordforms that have a different POS in different contexts.

In addition to achieving better results, the statistical Machine Learning approach also allows statistical taggers other than the one used by TagTeg to be trained on the same data. This ensures that the Welsh language is not tied to one specific piece of software, such as spaCy, in perpetuity. That being said, we believe that spaCy is a good choice to form the basis of a broader NLP framework for the Welsh language, as it is a modern, well-documented, accessible library that is available free of charge under a permissive open license. With this in mind we are investing further in building a modern NLP pipeline. This will include creating additional tools, such as a Welsh language dependency parser and an NER component, so that the current and future technical needs of the Welsh language are answered.

10. Acknowledgements

We are grateful to the Welsh Government for funding this work as part of the Text, Speech and Translation Technologies for the Welsh Language project.

11. Bibliographical References

Association for Computational Linguistics. (2019). Pos tagging (state of the art).

Brants, T. (2000). Tnt - a statistical part-of-speech tagger.

Choi, J. D., Tetreault, J., and Stent, A. (2015). It depends: Dependency parser comparison using a web-based evaluation tool. In *Proceedings of the 53rd Annual Meeting of the Association for Computational Linguistics and the 7th International Joint Conference on Natural Language Processing (Volume 1: Long Papers)*, pages 387–396. Association for Computational Linguistics.

Cole, R. A., Chief, I., Mariani, J., Uszkoreit, H., Zaenen, A., Zue, V., Varile, G., Zampolli, A., Cole, R., Zue, V., Zue, V., and Cole, R. (1997). Survey of the state of the art in human language technology. In *Studies In Natural Language Processing, XIIXIII*.

Cunliffe, D., Tudhope, D., Vlachidis, A., and Williams, D. (2017). Pecyn Cymorth Iaith Naturiol Cymru Fersiwn 2.2.

Cunliffe, D., Vlachidis, A., Williams, D., and Tudhope, D. (2022). Natural language processing for under-resourced languages: Developing a Welsh natural language toolkit. *Computer Speech Language*, 72:101311.

Hagerman, C. (2012). Evaluating the performance of automated part-of-speech taggers on an l2 corpus.

Jiang, R., Banchs, R. E., and Li, H. (2016). Evaluating and combining name entity recognition systems. In *Proceedings of the Sixth Named Entity Workshop*, pages 21–27. Association for Computational Linguistics.

Jurafsky, D. and Martin, J. H., (2021). *Sequence Labeling for Parts of Speech and Named Entities*. Stanford University, online.

Knight, D., Morris, S., Fitzpatrick, T., Rayson, P., Spasić, I., Thomas, E.-M., Lovell, A., Morris, J., Evas, J., Stonelake, M., Arman, L., Davies, J., Ezeani, I., Neale, S., Needs, J., Piao, S., Rees, M., Watkins, G., Williams, L., Muralidaran, V., Tovey-Walsh, B., Anthony, L., Cobb, T., Deuchar, M., Donnelly, K., McCarthy, M., and Scannell, K. (2020). CorCenCC: Corpws Cenedlaethol Cymraeg Cyfoes – the National Corpus of Contemporary Welsh.

Lamb, W. and Danso, S. (2014). Developing an automatic part-of-speech tagger for scottish gaelic. Proceedings of the First Celtic Language Technology Workshop, pages 1–5. Association for Computational Linguistics and Dublin City University.

Leech, G. and Wilson, A. (1996). Recommendations for the morphosyntactic annotation of corpora. Report.

Manning, C. D. (2011). Part-of-Speech Tagging from 97% to 100%: Is It Time for Some Linguistics? Computational Linguistics and Intelligent Text Processing, pages 171–189. Springer Berlin Heidelberg.

Neale, S., Donnelly, K., Watkins, G., and Knight, D. (2018). Leveraging lexical resources and constraint grammar for rule-based part-of-speech tagging in welsh. In *Proceedings of the Eleventh International Conference on Language Resources and Evaluation (LREC 2018)*. European Language Resources Association (ELRA).

Neale, S. (2022). Private Communication.

Nguyen, D. Q., Nguyen, D. Q., Pham, D. D., and Pham, S. B. (2016). A robust transformation-based learning approach using ripple down rules for part-of-speech tagging. *AI Communications*, 29(3):409–422, apr.

Paroubek, P., (2007). *Evaluating Part-of-Speech Tagging and Parsing*, pages 99–124. Springer Netherlands, Dordrecht.

Partalidou, E., Spyromitros-Xioufis, E., Doropoulos, S., Vologiannidis, S., and Diamantaras, K. (2019). Design and implementation of an open source Greek pos tagger and entity recognizer using spacy.

Sadredini, E., Guo, D., Bo, C., Rahimi, R., Skadron, K., and Wang, H. (2018). A scalable solution for rule-based part-of-speech tagging on novel hardware accelerators. In *Proceedings of the 24th ACM SIGKDD International Conference on Knowledge Discovery amp; Data Mining*, KDD '18, page 665–674, New York, NY, USA. Association for Computing Machinery.

Schmitt, X., Kubler, S., Robert, J., Papadakis, M., and Le Traon, Y. (2019). A replicable comparison study of NER software: StanfordNLP, NLTK, OpenNLP, SpaCy, Gate, 2019-10-22. ISET Engineering Sciences [physics]/AutomaticConference papers.

spaCy. (2022). Facts & figures.

Universal Dependencies. (2021a). Introduction.

Universal Dependencies. (2021b). Propn: proper noun.

Williams, D. (2017). Welsh Natural Language Toolkit.

12. Language Resource References

Cunliffe, D., Vlachidis, A., Williams, D., and Tudhope, D. (2022). Natural language processing for under-resourced languages: Developing a Welsh natural language toolkit. *Computer Speech Language*, 72:101311.

Deuchar, M., Carter, D., Davies, P., Donnelly, K., Herring, J., del, M., Stammers, J., Aveledo, F., Fusser, M., Jones, L., Lloyd-Williams, S., Prys, M., and Robert, E. (2009). Siarad corpus.

Donnelly, K. (2013). Eurfa.

Donnelly, K. (2018). Autoglosser2.

Ellis, N. C., O'Dochartaigh, C., Hicks, W., Morgan, M., and Laporte, N. (2001). Cronfa Electroneg o Gymraeg (CEG).

Gorrell, G., Maynard, D., and Roberts, A. (2010). Module 2: Introduction to IE and ANNIE.

Hepple, M. (2000). Independence and commitment: Assumptions for rapid training and execution of rule-based pos taggers. In *Proceedings of the 38th Annual Meeting of the Association for Computational Linguistics*, pages 278–277.

Hicks, W. J. (2004). Welsh proofing tools: Making a little nlp go a long way. In *the 1st Workshop on International Proofing Tools and Language Technologies*.

Jones, D. B., Robertson, P., and Prys, G. (2015). Gwasanaeth API Tagiwr Rhannau Ymadrodd Cymraeg.

Karlsson, F. (1990). Constraint grammar as a framework for parsing running text. In *Proceedings of the 13th Conference on Computational Linguistics - Volume 3*, COLING '90, page 168–173, USA. Association for Computational Linguistics.

Neale, S., Donnelly, K., Watkins, G., and Knight, D. (2018). Leveraging lexical resources and constraint grammar for rule-based part-of-speech tagging in Welsh. In *Proceedings of the Eleventh International Conference on Language Resources and Evaluation (LREC 2018)*. European Language Resources Association (ELRA).

Prys, D., Prys, G., and Watkins, G. L. (2020). Model Tagio Rhannau Ymadrodd Cymraeg/Welsh Language Part of Speech Tagging Model.

Prys, D., Jones, D. B., Prys, G., and Watkins, G. L. (2021). Lecsicon Cymraeg Bangor Welsh Lexicon.

Proceedings of the CLTW 4 @ LREC2022, pages 40–46
Marseille, 20-25 June 2022

Iterated Dependencies in a Breton treebank and implications for a Categorial Dependency Grammar

Annie Foret, Denis Béchet, Valérie Bellynck
IRISA& Univ. Rennes 1, Nantes University, Univ. Grenoble
Annie.Foret@irisa.fr, Denis.Bechet@univ-nantes.fr, Valerie.bellynck@imag.fr

Abstract

Categorial Dependency Grammars (CDG) are computational grammars for natural language processing, defining dependency structures. They can be viewed as a formal system, where types are attached to words, combining the classical categorial grammars' elimination rules with valency pairing rules able to define discontinuous (non-projective) dependencies. Algorithms have been proposed to infer grammars in this class from treebanks, with respect to Mel'čuk principles. We consider this approach with experiments on Breton. We focus in particular on "repeatable dependencies" (iterated) and their patterns. A dependency d is iterated in a dependency structure if some word in this structure governs several other words through dependency d. We illustrate this approach with data in the universal dependencies format and dependency patterns written in Grew (a graph rewriting tool dedicated to applications in natural Language Processing).

Keywords: Formal Grammar, Categorial Grammar, Treebank, Universal Dependencies, Breton, Repeatable Dependencies, Grammatical Inference, Graph Rewriting

1. Introduction

This paper discusses how a formal grammar in the class of categorial dependency grammars can be applied to under-resourced languages.

Previous works have proposed the categorial dependency framework for natural language modelling and processing, with nice formal and pratical properties: polynomial parsing complexity and algorithms to infer such grammars from dependency treebanks.

We conducted experiments in that direction on Breton. Using Grew with both CDG grammars and a treebank provides quickly specific views of the linguistic data: in our case views related to the interpretations of the Mel'čuk repeatable dependency principle. This helps to validate this repeatable principle for a language such as Breton and annotation guidelines.

Several dependency treebanks are developed for Celtic languages (Lynn and Foster, 2016; Batchelor, 2019; Heinecke and Tyers, 2019). In this work we consider the UD_Breton-KEB corpus [1] (Tyers and Ravishankar, 2018). We wrote programs with reproducible experiments on Breton annotated sentences following the Universal Dependencies scheme [2].

We focus in particular on iterated dependencies. A dependency d is iterated in a dependency structure if some word in this structure governs several other words through dependency d. The iterated dependencies are due to the basic principles of dependency syntax, on optional repeatable dependencies (Mel'čuk, 1988): All modifiers of a noun n share n as their governor and, similarly, all modifiers of a verb v share v as their governor. At the same time, the iterated dependencies have been a challenge for grammatical inference (Béchet and Foret, 2021): the class of k-valued CDG (at most k types per word) is not learnable (in the sense of Gold's (Gold, 1967) "identification in the limit"), while the class of k-valued "iteration-free" CDG is learnable.

The paper is organized as follows. Section 2 introduces Categorial Dependency Grammars (CDG). Section 3 provides an inference algorithm for CDG when we interprete the notion of iterated dependencies as consecutive outgoing edges separately on the left and on the right of a governor. We also discuss different possible interpretations of the notion of iterated dependencies, handled in extended CDG. Section 4 reports on experiments on a Breton corpus. Section 5 concludes. We provide code on CDG and UD available at the *cdg-ud* page[3].

2. Categorial Dependency Grammars

A CDG (Dekhtyar et al., 2015) is a formal grammar that defines a language of surface dependency structures. A surface dependency structure is a list of words linked together by dependencies. Each dependency has a name, a starting point called the governor and an ending point called the subordinate.

Figure 1 shows a surface dependency structure for the string *"This deal brought more problems than profits."*. The structure contains eight words (or punctuation symbols) and seven dependencies. The arrow between *brought* and *problems* defines a dependency of name $a-obj$ where *brought* is the governor and *problems* is the subordinate (this dependency indicates that *problems* is the object of *brought*). The root of the structure is the word *brought* (this word isn't the subordinate of any dependency). The CDG dependency

[1] V1.0 available at `https://universaldependencies.org/treebanks/br_keb/index.html`

[2] `https://universaldependencies.org/`

[3] `https://gitlab.inria.fr/foret/cdg-ud`

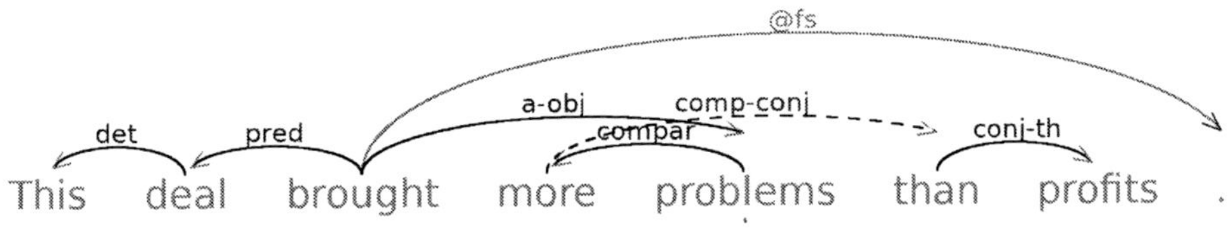

Figure 1: A Dependency Structure.

$\mathbf{L}^l$	$[C]^P[C\backslash\beta]^Q \vdash [\beta]^{PQ}$	(\ elimination)
$\mathbf{I}^l$	$[C]^P[C^*\backslash\beta]^Q \vdash [C^*\backslash\beta]^{PQ}$	(\ repetition)
Ω^l	$[C^*\backslash\beta]^P \vdash [\beta]^P$	(\ option)
$\mathbf{D}^l$	$\alpha^{P_1(\swarrow V)P(\nwarrow V)P_2} \vdash \alpha^{P_1PP_2}$	$P\ without \swarrow^V \nwarrow^V$

Table 1: The CDG Type Calculus (Left Rules)

structures are not necessarily dependency trees because certain dependencies called discontinuous dependencies are usually introduced together with an auxiliary dependency called an anchor [4]. In the example, there is a discontinuous dependency *comp–conj* but its anchor dependency is not shown here.

A CDG is defined mainly by a lexicon that associates types to words and punctuation symbols. The following lexicon shows a lexicon for the previous dependency structure (the anchor sub-types for the discontinuous dependency *comp–conj* are presented as $\#\searrow$ *comp–conj* in the types of *problems* and *than*):

this	$\mapsto$	$[det]$
deal	$\mapsto$	$[det\backslash pred]$
brought	$\mapsto$	$[pred\backslash S/@fs/a\text{–}obj]$
problems	$\mapsto$	$[compar\backslash a\text{–}obj/\#\searrow comp\text{–}conj]$
profits	$\mapsto$	$[conj\text{–}th]$
more	$\mapsto$	$[compar]^{\nearrow comp\text{-}conj}$
than	$\mapsto$	$[\#\searrow comp\text{–}conj/conj\text{–}th]^{\searrow comp\text{-}conj}$
.	$\mapsto$	$[@fs]$

in this CDG, *S* is for sentences, *@fs* is for the full stop.

CDG languages are defined by a dependency types calculus showed on Table 1 which constructs Dependency Structures. Figure 2 shows a proof tree for a simple sentence and typing (en, br). Figure 3 shows a subproof where labels are abreviated (en, br).

In comparison with CCG or Lambek grammars, CDG are written using flat types without type-raising mechanism. From a practical point of view, CDGLab (Béchet et al., 2014) implements a parser for CDG. The lab can also help to define a CDG together with corpora for a specific language. For instance, a large scale grammar and a corpus for French have been developed with this tool (Béchet and Lacroix, 2015).

[4] Formally a token could have several heads, but practically, token have one head or one main head and auxiliary heads (for anchors)

3. CDG Learning and Subclasses

The notion of K-star has been introduced to define learnable subclasses of CDG grammars allowing iterated dependencies. This constraint differs from the k-valued bound and does not impose a bound on the number of types associated to a word. A K-star constraint (for a number K) reflects an indiscernability principle between K repetitions of a same dependency d and its iterated form d^*. Different K-star criterions have been proposed, that enable grammatical inference in the presence of iterated dependencies; the first one "K-star revealing" is a complex non-constructive criterion, the two later proposals "Simple K-star" (Béchet and Foret, 2016b) and "Global Simple K-star" (Béchet and Foret, 2021) (the global variant does not impose the repetitions to be consecutive in a type) are both syntactic and easy to check on a given grammar. The inference of CDG with these properties is possible from a corpus using the algorithm in Figure 5 (where the set of atomic types depends from the corpus labels). The algorithm can be used to complete an existing CDG as well.

3.1. An Inference Algorithm from a Treebank

The algorithm we proposed in Béchet et al. (2010) first computes a "pre-type" for each word from a dependency structure, called a vicinity, following the outgoing dependencies in sentence order, but without marked iteration. This type is then generalized before expanding the grammar. This kind of algorithm is termed TGE-like for "Type-Generalize-Expand" (Béchet and Foret, 2021). The algorithm is shown in Figure 5.

3.2. Vicinity of a word on a dependency structure

Vicinity. The TGE method involves a first set of types without iteration, called vicinity, that can be directly obtained from a dependency structure. The *vicinity* $V(w, D)$ of a word w in a (labelled) dependency struc-

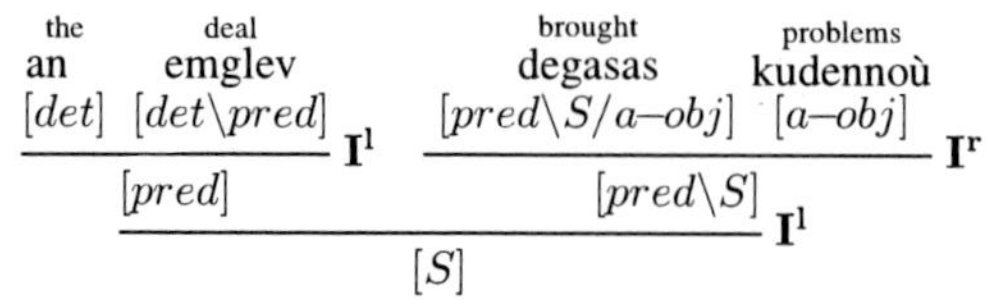

Figure 2: A Proof Tree.

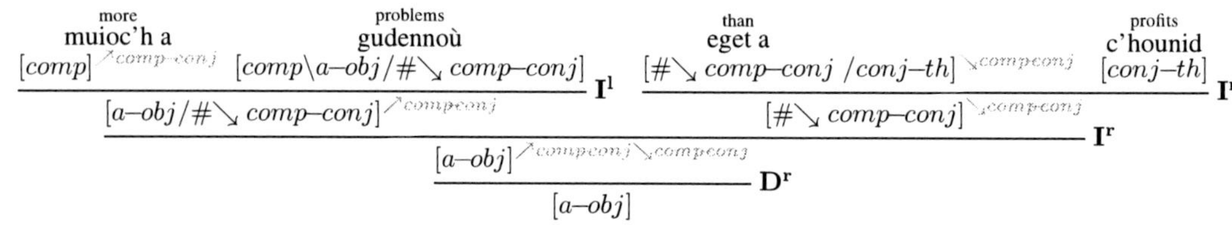

Figure 3: A Simplified Subproof Tree.

ture D, is the type

$$V(w,D) = [l_1\backslash \ldots \backslash l_k \backslash h / r_m / \ldots / r_1]^P,$$

such that D has:

- the incoming projective dependency or anchor h (or the axiom S for sentences),
- the left projective dependencies or anchors $l_k, \ldots, l_1$ (in this order),
- the right projective dependencies or anchors $r_1, \ldots, r_m$ (in this order),
- the discontinuous dependencies $d_1, \ldots, d_n$ with their respective polarities P to handle their start, their end and their orientation.[5]

3.3. TGE$^{(\mathbf{K})}$ Algorithm and Example.

Our learning algorithm is provided on Figure 5. From the dependency structure D (fragment) of Figure 4 for a sentence in French[6], we get these two vicinity types:

$V(partition, D) = [det\backslash a{-}obj/modif/attr/attr/modif]$,
$V(de, D) = [attr/prepos{-}g]$

If the "2-star repetition principle" applies to the $attr$ dependency, in the sense that if $attr$ occurs consecutively two times then it can occur consecutively any number of times, the previous vicinity of *partition* would be generalized by this CDG type:

$partition \mapsto [det\backslash a{-}obj/modif/attr^*/modif]$

3.4. Repetition Patterns

Grammar classes and TGE algorithm. The same TGE^K algorithm can be run to learn the class of simple K-star grammars. It can be adjusted to learn global K-star grammars by adding a final step replacing each type t of the output of TGE^K by its *global simple K-star generalization* $gs^{(K)}(t)$ obtained as follows (Béchet and Foret, 2021):

- for each d on the left, where $d\backslash$ occurs at least K times or if $d^*\backslash$ is present, then replace each $d\backslash$ with its starred version $d^*\backslash$
- for each d on the right, proceed similarly.

Variants and extended types. More flexible interpretations than the strict reading of repeatable optional dependencies as "consecutive repetitions" have been proposed.

- "Dispersed iteration" (Pogodalla and Prost, 2011), $\{d_1^*, \ldots, d_p^*\}$ represents the case where the subordinates through a repeatable dependency may occur in any position on the left (respectively, on the right) of the governor.
- "Choice iteration" (Pogodalla and Prost, 2011), $(d_1|\ldots|d_k)^*$ represents the case where the subordinates through one of several repeatable dependencies may occur in one and the same argument position. Using a similar approach in the dispersed case, an algorithm TGE^K_{disp} has been shown to learn K-star dispersed revealing grammars. A similar learning algorithm TGE^K_{ch} is provided for "choice iteration".
- CDGs with "sequence iteration" have later been proposed in Béchet and Foret (2016a) as a generalization of d^*: repeating $/\,d_2\,/\,d_1\,/\,d_2\,/\,d_1$, etc. as $/\,(d_1 \bullet d_2)^*$. An extended CDG-calculus and a TGE-like algorithm for sequences of length 2 is provided in Béchet and Foret (2016a)[7]. This extension seems relevant for treebanks.

4. Experiments

Experiments are reported in Béchet and Foret (2016a) to process vicinities from a French treebank and view patterns in a concept analysis tool[8]. In this paper, we

[5] P is a sequence of elements of the form: $\nwarrow d$ (start left) $\searrow d$ (end right), $\swarrow d$ (end left), $\nearrow d$ (start right).

[6] "On y trouve aussi une partition récente à récupérer de l'ONPL signée par lui." , meaning "There is also a recent score to recover from the ONPL signed by him."

[7] Sequence iteration does not introduce new string languages

[8] Camelis available at `http://www.irisa.fr/LIS/ferre/camelis`

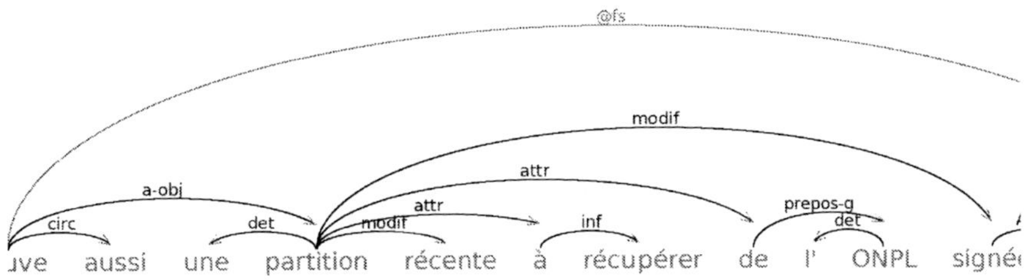

Figure 4: Part of a Dependency Structure.

Algorithm $\mathbf{TGE}^{(K)}$ (type-generalize-expand):
Input: σ, a training sequence of length N.
Output: CDG $\mathbf{TGE}^{(K)}(\sigma)$.

let $G_H = (W_H, \mathbf{C}_H, S, \lambda_H)$
  where $W_H := \emptyset$; $\mathbf{C}_H := \{S\}$; $\lambda_H := \emptyset$;
(loop) **for** $i = 1$ **to** N //loop on σ
  let D such that $\sigma[i] = \sigma[i-1] \cdot D$;
    // the i-th dependency structure of σ
  let $(X, E) = D$;
  (loop) **for every** $w \in X$
    // the order of this loop is not important
    $W_H := W_H \cup \{w\}$;
    let $t_w = V(w, D)$
    // the vicinity of w in D
    (loop) **while** $t_w = [\alpha\backslash l\backslash \mathrm{d}\backslash \cdots \backslash \mathrm{d}\backslash r\backslash \beta]^P$
      with at least K consecutive occurrences of d,
      $l \neq d$ (or $\alpha\backslash l\backslash$ not present)
      and $r \neq d$ (or $r\backslash$ not present)
        $t_w := [\alpha\backslash l\backslash \mathrm{d}^{*}\backslash r\backslash \beta]^P$
    (loop) **while** $t_w = [\alpha/l/\mathrm{d}/\cdots/\mathrm{d}/r/\beta]^P$
      with at least K consecutive occurrences of d,
      $l \neq d$ (or $/l$ not present)
      and $r \neq d$ (or $/r/\beta$ not present)
        $t_w := [\alpha/l/\mathrm{d}^{*}/r/\beta]^P$
    $\lambda_H(w) := \lambda_H(w) \cup \{t_w\}$;
      // lexicon expansion
  end end
return G_H

Figure 5: Algorithm $TGE^{(K)}$

use Grew[9] (Guillaume, 2021) to search[10] for patterns corresponding to the CDG vicinities and their possible generalizations; in other words, these express patterns on the successive dependencies outgoing from a given word.

4.1. Edge patterns on a corpus

We wrote patterns, in the Grew syntax, to select graphs (sentences) containing dependency name repetitions, depending on these parameters: a number K of repetitions, a repetition mode (anywhere/flex or consecutive/cons), a side (left, right, or both). We give some of them below, then an occurrence table on Breton data (we provide more patterns at the *cdg-ud* page[3]):

- 2 repetitions, anywhere, left or right (2rep flex l/r)

```
pattern { e: GOV -> DEP1;
f: GOV -> DEP2;
e.label = f.label ;
DEP1 << DEP2 }
```

- 3 repetitions, anywhere, left or right (3rep flex l/r)

```
pattern { e: GOV -> DEP1;
f: GOV -> DEP2;  g : GOV -> DEP3;
e.label = f.label ;
e.label = g.label ;
DEP1 << DEP2 ; DEP2 << DEP3}
```

- 2 repetitions, consecutive, right (2rep cons r)

```
pattern { e: GOV -> DEP1;
f: GOV -> DEP2;
e.label = f.label ;
DEP1 << DEP2 ;  GOV << DEP1 }
without { g: GOV -> DEP12 ;
DEP1 << DEP12 ; DEP12 << DEP2 }
```

- 2 repetitions, consecutive, left (2rep cons l)

```
pattern { e: GOV -> DEP1;
f: GOV -> DEP2;
e.label = f.label ;
DEP1 << DEP2 ;  DEP2 << GOV }
without { g: GOV -> DEP12 ;
DEP1 << DEP12 ; DEP12 << DEP2 }
```

[9] https://grew.fr

[10] We wrote other patterns related to CDG, we also wrote Grew rules that extend such patterns, to transform the corpus with http://transform.grew.fr/, with several outcomes compatible with the UD format: for marking repeatable dependencies on relevant edges, for adding the projective vicinities as node features, for the inference algorithm ; these files can be directly tested on the Grew site and can be provided on demand, see also the *cdg-ud* site[3].

UD e.label	2rep flex l/r 2 repetitions anywhere left or right	3rep flex l/r 3 repetitions anywhere left or right	2rep cons r 2 consecutive repetitions right	2rep cons l 2 consecutive repetitions left	3resp cons r 3 consecutive repetitions right
aux	268	35	107	105	1
advmod	133	22	5	8	
obl	119	16	53	2	7
punct	83	3	3	1	
conj	75	59	42		18
dep	16			11	
nmod:gen	16	1	14		1
det	13			13	
nmod	12	1	8		1
amod	10	1	7		1
flat:name	4		4		
case	3			2	
parataxis	3		2	1	
nsubj	2				
fixed	2		2		
acl	2		2		
advcl	2				
list	1		1		
SUD e.label					
mod	214	27	59	8	5
udep	88	8	64	2	8
punct	78	2	2	1	
unk	16			12	
mod@gen	16	1	14		1
det	13			13	
parataxis	3		2	1	
subj	2				
list	1		1		

Table 2: Occurrences of edge labels w.r.t. repetition patterns on Breton data, in UD and SUD formats

These results in table 2 apply to two versions of the Breton corpus, UD format (de Marneffe et al., 2021) and SUD format (Gerdes et al., 2018)[11], where we ask for e.label in the above patterns.
We can also check the amount of discontinuous (non-projective) dependencies in these formats, with:

```
global { is_not_projective }
pattern { e:GOV -> DEP }
without {f:X -> GOV}
```

We get few (19) in the UD format, and much more (296) in the SUD format. The SUD format seems relevant for further developments. This raises this question: what is the best amount of non-projectivity needed in Breton. CDG is a good formalism for discontinuity, this is not developed here.

4.2. Selected sentences and dependencies

We select here two sentences, to illustrate different repetition status.

[11] SUD stands for "Surface Syntactic Universal Dependencies", the SUD scheme is a recent alternative to the UD format, with possible automatic conversion main differences are that SUD favors functional heads, and has an more economical set of labels; a comparison summary can be found at `https://surfacesyntacticud.github.io/conversions/`

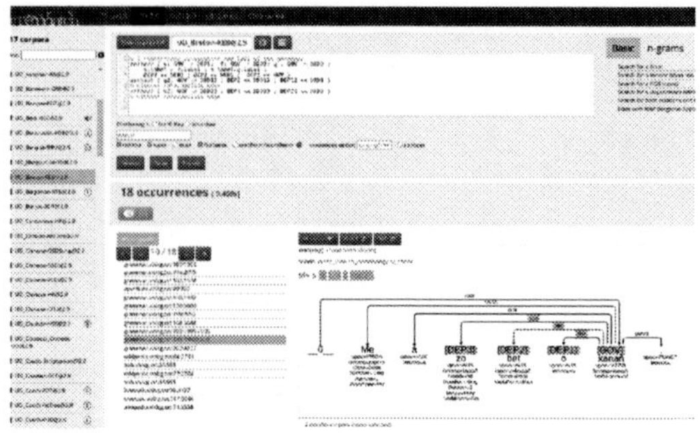

Figure 6: "Me a zo bet o kanañ" in UD format

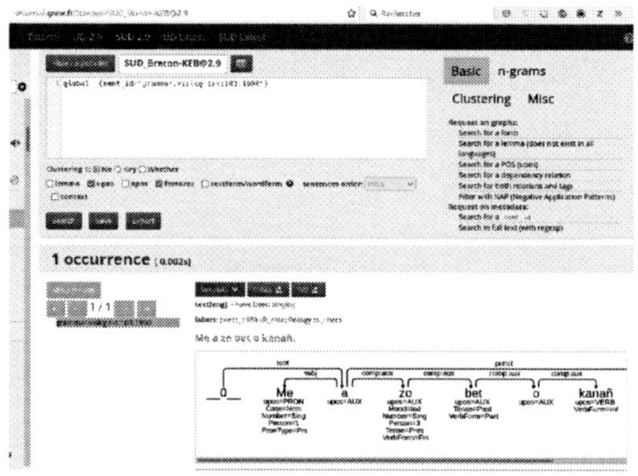

Figure 7: "Me a zo bet o kanañ" in SUD format

In the first sentence "Me a zo bet o kanañ." (meaning "I have been singing.", with sent_id="grammar.vislcg.txt:103:1990"), in the original UD format (Figure 6), 3 consecutive edges on the left of the same governor have the same label (aux); this does not happen in the SUD format (Figure 7). This dependency (aux) may preferably be kept non-repetitive on the left (in the consecutive or in a flexible reading).
In another sentence "Gant ur c'hresk a 35% eus ar veajourien dindan pemp bloaz, emañ Breizh e penn rannvroioù Frañs evit an TER" (with sent_id="oab.vislcg.txt:163:4313" , meaning "With a 35% increase in TER use in five years, Brittany ranks first among the regions of France."), 3 consecutive edges on the right of a same governor have the same label: $nmod$ in UD as in Figure 8, $udep$ in SUD as in Figure 9. This dependency ($nmod$) is preferably considered as repetitive on the right (in the consecutive reading).

5. Conclusion and further work

In this study we tried to answer the question: how to identify iterated dependencies on a Breton corpus and translate them into iterated types, to design a Categorial Dependency Grammar (CDG).

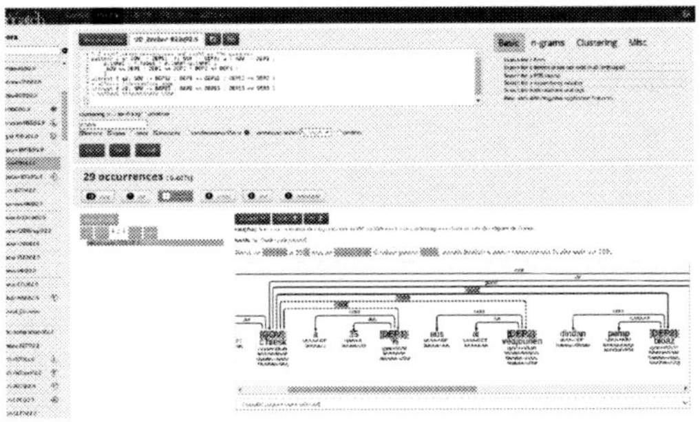

Figure 8: "Gant ur c'hresk a 35% eus ... " in UD

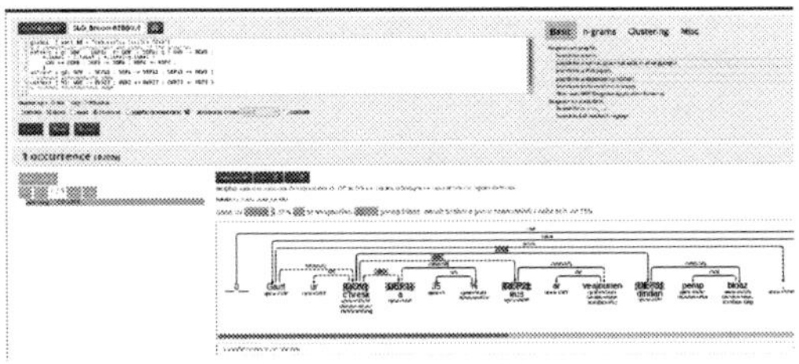

Figure 9: "Gant ur c'hresk a 35% eus ... " in SUD

One of the issues in grammatical design or in corpus annotation is to determine the good level of generalization and of automation. Through explorations and experiments, we also aim to provide some answers and recommendations both formally and practically.
Here are some other questions we wish to address for Breton:
- In the case of discontinuous dependencies in the corpus, how to treat them (for CDGs, how can we manage the introduction of polarized valencies and anchors); in case of absence of discontinuous dependencies, is it a weakness of the annotated corpus?
- How to use the information from a site such as Arbres (Jouitteau, 2009 2022), an online site describing the grammar of Breton?
- In documents, what are the levels and sources of ambiguity and how to deal with them?
- What processing chain should we develop to go from a text to a targeted semantics (case of the French-Breton language pair)?

6. Acknowledgements

This study has benefited from funds from CNRS and DGLFLF (LangNum-br-fr project) enabling a user study and several student internships (K. Kechis, P. Morvan, P. Martinet). We thank the reviewers for their helpful comments and M. Jouitteau, E. Hupel for useful discussions on Breton.

7. Bibliographical References

Batchelor, C. (2019). Universal dependencies for Scottish Gaelic: syntax. In *Proceedings of the Celtic Language Technology Workshop*, pages 7–15, Dublin, Ireland, August.

Béchet, D. and Foret, A. (2016a). Categorial dependency grammars with iterated sequences. In *Logical Aspects of Computational Linguistics, Nancy, France, December 5-7, 2016*, pages 34–51.

Béchet, D. and Foret, A. (2016b). Simple k-star categorial dependency grammars and their inference. In *Proceedings of the 13th International Conference on Grammatical Inference, ICGI 2016*, pages 3–14.

Béchet, D. and Foret, A. (2021). Incremental learning of iterated dependencies. *Machine Learning*, March.

Béchet, D. and Lacroix, O. (2015). CDGFr, un corpus en dépendances non-projectives pour le français. In *Actes de la 22e conférence sur le Traitement Automatique des Langues Naturelles, June 2015, Caen, France*, pages 522–528. Association pour le Traitement Automatique des Langues. Short paper in French.

Béchet, D., Dikovsky, A., and Foret, A. (2010). Two models of learning iterated dependencies. In Markus Egg, et al., editors, *Proceedings of the 15th International Conference on Formal Grammar (FG10), Copenhagen, Denmark, August 7-8, 2010*, pages 1–16.

Béchet, D., Dikovsky, A., and Lacroix, O. (2014). "CDG Lab": an integrated environment for categorial dependency grammar and dependency treebank development. In Kim Gerdes, et al., editors, *Computational Dependency Theory*, volume 258 of *Frontiers in Artificial Intelligence and Applications*, pages 153–169. IOS Press.

de Marneffe, M.-C., Manning, C. D., Nivre, J., and Zeman, D. (2021). Universal Dependencies. *Computational Linguistics*, 47(2):255–308, 07.

Dekhtyar, M. I., Dikovsky, A., and Karlov, B. (2015). Categorial dependency grammars. *Theor. Comput. Sci.*, 579:33–63.

Gerdes, K., Guillaume, B., Kahane, S., and Perrier, G. (2018). SUD or surface-syntactic universal dependencies: An annotation scheme near-isomorphic to UD. In Marie-Catherine de Marneffe, et al., editors, *Proceedings of the Second Workshop on Universal Dependencies, UDW@EMNLP 2018, Brussels, Belgium, November 1, 2018*, pages 66–74. Association for Computational Linguistics.

Gold, E. M. (1967). Language identification in the limit. *Information and control*, 10:447–474.

Guillaume, B. (2021). Graph Matching and Graph Rewriting: GREW tools for corpus exploration, maintenance and conversion. In *EACL 2021 - 16th conference of the European Chapter of the Association for Computational Linguistics*, Kiev/Online.

Heinecke, J. and Tyers, F. M. (2019). Development of a Universal Dependencies treebank for Welsh. In *Proceedings of the Celtic Language Technology Workshop*, pages 21–31, Dublin, Ireland, August. European Association for Machine Translation.

Jouitteau, M. (2009-2022). ARBRES, wikigrammaire des dialectes du breton et centre de ressources pour son étude linguistique formelle, IKER, CNRS. `http://arbres.iker.cnrs.fr`. Licence Creative Commons BY-NC-SA.

Lynn, T. and Foster, J. (2016). Universal dependencies for irish. In *Proceedings of the Celtic Language Technology Workshop*, Paris, France.

Mel'čuk, I. (1988). *Dependency Syntax*. SUNY Press, Albany, NY.

Sylvain Pogodalla et al., editors. (2011). *Logical Aspects of Computational Linguistics, 6th International Conference, LACL 2011, Montpellier, France, June 29 – July 1, 2011. Proceedings*, volume 6736 of *Lecture Notes in Computer Science (LNCS)*. Springer.

Tyers, F. M. and Ravishankar, V. (2018). A prototype dependency treebank for breton. In *Actes de la 25e conférence sur le Traitement Automatique des Langues Naturelles (TALN)*.

Proceedings of the CLTW 4 @ LREC2022 , pages 47–51
Marseille, 20-25 June 2022

Automatic Speech Recognition for Irish: the ABAIR-ÉIST System

Liam Lonergan[1], Mengjie Qian[2], Harald Berthelsen[1], Andrew Murphy[1], Christoph Wendler[1], Neasa Ní Chiaráin[1], Christer Gobl[1], Ailbhe Ní Chasaide[1]
[1]Phonetics and Speech Laboratory, School of Linguistic, Speech and Communication Sciences, Trinity College Dublin,
[2]Department of Engineering, Cambridge University
{llonerga, berthelh, murpha61,wendlec,nichiarn,cegobl,nichsid}@tcd.ie
mq227@cam.ac.uk

Abstract

This paper describes ÉIST, automatic speech recogniser for Irish, developed as part of the ongoing ABAIR initiative, combining (1) acoustic models, (2) pronunciation lexicons and (3) language models into a hybrid system. A priority for now is a system that can deal with the multiple diverse native-speaker dialects. Consequently, (1) was built using predominately native-speaker speech, which included earlier recordings used for synthesis development as well as more diverse recordings obtained using the MíleGlór platform. The pronunciation variation across the dialects is a particular challenge in the development of (2) and is explored by testing both Trans-dialect and Multi-dialect letter-to-sound rules. Two approaches to language modelling (3) are used in the hybrid system, a simple n-gram model and recurrent neural network lattice rescoring, the latter garnering impressive performance improvements. The system is evaluated using a test set that is comprised of both native and non-native speakers, which allows for some inferences to be made on the performance of the system on both cohorts.

Keywords: Irish, speech recognition, minority language

1. Introduction

This paper describes the ongoing work to develop automatic speech recognition (ASR) systems for Irish, as part of the ABAIR initiative on Irish speech technology. The current system, ÉIST is described, and the results of recent tests are presented, along with the pointers to issues that are pertinent to all Celtic (and other endangered) languages

2. Background

The development of automatic speech recognition (ASR) for Irish, is a current goal in the ABAIR ("to speak") research programme at the Phonetics and Speech Laboratory, Trinity College Dublin. ABAIR is concerned with developing speech technologies for Irish as well as applications that make the technology useful for the language community. Fundamental to this work is the provision of the linguistic research, that not only delivers resources that underpin the technology, but is also essential to the wider language research community and central to the building of 'intelligent' applications – i.e, applications that incorporate a knowledge of the language structure. Lingustic resource building has been a central feature of our work from the outset – from the original collaboration between Irish and Welsh researchers to develop speech resources for the two languages (the EU-Interreg project WISPR[1]).

In developing speech technology for Irish, and similarly for other Celtic (and endangered languages) one needs to consider that there is no one spoken standard – but rather three dialects which diverge considerably in lexicon, morphology, and especially in pronunciation. Whereas, in the 'major' widely spoken languages, technologies were developed for a standard variety (catering for other varieties came much later) this was/is not an option for Irish. Thus, developing text-to-speech synthesis was approached from the outset as a multi-dialect project, requiring the development of linguistic resources that could provide for a multi-dialect facility. Text-to-speech synthesis systems have been developed for the three main dialects of Irish: Ulster (Ul); Connacht (Co) and Munster (Mu). The synthetic voices, which are available on the ABAIR website[2] include male and female voices and the user has a choice of speech engines (currently deep neural network (DNN) and hidden Markov model speech synthesis (HTS) voices). Current work is focussed on extending the range of dialects covered, as well as exploring the rapidly evolving synthesis modalities.

In building core technology, such as speech synthesis or recognition, it makes sense to understand (i) what applications are most needed by the language community and (ii) who precisely the users might be. To date, ABAIR has been exploiting the synthetic voices in applications for (i) the *general public*, e.g., a web-reader that reads out any electronic text in your choice of dialect; (ii) for Irish language *teaching and learning,* e.g. learning platforms geared to different learner cohorts, different language skills and different language levels (Ní Chiaráin et al., 2022), and (iii) for *disability and access,* to enable the inclusion of this very neglected 'minority within the minority' (Barnes et al., 2022).

In building the ASR system, the diversity of the potential users/applications presents many challenges. As in the development of speech synthesis systems, it is a basic requirement that the system can deal equally well with the diversity of native dialects. Furthermore, one envisages many applications in the educational sphere, where recognition of learners' productions is desirable. This latter group is in itself a very diverse cohort – with different levels ranging from highly proficient speakers with near native-speaker pronunciation to beginners, to fluent speakers who have, nonetheless, a sound system more akin to that of English. Furthermore, for educational and disability applications, one will need recognition of children's voices.

[1] https://keep.eu/projects/2540/WISPR-EN/

[2] https://abair.ie

In ÉIST ("to listen"), we will be targeting all of these cohorts, but there are choices to be made as to the priorities in developing the initial resources. The most basic requirement is in our view to provide a facility that works for the native speaker communities – regardless of which dialect. For that reason, the system described here, and the resources on which our research has been focussed to date, is geared primarily to native speaker speech.

In testing the present system, test materials were used that contained both native-speaker (L1) speech and L2 speech (the latter from the Mozilla Common Voice[3] collection for Irish). This provides some indicators as to the likely performance of the current system with L1 and L2 speakers and provides some pointers for future work.

3. Resources

The initial efforts to build the ÉIST system drew heavily on the linguistic resources developed for synthesis.

3.1 Speech Corpora

The speech corpora recorded for the synthetic voices were a starting point for the system. These were quite extensive (c.25.2 hours) but involved only 8 speakers. The recordings were of the 3 main dialects referred to above and were based on readings of materials appropriate for each dialect. The quality of recordings was high, and the corpora were edited, cleaned, annotated and aligned – ready to be used in the ASR engine.

Additionally, speech corpora were collected, as part of an initiative MíleGlór[4] ("A Thousand Voices"). A platform was developed that can be used for live or crowdsourced recordings: given that our priority was to obtain data for native speakers of the different Gaeltachtaí (Irish speaking areas), the platform offered different materials, depending on the dialect of the speaker. The control over the text presented to users for recording is important. Ideally, we would like coverage of the sounds in all environments, and it is important to use natural, dialect-appropriate and relatively simple language to ensure it is easy for users to read. Most of the data collected was recorded live during successive Oireachtas gatherings (annual Irish language festival). This corpus is 20.8 hours in duration from 256 speakers reading from dialect-appropriate texts. Prior to recording, demographic information on the speakers is elicited e.g. whether they are native speakers, their dialect, approximate age etc.

We also had access to a corpus of spontaneous speech from 71 speakers, the Comhrá corpus (Uí Dhonnchadha et al., 2012). About 5.1 hours from this corpus has been edited and processed for recognition training, although only part of this is used in the system described below.

Finally, part of the Mozilla Common Voice corpus of Irish (54 speakers, 2.3 hours) was used as part of the Test set for system evaluation (see Section 6). Note that this corpus is of nearly all L2 speakers, and this is something we return to below.

3.2 Lexicon Building

ABAIR synthesis resources were used for building the pronunciation lexicons for the ÉIST system. These are the letter-to-sound (LTS) rules and the pronunciation lexicons for the dialects. The pronunciation lexicons for the text-to-speech systems are rather limited, as they are intended solely to cater for those irregular word forms, whose pronunciation cannot be predicted using the LTS rules. Nonetheless, combined, these provided ideal tools for constructing pronunciation lexicons.

As a strategy for dealing with the multiple dialects in building the synthesis systems, we developed a *Trans-dialect (Trans)* set of LTS rules, which capture the common core of the phonological system, while allowing for dialect-specific modules to capture dialect-specific differences in realisation (Ó Raghallaigh, 2010). From the *Trans* ruleset, we developed a *Trans* lexicon. We also had entirely separate sets of LTS rules for the three dialects, allowing us to build a *Multi-dialect (Multi)* lexicon comprising all forms in all dialects. These two approaches are tested in Section 6.

3.3 Text resources for language modelling

The text corpora used for language modelling included the *Corpus of Irish for Lexicography* (Ó Meachair, M. J. et al., 2021) using the 2021.1 version. It was developed by Gaois, DCU, with funding from Foras na Gaeilge, is referred to as Text A (72m words, 1.5m vocabulary). A version of the *National Corpus of Irish*, provided by Foras na Gaeilge, is referred to as Text B (52m words, c.0.25m vocabulary). The text from a spontaneous speech corpus of Irish is used and is referred to as Text C (c.4m words, c.0.08m vocabulary). Finally, Irish language text collected from Wikipedia is referred to as Text D (c.2.5m words, 0.13m vocabulary)

4. The current ÉIST ASR system

The ASR system is a hybrid system, in that it combines (1) an acoustic model, (2) a pronunciation lexicon and (3) a language model in a weighted finite state transducer (Mohri et al., 2002). We are continuously running experiments making use of various combinations of our speech data for acoustic model training as well as different configurations of lexicons and of the language models. The system described and tested here is built as follows:

4.1 Acoustic Model

The HMM-based neural network acoustic model is a Time-Delay Neural Network (TDNN) (Peddinti et al., 2015; Povey et al., 2018), that was trained on a subset of our speech corpora. This subset was balanced for the 3 dialects and totalled 37.2h, from 281 speakers. 85% of the total speech duration involved native (L1) speakers. Details of the training data are in Table 1. All experiments are done using the Kaldi toolkit (Povey et al., 2011).

[3] https://commonvoice.mozilla.org/

[4] https://abair.ie/mileglor/

Table 1: Details of speech datasets used. Duration is noted in hours.

dataset	#wav	#spk	#words	#vocab	#dur
Train	39,609	281	338,643	15,018	37.24
Test	1174	20	8224	2103	1.14

The data was initially aligned using a triphone GMM-HMM trained using MFCC features, applying linear discriminative analysis (LDA), maximum likelihood linear transformation (MLLT), feature space maximum likelihood linear regression (fMLLR) and speaker adaptive training (SAT). The features for training the TDNN model were 40-dimensional high-resolution MFCCs stacked with 100-dimensional online extracted i-vectors.

Two common, on-the-fly data augmentation techniques were used in training to augment the speech data: *speed perturbation* (Mubashir et al., 2013) and *spectral augmentation* (*SpecAug*) (Park et al., 2019). On-the-fly methods work by augmenting data during training, which both improves the flexibility of training and greatly saves disk space. Using speed perturbation, the training data was tripled using speed warping factors of 0.9, 1.0 and 1.1. *SpecAug* augments the log mel-spectrogram of an utterance, by randomly masking bands on the frequency domain and time domain. This method leads to impressive improvements.

The TDNN model consists of 13 factorized TDNN (TDNN-F) layers with a size of 1024 and a bottleneck size of 128 and was trained for 10 epochs. It was trained with lattice-free maximum mutual information (LF-MMI) (Povey et al., 2016).

System fusion is a common method to make use of multiple similar systems and achieve a stable performance. As the number of training epochs affects how much a system is fine tuned to the training data and as such, how robust it will be to unseen testing data, fusion of variants of acoustic models, trained using a different number of epochs is explored in the evaluation (Section 6), where it is compared to systems trained with a single acoustic model.

4.2 Lexicon

The complexity of pronunciation variation across dialects and speaker communities in Irish is a challenge when developing a pronunciation lexicon. As mentioned above, two different approaches to lexicon building were tested in the present system, a *Trans* lexicon, based on the *Trans* LTS rules, and a *Multi* lexicon, which simply included all dialect pronunciations. This *Trans* lexicon is more compact than the *Multi* lexicon, which has advantages in the size of the decoding lattices and the efficiency with which they can be searched. It would thus confer many advantages if it can perform equally well as the larger *Multi* lexicon. See Table 2 for details.

Table 2: Number of phones / abstract units (#phn) and entries (#lex) in Multi and Trans lexicons.

	Trans	Multi
#phn	92	118
#lex	540k	1006k

4.3 Language Model

The language model in the present hybrid system is a 3-gram model (Goodman, 2001) trained on all text corpora listed in Section 3.3 using the SRILM toolkit (Stolcke et al., 2011). Lattice-rescoring (Liu et al., 2016; Xu et al., 2018) using recurrent neural network language models (RNNLM) (Bengio et al., 2003; Mikolov et al., 2011) has been shown to be greatly beneficial. An RNNLM trained on Text A and Text D is used to rescore the hypotheses generated from the 3-gram language model.

5. System Evaluation

5.1 Test set

A test set was developed for the system evaluation. This consisted of materials taken from two sources. Firstly, a subset of speakers was taken from our own MíleGlór recordings, ensuring no overlap of speakers or utterance text between the training set and the test set. These speakers were virtually all native (L1) speakers. Secondly, part of the Mozilla Common Voice corpus for Irish was used. The data chosen were those where the speaker had declared a dialect preference and predominantly positive listeners' judgements were obtained. These speakers were however L2 speakers, which may partly be explained by the fact that a large cohort of the Irish-speaking online community are not native speakers. Over the two combined sets, efforts were made to balance for the dialects.

The fact that the two datasets used in the test data represented a clean L1/L2 divide is interesting in that it allows inferences to be drawn regarding the likely performance of the ÉIST ASR system for native and non-native speakers. See Table 1 for details of the test set.

5.2 Results

Table 3 presents the results obtained for the *Multi* and *Trans* lexicons. In a), the Overall Word Error Rate (WER) results are compared for: single systems, which are trained for 10 epochs using the baseline 3-gram LM; fused systems using the baseline 3-gram LM; and fused systems rescored using an RNNLM (see Section 4.1). The best results were obtained with the RNNLM, and the *Trans* lexicon performs as well as, or marginally better than the *Multi* lexicon.

Table 3: WER% for Multi and Trans lexicons. a) Overall WER% for all test speakers; b) breakdown of WER according to dialect affiliation of speakers; and c) breakdown of WER% for the two corpora used in the Test set.

a)	Multi	Trans
Single	13.1	13.38
Fused	12.6	12.5
+RNNLM	8.85	8.78
b)	**Multi**	**Trans**
Co spk	10.35	9.98
Mu spk	6.96	7.31
Ul spk	10.11	9.74
c)	**Multi**	**Trans**
MíleGlór	6.38	6.73
Mozilla	10.68	10.30

In part b) of Table 3, a breakdown of the Overall WER of systems with RNNLM rescoring is presented according to the dialect affiliation of the speakers. It should be noted that the dialect affiliation here refers to the actual dialect in the case of the native speakers (L1) but refers simply to the dialect preference of the L2 speakers, whose speech may approximate to dialect norms in varying degrees. The *Trans* lexicon yields a better performance for Co and Ul speakers, but the *Multi* performs better for Mu.

In part c) of Table 3, WER are compared for the two different corpora used in the Test set, the MíleGlór and Mozilla data. This comparison is of interest because in the former, native speakers dominate (80%) while in the latter all are L2 speakers. There is a consistently large WER difference, with performance being considerably better (lower WERs) for the MíleGlór speakers. This does suggest that the ÉIST system performs better for native-speaker speech. This is not surprising, as this was the intention behind the strong focus of native-speaker speech in the collection of data for the ASR training.

6. Current and future directions

The ÉIST system is available to try[5], although it is still a work in progress. Our current efforts and future aspirations include the following: Speech Corpus extension- we will be gathering a much larger corpus of speech data, focusing on a) Gaeltacht-based native speakers to include all the dialects and b) non-Gaeltacht speakers of Irish. The corpus will be collected in such a way that the different cohorts can be identified, both in terms of native / non-native distinction and the dialect of the speaker. We are currently extending the dialect-appropriate text materials used in MíleGlór for recording, to include much more varied sentences with greatly increased vocabulary.

Further to the current approach, we are also investigating the potential of End-to-End ASR systems (Gulati et al., 2020; Zhang et al., 2020) for dealing with the large variation in Irish speech, including the use of pretrained models, such as Wav2Vec 2.0 (Baevski et al., 2020).

Although not a current activity, we are keenly aware of the need to cater for children's speech, both for synthesis and recognition. This is particularly critical given that much of ABAIR's focus is on developing applications to support Irish language education and to ensure that those with disabilities are included in the Irish language educational, social and cultural spheres.

7. Acknowledgments

This work is part of the ABAIR initiative, which is supported by *An Roinn Turasóireachta, Cultúir, Ealaíon, Gaeltachta, Spóirt agus Meán*, with funding from the National Lottery, as part of the *Stráitéis 20 Bliain don Ghaeilge*.

8. Bibliographical References

Baevski, A., Zhou, H., Mohamed, A., & Auli, M. (2020). wav2vec 2.0: A Framework for Self-Supervised Learning of Speech Representations. *Advances in Neural Information Processing Systems*, *2020-Decem*, 1–12.

Barnes, E., Morrin, O., Ní Chasaide, A., Cummins, J., Berthelsen, H., Murphy, A., Nic Corcráin, M., O'Neill, C., Gobl, C., & Ní Chiaráin, N. (2022). AAC don Ghaeilge: the Prototype Development of Speech-Generating Assistive Technology for Irish. *Proceedings of the International Conference on Language Resources and Evaluation*.

Bengio, Y., Ducharme, R., Vincent, P., & Jauvin, C. (2003). A Neural Probabilistic Language Model. *Journal of Machine Learning Research*, *3*(6), 1137–1155.

Ní Chiaráin, N., Comtois, M., Nolan, O., Robinson-Gunning, N., Sloan, J., Berthelsen, H., & Ní Chasaide, A. (2022). Celtic CALL: Strengthening the Vital Role of Education for Language Transmission. *Proceedings of the International Conference on Language Resources and Evaluation*.

Goodman, J. T. (2001). A bit of progress in language modeling. *Computer Speech & Language*, *15*(4), 403–434.

Gulati, A., Qin, J., Chiu, C.-C., Parmar, N., Zhang, Y., Yu, J., Han, W., Wang, S., Zhang, Z., Wu, Y., & Pang, R. (2020). Conformer: Convolution-augmented Transformer for Speech Recognition. *Interspeech 2020*, 5036–5040.

Liu, X., Chen, X., Wang, Y., Gales, M. J. F., & Woodland, P. C. (2016). Two Efficient Lattice Rescoring Methods Using Recurrent Neural Network Language Models. *IEEE/ACM Transactions on Audio, Speech, and Language Processing*, *24*(8), 1438–1449.

Mikolov, T., Kombrink, S., Deoras, A., Burget, L., & Černocký, J. (2011). RNNLM --- Recurrent Neural Network Language Modeling Toolkit. *Proceedings of ASRU 2011*, 1–4.

Mohri, M., Pereira, F., & Riley, M. (2002). Weighted finite-state transducers in speech recognition. *Computer Speech & Language*, *16*(1), 69–88.

Mubashir, M., Shao, L., & Seed, L. (2013). Audio Augmentation for Speech Recognition Tom. *Neurocomputing*, *100*, 144–152.

Ó Meachair, M. J., Ó Raghallaigh, B., Bhreathnach, Ú., Ó Cleircín, G. & Scannell, K.. (2021). Corpus Creation for Lexicographical Research: Corpas Foclóireachta na Gaeilge (CFG 2020). *Teanga: The Journal of the Irish Association of Applied Linguistics.*, *28*, 278–305.

Ó Raghallaigh, B. T. C. D. (2010). Multi-dialect phonetisation for Irish text-to-speech synthesis : a modular approach. *Sciences-New York*, *September*.

Park, D. S., Chan, W., Zhang, Y., Chiu, C.-C., Zoph, B., Cubuk, E. D., & Le, Q. V. (2019). SpecAugment: A

[5] https://phoneticsrv3.lcs.tcd.ie/rec/irish_asr

Simple Data Augmentation Method for Automatic Speech Recognition. *Interspeech 2019*, *2019-Septe*, 2613–2617.

Peddinti, V., Povey, D., & Khudanpur, S. (2015). A Time-Delay Neural Network Architecture for Efficient Modeling of Long Temporal Contexts. *Proceedings of the Annual Conference of the International Speech Communication Association, INTERSPEECH*, *2015-Janua*, 2–6.

Povey, D., Cheng, G., Wang, Y., Li, K., Xu, H., Yarmohammadi, M., & Khudanpur, S. (2018). Semi-Orthogonal Low-Rank Matrix Factorization for Deep Neural Networks. *Interspeech 2018*, *2018-Septe*(2), 3743–3747.

Povey, D., Ghahremani, P., & Manohar, V. (2016). Purely Sequence-Trained Neural Networks for ASR Based on Lattice-Free MMI Transfer Learning for ASR View project Speech Recognition View project Purely sequence-trained neural networks for ASR based on lattice-free MMI. *Interspeech*, 2751–2755.

Povey, D., Ghoshal, A., Boulianne, G., Burget, L., Glembek, O., Goel, N., Hannemann, M., Motlicek, P., Qian, Y., Schwarz, P., Silovsky, J., Stemmer, G., & Vesely, K. (2011). The Kaldi Speech Recognition Toolkit. *IEEE Signal Processing Society*.

Stolcke, A., Zheng, J., Wang, W., & Abrash, V. (2011). SRILM at Sixteen : Update and Outlook. *Proceedings of the IEEE Automatic Speech Recognition and Understanding Workshop (ASRU)*, 5–9.

Uí Dhonnchadha, E., Frenda, A., & Vaughan, B. (2012). Issues in Designing a Corpus of Spoken Irish. *LREC-2012: SALTMIL-AfLaT Workshop on "Language Technology for Normalisation of Less-Resourced Languages"*, 1.

Xu, H., Chen, T., Gao, D., Wang, Y., Li, K., Goel, N., Carmiel, Y., Povey, D., & Khudanpur, S. (2018). A Pruned Rnnlm Lattice-Rescoring Algorithm for Automatic Speech Recognition. *2018 IEEE International Conference on Acoustics, Speech and Signal Processing (ICASSP)*, *2018-April*, 5929–5933.

Zhang, Q., Lu, H., Sak, H., Tripathi, A., McDermott, E., Koo, S., & Kumar, S. (2020). Transformer Transducer: A Streamable Speech Recognition Model with Transformer Encoders and RNN-T Loss. *ICASSP 2020 - 2020 IEEE International Conference on Acoustics, Speech and Signal Processing (ICASSP)*, *2020-May*(3), 7829–7833.

Proceedings of the CLTW 4 @ LREC2022, pages 52–59
Marseille, 20-25 June 2022

Development and Evaluation of Speech Recognition for the Welsh Language

Dewi Bryn Jones
Language Technologies Unit
Bangor University, Wales
d.b.jones@bangor.ac.uk

Abstract

This paper reports on ongoing work on developing and evaluating speech recognition models for the Welsh language using data from the Common Voice project and two popular open development kits – HuggingFace wav2vec2 and coqui STT. Activities for ensuring the growth and improvement of the Welsh Common Voice dataset are described. Two applications have been developed – a voice assistant and an online transcription service that allow users and organisations to use the new models in a practical and useful context, but which have also helped source additional test data for better evaluation of recognition accuracy and establishing the optimal selection and configurations of models. Test results suggest that in transcription good accuracy can be achieved for read speech, but further data and research is required for improving recognition results of freely spoken formal and informal speech. Meanwhile a limited domain language model provides excellent accuracy for a voice assistant. All code, data and models produced from this work are freely available.

Keywords: speech recognition, Welsh, Common Voice, wav2vec2, coqui STT

1. Introduction

Automatic speech recognition (ASR) is a technology that's transforming how people interact with computers and consume content. New products and services that cater to speakers of larger languages, that are facilitated by highly accurate automatic speech recognition systems, do not exist for speakers of less-resourced languages. The development of speech recognition with accuracies equivalent to that for larger languages has become ever more critical for any less-resourced languages' digital inclusion (Sayers, et.al., 2021).

This paper reports on ongoing work on developing and evaluating speech recognition for Welsh using primarily crowdsourced data and open-source development kits. It reports on how this work has contributed to ensuring the growth and quality of data crowdsourced from an international project as well as from two useful and practical applications developed by the Language Technologies Unit (LTU). The motivation and operation of the voice assistant application, Macsen, as well as the online transcription service, Trawsgrifiwr Ar-lein, are described in sections 1.1 and 1.2 respectively.

All data and source code for training models as well as for both applications are available from the Welsh National Language Technologies Portal (Prys et al., 2018) to any developer or user who may wish to integrate, customize or run local deployments.

1.1 Trawsgrifiwr Ar-lein – Transcription Service Website

Both the COVID pandemic and new United Kingdom Accessibility Legislation (The National Archives, 2018) created a greater demand for Welsh language speech content to be transcribed. The legislation mandates captions and subtitles for all teaching and student support resources used by universities to deliver blended learning[1] and came into effect during the COVID pandemic when provision of all university teaching moved to remote delivery and/or recorded lectures. Lecturers within Welsh universities and the Coleg Cymraeg Cenedlaethol[2] urgently required an application to help ensure compliance for their digital materials.

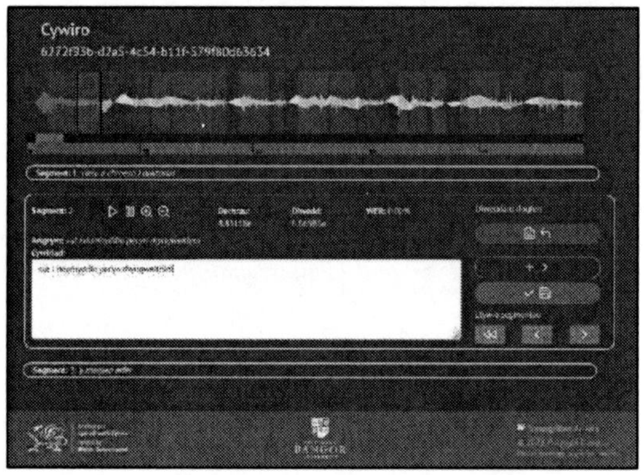

Figure 1: the Trawsgrifiwr Ar-lein interface for validating and correcting automatic transcriptions of Welsh language speech.

The LTU developed the Trawsgrifiwr Ar-lein website application[3] that allows users to submit an audio file or a link to a YouTube video of Welsh language speech for automatic transcribing. Users are required to accept terms and conditions each time before submitting content for transcription. These state that the service respects all privacy and copyright and automatically deletes submitted content after 30 days. No copies of their data are made in those 30 days nor is any other use made of it.

Each submission is added to a queue for processing. The audio is first segmented with an aggressive Voice Activation Detection algorithm (webrtcvad).[4] Each segment in turn is transcribed by the speech recognition

[1] Blended learning combines in-person and digital delivery of teaching. (see https://en.wikipedia.org/wiki/Blended_learning)

[2] The Coleg Cymraeg Cenedlaethol plans and supports Welsh language Higher Education provision. (see https://www.colegcymraeg.ac.uk/en)

[3] https://trawsgrifiwr.techiaith.cymru/

[4] https://github.com/wiseman/py-webrtcvad

model. In the meantime, users are given a unique URL that can be used to access the interface as seen in Figure 1, to listen, validate and correct the transcriptions in each segment. The interface provides a button to playback the segment's audio, its automatic transcription and a text box for entering corrections. If a segment requires no further corrections, the user clicks on the button which displays a tick and a disk icon to commit the correction and move to the next segment. Both next and previous segments are displayed for context, as well as the audio's waveform in order to correct segmentation. An additional button can also correct segments that are too short by merging the current segment to the next segment to form a larger segment. After all segments have been validated or corrected the interface provides buttons to download the transcription as files in SubRip (srt)[5] or TextGrid format - a file format for annotating speech files with Praat (Boersma et al., 2022).

Section 2.2.2 describes the data sourced with the aid of the transcription application.

1.2 Macsen – Voice Assistant App

Previous work on speech recognition for Welsh had been motivated solely by the development of Macsen, a voice assistant for Welsh speakers that can run on Android or iOS devices (Jones, 2020). Despite a lack of speech data, a functioning and everyday useful Welsh voice assistant was achieved, provided the assistant's speech recognition capability was constrained to recognizing only a closed set of commands and questions that trigger a small collection of the most practical and effective skills, such as for retrieving news, providing weather forecasts and playing music. This work was able to update Macsen's speech recognition model with a larger training dataset and expand its ability to support more new skills while not degrading the performance or the practicality of the app.

Figure 2 – the Macsen Voice Assistant with the Hyfforddi (Training) bottom navigation bar tab selected and a sentence provided for recording: "Switch off the lights in the living room"

The work also revised the four bottom navigation tabs (see Figure 2) that provide four screens or modes of operation within the app:

- Siarad (*Speak*) – the main screen providing the speech interface to the app's skills
- Trawsgrifio (*Transcribe*) – a new second screen that uses the models trained for transcription. Any speech is converted into text which can then be copied and pasted into any other application on the device, such as for messaging
- Hyfforddi (*Training*) – a screen, as seen in Figure 2, that provides an opportunity for users to record random sentences from the closed set of command and questions
- Help – a screen that lists all sentences from the closed set of commands and questions that the app recognizes. The list is categorized according to skill

Section 2.2.1 describes the data sourced with the aid of the Hyfforddi screen in Macsen voice assistant application.

2. Data

The data used for training Welsh speech recognition models was sourced from popular multilingual open speech and textual datasets. Additional data for evaluating new models was sourced with two applications developed by the LTU.

2.1 Common Voice

The primary speech data resource for training this work's speech recognition acoustic models was the Welsh language subset of Mozilla's Common Voice multilingual speech corpus (Ardila et al., 2020). Following previous attempts in crowdsourcing speech corpora (Prys et al., 2018; Cooper et al., 2019) Welsh has been fortunate to have been supported by the Common Voice project since its first multilingual expansion in June 2018 (Henretty, 2018). Since then, several campaigns to appeal to all speakers of Welsh to voluntarily record and validate recordings have been organized by the community while the LTU has monitored the growth and quality of Welsh Common Voice data for training Welsh language speech recognition.

	Published	Validated (hours)	Other (hours)	Speakers
CV1	Feb 2019	21	1	365
CV2	June 2019	41	6	738
CV3	June 2019	42	6	748
CV4	Dec 2019	59	18	1149
CV5.1	June 2020	83	13	1257
CV6.1	Dec 2020	95	29	1382
CV7	July 2021	110	31	1655
CV8	Jan 2022	116	29	1695

Table 1 – Welsh speech data in Common Voice releases (source: Common Voice website's datasets page).

Table 1 shows how Welsh has progressed through each Common Voice release since June 2018. The total amount of recordings that have been approved by volunteers (validated hours) have increased well with each release.

[5] Further information on the SubRip file format: https://docs.fileformat.com/video/srt/

Whilst the number of recordings that have not yet been validated ('other' hours) have also increased. This may suggest a need to prioritize validation efforts rather than recording new sentences in campaigns for subsequent Common Voice releases. No data from the 'other' split was used in this work since its quality is unknown.
Table 2 shows Mozilla's pre-defined splits of the validated recordings into training, validating and testing sets. Each split contains only one recording per distinct sentence. As noted in Jones (2020), initial versions of Welsh Common Voice consisted of a low number of distinct sentences with a high number of multiple recordings. This consequently created pre-defined splits from Mozilla that were much smaller in size when compared to the overall size of all validated recordings.

	train (minutes)	validation (minutes)	test (minutes)
CV1	34	35	37
CV2	37	37	40
CV3	37	36	41
CV4	66	55	59
CV5.1	311	259	253
CV6.1	557	411	425
CV7	547	439	432
CV8	627	461	469

Table 2 - Welsh data in Mozilla pre-defined splits in all releases.

The only way to remedy such low utilization of contributions into pre-defined splits as set by Mozilla was to ensure that enough distinct sentences are available to the Common Voice website for recording only once by any volunteer. Thus began, after CV3 a concerted effort by members of the LTU to remedy the situation by adding significant amounts of distinct Welsh sentences to Common Voice. Sentences were collected from out-of-copyright materials such as novels and essays as well as from copyrighted texts gifted by individuals[6] and submitted via Mozilla's Common Voice SentenceCollector website. By CV6.1, 14,857 sentences had been added and the size of the Welsh pre-defined training split increased by approximately 1400% from 37 minutes in CV3 to 557 minutes. This provided a larger training set for this work's initial attempts at training models. The next release however, CV7, saw a reduction in the pre-defined training split, with its size decreasing to 547 minutes, indicating there were no new distinct sentence recordings meaning an urgent need for more distinct sentences for improving CV8. Fortunately, the CoVoST 2 corpus (Wang et al., 2020) contains 232,037 unique Welsh sentences created by professional translation of English sentences from version 4 of Common Voice. The CoVoST project conducted sanity checks on all translated sentences by means of language model perplexity and length ratio heuristics with lowest scoring sentences sent for re-translation.

For submission of CoVoST translated sentences back into Welsh Common Voice for recording, this work excluded 130,502 sentences[7] that did not meet the following criteria as set by the Common Voice project or by editors in the LTU:

- sentences should contain less than 15 words
- sentences should not include numbers, acronyms or abbreviations
- all words must be present in a Welsh language lexicon (Prys et al., 2021) or in a list of 20,000 additionally permitted words.

The lexicons facilitated the exclusion of a high number of sentences containing American English proper nouns. In the opinion of the editors in the LTU such sentences were not relevant for speech recognition in a Welsh cultural context. Certain English words, as well as company names and products were judged to be commonly used in Welsh speech and were included in the list of additional permitted words, thus retaining their sentences.
The remaining 101,535 sentences were validated according to Mozilla's recommended method for bulk submissions[8] requiring human editors to proofread a statistically significant random sample of sentences and confirm that a maximum of 5% of sentences were problematic and not appropriate for recording.[9] The sentences were accepted by Mozilla shortly after the CV7 release. Consequently, the size of the pre-defined training split increased by 14.6% a few months later in CV8.

2.2 New Test Sets from LTU Applications

Mozilla Common Voice already provides a test set from its pre-defined splits for researchers to use for measuring their models' recognition accuracy. As shown in Table 2 it is comparable in size to the validation set and by CV8 was 469 minutes in size. This is useful for measuring model accuracy across training sessions and for comparing with models by other researchers. However, since it contains recordings similar in nature to those in the pre-defined training and validation sets, it may not be sufficient for measuring accuracy and suitability in real life application scenarios.
This work collected two test sets from two applications to form a single open resource for testing Welsh speech recognition called the Corpws Profi Adnabod Lleferydd (Speech Recognition Test Corpus) which can be accessed from the LTUs gitlab repositories website.[10]

2.2.1 Voice Assistant Test Set

Within its 'Hyfforddi' (Training) tabbed screen, as shown in Figure 2, the Macsen voice assistant app provides a simple interface that allows users to contribute recordings of sentences randomly selected from the closed set of commands and questions that trigger a response from any of its supported skills. The user touches the microphone button to start and stop recording. Stopping the recording uploads the audio immediately and provides the user with the next sentence for recording. There is no support for

[6] https://github.com/techiaith/brawddegau-adnabod-lleferydd/blob/master/README_en.md
[7] https://github.com/techiaith/brawddegau-adnabod-lleferydd/blob/master/docker/README.md
[8] https://github.com/common-voice/common-voice/blob/main/docs/SENTENCES.md#bulk-submission
[9] https://github.com/common-voice/common-voice/pull/3239
[10] https://git.techiaith.bangor.ac.uk/data-porth-technolegau-iaith/corpws-profi-adnabod-lleferydd

listening and/or re-recording before submitting. The list of possible sentences for recording can be seen within the app under its 'Help' tabbed screen.

Since its release in 2020, approximately 700 recordings have been submitted. Quality control and validation for inclusion into a test set corpus consisted of LTU members listening to each recording and comparing with the original sentence. It was not possible to validate every submission but 300 recordings from 25 users, with a total duration of 17 minutes, were accepted.

The data can be found in the `data/macsen` sub-directory of the Corpws Profi Adnabod Lleferydd gitlab repository.[10]

2.2.2 Transcriptions Test Set

As noted in section 1.1, all submitted audio and corrected transcriptions are deleted after 30 days by the Trawsgrifiwr Ar-lein website and are not used for any other purposes in the meantime. The website however does invite users, through a section included in the terms and conditions displayed each time the website is initially opened, to contact the LTU and to discuss providing permission for contributing their audio and corrected transcriptions into the Corpws Profi Adnabod Lleferydd. Another strategy involved commissioning the use of the Trawsgrifiwr Ar-lein website to transcribe recorded sessions from an online conference hosted by the LTU. All speakers had indicated their permission for including transcriptions of their speech into the Corpws Profi Adnabod Lleferydd.

Table 8 in the appendix lists details of 13 YouTube videos that have been transcribed and included into Corpws Profi Adnabod Lleferydd. They include numerous videos from the online conference, but also from teaching resources by various departments at Bangor University, short videos and podcasts for young people by S4C[11] (a Welsh language broadcaster) as well as gaming videos by Menter Iaith Sir Caerffili[12] (a language promotion community group in Caerffili county borough).

Table 9 in the appendix provides information regarding the variations in speech such as gender and accent. All recordings were of native speakers. Accents were generalised as being either 'North' or 'South', although there exist smaller variations of accents for Welsh (Cooper, et al., 2019). This work additionally categorised speech into three types which also took into consideration as to whether transcriptions would be verbatim or non-verbatim, meaning filler words, disfluencies or any small linguistic errors produced during speech were removed or corrected in order to make subtitles as readable as possible.

- Read-Speech – speech by a person reading from a prepared text. Linguistic errors in speech would be minimal with a non-verbatim transcription closer to the actual speech
- Formal-Spoken – speech using a formal register with the assistance of very little or no prepared text. Linguistic errors are more probable, but a non-verbatim transcription would be further from a corrected transcription
- Free-Spoken – speech from speaking freely in an informal register and occasionally some code switching with English. Non-verbatim transcriptions would be furthest from actual speech

Non-verbatim transcriptions may not be as optimal as verbatim transcriptions for evaluating models. A total of 266 segments were found to contain indistinguishable speech, multiple speakers, music, singing or interjections and were therefore excluded from this work's evaluation of models. Table 7 in the appendix lists the tags used to annotate and locate such features in excluded segments.

The transcriptions test set can be found in the `data/trawsgrifio` sub-directory of Corpws Profi Adnabod Lleferydd gitlab repositorty.[10]

2.3 Text Corpora

This work also used the following text corpora for training n-gram language models.

2.3.1 Macsen Texts Corpus

The Macsen voice assistant's closed set of questions and commands can serve as a text corpus for training a domain specific language model (Jones, 2020). Sentences can be easily generated from filling slots in template sentences with each possible entry from associated slot value entity files (for example files with lists of topics for the news or names of Welsh language bands). Both template sentences and slot entity values were composed by members of the LTU to facilitate an effective but as natural as possible collection of sentences for users to speak to their Welsh voice assistant. The resulting corpus of 1098 sentences can be downloaded from an API. [13]

2.3.2 OSCAR

The OSCAR corpus (Suárez et al., 2019) of texts crawled from the internet was used to provide a text corpus for training general purpose n-gram Welsh language models. Texts were left deduplicated and unshuffled with no segmentation, special filtering, normalization or tokenization undertaken. This corpus was approximately 23 million words in size.

3. Method

Several acoustic models for Welsh speech recognition have been trained with data from version 8 of Common Voice and open-source speech recognition development kits by coqui STT and HuggingFace. The entry for CV8 in Table 2 provides the duration of each pre-defined split. Common Voice's pre-defined set for testing, as well as the additional test sets as described in section 2.2 were used to measure word and character error rates. Measurements were made of greedy decoding, CTC beam search decoding and decoding with n-gram language model support (Graves et al., 2006).

All training and tests were conducted on a single workstation containing a single NVIDIA Titan 2080 RTX graphics card with 24Gb of RAM.

3.1 coqui STT

Previous work on speech recognition for a voice assistant (Jones, 2020) relied on the then Mozilla DeepSpeech speech recognition kit and its support for transfer learning from an English pre-trained model. In April 2021, Mozilla decided to end all work before its version 1.0 release leaving the start-up coqui AI to continue development.

[11] https://www.s4c.cymru

[12] http://www.mentercaerffili.cymru/

[13] Macsen corpus can be obtained from: https://api.techiaith.org/assistant/get_all_sentences

Previous work had demonstrated that despite a high number of repeated recordings of sentences, risking over fitting to the sentences in Common Voice, training with all 'validated' recordings (116 hours in CV8 as seen in Table 1) and the 'drop_source_layers' transfer learning hyperparameter value set to 2, was found to be optimal for the Macsen voice assistant app. This work would repeat the same training method to train acoustic models with version 1.2 of the coqui STT kit as well as with more recent and larger datasets from CV8.

All scripts for training and inference, as well as the optimal models produced from this work are available from a LTU GitHub repository.[14]

3.2 wav2vec 2.0

Recent work on wav2vec 2.0 at Facebook AI (Baevski et al., 2020) has made it possible to realise effective speech recognition with smaller quantities of transcribed speech. Representations of speech are initially learnt from large collections of raw speech audio which are then finetuned with transcribed speech data to perform speech recognition. Initial research with English speech recognition demonstrated that just ten minutes of transcribed speech could finetune a model pre-trained with 53,000 hours of raw speech audio and achieve a word error rate of 4.8.

Further work, given the lack of transcribed speech for the majority of the world's 7000 languages, has focused on learning speech representations from multiple languages (Conneau et al., 2020) and has demonstrated that cross-lingual pre-training outperforms monolingual training. The following multilingual models have been pre-trained by Facebook AI and published via the HuggingFace hub[15] for other researchers to finetune for their own languages using their own transcribed speech datasets:

- wav2vec2-large-xlsr-53 (Conneau et al., 2020): pre-trained from 56k hours of raw speech audio in 53 languages.
- wav2vec2-xls-r (Babu et al., 2021): pre-trained from 436k hours of raw speech audio in 128 languages. Models are provided in increasing sizes, from 300 million parameters, to 1 and 2 billion.

Both types of pre-trained models have been exposed to Welsh speech audio from Common Voice. In this work's experiments, all pre-trained models were finetuned for 30 epochs using a concatenation of Common Voice's pre-defined training and validation sets. Identical training hyperparameters values were used for all finetuning training runs with only the name of the pre-trained model varying.

The HuggingFace library support for wav2vec 2.0 speech recognition did not initially support decoding with CTC beam search nor decoding with the support of n-gram language models. Given the urgency for the Trawsgrifiwr Ar-lein transcription application at the time, this work undertook integrating the CTC decoding library from Parlance[16] as well as adding support for training and optimizing n-gram language models.

All scripts for training and inference as well as optimal models are available from a LTU GitHub repository.[17]

3.3 Language Model

Various n-gram language models were created with the KenLM library (Heafield, 2011) using the text corpora described in section 2.3. Optimal values for alpha and beta hyperparameters for CTC with language model decoding were found after 100 trail runs against the CV8 pre-defined test set.

4. Results

Table 3 presents results from evaluating coqui STT and wav2vec2 based models with the CV8 test set. Unfortunately, finetuning a wav2vec2-xls-r-2b pre-trained model, with 2 billion parameters, was not possible due to insufficient GPU hardware. Unsurprisingly however, all wav2vec2 self-supervised based models outperformed the supervised models from coqui STT. A WER as low as 22.4% by a model finetuned from the wav2vec2-xls-r-1b pre-trained model with only greedy decoding is very promising. The addition of a language model trained with the OSCAR corpus with optimized alpha and beta hyperparameters decreased its WER by 39.79% to 13.33 (as highlighted in bold in Table 3). coqui STT's WER, despite having been trained with all of Common Voice's validated recordings, as described in section 3.1, is much higher. However, a larger decrease of 52.01% is achieved with the support of a similar language model. The language model does not decrease each model's CER as significantly - 27.30% decrease for wav2vec2-xls-r-1b and 30.30% for coqui STT.

Model(s)	WER	CER
wav2vec2-large-xlsr-53	24.03	6.74
wav2vec2-large-xlsr-53 + CTC	24.01	6.71
wav2vec2-large-xlsr-53 + CTC + LM	13.79	4.77
wav2vec2-xls-r-300m	25.31	7.01
wav2vec2-xls-r-300m + CTC	25.19	6.98
wav2vec2-xls-r-300m + CTC + LM	14.41	5.03
wav2vec2-xls-r-1b	22.14	6.19
wav2vec2-xls-r-1b + CTC	21.95	6.16
wav2vec2-xls-r-1b + CTC + LM	**13.33**	**4.5**
wav2vec2-xls-r-2b	-	-
coqui STT (AM)	83.33	28.21
coqui STT (AM+LM)	39.99	19.66

Table 3 – Acoustic models test results against CV8 test set. n-gram language model (n=5) trained with the OSCAR corpus.

Table 4 provides recognition results from evaluating coqui STT and wav2vec2 models with the transcription test set from the Corpws Profi Adnabod Lleferydd. Results imply that all models are not as effective and as accurate when applied to a real-world application scenario such as transcribing. As highlighted in bold in Table 4, the best achieved accuracy is a WER of 32.96 by a finetuned wav2vec2-xls-r-1b based model with the support of a language model. Table 6 provides a break-down of results from evaluating the best wav2vec2-xls-r-1b based model with each YouTube video. Accuracy performance varies considerably. Videos of read speech, such as Pl16jPn0Jy4

[14] https://github.com/techiaith/docker-coqui-stt-cy/tree/22.02

[15] https://huggingface.co/models?other=wav2vec2

[16] https://github.com/parlance/ctcdecode

[17] https://github.com/techiaith/docker-wav2vec2-xlsr-ft-cy

and UdWqyWDZ4Y, are transcribed with an accuracy consistent to accuracies reported in Table 3. Other types of speech however are not transcribed as accurately with free spoken speech videos suffering very poor WER scores.

Model(s)	WER	CER
wav2vec2-large-xlsr-53	45.90	16.94
wav2vec2-large-xlsr-53 + CTC	45.66	16.90
wav2vec2-large-xlsr-53 + CTC + LM	34.98	16.47
wav2vec2-xls-r-1b	42.44	15.78
wav2vec2-xls-r-1b + CTC	42.53	15.88
wav2vec2-xls-r-1b + CTC + LM	**32.96**	**15.15**
coqui STT (AM)	92.32	43.26
coqui STT (AM+LM)	71.86	45.68

Table 4 – Model performance on the Transcription test set. n-gram LM with n=5 and trained with the OSCAR text corpus.

Table 5 shows results from using the Corpws Profi Adnabod Lleferydd's Macsen voice assistant test set to evaluate two candidate models for current and future versions of the app. The first candidate was the best performing wav2vec2-xls-r-1b based acoustic model supported by a general-purpose language model. The second candidate was the coqui STT model from previous experiments supported by a domain specific language model trained from the Macsen text corpus as described in section 2.3.1. As highlighted in bold in Table 5, a coqui STT based model with a domain specific language model has considerable better accuracy than the best general purpose wav2vec2-xls-r-1b based models.

Model(s)	WER	CER
wav2vec2-xls-r-1b + CTC + LM	18.06	5.11
coqui STT (AM + domain specific LM)	**4.18**	**2.4**

Table 5 - Model performance on the Macsen Welsh language Voice Assistant test set.

5. Conclusion

This paper has described the development of speech recognition for the Welsh language using speech data from the Mozilla Common Voice project and two popular open-source development kits from HuggingFace and coqui AI. Work on supporting the growth and quality of data in Welsh Common Voice with submissions of thousands of unique and readable sentences is also described. Two new test datasets were constructed from two real world application scenarios – a voice assistant and a transcriber – and used in further evaluation of models.

Results showed that wav2vec2 based models provide impressive accuracy, especially when evaluated with the Common Voice pre-defined test set. This is understandable since models were trained with similar data from other Common Voice pre-defined sets.

Evaluation with a new transcription test set from this work's new Corpws Profi Adnabod Lleferydd suggests that wav2vec2 models may be considered as sufficiently accurate for automatically transcribing read speech. However further research and different types of speech training data is required for improving the accuracy of recognition for free spoken, formal and informal speech. Results suggest that larger models pre-trained from a greater number of hours of raw audio in a greater number of languages can facilitate more accurate acoustic models for Welsh speech recognition after finetuning.

YouTube ID	Decode	WER	CER
Pl16jPn0Jy4	greedy	30.61	9.34
	CTC	30.24	9.19
	CTC+LM	19.91	8.13
4kIby51XL1E	greedy	33.27	10.29
	CTC	33.07	10.26
	CTC+LM	20.99	8.26
0P3VrE-VoOE	greedy	49.87	20.13
	CTC	49.79	20.35
	CTC+LM	40.57	19.8
_UdWqyWDZ4Y	greedy	28.08	8.93
	CTC	27.91	8.92
	CTC+LM	18.41	7.33
TJkVrsNaeY0	greedy	34.48	11.5
	CTC	34.5	11.58
	CTC+LM	27.12	10.62
xSs8TJiD5-Q	greedy	45.4	18.05
	CTC	45.17	17.98
	CTC+LM	37.11	17.69
06Gt5n0BWkw	greedy	49.55	19.35
	CTC	49.34	19.38
	CTC+LM	39.29	18.05
E7qGxNhGP9U	greedy	30.65	10.41
	CTC	30.43	10.43
	CTC+LM	21.3	8.48
BIG0OJ_Kbl4	greedy	54.98	21.0
	CTC	54.68	20.79
	CTC+LM	50.43	25.36
wMMm6rcSpnU	greedy	41.89	14.52
	CTC	40.85	14.44
	CTC+LM	31.08	13.48
C9VnfalWr44	greedy	70.33	26.76
	CTC	69.11	26.9
	CTC+LM	64.74	29.9
yxM1q3AzPJI	greedy	56.35	23.07
	CTC	56.77	23.06
	CTC+LM	44.96	23.25
jdYIrb9L_Tc	greedy	141.2	150.9
	CTC	212.2	189.7
	CTC+LM	102.8	117.4

Table 6 – Test results of a wav2vec2-xls-r-1b based speech recognition model on each video in the transcription test set.

Evaluation of models with the Corpws Profi Adnabod Lleferydd Macsen voice assistant test set suggest coqui STT with a limited domain language model can serve as a very accurate speech recognition component for recognizing sentences for all current skills in the Macsen voice assistant app. Coqui STT's relatively inexpensive computational demands are also attractive since the assistant may be required to run on local and on offline devices. Results have informed on the feasibility of utilizing wav2vec2 models with a general-purpose language model for all current skills. Users would perceive a significant degradation in recognition of sentences. Further work will aim to improve speech recognition that will allow reliable recognition of a greater number of skills and/or a more open set of commands and questions.

Comparing this work's methods and models with that for other Celtic languages is limited by the fact that only Irish and Breton are supported by the Mozilla Common Voice project. Both coqui STT and HuggingFace wav2vec2 models have been trained and reported for both languages. In Tyers et al. (2021) both Irish and Breton coqui STT models were trained with Common Voice data. By utilizing the same transfer learning mechanism as described in section 3.1, word error rates of approximately 94 were reported for both languages' acoustic models. The addition of an n-gram language model is reported to have improved results to 70.73 for Irish and 68.37 for Breton. Numerous attempts have been made by individuals at finetuning the wav2vec2 pre-trained models listed in section 3.2 for both languages, with word error rates of 42.34 for Irish and 41.71 for Breton for acoustic models reported on the 'Papers With Code' website.[18] Both languages have much smaller total hours of speech than Welsh in Common Voice and would need to ensure both significant amounts of distinct and readable sentences are available as well as to collaborate to appeal to the wider language community for contributions. Other speech data sets may be available and viable for finetuning. Similar approaches to crowdsource data with applications may also be possible using the code from this work.

The best Welsh language coqui STT and wav2vec2 based models from this work have been published to the LTU's GitHub pages[19] as well as to each speech development kit's respective public model repositories.[20] [21] All are licensed with open and permissive licensing in order to provide as many opportunities as possible for discoverability and integration of models by developers of into their software products and services with the least restrictions. Models will be updated for as long as this work continues to improve training of models with both coqui STT and HuggingFace speech recognition development kits. Work will also continue to collect more data through supporting Mozilla Common Voice, the LTUs own applications and from other sources.

6. Acknowledgements

This work was funded by the Welsh Government as part of its implementation of its Welsh Language technology plan (Welsh Government, 2018).

This work has been greatly supported by Rhoslyn Prys who undertook on a voluntary basis several crowdsourcing campaigns, to the Mentrau Iaith, Gwynedd Council, the National Library of Wales who worked with Rhoslyn on some of these campaigns, to the Welsh Government, and to the many participants across Wales and beyond who have contributed their voices to the Welsh Common Voice datasets.

Sentences for Welsh Common Voice were edited and proofread by Professor Delyth Prys and Gruffudd Prys.

The Trawsgrifiwr Ar-lein online transcription website was developed by Stephen Russell and used by Tegwen Bruce-Deans in the construction of the Corpws Profi Adnabod Lleferydd transcription test set.

7. Bibliographical References

Ardila, R., Branson, M., Davis, K., Henretty, M., Kohler, M., Meyer, J., Morais, R., Saunders, L., Tyers, F.M., & Weber, G. (2020). Common Voice: A Massively Multilingual Speech Corpus. LREC.

Babu, A., Wang, C., Tjandra, A., Lakhotia, K., Xu, Q., Goyal, N., Singh, K., Platen, P. V., Saraf, Y., Pino, J., Baevski. A., Conneau, A., Auli, M. (2021). XLS-R: Self-Supervised Cross-Lingual Speech Representation Learning at Scale. ArXiv, abs/2111.09296.

Baevski, A., Zhou, H., Mohamed, A., Auli, M. (2020). wav2vec 2.0: A Framework for Self-Supervised Learning of Speech Representations. ArXiv, abs/2006.11477.

Boersma, P., Weenik, D. (2022) Praat: Doing phonetics by computer [Computer Program]. Version 6.2.10. http://www.praat.org/

Conneau, A., Baevski, A., Collobert, A., Mohamed, R., Auli, M. (2020). Unsupervised Cross-lingual Representation Learning for Speech Recognition. ArXiv, abs/2006.13979

Cooper,S. Jones, D.B. and Prys, D. (2019). Crowdsourcing the Paldaruo Speech Corpus of Welsh for Speech Technology. Information, 10(8), p.247. Available at: http://dx.doi.org/10.3390/info1008024

Graves, A., Fernández, S., Gomez, F., Schmidhuber, J. (2006). Connectionist temporal classification: Labelling unsegmented sequence data with recurrent neural networks. p 369-376 ICML 2006 – Proceedings of the 23rd International Conference on Machine Learning.

Heafield, K. (2011). KenLM: Faster and Smaller Language Model Queries. WMT@EMNLP.

Henretty, M. (2018). More Common Voices. https://medium.com/mozilla-open-innovation/more-common-voices-24a80c879944 [Accessed March 31, 2022]

Prys,D. Jones, D.B. (2018). Gathering Data for Speech Technology in the Welsh Language: A Case Study. Proceedings of the LREC 2018 Workshop "CCURL 2018 – Sustaining Knowledge Diversity in the Digital Age", p.56. Claudia Soria, Laurent Besacier and Laurette Pretorius (eds.). Available at: http://lrec-conf.org/workshops/lrec2018/W26/pdf/book_of_proceedings.pdf

Prys,D., Jones, D.B. (2018). National Language Technologies Portals for LRLs: A Case Study. In: Vetulani, Z., Mariani, J., Kubis, M. (eds) Human Language Technology. Challenges for Computer Science and Linguistics. LTC 2015. Lecture Notes in Computer Science(), vol 10930. Springer, Cham. https://doi.org/10.1007/978-3-319-93782-3_30

Sayers, D., R. Sousa-Silva, S. Höhn et al. (2021). The Dawn of the Human-Machine Era: A forecast of new and emerging language technologies. Report for EU COST Action CA19102 'Language In The Human-Machine Era'. https://doi.org/10.17011/jyx/reports/20210518/1

[18] https://paperswithcode.com/dataset/common-voice

[19] https://github.com/techiaith/docker-wav2vec2-xlsr-ft-cy/releases

[20] https://huggingface.co/techiaith/wav2vec2-xlsr-ft-cy

[21] https://coqui.ai/models

The National Archive (2018). The Public Sector Bodies (Websites and Mobile Applications) Accessibility Regulations 2018. Available at: https://www.legislation.gov.uk/uksi/2018/852 [Accessed March 31, 2022]

Tyers, F., Meyer, J. (2021). What shall we do with an hour of data ? ArXiv, abs/2105.04674

Welsh Government (2018). Welsh language technology action plan. Available at: https://gov.wales/sites/default/files/publications/2018-12/welsh-language-technology-and-digital-media-action-plan.pdf [Accessed March 31, 2022]

8. Language Resource References

Wang, C., Wu, A., Pino, J. (2020) CoVoST 2: A Massively Multilingual Speech-to-Text Translation Corpus. Available via GitHub: https://github.com/facebookresearch/covost

Prys, D., Jones, D. B., Prys, G., & Watkins, G. L. (2021). Lecsicon Cymraeg Bangor Welsh Lexicon (Version 21.10) [Dataset]. https://github.com/techiaith/lecsicon-cymraeg-bangor

Suárez, P., Sagot, B., Romary, L. (2019). Asynchronous pipelines for processing huge corpora on medium to low resource infrastructures. In CMLC-7 (pp. 9 – 16). Leibniz-Institut für Deutsche Sprache.

9. Appendix

Tag	Meaning
[cerddoriaeth]	Segment contains music
[en_start]	Start of English language speech
[en_finish]	End of English language speech
[canu]	Segment is singing
[siaradwyr lluosog]	Multiple speakers
[ebychiad]	Burst / interjection
[chwerthin]	Laughter
[sŵn y gêm]	Sound of a computer game
[siarad]	Indistinguishable speech

Table 7 - Tags used to annotate the Corpws Profi Adnabod Lleferydd transcriptions test set.

ID	Segments	Voices	Duration Total (min)	Duration Avg (secs)
Pl16jPn0Jy4	79	1	19.22	14.6
4kIby51XL1E	78	1	20.82	16.02
0P3VrE-VoOE	77	1	30.62	23.87
_UdWqyWDZ4Y	182	1	15.95	5.26
TJkVrsNaeY0	144	1	24.42	10.18
xSs8TJiD5-Q	227	1	24.56	6.49
06Gt5n0BWkw	244	1	24.85	6.11
E7qGxNhGP9U	128	7	10.64	4.99
BIG0OJ_Kbl4	8	2	1.74	13.11
wMMm6rcSpnU	70	1	7.42	6.36
C9VnfalWr44	6	12	1.74	17.42
yxM1q3AzPJI	35	2	6.35	10.89
jdYIrb9L_Tc	99	5	4.2	2.55

Table 8 – Corpws Profi Adnabod Lleferydd Transcription Test Set Properties.

ID	Gender	Accent	Type of Speech
Pl16jPn0Jy4	F	S	Read speech
4kIby51XL1E	F	S	Read speech
0P3VrE-VoOE	M	N	Formal Spoken
_UdWqyWDZ4Y	M	N	Read speech
TJkVrsNaeY0	M	N	Formal Spoken
xSs8TJiD5-Q	F	N	Formal Spoken
06Gt5n0BWkw	M	N	Formal Spoken
E7qGxNhGP9U	M+F	N	Formal Spoken
BIG0OJ_Kbl4	M+F	N	Formal Spoken
wMMm6rcSpnU	M	N	Formal spoken
C9VnfalWr44	M+F	N+S	Free spoken
yxM1q3AzPJI	F	S	Free spoken
jdYIrb9L_Tc	M	S	Free spoken

Table 9 - Speech variations in transcription test set - Gender: F=Female, M=Male Accent: S=South Wales, N=North Wales.

Proceedings of the CLTW 4 @ LREC2022 , pages 60–70
Marseille, 20-25 June 2022

Handwriting Recognition for Scottish Gaelic

Mark Sinclair, William Lamb, Beatrice Alex
Quorate Technology Ltd, University of Edinburgh, University of Edinburgh
mark.s.sinclair@gmail.com, w.lamb@ed.ac.uk, b.alex@ed.ac.uk

Abstract

Like most other minority languages, Scottish Gaelic has limited tools and resources available for Natural Language Processing research and applications. These limitations restrict the potential of the language to participate in modern speech technology, while also restricting research in fields such as corpus linguistics and the Digital Humanities. At the same time, Gaelic has a long written history, is well-described linguistically, and is unusually well-supported in terms of *potential* NLP training data. For instance, archives such as the School of Scottish Studies hold thousands of digitised recordings of vernacular speech, many of which have been transcribed as paper-based, handwritten manuscripts. In this paper, we describe a project to digitise and recognise a corpus of handwritten narrative transcriptions, with the intention of re-purposing it to develop a Gaelic speech recognition system.

Keywords: Scottish Gaelic, Handwriting Recognition, minority languages, Low-Resource NLP, Digital Humanities

1. Introduction

Few minority languages have progressed beyond an inchoate developmental stage in language technology and Natural Language Processing (NLP). As the emphasis in these fields has shifted from rule-based approaches to deep-learning, the challenges for most minority languages have intensified. For many, the requisite training data do not exist. For some, the data are available, but must be digitised – a less imposing, but still significant barrier. In this latter category is Scottish Gaelic, a minority language spoken by 57,000 people in Scotland (National Records of Scotland, 2015).[1] A wealth of transcribed spontaneous speech and corresponding audio exist in Gaelic, but these transcriptions generally occur as handwritten manuscripts. Thus, to use these data for training an automatic speech recognition (ASR) system, for instance, one must first convert them to digital text.

Most of the transcriptions of natural language available in Gaelic are paper-based and stem from linguistic and ethnological fieldwork carried out in the mid-20th century by the School of Scottish Studies (University of Edinburgh).[2] Although some of these documents are typed, the majority are handwritten.[3]

Optical character recognition (OCR) for roman type is considered less challenging than handwriting recognition (HWR) due to language-specific parameters, variability in handwriting styles and the character-touching problem (Chen et al., 2021). If a robust HWR tool could be developed for Gaelic, it would unlock a vast trove of data useful both to the Digital Humanities and NLP research.

This paper reports on a one-year pilot study[4] to develop such a tool, by utilising the configurable HWR platform, Transkribus (Kahle et al., 2017), which is described further below. A Scottish Gaelic HWR resulting from our work is publicly available on the Transkribus site.[5]

Central to the effort were three research questions:

1. Given that most of the transcriptions were from one hand, to what extent would models developed using that hand alone generalise to the other hands in the dataset?

2. Manual annotation is by nature costly: How much data is required to produce a model that is accurate enough to allow a semi-supervised or unsupervised approach (i.e. one requiring little further editing)?

3. What impact do other resources (e.g. a lexicon and language model) have on error rates vis-à-vis training data alone (i.e. what is the most efficient combination of parameters to produce a usable model quickly)?

[1] `https://www.scotlandscensus.gov.uk/census-results/at-a-glance/languages/`

[2] `https://www.ed.ac.uk/information-services/library-museum-gallery/cultural-heritage-collections/school-scottish-studies-archives`

[3] A recent survey of the transcriptions held by the School of Scottish Studies' Tale Archive indicates that 77% are handwritten and 23% are typed

[4] We gratefully acknowledge funding from the University of Edinburgh's Challenge Investment Fund towards this project.

[5] `https://readcoop.eu/model/scottish-gaelic-1949-1979/`

2. Related Work

2.1. Speech and Language Processing for Scottish Gaelic

Given the lack of available electronic data for Scottish Gaelic, speech and language processing research for the language remains fairly limited. However, there has been recent work to develop: a Scottish Gaelic part-of-speech tagger (Lamb and Danso, 2014); an online linguistic analyser (Boizou and Lamb, 2020); a dependency treebank and parser (Batchelor, 2019); an automatic speech recognition system (Rasipuram et al., 2013); machine translation from Gaelic to Irish (Murchú, 2019);[6] an embedding model for Scottish Gaelic (Lamb and Sinclair, 2016); a derivation of a categorical grammar (Batchelor, 2016; Batchelor, 2019); a wordnet (Bella et al., 2020) and a text-to-speech system (developed by Cereproc).[7] Akhmetov et al. (2020) have also included Scottish Gaelic in their experiments on language-independent word lemmatisation.

Aside from existing speech and language processing work, there are digital corpora and lexical resources for Scottish Gaelic, including the Digital Archive of Scottish Gaelic (DASG) (O Maolalaigh, 2016)[8], the Annotated Representative Corpus of Scottish Gaelic (ARCOSG)[9] and the online dictionary, Am Faclair Beag (Bauer and MacDhonnchaidh,)[10].

2.2. Handwriting Recognition

Methods for HWR, also referred to as Handwritten Text Recognition, were first developed in the 1950s (Dimond, 1957). Since then, HWR has developed into an extremely active research field in computer science, which has been covered by a series of surveys and reviews (Hull, 1994; Plamondon and Srihari, 2000; Santosh and Nattee, 2010; Tagougui et al., 2012; Parvez and Mahmoud, 2013; Pal et al., 2012; Manoj et al., 2016; Al-Salman and Alyahya, 2017; Choudhary et al., 2017; Kumbhar and Kunjir, 2017; Das et al., 2018; Ramzan et al., 2018; Wang et al., 2021). A number of approaches including machine learning (Xu et al., 1992; Marti and Bunke, 2001) and neural network based learning (Graves et al., 2009; Boquera et al., 2011; Bluche, 2015; Wu et al., 2017; Naz et al., 2015; Voigtlaender et al., 2016; Chowdhury and Vig, 2018; Pham et al., 2014), or combinations thereof, have been applied to this task. The state-of-the-art is driven by regular international competitions on HWR and the availability of public datasets to compare performance of systems developed by different research groups (Menasri et al., 2011; Yin et al., 2013; Sánchez et al., 2014; Sánchez et al., 2017; Nguyen et al., 2018; Potanin et al., 2021). While HWR tended to be applied for financial or commercial purposes (Pal et al., 2012; Dimauro et al., 1997; Hafemann et al., 2017), with the increasing availability of digitised manuscript collections made available by libraries and archives, it has more recently been applied to historical manuscripts (Terras, 2006; Fischer et al., 2009; Fischer et al., 2014; Bhunia et al., 2019; Firmani et al., 2018; Chammas et al., 2018). There is also related work on applying HWR to different languages (Alipour et al., 2016; Zhang et al., 2018; Altwaijry and Al-Turaiki, 2020) or devising methods which work for multiple languages (Mondal et al., 2010; Keysers et al., 2017; Carbune et al., 2020). Carbune et al. (2020) are the only group we are aware of with a system that supports Scottish Gaelic alongside 101 other languages. They found that, compared to their previous segment-and-decode method, their Long Short-Term Memory (LSTM) based algorithm reduced the character error rate by between 20-40%, but they reported only for languages for which they had sufficient evaluation data (Figure 7 in Carbune et al. (2020)). They did not provide evaluation results for Scottish Gaelic. To the best of our knowledge, our paper is the first to report performance of HWR models applied to Scottish Gaelic text.

Transkribus (see Section 5) uses a deep neural network based algorithm for HWR (Muehlberger et al., 2019) and currently provides access to over 80 publicly available HWR models for different languages, each time reporting their character error rates against a validation set.[11] The platform has been used for training models for a series of languages, including low resource languages and scripts such as dialectal Finnish (Blokland et al., 2019), South Tyrolean (König et al., 2020), Low Saxon (Siewert et al., 2021), Evenki and Russian (Arkhipov et al., 2021), Greek, Slavic and Latin (Thompson and others, 2021), 16th century Romanian (Burlacu and Rabus, 2021) and Croatian Glagolitic (Rabus, 2022), to name but a few. Terras (2022) surveyed the registered users of Transkribus in early 2019 and examined how HWR had been by adopted libraries, archives and academia. Her work clearly shows that most of the documents processed by Transkribus projects were in German, Latin, English and French. A lot less material in other languages was processed at that point. Since the survey was conducted the user base has more than doubled and many more languages have been included, showing the potential and demand of HWR technology.

3. Digitisation and Correction of the Corpus

The training data for the current study came from a subset of the School of Scottish Studies Archives (University of Edinburgh) known as the Tale Archive. The

[6]NB: Gaelic also was added to Google Translate in 2016.

[7]https://www.cereproc.com

[8]https://dasg.ac.uk/

[9]https://github.com/Gaelic-Algorithmic-Research-Group/ARCOSG

[10]https://www.faclair.com/

[11]https://readcoop.eu/transkribus/public-models/

Tale Archive is an extensive collection of traditional narrative texts (c30k pages), most of which are entirely or partly in Scottish Gaelic.[12] Together, they represent the largest collection of transcribed Scottish Gaelic in the world. Although most of the participants from whom they were recorded lived in areas that continue to be Gaelic-speaking at the time this paper was written, many participants spoke regional variants that are now moribund or no longer extant. Thus, these data are uniquely valuable for their linguistic and ethnological content, as much as their potential to provide robust speech data for language technology applications.

We began the project by manually recording key metadata about the transcripts. Following this, we randomly selected documents totalling 2724 pages for digitisation. The transcripts were originally gathered between 1949 and 1979 and the distribution across that time period is shown in Figure 1. Here we can see some spikes in frequency corresponding to periods of increased activity for the project.

Despite spanning several decades, the narratives were predominantly transcribed by a single principal hand (approximately 85%) with the remaining portion (approximately 15%) distributed across 10 other hands. Given the over representation of this single hand in the data, a particular theme of our research was to examine how this imbalance would affect the potential generalisation of the HWR system.

The digitisation process involved converting the paper texts to a multi-page PDF format using a feed-based scanner and single-page scanning booth, depending on whether the source was an original or photocopy. Subsequently, the texts were uploaded to Transkribus for manual editing by a Domain Expert and, eventually, automatic recognition. The following section outlines the segmentation and transcription process in detail.

4. Handwriting Recognition

The task of Handwriting Recognition (HWR) involves automatically transcribing handwritten text into a digital form. HWR is similar to the task of Optical Character Recognition (OCR). The main difference is that the latter involves the recognition of printed text which, due to its uniformity, is typically less challenging to recognise automatically than handwriting.
Before carrying out HWR, handwritten documents must be captured as digital images, typically using digital imaging technologies such as scanners or cameras. Generally, modern HWR systems will them process these images in two main stages: *Segmentation* and *Transcription*.

[12]Roughly 75% are primarily in Gaelic, with another 25% mainly in Scots, English or Irish.

Segmentation is the task of removing non-relevant information from an image. This is typically achieved by defining tight geometric boundaries around areas of the image that are hypothesised to contain handwritten text. The purpose of this stage is to reduce noise in the input as well as to reduce the search space of any recognition algorithm in order to increase efficiency. An example is shown in Figure 2a.

Transcription is the task of estimating the text within each text segment and providing the results as standard digitised text. An example is shown in Figure 2b.

5. Transkribus

Transkribus is a software platform that helps to facilitate both manual and automatic transcription of historical written documents, as well as providing tools for searching and archiving. The main components of Transkribus include:

- An editing tool for manual and automatic segmentation, transcription and searching of documents.
- Cloud services that provide compute and storage resources for automated system components, including training HWR models.
- Web-based documentation and 'how-to' guides

5.1. Automatic Text Segmentation

The Transkribus platform provides an automatic text segmentation tool that is limited to Latin character sets, but is otherwise language-independent. This means that the tool is able to automatically find the boundaries of any text regions within Gaelic handwritten documents without the need for a specialised model. An example of fully automatic Transkribus segmentation on Scottish Gaelic is shown in Figure 3.

The text segmentation system component is not guaranteed to be error free and may require manual edits to be regarded as 'gold standard'. On the other hand, it is likely that such efforts will be minimal.

5.2. Manual HWR

Transkribus provides functionality for manually transcribing documents by means of an editor tool. This is a graphical interface that focuses an image viewer on each text segment and allows a human transcriber to easily type in the correct matching transcript.

5.3. Automatic HWR

Transkribus also facilitates automatic HWR. This system, however, relies on language-dependent neural network models in order to function accurately. Models are provided for a limited set of languages, including English and German, but no known Transkribus model for Gaelic existed before the current study. In order to

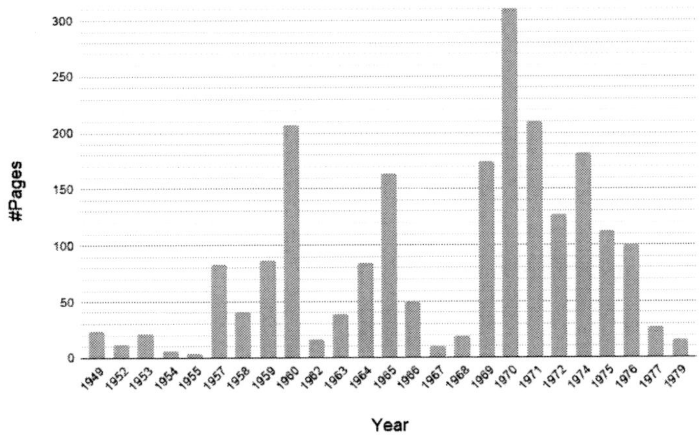

Figure 1: Distribution of complete training corpus data over year of collection.

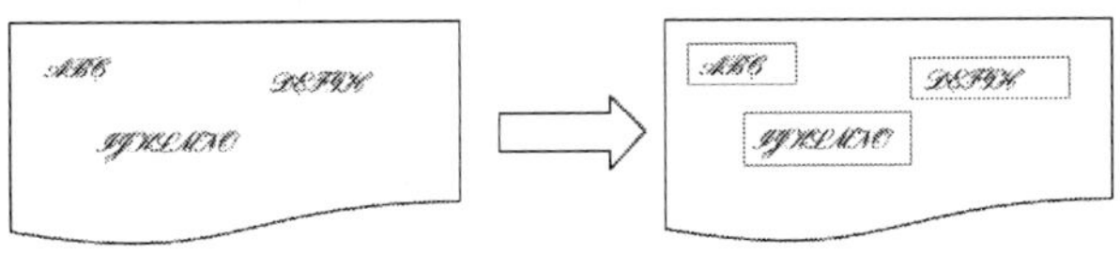

(a) Segmentation

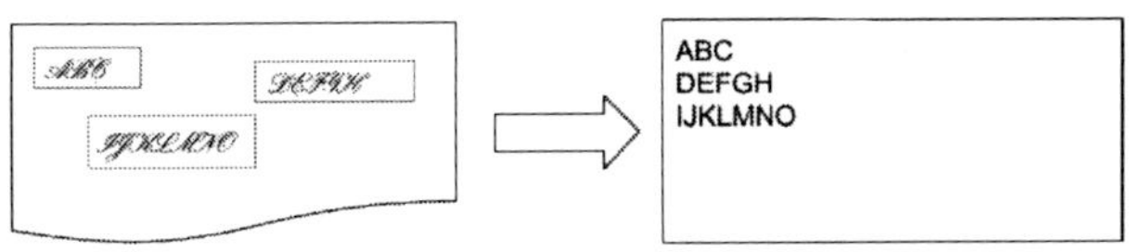

(b) Transcription

Figure 2: Examples of the Segmentation and Transcription tasks for HWR

provide a Gaelic model, it would have to be trained. This training process is described in Section 6 below.

In Figures 4a and 4b we provide examples of how the output quality of a Scottish Gaelic HWR model can vary depending on whether it is applied to the writing of the principal hand, or one with little or no training data. While the model performs fairly well on the principal hand it does extremely badly on the other hand. We think that this is mainly due to an unseen writing style, especially the way some of capital letters are curved, as well as the spaced out writing in this case.[13] Transkribus seems to fail to recognise that this is a sequence of text and only recognises a few, individual words. The latter example is one of the worst outputs we have encountered and we include it here to illustrate that HWR is not a solved problem. However, our evaluation results presented in Section 7 show that our models can yield promising results on unseen test data, especially when using larger training datasets and a language model.

6. Model Training Workflow

The workflow of the project comprised an iterative process of manual and automatic tasks. A systematic representation of the workflow is shown in Figure 5.

The sequence of tasks are as follows:

- A large quantity (1000s) of documents are scanned or photographed[14]
- Documents are loaded into Transkribus and are automatically segmented
- A Gaelic Domain Expert transcribes a portion of the documents (100s; using the Transkribus interface)

[13]See Lamb (2012, 121, fn 24) for more information on this transcriber.

[14]Transkribus provides an Android app to facilitate document photography.

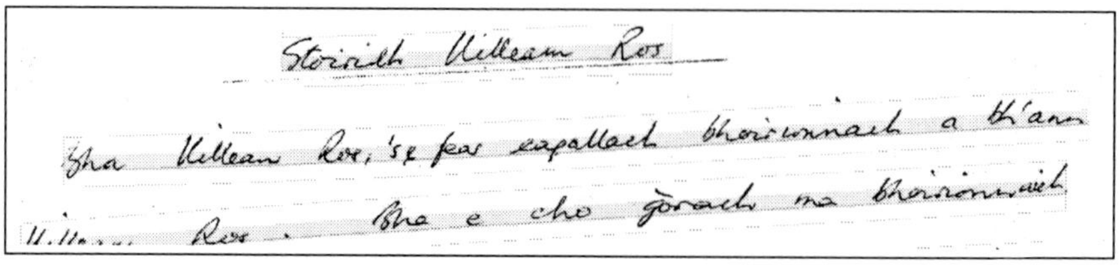

Figure 3: An example of automatic segmentation of Scottish Gaelic from the Transkribus software platform

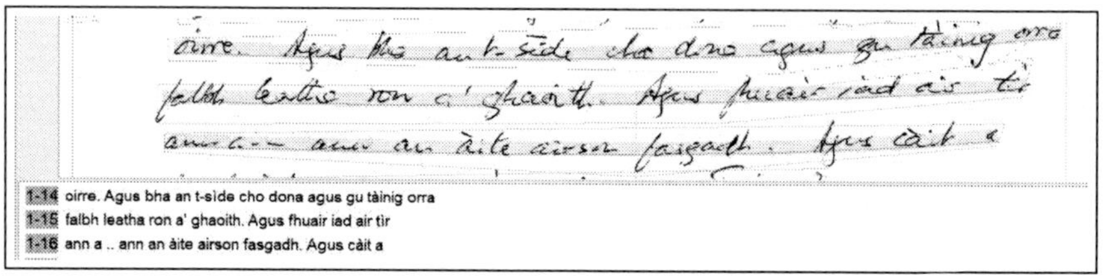

(a) Good quality output for the principal hand

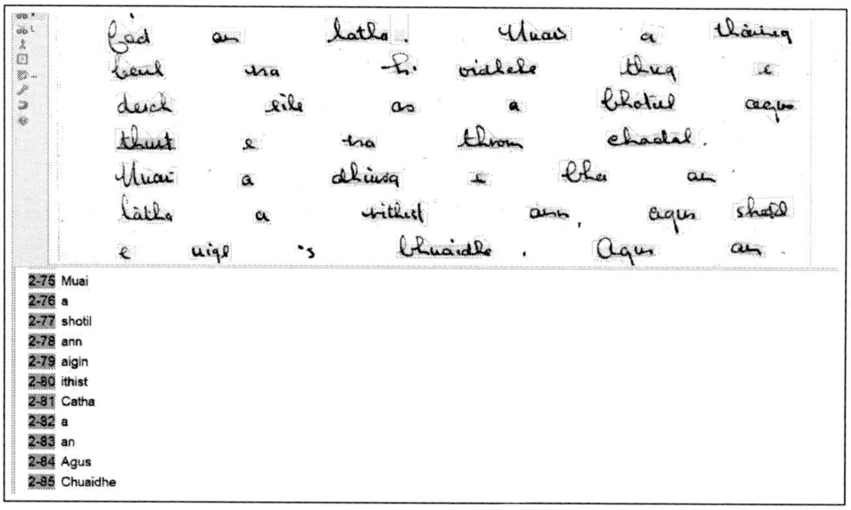

(b) Bad quality output for a hand with little training data

Figure 4: HWR output examples for the Scottish Gaelic Transkribus model

- Transcribed documents are divided into a training set (90%) and an evaluation set (10%)
- The training set is used to train a Transkribus neural network model for Scottish Gaelic
- The first (seed) model is used to transcribe the evaluation set
- Transkribus hypothesis on the evaluation set is scored against the manual transcription, i.e. Word Error Rate (WER) and Character Error Rate (CER) are computed
- If the error is unacceptable (above some defined threshold)
  - Auto-transcribe more training data (100s of pages) from the scanned documents that have not already been transcribed
  - The Gaelic Domain Expert corrects errors of Transkribus transcriptions
  - The corrected data augments the existing training set
  - Training and evaluation are repeated
- Else, if error is acceptable (below some defined threshold)
  - Auto transcribe all remaining scanned documents

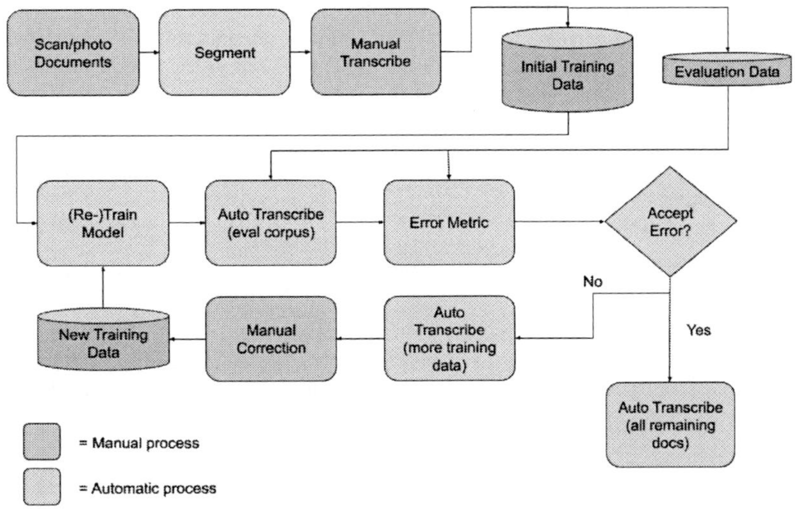

Figure 5: An overview of the machine-assisted transcription workflow. Red components are manual processes and blue components are automated. The system is initialised with the first manual transcription process, then enters the iterative feedback cycle where new data is automatically transcribed, manually corrected and fed back into training a new model.

The whole process begins with a small manual investment. The principle is that the manual correction phase gets easier at each iteration, because the automated system is improving its hypothesis. That is, there should be fewer mistakes to correct and, over time, more transcription data can be brought up to a manually-corrected standard with the same effort. The nature of neural network training methods suggests that we should expect an exponential decay in error until the limits of the model are reached. This means that there will likely be diminishing returns and a natural point will be found where the value of further transcribing/correcting data for the purpose of training the model is no longer economical. At this point, if the model performance is sufficiently acceptable, it can be used to automatically transcribe any remaining documents without the need for manual correction.

7. Experimental Results

7.1. Machine Assisted Transcription

In total, we completed three iterations through the workflow: a 75-hour initialisation iteration involving fully-manual transcription, followed by two further iterations with 75 and 380 hours of manual effort respectively, where HWR models were trained and used as the basis for manual correction. Table 1 shows the resulting transcription yield from each of the three stages. The first 75 hours of manual effort produced 18,158 words, making a yield of 242.11 words per hour. This initial tranche of data was used to train our first HWR model (**118_P_LM**), which was then used to generate an automatic transcription. The next 75 hours of manual effort in the second iteration were used to correct the output.

The second iteration produced an additional 18,397 words, making a yield of 245.29 words per hour: this was only slightly higher than the first. This suggested that, with the initial model, the machine assisted transcription had a very similar yield to a fully-manual transcription approach, i.e. it was taking just as long to correct the errors as it would have taken to transcribe from scratch, unassisted.

Combining all of the data from the first and second iterations, making a total of 36,555 words, we trained a second model (**221_P_LM**). It was clear at this point that the second model had performed much better than the first and was providing substantially greater assistance to the manual transcription process. For this reason, we decided to perform automated recognition on all remaining documents and focus the remaining manual transcription time budget on correction of the output. An additional 340,237 words were transcribed during this iteration, over 380 hours, making a yield of 895.36 words per hour. This means that with a modest investment of 150 hours of manual effort, we increased our transcription yield by a factor of over 3.5 times.

Table 1: Yield from manual transcription effort across 3 iterations of the workflow shown in Figure 5. The *Segmentation Only* row is the initial fully-manual transcription and subsequent rows were seeded with an automated transcription hypothesis using a model trained on the data from the previous row. The model name represents some information about the model separated by underscores: the number of pages used in training the model, that the data came from the (P)rincipal hand, and a Language Model (LM) was used – see subsequent sections for more detail.

HWR Seed Model	Manual Hours	Words Transcribed	Words per Hour
Segmentation Only	75	18,158	242.11
118_P_LM	75	18,397	245.29
221_P_LM	380	340,237	895.36
Total/Average	530	376,792	710.93

Table 2: Experimental results for HWR models with different quantities of training data (118, 221, 1678 or 1917 pages), Principal or Mixed hands (P or M), and with Lexical support from a Language Model (LM), (150k) word vocabulary dictionary or None. Results show Character Error Rate (CER) and Word Error Rate (WER) for Principal (P) and Other (O) hands evaluation data. The best results for each evaluation condition are highlighted in bold.

Model Code	#Pages	#Words	Mixed	Lex.	CER(P)	WER(P)	CER(O)	WER(O)
1917_M_None	1,917	376,792	TRUE	None	2.19	6.75	5.89	17.65
1917_M_150k	1,917	376,792	TRUE	150k	4.5	12.88	8.18	24.02
1917_M_LM	1,917	376,792	TRUE	LM	1.7	5.04	**5.01**	**14.86**
1678_P_None	1,678	318,967	FALSE	None	2.07	6.38	25.76	49.59
1678_P_150k	1,678	318,967	FALSE	150k	4.4	12.56	25.62	47.69
1678_P_LM	1,678	318,967	FALSE	LM	**1.67**	**4.94**	23.06	43.54
221_P_None	221	36,555	FALSE	None	2.58	7.53	25.07	49.68
221_P_150k	221	36,555	FALSE	150k	3.68	9.2	25.19	47.76
221_P_LM	221	36,555	FALSE	LM	2.53	7.28	24.14	47.34
118_P_None	118	18,158	FALSE	None	4.97	14.44	30.05	57.08
118_P_150k	118	18,158	FALSE	150k	5.62	14.84	29.78	54.28
118_P_LM	118	18,158	FALSE	LM	4.75	13.76	29.16	54.95

Ultimately, after 530 hours of manual effort we managed to achieve a total of 376,792 transcribed words. Assuming our initial fully-manual yield of 242.11 words per hour, the same quantity of transcription would have otherwise taken around 1,556 hours of manual effort. This means that the machine-assisted approach presents a significant reduction to costs, vis-à-vis manual handwriting transcription.

7.2. Lexical Support for HWR Models

The HWR models learnt to predict the most likely characters of the texts, given observation features derived from their images. HWR models are typically purely optical models that have no specific knowledge of the language they are transcribing, other than its character set. However, it is also possible to supplement models with information from additional lexical models in order to support, and potentially improve, the hypothesis. In particular, the Transkribus platform allows the provision of a lexicon or language model during the recognition inference.

The lexicon essentially provides an *allow*-list of tokens that can be permitted in the hypothesis. If an HWR hypothesis predicts a character sequence that does not correspond to an entry in the lexicon, then it can be rejected in favour of an another hypothesis that is represented. Each token is also weighted according to its prior probability, meaning that in cases of ambiguity, tokens that are more common are more likely to be selected. This can help to remove illegitimate character sequences (non-valid tokens) from the hypothesis but, conversely, any legitimate tokens that happen to be out-of-vocabulary in the lexicon may never be predicted. Therefore, it is important that the lexicon is comprehensive.

The language model differs in comparison to the lexicon in that it is not simply a model of tokens in isolation, but predicts the most likely sequences of tokens. This means that if there is ambiguity in a hypothesis, or noise in the input features, the lexical context can help to inform the most likely token that would have come next. By modelling more intrinsic information about the structure of a language in this way, we typically have more powerful lexical support than the basic lexicon. Each time Transkribus is used to train a HWR model, it also trains a language model using the same reference text as training data. These language and HWR models are tied in a way that they cannot be mixed and matched between different training runs.

8. Discussion

Our results show that increasing the quantity of data helped to improve recognition performance. For example, going from our **118_P_LM** through **221_P_LM** to **1678_P_LM**, we see a reduction in WER from 13.76% through 7.28% to 4.94% for the principal hand evaluation case. This suggests a non-linear relationship between data quantity and error reduction, i.e. reducing the error rate by a constant factor would require increasing the data quantity factor. However, we do not have enough data points to estimate the true nature of this relationship.

The lexicon does not seem to help to improve recognition accuracy. However, we believe this is because our lexicon contains mostly base dictionary form words, i.e. it does not contain a lot of morphological permutations. For that reason, restricting the output to the lexicon entries is likely to create a lot of out-of-vocabulary (OOV) issues where words that are not present are assigned another word that has a similar character sequence. This is supported by the fact that the WER degraded more significantly than the CER when introducing the lexicon, i.e. the OOV word substitution can still result in getting most of the characters correct even if the word is incorrect.

Introducing the Language Model (LM) as a lexical support does help to improve recognition accuracy for both CER and WER. While the LM always improved accuracy, it demonstrated a more substantial improvement for the HWR models trained on more data. The LM can be particularly useful when the HWR hypothesis has fewer alternatives to choose from. As the HWR model improves, it is more likely to correctly recognise sub-word units of words (e.g. stems and affixes) that were previously poorly recognised. This can narrow the hypothesis and make it more likely for the LM to select the correct result. The introduction of a portion of mixed hand data resulted in substantial improvements on mixed hand evaluation data with only a negligible reduction in performance on the principal hand evaluation data: e.g. the WER reduced from 43.54% to 14.86% on mixed hands between **1678_P_LM** and **1917_M_LM** respectively, while only increasing from 4.94% to 5.04% for the same models.

9. Conclusion

We have shown that the use of machine-assisted handwriting recognition can significantly improve transcription efficiency with a modest manual effort investment. The data that has been digitised is now available to be easily searched and archived for humanities research. It can also be used as a data resource for other NLP tasks such as Automatic Speech Recognition (ASR), language modelling and entity extraction.

We believe that the iterative framework that we employed for this task could be re-purposed for other low-resource languages where the lack of an initial HWR requires such a bootstrapping approach. The acceleration in yield could have been improved further by re-training the model more often so as to gain the benefits at a more frequent cadence. The framework also supports the possibility of multiple manual transcribers and an asynchronous approach to model updates and manual effort, i.e. training a new model is not blocked by waiting for all transcribers to finish their current tasks.

10. Future Work

While the models developed for this project proved valuable for improving the efficiency of transcription on our target corpus, we would like to investigate how well the approach would generalise to corpora in other domains. In particular, we would like to create a general Scottish Gaelic HWR model than can be used as a reliable resource for digitising handwritten documents. This work would involve acquiring new datasets both to evaluate our existing models against and develop contrasting systems.

We were able to demonstrate that increasing data quantity improved model performance, but we did not have enough data to accurately estimate the trend. As with many machine learning tasks, it is likely that there will be an issue with diminishing gains where equivalent performance improvements may require exponential increases in data. Having enough data and examples of models trained with different quantities to estimate this would be useful when designing future experiments.

Another interesting approach is to consider the use of multi-lingual training data. Handwriting corpora for the related Goidelic language, Irish, could be used to supplement our training data; their character sets and many aspects of their grapheme distribution are similar. This kind of data could also help to act as a kind of natural regularisation for our models and prevent over-fitting to certain hands that are over-represented in our data. The combined data could be used to develop a multi-lingual model that can handle more general Gaelic-language handwriting.

11. Acknowledgements

We gratefully acknowledge funding received from the University of Edinburgh's Challenge Investment Fund. We would like to thank Prof James Loxley (University of Edinburgh) for his contributions to the early stages of the project, Prof Melissa Terras (University of Edinburgh) for her advice and putting us in touch with Transkribus, and Michael Bauer, who carried out the recognition and editing of the Gaelic text. Finally, our sincere thanks to the staff at Transkribus and the School of Scottish Studies Archives, for their excellent support and assistance.

12. Bibliographical References

Akhmetov, I., Pak, A., Ualiyeva, I., and Gelbukh, A. (2020). Highly language-independent word lemmatization using a machine-learning classifier. *Computación y Sistemas*, 24(3):1353–1364.

Al-Salman, A. S. and Alyahya, H. (2017). Arabic online handwriting recognition: a survey. *Proceedings of the 1st International Conference on Internet of Things and Machine Learning*.

Alipour, S. A., Tabatabaey-Mashadi, N., and Abbassi, H. (2016). Recent approaches in online handwriting recognition for persian and arabic right-to-left languages. *2016 2nd IEEE International Conference on Computer and Communications (ICCC)*, pages 358–364.

Altwaijry, N. and Al-Turaiki, I. M. (2020). Arabic handwriting recognition system using convolutional neural network. *Neural Computing and Applications*, pages 1–13.

Arkhipov, A., Barinskaya, A., and Shtefura, R. (2021). Using handwritten text recognition on bilingual evenki-russian manuscripts of konstantin rychkov1. *Scripta & E-Scripta*, 21.

Batchelor, C. (2016). Automatic derivation of categorial grammar from a part-of-speech-tagged corpus in scottish gaelic. *PARIS Inalco du 4 au 8 juillet 2016*, page 1.

Batchelor, C. (2019). Universal dependencies for scottish gaelic: syntax. In *Proceedings of the Celtic Language Technology Workshop*, pages 7–15.

Bauer, M. and MacDhonnchaidh, U. (????). Am faclair beag. Online; accessed 19-February-2022.

Bella, G., McNeill, F., Gorman, R., O Donnaile, C., MacDonald, K., Chandrashekar, Y., Freihat, A. A., and Giunchiglia, F. (2020). A major Wordnet for a minority language: Scottish Gaelic. In *Proceedings of the 12th Language Resources and Evaluation Conference*, pages 2812–2818, Marseille, France, May. European Language Resources Association.

Bhunia, A. K., Das, A., Bhunia, A. K., Kishore, P. S. R., and Roy, P. P. (2019). Handwriting recognition in low-resource scripts using adversarial learning. *2019 IEEE/CVF Conference on Computer Vision and Pattern Recognition (CVPR)*, pages 4762–4771.

Blokland, R., Partanen, N., Rießler, M., and Wilbur, J. (2019). Using computational approaches to integrate endangered language legacy data into documentation corpora: Past experiences and challenges ahead. In *Workshop on Computational Methods for Endangered Languages, Honolulu, Hawai'i, USA*, volume 2, pages 24–30.

Bluche, T. (2015). *Deep neural networks for large vocabulary handwritten text recognition*. Ph.D. thesis, Paris 11.

Boizou, L. and Lamb, W. (2020). An online linguistic analyser for scottish gaelic. In *Human Language Technologies–The Baltic Perspective: Proceedings of the Ninth International Conference Baltic HLT 2020*, volume 328, page 119. IOS Press.

Boquera, S. E., Bleda, M. J. C., Gorbe-Moya, J., and Zamora-Martínez, F. (2011). Improving offline handwritten text recognition with hybrid hmm/ann models. *IEEE Transactions on Pattern Analysis and Machine Intelligence*, 33:767–779.

Burlacu, C. and Rabus, A. (2021). Digitising (romanian) cyrillic using transkribus: new perspectives. *Diacronia*, 2021(14):A196–A196.

Carbune, V., Gonnet, P., Deselaers, T., Rowley, H., Daryin, A. N., Lafarga, M. C., Wang, L.-L., Keysers, D., Feuz, S., and Gervais, P. (2020). Fast multi-language lstm-based online handwriting recognition. *International Journal on Document Analysis and Recognition (IJDAR)*, 23:89–102.

Chammas, E., Mokbel, C., and Likforman-Sulem, L. (2018). Handwriting recognition of historical documents with few labeled data. *2018 13th IAPR International Workshop on Document Analysis Systems (DAS)*, pages 43–48.

Chen, X., Jin, L., Zhu, Y., Luo, C., and Wang, T. (2021). Text recognition in the wild: A survey. *ACM Computing Surveys (CSUR)*, 54(2):1–35.

Choudhary, U., Bhosale, S., Bhise, S., and Chilveri, P. G. (2017). A survey: Cursive handwriting recognition techniques. *2017 2nd IEEE International Conference on Recent Trends in Electronics, Information & Communication Technology (RTEICT)*, pages 1712–1716.

Chowdhury, A. and Vig, L. (2018). An efficient end-to-end neural model for handwritten text recognition. In *BMVC*.

Das, Y. K., Jain, P., and Sreekumar, K. G. (2018). Comprehensive survey on machine learning application for handwriting recognition. *International Journal of Applied Engineering Research*, 13(8):5823–5830.

Dimauro, G., Impedovo, S., Pirlo, G., and Salzo, A. (1997). Automatic bankcheck processing: A new engineered system. *Int. J. Pattern Recognit. Artif. Intell.*, 11:467–504.

Dimond, T. (1957). Devices for reading handwritten characters. In *IRE-ACM-AIEE '57 (Eastern)*.

Firmani, D., Maiorino, M., Merialdo, P., and Nieddu, E. (2018). Towards knowledge discovery from the vatican secret archives. in codice ratio - episode 1: Machine transcription of the manuscripts. *Proceedings of the 24th ACM SIGKDD International Conference on Knowledge Discovery & Data Mining*.

Fischer, A., Wuthrich, M., Liwicki, M., Frinken, V., Bunke, H., Viehhauser, G., and Stolz, M. (2009). Automatic transcription of handwritten medieval documents. *2009 15th International Conference on Virtual Systems and Multimedia*, pages 137–142.

Fischer, A., Baechler, M., Garz, A., Liwicki, M., and Ingold, R. (2014). A combined system for text line extraction and handwriting recognition in historical documents. *2014 11th IAPR International Workshop on Document Analysis Systems*, pages 71–75.

Graves, A., Liwicki, M., Fernández, S., Bertolami, R., Bunke, H., and Schmidhuber, J. (2009). A novel connectionist system for unconstrained handwriting recognition. *IEEE Transactions on Pattern Analysis and Machine Intelligence*, 31:855–868.

Hafemann, L. G., Sabourin, R., and Oliveira, L. (2017). Offline handwritten signature verification — literature review. *2017 Seventh International Conference on Image Processing Theory, Tools and Applications (IPTA)*, pages 1–8.

Hull, J. J. (1994). A database for handwritten text recognition research. *IEEE Trans. Pattern Anal. Mach. Intell.*, 16:550–554.

Kahle, P., Colutto, S., Hackl, G., and Mühlberger, G. (2017). Transkribus-a service platform for transcription, recognition and retrieval of historical documents. In *2017 14th IAPR International Conference on Document Analysis and Recognition (ICDAR)*, volume 4, pages 19–24. IEEE.

Keysers, D., Deselaers, T., Rowley, H., Wang, L.-L., and Carbune, V. (2017). Multi-language online handwriting recognition. *IEEE Transactions on Pattern Analysis and Machine Intelligence*, 39:1180–1194.

König, A., Lyding, V., Gorgaini, E., Grote, G., and Pretti, M. (2020). Community involvement for transcribing historical correspondences of south tyrolean interest: A di-öss use case. Technical report, -.

Kumbhar, O. and Kunjir, A. (2017). A survey on optical handwriting recognition system using machine learning algorithms. *International Journal of Computer Applications*, 175:28–31.

Lamb, W. and Danso, S. (2014). Developing an automatic part-of-speech tagger for scottish gaelic. In *Proceedings of the First Celtic Language Technology Workshop*, pages 1–5.

Lamb, W. and Sinclair, M. (2016). Developing word embedding models for scottish gaelic. In *Actes de la conférence conjointe JEP-TALN-RECITAL*, volume 6, pages 31–41.

Lamb, W. (2012). The storyteller, the scribe, and a missing man: Hidden influences from printed sources in the gaelic tales of duncan and neil macdonald. *Oral Tradition*, 27(1):109–160.

Manoj, A., Borate, P., Jain, P., Sanas, V., and Pashte, R. (2016). A survey on offline handwriting recognition systems. *International journal of scientific research in science, engineering and technology*, 2:253–257.

Marti, U.-V. and Bunke, H. (2001). Using a statistical language model to improve the performance of an hmm-based cursive handwriting recognition system. *Int. J. Pattern Recognit. Artif. Intell.*, 15:65–90.

Menasri, F., Louradour, J., Bianne-Bernard, A.-L., and Kermorvant, C. (2011). The a2ia french handwriting recognition system at the rimes-icdar2011 competition. In *Electronic Imaging*.

Mondal, T., Bhattacharya, U., Parui, S. K., Das, K., and Mandalapu, D. (2010). On-line handwriting recognition of indian scripts - the first benchmark. *2010 12th International Conference on Frontiers in Handwriting Recognition*, pages 200–205.

Muehlberger, G., Seaward, L., Terras, M., Oliveira, S. A., Bosch, V., Bryan, M., Colutto, S., Déjean, H., Diem, M., Fiel, S., Gatos, B., Greinoecker, A., Grüning, Tobias, Hackl, G., Haukkovaara, V., Heyer, G., Hirvonen, L., Hodel, T., Jokinen, M., Kahle, P., Kallio, M., Kaplan, F., Kleber, F., Labahn, R., Lang, E. M., Laube, S., Leifert, G., Louloudis, G., McNicholl, R., Meunier, J.-L., Michael, J., Mühlbauer, E., Philipp, N., Pratikakis, I., Puigcerver Pérez, J., Putz, H., Retsinas, G., Romero, V., Sablatnig, R., Sánchez, J. A., Schofield, P., Sfikas, G., Sieber, C., Stamatopoulos, N., Strauss, T., Terbul, T., Toselli, A. H., Ulreich, B., Villegas, M., Vidal, E., Walcher, J., Weidemann, M., Wurster, H., and Zagoris, K. (2019). Transforming scholarship in the archives through handwritten text recognition: Transkribus as a case study. *Journal of documentation*.

Murchú, E. P. Ó. (2019). Using intergaelic to pre-translate and subsequently post-edit a sci-fi novel from scottish gaelic to irish. In *Proceedings of the Qualities of Literary Machine Translation*, pages 20–25.

National Records of Scotland. (2015). Scotland's census 2011: Gaelic report (part 1). Technical report, National Records of Scotland, Edinburgh.

Naz, S., Umar, A. I., Ahmad, R., Ahmed, S. B., Shirazi, S. H., and Razzak, M. I. (2015). Urdu nasta'liq text recognition system based on multi-dimensional recurrent neural network and statistical features. *Neural Computing and Applications*, 28:219–231.

Nguyen, H. T., Nguyen, C. T., and Nakagawa, M. (2018). Icfhr 2018 – competition on vietnamese online handwritten text recognition using handsvnondb (vohtr2018). *2018 16th International Conference on Frontiers in Handwriting Recognition (ICFHR)*, pages 494–499.

O Maolalaigh, R. (2016). Dasg: Digital archive of scottish gaelic/dachaigh airson stòras na gàidhlig. *Scottish Gaelic Studies*, 30:242–262.

Pal, U., Jayadevan, R., and Sharma, N. (2012). Handwriting recognition in indian regional scripts: A survey of offline techniques. *ACM Trans. Asian Lang. Inf. Process.*, 11:1:1–1:35.

Parvez, M. T. and Mahmoud, S. A. (2013). Offline

arabic handwritten text recognition: A survey. *ACM Comput. Surv.*, 45:23:1–23:35.

Pham, V., Kermorvant, C., and Louradour, J. (2014). Dropout improves recurrent neural networks for handwriting recognition. *2014 14th International Conference on Frontiers in Handwriting Recognition*, pages 285–290.

Plamondon, R. and Srihari, S. N. (2000). On-line and off-line handwriting recognition: A comprehensive survey. *IEEE Trans. Pattern Anal. Mach. Intell.*, 22:63–84.

Potanin, M. B., Dimitrov, D., Shonenkov, A., Bataev, V., Karachev, D., and Novopoltsev, M. (2021). Digital peter: Dataset, competition and handwriting recognition methods. In *HIP@ICDAR*.

Rabus, A. (2022). Handwritten text recognition for croatian glagolitic. *Slovo: časopis Staroslavenskoga instituta u Zagrebu*, 72(1):181–192.

Ramzan, M., Khan, H. U., Akhtar, W., Zamir, A., Awan, S. M., Ilyas, M., and Mahmood, A. (2018). A survey on using neural network based algorithms for hand written digit recognition. *environment*, 9(9).

Rasipuram, R., Bell, P., and Doss, M. M. (2013). Grapheme and multilingual posterior features for under-resourced speech recognition: a study on scottish gaelic. In *2013 IEEE International Conference on Acoustics, Speech and Signal Processing*, pages 7334–7338. IEEE.

Sánchez, J.-A., Romero, V., Toselli, A. H., and Vidal, E. (2014). Icfhr2014 competition on handwritten text recognition on transcriptorium datasets (htrts). *2014 14th International Conference on Frontiers in Handwriting Recognition*, pages 785–790.

Sánchez, J.-A., Romero, V., Toselli, A. H., Villegas, M., and Vidal, E. (2017). Icdar2017 competition on handwritten text recognition on the read dataset. *2017 14th IAPR International Conference on Document Analysis and Recognition (ICDAR)*, 01:1383–1388.

Santosh, K. C. and Nattee, C. (2010). A comprehensive survey on on-line handwriting recognition technology and its real application to the nepalese natural handwriting. *Kathmandu University Journal of Science, Engineering and Technology*, 5:31–55.

Siewert, J., Scherrer, Y., and Tiedemann, J. (2021). Towards a balanced annotated low saxon dataset for diachronic investigation of dialectal variation. In *Proceedings of the 17th Conference on Natural Language Processing (KONVENS 2021)*, pages 242–246.

Tagougui, N., Kherallah, M., and Alimi, A. M. (2012). Online arabic handwriting recognition: a survey. *International Journal on Document Analysis and Recognition (IJDAR)*, 16:209–226.

Terras, M. (2006). *Image to interpretation: an intelligent system to aid historians in reading the Vindolanda texts*. OUP Oxford.

Terras, M. (2022). Inviting AI into the archives: The reception of handwritten recognition technology into historical manuscript transcription. transcript Verlag.

Thompson, W. et al. (2021). Using handwritten text recognition (HTR) tools to transcribe historical multilingual lexica. *Scripta & e-Scripta*, 2021(21):217–231.

Voigtlaender, P., Doetsch, P., and Ney, H. (2016). Handwriting recognition with large multidimensional long short-term memory recurrent neural networks. *2016 15th International Conference on Frontiers in Handwriting Recognition (ICFHR)*, pages 228–233.

Wang, Y., Xiao, W., and Li, S. (2021). Offline handwritten text recognition using deep learning: A review. *Journal of Physics: Conference Series*, 1848.

Wu, Y.-C., Yin, F., and Liu, C.-L. (2017). Improving handwritten chinese text recognition using neural network language models and convolutional neural network shape models. *Pattern Recognit.*, 65:251–264.

Xu, L., Krzyżak, A., and Suen, C. Y. (1992). Methods of combining multiple classifiers and their applications to handwriting recognition. *IEEE Trans. Syst. Man Cybern.*, 22:418–435.

Yin, F., Wang, Q.-F., Zhang, X.-Y., and Liu, C.-L. (2013). Icdar 2013 chinese handwriting recognition competition. *2013 12th International Conference on Document Analysis and Recognition*, pages 1464–1470.

Zhang, X.-Y., Yin, F., Zhang, Y., Liu, C.-L., and Bengio, Y. (2018). Drawing and recognizing chinese characters with recurrent neural network. *IEEE Transactions on Pattern Analysis and Machine Intelligence*, 40:849–862.

Proceedings of the CLTW 4 @ LREC2022 , pages 71–76
Marseille, 20-25 June 2022

Celtic CALL: Strengthening the Vital Role of Education for Language Transmission

Neasa Ní Chiaráin, Madeleine Comtois, Oisín Nolan, Neimhin Robinson-Gunning, John Sloan, Harald Berthelsen, Ailbhe Ní Chasaide
Trinity College Dublin
The Phonetics and Speech Laboratory, School of Linguistic, Speech and Communication Sciences

{neasa.nichiarain, comtoism, oinolan, nrobinso, sloanjo, berthelh, anichsid}@tcd.ie

Abstract

In this paper, we present the Irish language learning platform, *An Scéalaí*, an intelligent Computer-Assisted Language Learning (iCALL) system which incorporates speech and language technologies in ways that promote the holistic development of the language skills - writing, listening, reading, and speaking. The technologies offer the advantage of extensive feedback in spoken and written form, enabling learners to improve their production. The system works equally as a classroom-based tool and as a standalone platform for the autonomous learner. Given the key role of education for the transmission of all the Celtic languages, it is vital that digital technologies be harnessed to maximise the effectiveness of language teaching/learning. *An Scéalaí* has been used by large numbers of learners and teachers and has received very positive feedback. It is built as a modular system which allows existing and newly emerging technologies to be readily integrated, even if those technologies are still in development phase. The architecture is largely language-independent, and as an open-source system, it is hoped that it can be usefully deployed in other Celtic languages.

Keywords: Irish, intelligent-Computer-Assisted Language Learning (iCALL), Modular Design

1. Introduction

This paper introduces an iCALL platform for the teaching/learning of Irish - *An Scéalaí*, ('the Storyteller'), available at abair.ie/scealai. It is built as a modular system which integrates speech and language technologies as they emerge and strives to enable parallel development of all language skills, including speaking, writing, listening and reading. Section 4 below gives a detailed overview of the system architecture, describing its modular nature and discussing how it can, in principle, be used as a language-independent platform that could be deployed by other Celtic language communities. Sections 2 and 3 first situate this iCALL platform in the current Irish educational context and then in the wider context of speech and language technology resource development for endangered and minority languages.

2. The Irish language educational context

In February 1922 the Provisional Government of the newly established State placed the Irish language at the centre of their vision for education in the Free State. From the beginning of the independent State the Irish public supported the 'expectation that the Gaelicisation of Ireland... would be achieved through its education system' (Hyland and Milne, 1992).

Despite this, the outcomes of Irish language education in the majority of schools (English-medium) are poor. Over the last two decades, the situation has continued to worsen and pupils' learning outcomes in Irish are still of concern (Department of Education, 2022).

There are many challenges. The Irish speaking community is quite small. A recent report commissioned by Glór na nGael, estimated that there were c. 7,000 Irish speaking families, including some 16,000 children in the whole of Ireland, with a quarter located in Gaeltacht areas (Seoighe et al., 2021). Effectively the teacher carries enormous responsibilities for the transmission and promotion of the language, particularly at primary level. Most teachers are themselves second language learners and there are issues concerning their own motivation levels and proficiency (Dunne, 2019). Learner engagement is critically dependent on the classroom teacher (Devitt et al., 2018) but many teachers feel that they are poorly supported in this important aspect of their mission (Dunne, 2019).

For most learners the classroom presents the only opportunity to connect with the language (Ó Murchú, 2016) and the majority never have an opportunity to converse with a native speaker. Thus, pupils have insufficient access to native speaker models of the language. An aspiration in the 2022 Chief Inspector's Report is to "develop pupils' academic, cognitive and social language to enable them to use the language more independently, confidently and creatively". This report also recommends that "schools should make further use of school self-evaluation and assessment processes to develop pupils' literacy and communication skills in Irish to support their accurate use of the language" (Department of Education, 2022).

Related to the above, the teaching of the spoken language and pronunciation is frequently seen as a particular failure in Irish language teaching. Most learners have a poor grasp of the sound system of the language and little sense of how the sounds relate to the writing system (the phonics of Irish).

When it comes to reading, there is often a complete focus on a single textbook for the entire year and reading for pleasure is typically not considered. The materials used for teaching often tend to compare badly with the attractive, interactive materials available in other subject areas.

Given the short time allotted to Irish lessons, (in English-medium schools) and the high pupil-teacher ratio, there is limited opportunity for the individual to engage with the teacher and to get personalised feedback on progress.

3. The Role of Speech and Language Technology

Despite the dire situation of current Irish language education, it remains true that the population at large has a positive attitude to the language. This is reflected partly in the rapid growth of Irish medium schools, which has grown to 8.1% of the total number of schools (Gaeloideachas, 2022). Furthermore, there is a very positive attitude to the use of technology in the classroom.

The *An Scéalaí* platform described here is part of a broader initiative (ABAIR, 2022), involving the development of speech and language resources. Core technologies developed to date include synthetic (male and/or female) voices for the three main dialects and a first speech recognition system is now available (ÉIST, 2022).

A core part of ABAIR's mission is to serve the needs of the language community and consequently, in parallel with core technology development, applications are being built for the public, for those with disabilities and for Irish language education. Initial exploration in this latter area has included proof-of-concept development of interactive language learning games, such as *Taidhgín*, an animated chatbot and *Digichaint*, an interactive adventure game. These proved to be popular with school-going pupils and showed an appetite for this approach (Ní Chiaráin and Ní Chasaide, 2020). Building on these prototypes, we are now developing a comprehensive platform, *An Scéalaí*, that exploits all the technologies currently available in an integrated platform, that is user-friendly for both learners and teachers. This learning platform is also seen as a research tool which will harvest learner and teacher data, leading to iterative longer-term development of intelligent-CALL (iCALL) for the Irish language.

In recent years, the gap between the performance of high and low resource speech and language technologies has widened. This is due, primarily, to the vast amounts of data required by the deep learning models which have generated the improvements in high resource languages (Lugosch et al., 2019). The same levels of data are typically not currently available for low resource languages. Additionally, while high resource languages have a large pool of expertise to call on, low resource languages may have few, or even none in certain areas. This has led to a significant relative deficit in the available resources, which has been described as a *'digital timebomb'* for those languages that cannot keep pace (Ní Chasaide et al., 2020).

For developers of CALL applications for low-resource languages, the availability and quality of speech and language technologies is often the deciding factor in the functionality which can be presented to end users. If a language has a great speech recognition engine, but lacks synthesis, a CALL application using the available resources will have to focus on the affordances provided by the recognition, e.g. pronunciation training. Conversely, a language with strong synthesis but not recognition will be inclined to favour listening exercises. The design of the application will necessarily follow the resources at hand.

It is not possible to predict whether the quality of speech and language technologies for low resource languages will catch up to the standard being set by the high resource ones. This uncertainty means development of CALL applications for low resource languages is governed, in large part, by what is usable now. This leads to two pertinent issues. First, uncertainty needs to be built in to CALL applications for low resource languages. They need to be ready to incorporate new or improved functionality as soon as it arrives. If, for example, an application was built purely for a language with no speech technologies, but then a good recognition engine became available, the application should be structured in a way that this new functionality could easily be slotted in. Therefore, CALL applications for low resource languages need to be extremely adaptable. Second, these platforms should be constructed to be as language independent as possible. The elements of a CALL platform for one language should be made easily portable for another. This should be particularly the case for closely related languages, e.g. the Celtic family.

In this paper, we introduce *An Scéalaí*, an open source CALL application for Irish which has been designed to be language independent and highly adaptable to future changes in speech and language technologies. It aims to serve both as a template of a successful, practical CALL application for a low-resource language, and also as a codebase for developers to clone and slot in their own resources.

4. The *An Scéalaí* Platform

An Scéalaí (abair.ie/scealai/) is a web application where learners can write stories, listen to a synthetic voice read their story in any one of the three main dialects, record their own voice, consult a dictionary, get feedback from teachers, and receive automated grammatical feedback on common errors. As shown in Figure 2, all this functionality is available by clicking on the re-

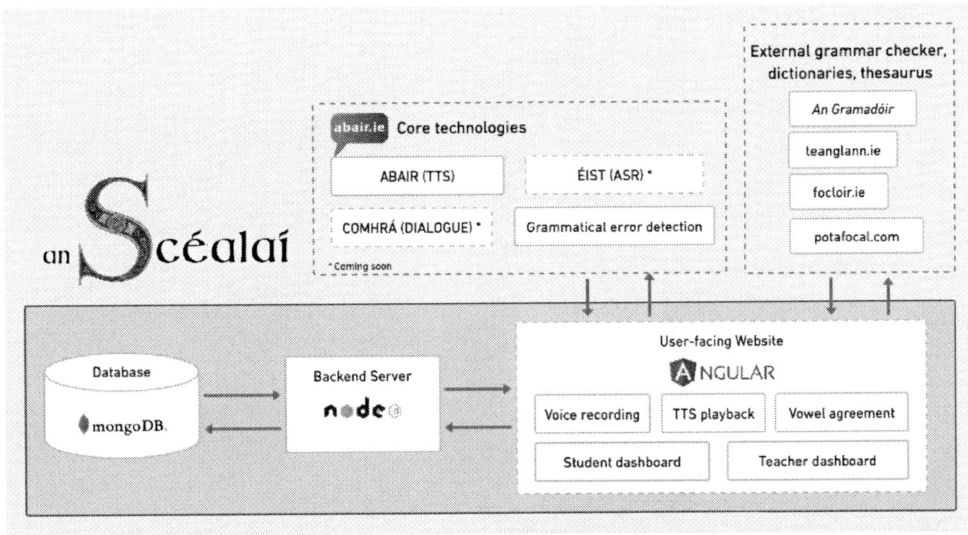

Figure 1: System architecture: an overview of how individual components are combined in *An Scéalaí*.

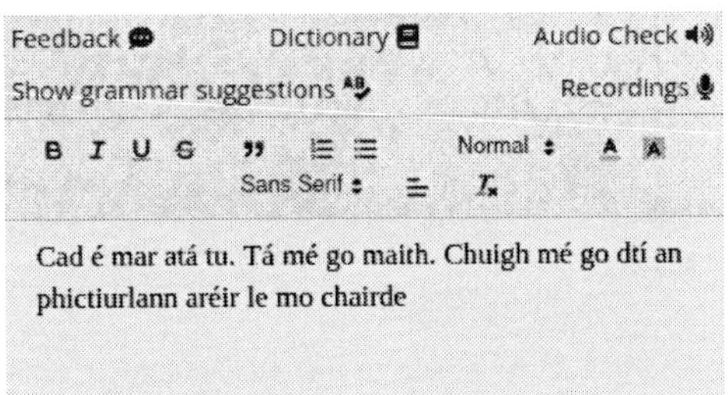

Figure 2: Learner interface for *An Scéalaí* (English version).

lated buttons positioned above the learner's story. Since its inception in 2019, *An Scéalaí* has seen over 4,000 learners write over 40,000 stories, totalling over 5 million words.

The popularity of *An Scéalaí* is due, in part, to its appeal to both sides of the educational divide. Learners are attracted to the platform because it provides spoken synthesis of their own sentences with instantaneous grammatical feedback. Irish, as a Celtic language, contains complex pronunciation and grammatical rules which are quite different from most learners' native language (typically English). Irish has a complex sound system and an opaque writing system. For the learner of Irish (and most teachers), the link between the sounds and the written forms is generally not appreciated. This can make it difficult for the learner to determine correct pronunciation from written text alone, and certain 'basic' grammatical errors persist in many learners' production even at intermediate and advanced levels. *An Scéalaí* provides these learners with opportunities to privately self-correct and improve their production. These features answer to the aspiration set out by the 2022 Chief Inspector's Report to enable pupils "to use the language more independently, confidently and creatively", using self-evaluation to develop literacy, communication skills and a more accurate use of the language (Department of Education, 2022)

An Scéalaí has proven popular with pupils but also with their teachers. Self-correction facilities reduces the teachers' workload, as it guides learners towards native-like pronunciation and grammatical forms, even without their direct intervention, and the drafts submitted to them are of a much higher standard. As most Irish teachers are not, themselves, native speakers, many report using the platform to check their own notes/feedback before sending it on to learners or parents.

4.1. Modular Approach

An Scéalaí has been designed with modularity at the heart of its design to allow flexibility for changing technologies, user requirements and personnel (see (Figure 1) for an overview of how the various components are combined). It is built using the Angular web framework (https://angular.io/), which utilizes *modules* and *components* to separate functionality into discrete building blocks. These can be developed and tested independently, then easily inserted into the main application. This structure has allowed a diverse range of people to actively contribute to the project, e.g. undergraduate and graduate students, web developers, software engineers, etc. It also has enabled the rapid incorporation of teacher and learner feedback into the platform. Each of these individual modules and their functionality is described below.

4.2. Text-to-Speech Synthesis

A REST API call is made to generate the speech synthesis from the sentences written by the learner. These are available in the three main dialects of Irish through the ABAIR TTS engine (Ní Chasaide et al., 2017). On the learner interface, they appear as buttons beneath the main story (Figure 3). When clicked, they play an audio file. This functionality is designed to guide the learner towards native-like pronunciation in Irish. Common pronunciation problems emerge from an over-reliance on the mapping of the English sound system onto Irish orthography. Most Irish learners do not have ready access to native speaker pronunciation, especially on examples of their own spontaneous output.

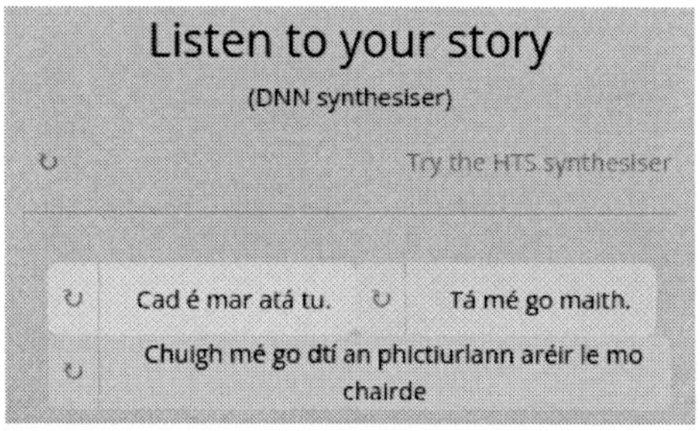

Figure 3: Buttons play synthesised audio for each sentence (English version).

4.3. Recording Audio

To increase the benefit provided to the learner through listening to the synthetic voice, there is also functionality included to allow recording and listening to their own voice (see Figure 4). They can then compare this recording to the synthesised audio. This is achieved by using the browser's MediaStream Recording API.

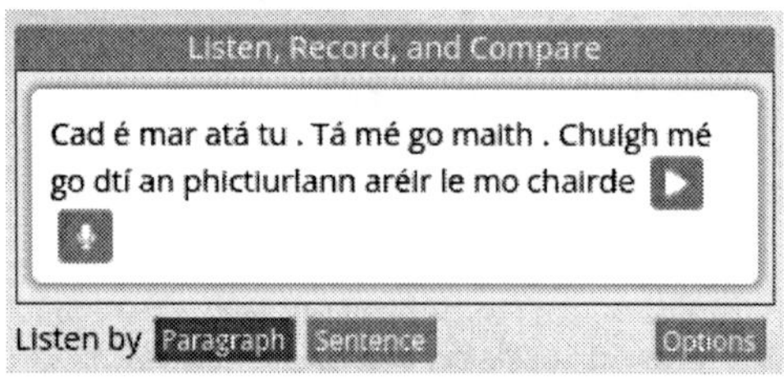

Figure 4: Options for recording one's own voice, listening back and comparing to the (synthetic) native-like version (English version).

4.4. Dictionary

The teanglann Irish dictionary (www.teanglann.ie) is included as a HTML *i-frame*. It appears beneath the story on the main interface and allows learners to access this resource without needing to navigate away from the page (Figure 5).

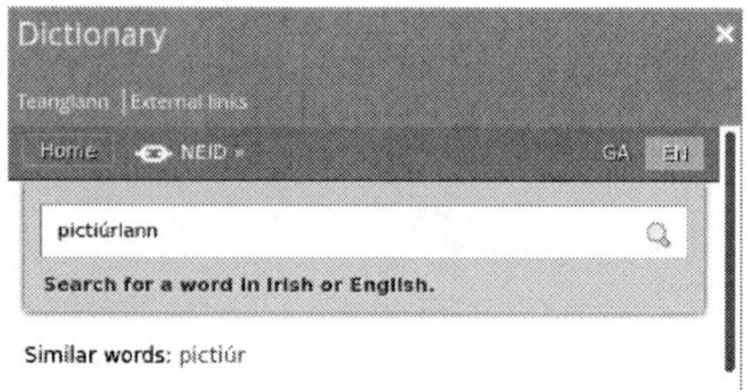

Figure 5: The *teanglann.ie* dictionary is available to search while working on a composition (English version).

4.5. Automated Grammar Correction

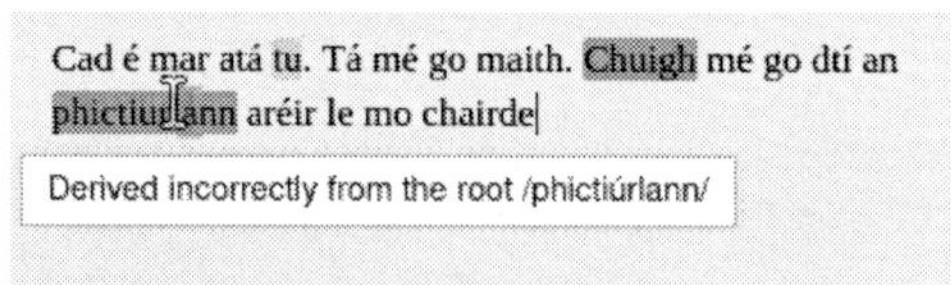

Figure 6: Errors highlighted with colour coding. Suggestions available on hover (English version).

Learners have access to the *An Gramadóir* (Scannell, 2013) grammar checker. Clicking the *show grammar suggestions* button sends a REST API call to the resource, which returns the location, error type, and suggestions as to the nature of the error and how it may be resolved (see Figure 6). Additional algorithms are being added to help with common spelling errors, and more are currently under development to deal with more complex grammatical structures not covered by *An Gramadóir*. These errors are then displayed to the learner by highlighting words (colour-coded by error-typev), with suggestions available if hovered by the cursor (see Figure 6).

4.6. Teacher Feedback

Teachers can create classrooms and assign learners to their class. Here, they are able to view the learners' stories and send feedback. This is then available to the learner through the feedback button on the main interface (Figure 7).

5. Structure for Modification and Developments

The *An Scéalaí* platform is structured so that individual speech and language technologies can easily be inserted and removed from the main story interface. In

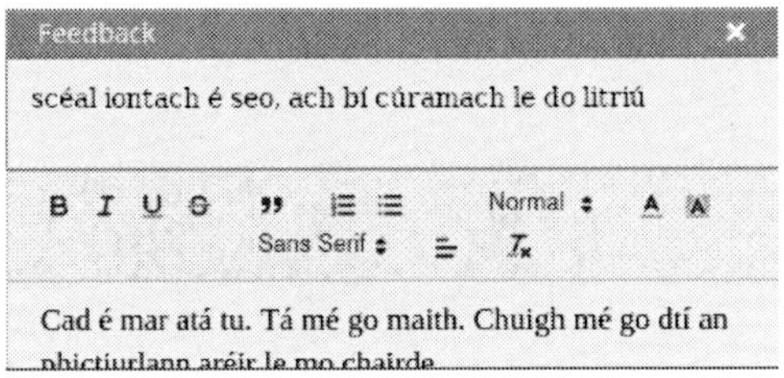

Figure 7: Teacher feedback on the story displayed to the learner in upper window (English version).

each example in the previous section, the relevant technology was displayed to the learner beneath their story. There is no interference from the individual technologies on each other, or the core function. Rather, they serve to enhance the learning experience and outcomes. One notable absence in the technologies available on *An Scéalaí* so far is speech recognition. Until recently, the word error rate of the ABAIR-ÉIST speech recognition (ASR) system was too high to enable inclusion. However, the rapid advances in our current system mean we expect it to be of a sufficiently high standard to be included as a module in the main *An Scéalaí* interface (see (Lonergan et al., 2022) for more detail). This will open up many new opportunities for learning activities. For example, it will make the *An Scéalaí* platform accessible for those who do not (yet) have typing skills / literacy difficulties. It will also open up the field of Computer-Assisted Pronunciation Training (CAPT) comparing learner utterances with the native speaker models. Most of all, it will form the crux of dialogue capacity, enabling the learner to have spoken interactions with virtual native speakers. This will help alleviate the currently limited opportunities learners have to engage in spoken communication.

Due to the modular design, this addition can largely be modelled on those already added. A learner can click a button, and beneath their story a microphone button for recording their voice will appear. After recording, a REST API call to the recognition service will be made, and the text delivered in response can be displayed. This then leads on to possibilities for additional functionality related to pronunciation, particularly when the resulting text does not match the target. Whatever form this will take, it can be developed independently and added to the main interface in exactly the same way.

6. Conclusion

An Scéalaí has now been used by large numbers and formal evaluation is currently being processed. Although it will take time to compile the results, it is clear that the response is overwhelmingly positive from both learners and teachers (some preliminary results are presented in (Ní Chiaráin et al., 2022)).

The beauty of this platform is that it has a simple, modular architecture, which means that as the technologies evolve, they can easily be incorporated to enhance its scope. As an open source platform, built with replicability in mind, we hope that it can be deployed by other Celtic languages, regardless of the level of currently available speech and language technology resources. Our experience tells us that even while resources are at a very rudimentary stage, it can have a big impact on the learning process. The key factor is not necessarily the technology but that its use is guided by the pedagogical aims and the platform and technologies are developed in partnership with the pedagogical and linguistic experts.

Our experience has also shown that even a very embryonic prototype tends to generate interest and a demand for more development, with a snowball effect. This draws in more teachers, learners, content developers, and so on.

We would like to think that *An Scéalaí* matches the aspirations of the Department of Education cited above. It marries well with the current curriculum and reflects our growing capacity to use digital technology to support teaching and learning. Ultimately, we are hopeful that *An Scéalaí* will contribute to the effective transmission of the language, whether in Irish- or English-medium schools, or in the context of the autonomous learner.

7. Acknowledgements

This work is part of the ABAIR initiative which is supported by An Roinn Turasóireachta, Cultúir, Ealaíon, Gaeltachta, Spóirt agus Meáin, with funding from the National Lottery as part of Stráitéis 20 Bliain don Ghaeilge, 2010-2030. We also gratefully acknowledge the support of An Chomhairle um Oideachas Gaeltachta agus Gaelscolaíochta (COGG), *An Corpas Cliste* Project.

8. Bibliographical References

ABAIR, (2022). *ABAIR: An Sintéiseoir Gaeilge - The Irish Language Synthesiser ABAIR*. `www.abair.ie`. As of 14 April 2022.

Department of Education, (2022). *Chief Inspector's Report, September 2016 – December 2020.*

Devitt, A., Condon, J., Dalton, G., O'Connell, J., and Ní Dhuinn, M. (2018). An maith leat an Ghaeilge? An analysis of variation in primary pupil attitudes to Irish in the Growing up in Ireland study. In *International Journal of Bilingual Education and Bilingualism*, volume 21, pages 105–117.

Dunne, C. M. (2019). Primary teachers' experiences in preparing to teach Irish: views on promoting the language and language proficiency. *Studies in Self-Access Learning*, 10(1):21–43.

ÉIST, (2022). *ÉIST: Aithint Chainte na Gaeilge: The Irish Language Recogniser ÉIST*. `https://phoneticsrv3.lcs.tcd.ie/rec/irish_asr`. As of 14 April 2022.

Gaeloideachas, (2022). *Statistics*. https://gaeloideachas.ie/i-am-a-researcher/statistics/. As of 14 April 2022.

Hyland, Á. and Milne, K., (1992). *Irish Educational Documents, Volume II, Dublin: C.I.C.E.*

Lonergan, L., Qian, M., Berthelsen, H., Murphy, A., Wendler, C., Ní Chiaráin, N., Gobl, C., and Ní Chasaide, A. (2022). Automatic Speech Recognition for Irish: the ABAIR-ÉIST system. In *The 4th Celtic Language Technology Workshop, LREC 2022*.

Lugosch, L., Ravanelli, M., Ignoto, P., Tomar, V. S., and Bengio, Y. (2019). Speech model pre-training for end-to-end spoken language understanding. *arXiv preprint arXiv:1904.03670*.

Ní Chasaide, A., Ní Chiaráin, N., Wendler, C., Berthelsen, H., Murphy, A., and Gobl, C. (2017). The ABAIR Initiative: Bringing spoken Irish into the digital space. In *INTERSPEECH*, pages 2113–2117.

Ní Chasaide, A., Ní Chiaráin, N., Berthelsen, H., Wendler, C., Murphy, A., Barnes, E., and Gobl, C. (2020). Can we defuse the digital timebomb? linguistics, speech technology and the irish language community.

Ní Chiaráin, N., Nolan, O., Comtois, M., Robinson Gunning, N., Berthelsen, H., and Ní Chasaide, A. (2022). Using Speech and NLP resources to build an iCALL platform for a minority language: the story of *An Scéalaí*, the Irish experience to date. In *The Fifth Workshop on the Use of Computational Methods in the Study of Endangered Languages, ACL 2022*.

Ní Chiaráin, N. and Ní Chasaide, A. (2020). The potential of text-to-speech synthesis in computer-assisted language learning: A minority language perspective. In Alberto Andujar, editor, *Recent Tools for Computer- and Mobile-Assisted Foreign Language Learning*, chapter 7, pages 149–169. IGI Global, Hershey, PA.

Scannell, K., (2013). *An Gramadóir*. https://cadhan.com/gramadoir/. As of 14 April 2022.

Seoighe, S., Smith-Christmas, C., and Ó hIfearnáin, T., (2021). *Líon agus Lonnaíocht na dTeaghlach atá ag tógáil clainne le Gaeilge lasmuigh den Ghaeltacht*. https://www.glornangael.ie/wp-content/uploads/2022/04/Lion-agus-Lonnaiocht-na-dTeaghlach-a-labhraionn-Gaeilge-19-Samhain-2021.pdf/. As of 14 April 2022.

Ó Murchú, H. (2016). *Irish: The Irish language in education in the Republic of Ireland*. The Netherlands: Mercator European Research Centre on Multilingualism and Language Learning, Regional Dossiers Series, Cambridge.

Proceedings of the CLTW 4 @ LREC2022, pages 77–84
Marseille, 20-25 June 2022

Cipher – Faoi Gheasa: A Game-with-a-Purpose for Irish

Elaine Uí Dhonnchadha[1], Monica Ward[2], Liang Xu[2]
[1] Trinity College Dublin, Ireland
[2] Dublin City University, Ireland
uidhonne@tcd.ie, monica.ward@dcu.ie, liang.xu6@mail.dcu.ie

Abstract

This paper describes *Cipher – Faoi Gheasa*, a 'game with a purpose' designed to support the learning of Irish in a fun and enjoyable way. The aim of the game is to promote language 'noticing' and to combine the benefits of reading with the enjoyment of computer game playing, in a pedagogically beneficial way. In this paper we discuss pedagogical challenges for Irish, the development of measures for the selection and ranking of reading materials, as well as initial results of game evaluation. Overall user feedback is positive and further testing and development is envisaged.

Keywords: CALL, game-based language learning, reading pedagogy, text ranking measures, adaptive learning.

1. Introduction

This paper describes *Cipher – Faoi Gheasa*, a 'game with a purpose' (Von Ahn, 2006, Vajjala, 2021) designed to support the learning of Irish in a fun and enjoyable way. The aim of the game is to promote 'noticing' (Skehan, 2013) and to combine the benefits of reading with the enjoyment of computer game playing, in a pedagogically beneficial way. As electronic game playing is a popular leisure time activity, a 'game with a purpose' such as *Cipher – Faoi Gheasa* facilitates language learning while playing a digital game. The game has been piloted in a two primary schools to date (see section 4) and initial feedback from students and teachers is positive. Although this game has been developed for Irish, we believe that this model can be adapted for use with any language.

Irish is an endangered language (Moseley, 2012) with most users learning it as a second language at school. Students have limited opportunities to use the language outside of the classroom. However, success in second language acquisition has been linked to the quantity and quality of language input (De Cat, 2020). This game provides exposure to valuable language input in the form of stories and myths. Reading is widely acknowledged to be an effective way of increasing vocabulary, and in the case of L2 language learners, it is a particularly important way of gaining exposure to grammatical structures (Heilman et al., 2007). Playing this game involves reading and paying attention to the spelling of the words, which promotes 'noticing' of word forms, an important aspect of language learning.

The game is designed to be adaptive to the learner's level of language proficiency. When a player plays the game for the first time, they provide their age (or 18+ for adults), class/year and type of school. Based on this information, a first-time player is assigned a story with a suitable level of challenge, and depending on their performance in the game, they will subsequently see harder or easier stories.

In section 2 we discuss some of the challenges in teaching and learning Irish, and review the role of reading in language learning, 'games with a purpose' and readability and complexity measures used in the ranking of reading materials. In section 3 we describe the game in more detail and in section 4 we present some results of a pilot study in a primary school. Section 5 presents conclusions and future work.

2. Background and Related Research

2.1 Irish – Some Pedagogical Challenges

Irish, apart from some exceptions, is a compulsory subject for most primary and secondary school children in Ireland. Most L2 Irish learners are L1 English speakers, which means that they learn Irish through an English speaker's lens. One area where this causes difficulties for learners is with Irish orthography. English orthography is very opaque and schoolchildren spend a lot of class time in the early years of primary school learning sound/orthography combinations. Irish orthography, though complex, is relatively regular (Hickey and Stenson, 2011). However, there is a general perception that it is irrelevant and not transparent (Ward, 2016). Teachers are often unaware of the logic behind the patterns in Irish spellings and they do not teach them to their students. This leaves students with gaps in their knowledge, which they fill with intuitions from English. For example, the Irish word *seachtain* 'week' could be pronounced as 'say-ach- tayne' on first reading by an L1 English speaker. However, the actual pronunciation is closer to 'shokht-en' or 'shocht-en' (ʃaxtˠənʲ). The 'e' after the 's' in *seachtain* indicates that the 's' should be pronounced as /ʃ/ ('sh') and the 'e' itself does not reflect an actual vowel. Irish language learners are generally not taught about these types of patterns and thus often mispronounce Irish words on first sight. Irish language learners often 'ignore' the accents on vowels, as they do not understand their importance. An accent lengthens a vowel, so that 'á' is pronounced /ɑː/ 'aw', whereas 'a' is pronounced /ə/ 'ah'. '*Mo*' means 'my' whereas '*mó*' means 'more'. Another challenging feature for learners of Irish is the presence of unusual combinations of letters, especially when marking initial mutations such as eclipsis at the start of words, e.g., *bp, mb, bhf, dt, nd, gc*, and *ng*. Hickey and Stenson (2011) recommend that these be taught explicitly but unfortunately this does not always happen. There are also digraph combinations that can cause difficulties for students including *ei, ea(i), eo(i), ae(i)*, and *ao(i)*, as well as unstressed final syllables e.g. *-(a)igh, -(a)idh, amh, -adh*. These letter combinations look confusing to students, but there is logic behind them and if learners knew more about these patterns it would increase their understanding and enjoyment of reading texts in Irish. Table 1 summarises of some of the orthographic issues for Irish language learners – see Hickey and Stenson (2011) for more details.

Issue	Example
Different orthography from English	Seachtain - 'e' indicates 's' should be pronounced 'sh'
Accents indicate vowel length	'*mo*' is different from '*mó*'
Unusual consonant combinations due to eclipsis	*bp, mb, bhf, dt, nd, gc*, and *ng*
Unusual digraph combinations	*ei, ea(i), eo(i), ae(i)*, and *ao(i)*
Unstressed final syllables	*-(a)igh, -(a)idh, -amh, -adh*

Table 1: Some orthography related issues for Irish language learners

Another aspect of Irish grammar which receives surprisingly little attention is noun gender. All nouns in Irish have either feminine or masculine gender, which has wide ranging consequences in the grammar and spelling. Many initial mutations and modifier agreements vary according to the gender of the noun. In the Cipher – Faoi Gheasa game, we draw particular attention to spelling including initial mutations and to the gender of nouns.

2.2 Reading and Readability Measures

Reading practice is a vital component of first and second language learning, particularly for vocabulary learning (Hafiz and Tudor, 1989, cited in (Heilman et al., 2008)). Matching the level of the text with the language proficiency of the learner is particularly important. Harris et al. (1996) suggest that the language input needs to be challenging to provide opportunities for learning, and they caution against over-simplification of written texts, which can result in stories that are bland and unnatural. They note that there is scope for using more complex language in the context of stories which are already familiar to the learners. For the beginner levels we use well known fairy tales, which will be familiar in the learner's first language (L1), followed by less well-known folktales and myths that are presented as they progress through the levels in the game.

However, choosing reading material of an appropriate level for the learner is a complex task which needs to take several factors into account, including both reading ability and reading interests. Both readability and complexity measures have been used in attempting to match the reading materials with the learner's proficiency level. Readability measures tend to focus on the text and its characteristics, while complexity measures focus on language learner output (Vajjala and Meurers, 2012). Commonly used text-based readability measures include average sentence length, average word length in characters or syllables (Flesch, 1948, Kincaid et al., 1975), and word frequency lists (Dale and Chall, 1948). Discourse features and text cohesion are also used in some readability measures (Graesser et al., 2014). Complexity measures which focus more on the learner's capabilities tend to measure lexical diversity, number and types of clause per sentence or other unit, and other features such as verb tense, mood, voice etc. Vajjala and Meurers (2012) maintain that both types of measure are important for choosing appropriate learning materials. Of the lexical and syntactic measures they implemented for English, they found type-token ratios, verb variation, modifier variation, and number of characters/syllables per word to be among the most useful lexical measures. Mean length of clause, as well as number of co-ordinate phrases or complex nominals per clause were among the most useful syntactic measures. See (Vajjala, 2021) for a survey of the most recent automatic readability assessment research. Gutierrez-Vasques et al. (2018) discuss measures of morphological complexity measures. This topic is of relevance to languages such as Irish which encode substantial semantic and grammatical information in their inflectional paradigms.

Ó Meachair (2019) investigated a range of complexity metrics for Irish educational materials using the EduGA corpus compiled for this purpose. These measures include (a) a comparative frequency of prescribed lexico-grammatical features, (b) an analysis of sentence and word length, and (c) an analysis of terminology topicality. Of particular interest to our research are the sentence and word length metrics. He found that sentences in lower-level Irish educational materials contained fewer words on average than sentences in higher levels materials, indicating that this metric behaves as an indicator of increasing complexity for Irish educational materials. This finding is in line with results for other languages. However, he found that increases in average word length did not correlate with increases in educational materials level, and average word lengths fluctuated significantly across all sub-corpora.

Hickey (2007) discusses the importance of developing fast, accurate, word recognition skills in young readers, which facilitates satisfying independent reading. She echoes Gardner's (2004) view that "high-frequency words must be mastered in order to achieve minimum levels of reading proficiency in both L1 and L2". She analyses a list of the 100 most frequent words in a corpus of Early Reader books (18K words) for 7-13 years and suggests ways of teaching the most frequent words.

2.3 Digital Educational Games for Language Learning

Digital Educational Games (DEGs) are a type of informal learning which have been proven to be beneficial to learners, particularly children in school (Sørensen and Meyer, 2007). In recent years, DEGs designed for language learning and teaching have become increasingly popular. This type of game is often used to motivate students to practise authentic communications in the target language. According to Gee (2005), this works because DEGs can provide a learning experience that schools normally do not offer to students. Many studies have shown that games can be used to help language learning. This research area is also known as digital game-based language learning (DGBLL) (Dixon et al., 2022). However, Dixon suggests that games designed specifically for language learning still need improvements in terms of engagement and authentic language interaction, as DEG development is relatively underdeveloped compared to the enormous effort that has been put into games designed for entertainment.

Games with a purpose (GWAP) (Von Ahn, 2006) have been used to collect data for solving real-world problems, such as labelling images (Von Ahn and Dabbish, 2008), identifying semantic connections (Chamberlain et al., 2008), correcting optical character recognition (OCR) errors (Chrons and Sundell, 2011) and so on. These tasks often involve language annotations, which can provide useful resources for natural language processing (NLP). The *Cipher – Faoi Gheasa* game is inspired by the game developed by Xu and Chamberlain (2020) to find errors in English Corpora using GWAP methodology and crowdsourcing. In the next section we describe *Cipher – Faoi Gheasa*, a digital game with the purpose of supporting the learning of Irish in a fun and enjoyable way.

3. *Cipher – Faoi Gheasa*: A Game-with-a-Purpose

3.1 Game Narrative

The game is set in a magical world where an evil spirit '*Syfer*' has put the ancient tales and myths under a variety of spells (*faoi gheasa* in Irish) causing them to be forgotten over time. The challenge for the player then is to defeat the evil spirit and restore the tales by discovering the enchanted words and identifying which evil spells (ciphers) were used.

The ciphers change the spelling of words in systematic ways. For example, the "Double Tail" cipher doubles the last letter of a word. This quite an easy cipher to find, but the player must be wary as not all words ending in a double letter are enchanted. In Figure 1 we see a page from a story where the Reverse (*Taobh Thiar Aniar*) spell has affected the words *suga* (agus), *rabot* (tobar) and *ehtiannaeb* (beannaithe) and the Bottom-Up (*Tóin Aníos*) spell has swapped the first and last letter of the words *hacacb* (bacach), *neab* (bean) and *r'iard* (d'iarr). Figure 2 shows a help message associated with these two ciphers.

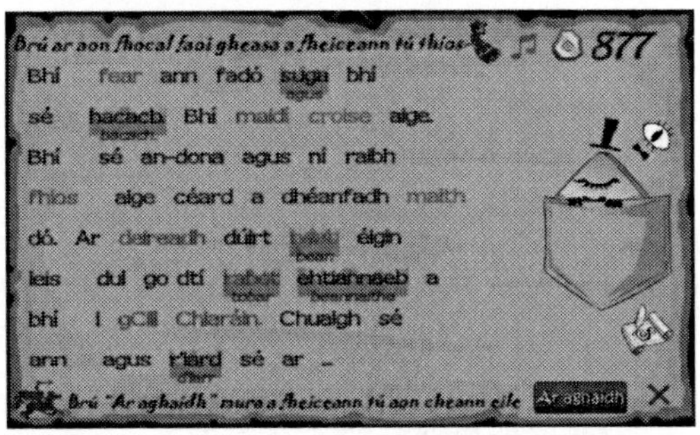

Figure 1: A page of ciphered text with noun gender highlighting

In Figure 1 the correct forms (green text) are shown for illustrative purposes. They are not normally present unless the player uses power-ups to make them visible. However, using power-ups will cost them points.

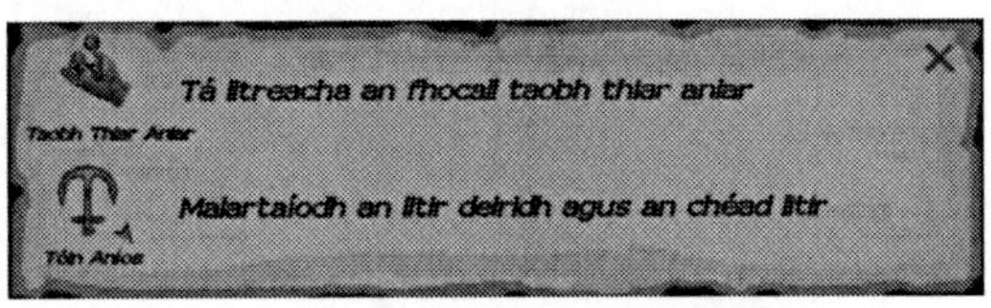

Figure 2: Ciphers - "Reverse" and "Bottom-up"

Note that the nouns in Figure 1 have gender highlighting. In the game narrative, feminine nouns are ruby red because they are loyal to the Spirit of Fire, and masculine nouns are sapphire blue because they are loyal to the Spirit of Water (see Figure 3).

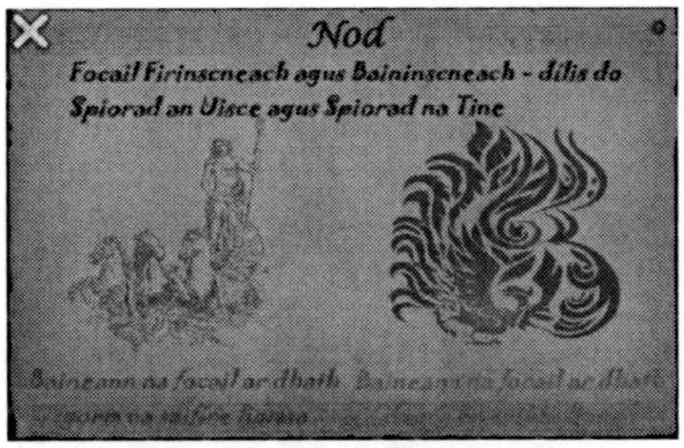

Figure 3: Spirits of Water and Fire

3.2 Pedagogical Features

Cipher: Faoi Gheasa has several pedagogical features that are helpful for Irish language learning. It encourages players to 'notice' spelling errors (or ciphers) in the texts. Often, Irish language learners ignore errors or are not aware there is an problem (Stenson and Hickey, 2018). The focus of *Cipher* is to get the players to notice the ciphers in the texts. They must pay attention to the words and decide if a word is spelt correctly or not. Orthographical features such as accents can either make a word correct or incorrect and players will have to carefully decide if a word is a cipher or not each time they read texts.

Another pedagogical benefit of this game is that it encourages the reading of Irish texts. Schoolchildren in English medium schools (most Irish schoolchildren) are only exposed to Irish during the Irish lessons. They neither hear nor read Irish outside of school. *Cipher: Faoi Gheasa* presents texts in a game context so that players are more inclined to read the texts (as compared to 'dry' text in a textbook).

Most Irish language learners are unaware of the fact that Irish words have an associated gender - either masculine or feminine. This means that they are prone to making errors in the initial mutations on lexical words following functional words such as articles and prepositions, and in agreement marking on modifiers such as adjectives and nouns. *Cipher: Faoi Gheasa* highlights masculine words in sapphire blue and feminine words in ruby red. This indicates to players that there are two categories of words and they will become familiar with the concept of two types of noun. They will see its word's colour each time it appears in a text. Meurers et al. (2010) refer to the highlighting of such language features as "input enhancement".

For many Irish school children, Irish is not the most popular subject and sometimes teachers struggle to make it interesting for their students (Ward et al., 2019) There are very few digital resources available for Irish, particularly for schoolchildren. *An Scéalaí* developed by Ní Chiaráin & Ní Chasaide (2019) allows students to write their own stories. However, most of their learning takes place via textbooks which are static resources that leave little room for variable-paced teaching and learning. *Cipher: Faoi Gheasa* is a digital game and, although it has an olde world feel about it, it is a modern game. Students are used to playing digital games (Dixon *et al.*, 2022) and initial feedback (Xu et al., 2022) suggests that they enjoy learning Irish with something other than a textbook. They can gain points when they correctly identify a cipher and move through the levels, which is motivational for them. Players can progress through the game at their own pace - more capable students can move through the texts faster than other students. Table 2 summarises some of the pedagogical benefits of *Cipher: Faoi Gheasa*.

Feature	Benefit
Reading	Students can read Irish outside of textbooks and can benefit from increased language exposure and vocabulary
Noticing of errors	Students have to pay attention to spellings (detect ciphers)
Gender highlighting	Students can become aware of the concept noun gender and the gender of individual nouns
Digital game	Students are not restricted to static textbooks as they would normally be
Personalisation	Students can progress at their own pace

Table 2: Pedagogical features and benefits of Cipher: Faoi Gheasa

3.3 Adaptivity

Cipher is an 'adaptive' game. Texts are chosen to suit the individual learner's level of Irish and, depending on how they perform in the game, they will be presented with easier or more challenging texts. This personalisation of learning is recognised as an important element in motivating students (Sanacore, 2007). Ciphers are also graded according to difficulty and become more challenging as the game progresses.

3.4 Choice of Materials

We chose to use stories with a magical or mythological theme for several reasons. Firstly, we believe these types of stories will appeal to language learners both young and old, and will help to overcome the common dilemma for L2 learners that their language abilities often lag behind their reading interests (Heilman et al., 2006). Secondly, a mythological theme can be made culturally relevant in different language settings. In this way we hope that the game can be adapted for other languages and that the stories will be interesting and relevant for learners. We also hope that folktales and mythology will raise the language learners' cultural awareness and pride in their heritage (Restoule et al., 2010). In addition, in order to build up a bank of stories, it is practical to use stories and tales which are free from copyright restrictions whenever possible.

As the Cipher game centres around tales and myths which have been enchanted by the evil spirit, *Syfer*, it is important to build up a collection of stories. As this is an 'adaptive' game the stories need to be ranked from easiest to most challenging. In the following sections we describe the sourcing and pre-processing of story texts and the metrics used to rank them.

3.5 Sources of Materials

Currently, our main sources of data are online archives. *Bailiúchán na Scol* (The Schools Collection) made available online by the Dúchas Community Transcription Project, dúchas.ie, is a valuable source of material for this DEG project. The Schools Collection contains folklore, stories and myths which were written down by primary school children aged 12-14 years of age and are therefore very appropriate for our purposes. As these children were native speakers of Irish, the language is intermediate to advanced level. There is also a small amount of Irish material on Gutenberg.org, which is also at advanced level. For the lower levels we have created Irish versions of common English fairy tales. The familiarity of the story in their L1 helps the less proficient players to understand the stories more easily and facilitates 'scaffolded' learning.

3.6 Pre-processing of Materials

As the texts in "The Schools Collection" on dúchas.ie are from the 1930's and the Irish texts on Gutenberg.org are from the 1900s, they were written before the official language standards were published (Rannóg an Aistriúcháin, 1958, Tithe an Oireachtas, 2017). This means that the spelling and grammar of the material in both archives requires standardisation.

The following is an example of the original transcribed text from Dúchas.ie with pre-standard forms and spelling mistakes underlined:

1) *Bhí daoine amuigh ag <u>iasgaireacht</u> <u>oidhche</u> amháin. Bhí siad ag <u>iasgaireacht</u> <u>sghadán</u>. Nuair a bhí siad ag teacht <u>'na</u> <u>bháile</u>. <u>Chonaich</u> siad trí <u>tonna</u> ag <u>tarraint</u> <u>ortha</u>.*

'People were out fishing one night. They were fishing for herring. When they were coming home. They saw three waves drawing towards them'

Manually standardised text:

2) *Bhí daoine amuigh ag iascaireacht oíche amháin. Bhí siad ag iascaireacht scadán. Nuair a bhí siad ag teacht abhaile chonaic siad trí thonn ag tarraingt orthu.*

In the case of the Gutenberg.org Irish texts the Gaelic font characters also needed to be converted, e.g., *Ḃ* to *Bh* etc. The following is an example from Gutenberg Project:

1) *<u>Ḃí</u> cú <u>breáġ</u> ag Fionn. Sin Bran. <u>Ċualaiḋ</u> <u>tu</u> caint <u>air</u> <u>Ḃran</u>.*
   'Fionn had a fine hound. That is Bran. You have heard talk about Bran.'

2) *Bhí cú breá ag Fionn. Sin Bran. Chuala tú caint ar Bhran.*

The updated texts were manually checked for accuracy using the online the electronic version of *Ó Dónaill's Irish English Dictionary*[1] and *Gramadóir*[2] spelling and grammar checker for Irish, and put in sentence-per-line format. They were automatically tagged using the Irish rule-based POS tagger (Uí Dhonnchadha and van Genabith, 2006), and the POS-tagged output was manually checked and corrected.

[1] https://www.teanglann.ie/en/fgb/

[2] https://cadhan.com/gramadoir/foirm-en.html

3.7 Ranking of Reading Materials

A number of lexical, grammatical and frequency statistics are calculated and combined in order to rank the materials from easy to more challenging.

3.7.1 Lexical Measures

Lexical diversity is a measure of the number of different words used in a text. There are a variety of measures in use. Type/token ratio (TTR) is the ratio of unique words (types) to total words (tokens) in a text. This measure is sensitive to text length, as longer texts will have repeated function words which reduce the type-token ratio, resulting in a lower lexical diversity for longer texts. This can be overcome to an extent by using a fixed sample of the text. We calculate TTR100 using the first 100 words only, in order to standardise across texts of different lengths, however this will not capture the effects on lexical diversity of repetition which is a common feature of fairy tales. We therefore calculated the CTTR and Uber/Maas Indices (Malvern et al, 2004) which are independent of text length. Morphological diversity is a measure of the number of inflected or derived words per lemma used in a text. As Irish texts may contain several inflected forms (and derived forms) associated with the same lemma, we calculate Lemma/Token ratio (LTR) i.e., the ratio of lemmas (headwords) to total words, as a measure of morphological diversity.

3.7.2 Grammatical Measures

A number of statistics, which are indicators of readability and grammatical complexity, are calculated:

- Average sentence length in words and syllables. Longer sentences are a good indicator of more grammatically complex language.
- Maximum sentence length. This is calculated as a text may have a mix of long and short sentences and the average length might not fully reflect the complexity of a text.
- Average word length in characters and syllables.
- Average number of clauses per sentence, as indicated by the number of verbs per sentence.
- Average number of modifiers per sentence, as indicated by the number of adjectives/adverbs per sentence.
- Average number of complex nominals per sentence, as indicated by the number of nouns in the genitive case.

3.7.3 Word Frequency Measures

As a measure of the semantic challenge for learners, we use vocabulary frequency lists which help us to distinguish the proportion of familiar words (i.e., frequently used) and less frequently-used words in a story. The word types in each story are compared with frequency wordlists based on a subset of the NCI[3] corpus (Kilgarriff et al., 2007) and Breacadh wordlists. Texts in the NCI corpus are categorised under two broad genre categories: 'imaginative' and 'informative'. We use a frequency word list based on 'imaginative' writings only (6.6 million words), which excludes non-fiction writing such as reports, newspapers, textbooks and legal documents. Breacadh, an organisation which promotes adult literacy in Irish, published Liostaí Bhreacadh which contains a number of frequency words lists (Breacadh, 2007). We use the frequency lists drawn from writings for 0-6 year olds, 7-11 year olds and teenagers. We compare the word types in each story with frequency wordlists from NCI and Breacadh, and calculate the proportion of words that are among the 100, 300, 500, 1000, 5000 and 5000+ most frequent words. Additional relevant sources of frequency wordlists include the EduGA Corpus (Ó Meachair, 2019) and the CLGP Corpus (Hickey, 2007).

3.7.4 Testing of Ranking Measures

The Lexical, Grammatical and Frequency measures are combined to provide a ranking for the stories currently in the Cipher story bank. We tested the efficacy of the measures against 10 stories from the Taisce Tuisceana[4] graded collection of reading comprehension material, using samples from the Sraith 1 (A, B and C) collections of reading material which are aimed at 7/8 year olds, and Sraith 2 (D and E) collections aimed at 9/10 year olds.

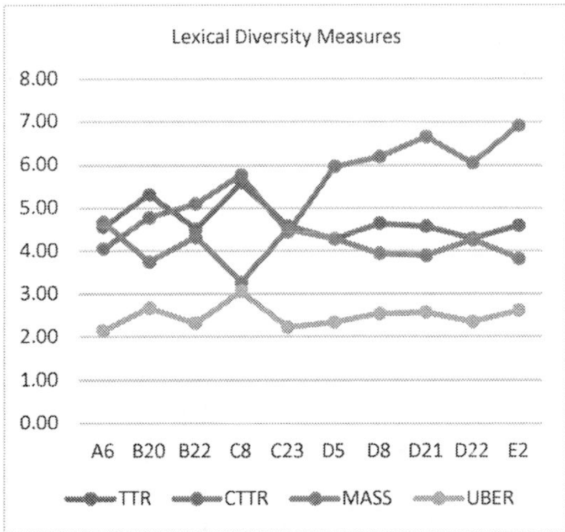

Figure 4: Lexical Diversity Measures for Taisce Tuisceana texts

In Figure 4, the preliminary results show that the CTTR measure indicates an overall increase in lexical diversity in the 10 short stories from Sraith 1 (A-C) and Sraith 2 (D-E) of Taisce Tuisceana. The TTR, Mass and Uber indices are inconclusive. Further testing with a larger data set is required to investigate which are the most appropriate lexical density measures.

[3] http://corpas.focloir.ie/

[4] https://www.cogg.ie/taisce-tuisceana/

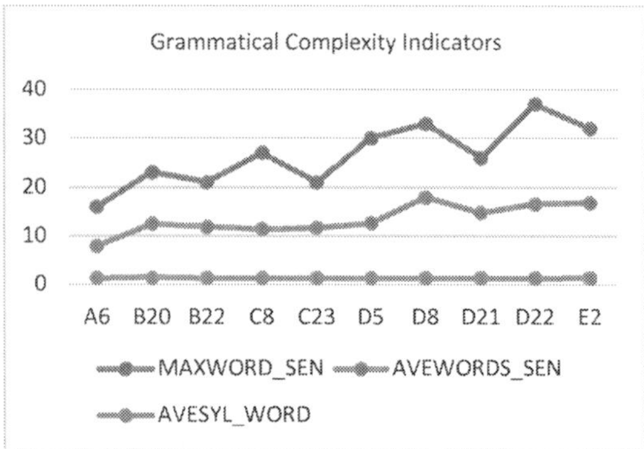

Figure 5: Grammatical Diversity Measures for Taisce Tuisceana texts

Figure 5 shows that for this small sample, the average words per sentence indicates an overall increasing grammatical complexity. Maximum words per sentence also shows an increasing trend but with fluctuations. Average syllables per word remains relatively constant for all texts.

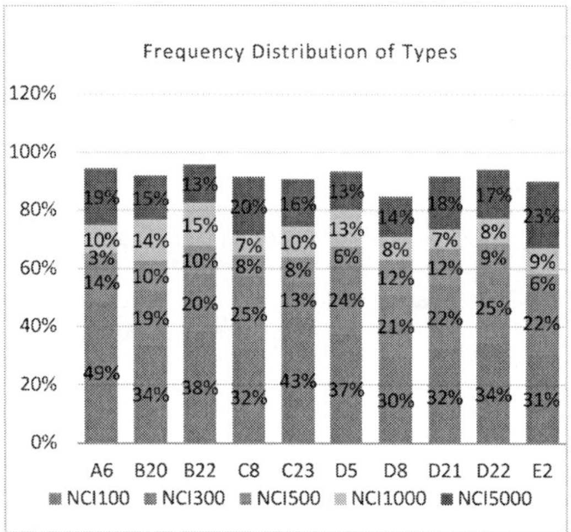

Figure 6: Frequency Distribution for Taisce Tuisceana texts.

Figure 6 shows the percentage of word types that are in the 100, 300, 500, 1000 and 5000 most frequent words in the NCI wordlists. For example, for text A6, 49% of word types are within the 100 most common words, and in total 95% of word types are within the 5000 most frequent words, with the remaining 5% being outside of the 5000 most frequent words. Overall, there is a trend for lower level texts (A, C and C) to have a greater proportion of more frequent words than the higher level texts (D and E). However, for this data sample this is quite a weak trend, with relatively little variation overall.

4. Game Evaluation

The game has been tested in two primary schools in Dublin. Initial testing took place in a Gaelscoil. Following user feedback, the game was improved and the following year was tested in an English-medium school. This paper focuses on the second test.

A total of nine classes participated in the experiment, with 20-30 students in each class. The students were aged 10-12 and were in 4th, 5th or 6th grade, with each grade having three classes. The experiment was run over two consecutive weeks. For each class, students had at least 30 minutes to play the game each week. Students were paired to play the game due to limited available laptops. In some smaller classes, individual students each had a laptop. However, it is interesting to note that students generally had a better gaming experience when playing in pairs. Afterwards participants were asked to fill out a questionnaire. In total, 64 questionnaire responses were collected. Figures 7 to 9 present the answers to some of the questions that were asked in the questionnaire.

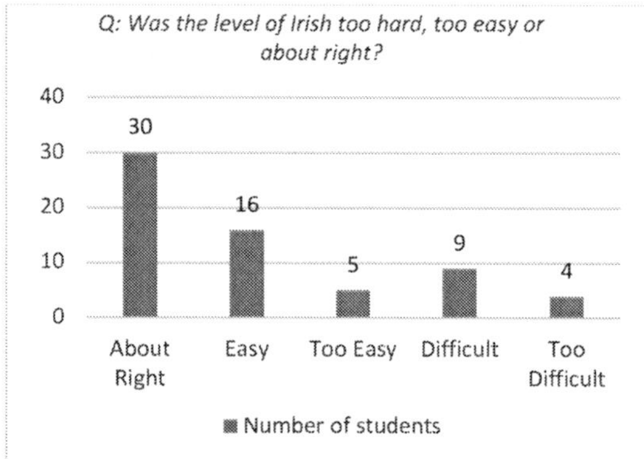

Figure 7: Students' opinion on text difficulty

In Figure 7 we see that most respondents felt that the difficulty level of the texts was appropriate, while in Figure 8 we see that most of the respondents enjoyed playing the game.

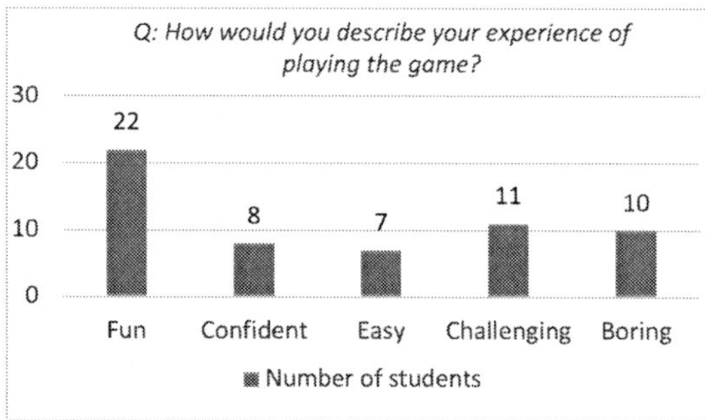

Figure 8: Students' opinion on their gaming experience

5. Conclusions and Further Work

The overall feedback received from students was positive. After the game testing session in class, many students asked the researchers if this game was publicly available online and so they could play at home. Some teachers also provided positive feedback regarding students' overall reactions to the game in class. In Figure 9 we see that more than 50% of students felt it was "very good" or "good" to learn Irish through the game compared to learning Irish in the classroom.

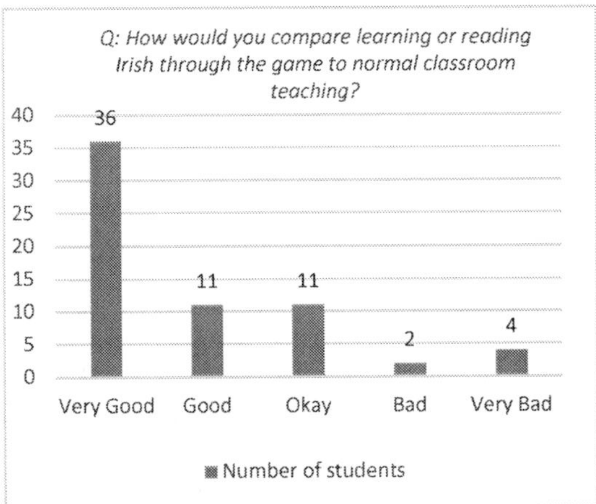

Figure 9 Students opinion of learning Irish through a game

These responses indicate a strong need for games like *Cipher* in Irish language learning education. Enjoyable language learning games have great potential for engaging children in learning a language.

The Cipher game is flexible and can easily be adapted for other languages. It is easily extensible in that new texts and new ciphers can be added at any time. Given the positive feedback received to date, we intend to carry out further development and testing in schools and also to trial it with adult learners. Testing of measures for ranking texts is ongoing, and while these results are tentative, results to date are promising.

6. Acknowledgements

This work was conducted with the financial support of the Science Foundation Ireland Centre for Research Training in Digitally-Enhanced Reality (d-real) under Grant No. 18/CRT/6224. For the purpose of Open Access, the author has applied a CC BY public copyright licence to any Author Accepted Manuscript version arising from this submission. We would like to express our special thanks to Tianlong Huang, who provided support for game development. We would also like to thank our anonymous reviewers for their helpful comments and suggestions.

7. Bibliographical References

Breacadh. (2007). "Liostaí Bhreacadh: Focail Choitianta sa Ghaeilge." In Acmhainn Aosoideachais trí Ghaeilge sa Ghaeltacht. Casla, Galway: Breacadh.

Chamberlain, J., Poesio, M., and Kruschwitz, U. (2008). Phrase detectives: A web-based collaborative annotation game. In Proceedings of the International Conference on Semantic Systems (I-Semantics' 08), pages 42–49.

Chrons, O. and Sundell, S. (2011). Digitalkoot: Making old archives accessible using crowdsourcing. In Workshops at the Twenty-Fifth AAAI Conference on Artificial Intelligence.

Dale, E. & Chall, J. (1948). A Formula for Predicting Readability. Educational Research Bulletin, 27, 11-20.

De Cat, C. (2020). Predicting Language Proficiency In Bilingual Children. Studies in Second Language Acquisition, 42, 279-325.

Dixon, D., Dixon, T. & Jordan, E. (2022). Second language (L2) gains through digital game-based language learning (DGBLL): A meta-analysis. Language Learning & Technology, 26.

Flesch, R. (1948). A New Readability Yardstick. Journal of Applied Psychology, 32.

Gardner, D. (2004). Vocabulary input through extensive reading: A comparison of words found in children's narrative and expository reading materials. Applied linguistics, 25(1), 1-37.

Gee, James Paul (2005) Pleasure, Learning, Video, Games, and Life: the projective stance" E-Learning Vol 2, number 3

Gutierrez-Vasques, X. & Mijangos, V. (2018). Comparing morphological complexity of Spanish, Otomi and Nahuatl. Workshop on Linguistic Complexity and Natural Language Processing, Santa Fe, New Mexico, USA.

Graesser, A., McNamara, D., Cai, Z., Conley, M., Li, H. & Pennebaker, J. (2014). Coh-Metrix measures Text Characteristics at Multiple Levels of Language and Discourse. The Elementary School Journal, 115.

Heilman, M., Collins-Thompson, K., Callan, J. & Eskenazi, M. (2006) Classroom success of an intelligent tutoring system for lexical practice and reading comprehension. InterSpeech 2006 ICSLP, Pittsburgh, PA, USA.

Heilman, M., Collins-Thompson, K., Callan, J. & Eskenazi, M. (2007). Combining Lexical and Grammatical Features to Improve Readability Measures for First and Second Language Texts. NAACL HLT 2007, Rochester, NY. Association for Computational Linguistics.

Heilman, M., Zhao, L., Pino, J. & Eskenazi, M. (2008) Retrieval of Reading Materials for Vocabulary and Reading Practice. Third ACL Workshop on Innovative Use of NLP for Building Educational Applications, Columbus, Ohio. ACL, 80–88.

Hickey, T. (2007) Fluency in Reading Irish as L1 or L2: Promoting High-frequency Word Recognition in Emergent Readers, International Journal of Bilingual Education and Bilingualism, 10:4, 471-493, DOI: 10.2167/beb455.0

Hickey, T. & Stenson, N. (2011). Irish orthography: what do teachers and learners need to know about it, and why? Language, Culture and Curriculum, 24, 23-46.

Kilgarriff, A., Rundell, M. & Uí Dhonnchadha, E. (2007). Efficient corpus creation for lexicography. Language Resources and Evaluation Journal.

Kincaid, J., Fishburne, R., Rogers, R. & Choissom, B. (1975). Derivation of new readability formulas (automated readability index, fog count, and Flesch reading ease formula) for Navy enlisted personnel. Research Branch Report 8–75.

Malvern, D., Richards, B., Chipere, N. & Durán, P. (2004). Lexical Diversity and Language Development: Quantification and Assessment, Springer.

Meurers, D., Ziai, R., Amaral, L., Boyd, A., Dimitrov, A., Metcalf, V. & Ott, N. (2010). Enhancing Authentic Web Pages for Language Learners. NAACL HLT 2010 Fifth Workshop on Innovative Use of NLP for Building Educational Applications, Los Angeles, California.

Moseley, C. (2012). The UNESCO atlas of the world's languages in danger [Online]. http://www.unesco.org/languagesatlas/index.php?hl=en &page=atlasmap. [Accessed 2022].

Ní Chiaráin, N. & Ní Chasaide, A. (2019). An Scéalaí: autonomous learners harnessing speech and language technologies. SLaTE 2019: 8th ISCA Workshop on Speech and Language Technology in Education. Graz, Austria: ISCA,.

Ó Meachair, M. J. (2019). The Creation and Complexity Analysis of a Corpus of Educational Materials in Irish (EduGA). PhD, University of Dublin, Trinity College.

Rannóg an Aistriúcháin (1958). Gramadach na Gaeilge agus Litriú na Gaeilge: An Caighdeán Oifigiúil, Baile Átha Cliath, Oifig an tSoláthair.

Restoule, J., Archibald, J., Lester-Smith, D., Parent, A. & Smillie, C. A. (2010). Connecting to spirit in indigenous research. Canadian Journal of Native Education, 33.

Sanacore, J. (2007). Needed: Critics of literacy education with a more inclusive perspective. International journal of progressive education, 3(1), 29-43.

Sørensen, B. H., & Meyer, B. (2007). Serious Games in language learning and teaching-a theoretical perspective. In DiGRA Conference (pp. 559-566).

Skehan, P. (2013). Nurturing noticing. Noticing and second language acquisition: Studies in honor of Richard Schmidt.

Stenson, Nancy, and Tina Hickey. (2018). Understanding Irish Spelling: A Handbook for Teachers and Learners. 92

Tithe an Oireachtas. (2017). Gramadach na Gaeilge: An Caighdeán Oifigiúil.

Uí Dhonnchadha, E. & Van Genabith, J. (2006). A Part-of-speech tagger for Irish using Finite-State Morphology and Constraint Grammar Disambiguation. LREC 2006, May 2006 Genoa.

Vajjala, S. (2021). Trends, Limitations and Open Challenges in Automatic Readability Assessment Research. arXiv: Computer Science, Computation and Language [Online], https://arxiv.org/abs/2105.00973.

Vajjala, S. & Meurers, D. (2012). On Improving the Accuracy of Readability Classification using Insights from Second Language Acquisition. 7th Workshop on the Innovative Use of NLP for Building Educational Applications, 2012 Monréal, Canada. ACL, 163-173.

Von Ahn, L. (2006). Games with a purpose. Computer, 36, 92–94.

Von Ahn, L. and Dabbish, L. (2008). Designing games with a purpose. Communications of the ACM, 51(8):58–67.

Ward, M. (2016). Using animated visualisation in Computer Assisted Language Learning. In 2016 9th International Conference on Human System Interactions (HSI) (pp. 38-44). IEEE.

Ward, M., Mozgovoy, M., & Purgina, M. (2019). Can WordBricks make learning Irish more engaging for students?. International Journal of Game-Based Learning (IJGBL), 9(2), 20-39.

Xu, L., Uí Dhonnchadha, E., and Ward, M. (2022). User Experience Study of "Cipher: Faoi Gheasa": A Digital Educational Game for Language Learning and Student Engagement. In ACM GameSys'22. May 2022, Athlone, Ireland.

Proceedings of the CLTW 4 @ LREC2022 , pages 85–93
Marseille, 20-25 June 2022

Towards Coreference Resolution for Early Irish

Mark Darling[1], **Marieke Meelen**[2], **David Willis**[1]
[1]University of Oxford, [2]University of Cambridge
{mark.darling,david.willis}@ling-phil.ox.ac.uk, mm986@cam.ac.uk

Abstract

In this article, we present an outline of some of the issues involved in developing a semi-supervised procedure for coreference resolution for early Irish as part of a wider enterprise to create a parsed corpus of historical Irish with enriched annotation for information structure and anaphoric coreference. We outline the ways in which existing resources, notably the POMIC historical Irish corpus and the Cesax annotation algorithm, have had to be adapted, the first to provide suitable input for coreference resolution, the second to cope with specific aspects of early Irish grammar. We also outline features of a part-of-speech tagger that we have developed for early Irish as part of the first task and with a view to expanding the size of the future corpus.

Keywords: Old Irish, Middle Irish, Information Structure, Coreference Resolution, Low-Resource NLP

1. Introduction

Because of their unique position, having both lexical and functional characteristics, pronouns form an excellent starting point for both diachronic as well as crosslinguistic research as they are widely assumed to proceed through a cycle of reduction from independent pronoun to inflectional affix and zero elements or 'null pronouns' (Siewierska, 1999; Van Gelderen, 2011). Links of pronouns to their referents are established through either linguistic, contextual licensing or extra-linguistic factors related to discourse. Much of the literature on pronouns, however, is either grammar-oriented, focusing on the correlations of, for example, null pronouns with other parts of the grammar ('rich agreement', a rich determiner system, or word order). Other authors focus solely on the information structure (IS) of anaphor–antecedent relations and contextual licensing. A crucial question that needs to be answered, however, is if and how these morphosyntactic and information-structure dimensions interact. In order to investigate how the presence or absence of subject pronouns reflects the flow of new and old information and of changing topics of discourse, we need a deeply annotated corpus, enriched with morphosyntactic and information-structural annotation. In this article, we report on how such a corpus can be developed for early Irish using rich annotation and semi-supervised coreference resolution.

Coreference resolution is an NLP task developed in the 1960s that involves determining all referring expressions that point to the same real-world entity. A referring expression in this case is often either a noun phrase (NP) (*the woman*, *Mary*) or a pronoun (*she*), either of which refer to an entity in the real world known as the referent (a specific woman evident in the context) (Sapena et al., 2013). The goal of a coreference-resolution system is to output all the coreference chains of a given text, thus identifying *a woman*, *Mary* and *she* as coreferring in the sequence *A woman walked in. It was Mary. She started to speak.*. This may allow us to gain insights into not only pronominal forms and functions, but also into topic chains and shifts (if the text continues *When she had finished, John asked a question*, then the topic has shifted from Mary to John). Irish is particularly interesting within this context, since its use of subject pronouns has changed considerably over time, it having been essentially a null-subject language in the earliest documentation, and gradually developing a requirement for overt subject pronouns in most parts of the verbal paradigm.

In this article, we focus on developing semi-automatic coreference resolution for Old Irish. We start by evaluating existing language resources for early Irish and assessing how these need to be extended to be suitable for our task (Section 2). In Section 3, we outline the necessary preprocessing stages as well as presenting an automatic part-of-speech (POS) tagger for Old Irish, before turning to our main task of coreference resolution in Section 4.

2. Current Irish Corpora

One aspect of the workflow is the building of a diachronic corpus of Irish, annotated with part of speech and information-structural features. Existing Irish corpora can be divided into two categories. First, there are large online text corpora, with minimal annotation. These include:

- the Thesaurus Linguae Hibernicae (TLH) (Kelly and Fogarty, 2006);
- the Corpus of Electronic Texts (CELT);
- the Historical Irish Corpus.

Where these are annotated at all, this annotation is generally limited to standard Text Encoding Initiative (TEI) annotation for text structure, and does not extend to POS tagging or annotation of syntactic features. Second, there are a few linguistically annotated corpora. Examples of this type of corpus include:

- Parsed Old and Middle Irish Corpus (POMIC) (Lash, 2014), a selection of fourteen short texts, largely from the Old Irish period, manually annotated with POS tags and constituent structure;
- the Universal Dependency (UD) treebanks of Old Irish and Middle Irish, which are currently works in progress, and are not included in version 2.10 of the UD treebanks. The Old Irish treebanks currently available consist of the St Gall glosses on Priscian (around 22,000 tokens), while for Middle Irish there are around 800 tokens of *Scéla Mucce Meic Dathó* (The Tale of Mac Dathó's Pig), not all of which have been tagged;
- The online database of the St Gall glosses, on which the UD Old Irish treebanks of the same text are based;
- The Corpus Palaeohibernicum, which contains over 70 annotated Old and Middle Irish texts, in spreadsheet form.

Clearly, none of the large online corpora are sufficient as they stand for research into the diachrony of subject pronouns in Irish, but they do provide a valuable resource of digitised texts. Of the existing annotated corpora, POMIC is the most immediately useful for our purposes, as it consists of Penn-style tagged and parsed texts. It lacks IS annotation, however, which is required for our study of how the use of subject pronouns changes over time in Irish. We are therefore building a larger, POS-tagged corpus, which will be augmented with IS annotation. The other linguistically annotated resources detailed above may, however, prove useful as training data for a POS tagger, and as future target texts for incorporation into the corpus. This corpus is being built to conform to the standards of the ongoing Parsed Historical Corpus of the Welsh Language (PARSHCWL) (Meelen and Willis, 2021; Meelen and Willis, 2022), a Penn-style treebank of historical Welsh (Willis and Mittendorf, 2004b) based on the Historical Corpus of the Welsh Language 1500–1850 (HCWL) (Willis and Mittendorf, 2004a).

2.1. POMIC

POMIC consists of fourteen manually annotated texts with a Penn-style tagset adapted for Old and Middle Irish. The annotation scheme was adapted from the 2010 version of the manual for the Penn Corpora of Historical English (Santorini, 2022). The texts span the period between around 700 and 1100 CE. We use POMIC as a starting point. The majority of the texts – ten of fourteen – are at least arguably of Old Irish date, meaning that they most likely predate the 10th century CE, generally taken as when Old Irish gives way to Middle Irish (McCone, 1996, p. 140). In practice, distinguishing Old from Middle Irish is not simple, but the preponderance of Old Irish material in the POMIC data means that it can be used to train a reasonably accurate tagger for Old Irish.

2.2. Necessary Extensions

Although useful as a starting point, POMIC requires a number of extensions for our purposes. In the first place, the manual tagging process understandably led to some errors, which need correcting in order to use POMIC as a training corpus for a POS tagger. For example, the tag and token of the perfective particle *ro*, normally `(RO ro)` in POMIC, are occasionally inverted, giving `(ro RO)`. The POS tagger is case-sensitive, so this will be interpreted as a separate token and tagset, reducing the overall accuracy. Furthermore, the annotation scheme, and particularly the use of compound tags, leads to a very large number of discrete tags, significantly complicating the process of training a tagger. We therefore reduce the number of tags by either splitting the compound tags into individual tokens or by reducing them to a single tag, detailed further below. We also remove discrete tags for initial-consonant mutations (tagged by Lash as `NAS`, `LEN`, and `GEM`).

We also need to add information not included in the POMIC annotation scheme. The existing tagged texts lack the following information which could be salient for the research questions we want to answer:

- person–number information for verbal forms: this information will be useful for investigating whether there are any patterns in the use of pronouns that correlate to specific persons and numbers of subjects;
- individual tokens for infixed and suffixed pronouns – these are particularly important, as they can be involved in coreference chains, and can refer to separate entities from the verb with which they form a single prosodic word;
- person–number information for pronominal forms and conjugated prepositions, which will be useful for establishing coreference further downstream.

3. Preprocessing and POS tagging

Creating a POS tagger or any other dedicated NLP tool for a historical language is challenging for a number of reasons. First and foremost, there are issues of data scarcity: historical languages are often classified as extremely low-resource from an NLP point of view,[1] because the amount of data is necessarily finite due to the surviving attestation, and often also limited in range. In addition, not all data is easily available or accessible. Finally, if material is available, it often requires much preprocessing, because orthography is not standardised.

The situation is further complicated by the fact that historical languages are not only low-resource but also under-researched from an NLP point of view: whereas there are numerous off-the-shelf tools available for basic preprocessing and annotation in modern varieties (even modern varieties of Irish and other Celtic languages), this is not the case for their historical counterparts. Since Old Irish differs significantly from Present-Day Irish, we cannot simply apply or even easily modify existing tools, e.g. tokenisers, morphological transducers and POS taggers (Uí Dhonnchadha, 2002; Uí Dhonnchadha et al., 2003; Uí Dhonnchadha and Van Genabith, 2006).[2]

The lack of NLP resources for early Irish ultimately reflects the fact that the extremely complex inflectional system, the phonological challenges of mutated initial consonants, and the orthographic inconsistencies, even of edited texts, significantly complicate the processing of early Irish source material. There has been some work on producing a general POS tagger for early Irish (Lynn, 2012), but this was, by the author's own admission, "rudimentary": the results published show that the tagger could only differentiate between types of part of speech (verb, noun, etc.), but no finer detail of inflection could be distinguished. More recently, there has been work to develop computational methods for identifying and tagging Old Irish weak verbs, building on Uí Dhonnchadha's work on Modern Irish (Fransen, 2019; Fransen, 2020b; Fransen, 2020a). While this work deals with the right period in the history of Irish for our work, we require a tagger that functions more comprehensively, meaning that we cannot make use of Fransen's previous work in this area.

Efforts have been made in recent years to develop an Old Irish lemmatiser (Dereza, 2016; Dereza, 2018; Dereza, 2019), trained on the Dictionary of the Irish Language, but even the most recent version cannot lemmatise everything (accuracy ranges from 64.9% for unknown tokens to 99.2% for known tokens) and it was tested on a rather small corpus ($83k$ tokens). We use this for new texts as, despite the error rate, it is still an improvement on the complete absence of lemmatisation. It does not, however, address normalisation of orthography, which is why we deal with this separately, both for POMIC, used as a starting point, as well as for new texts.

In the following subsections we discuss all stages of preprocessing and POS tagging, which are necessary prerequisites to successful performance of coreference Resolution.

3.1. Normalisation

Even in POMIC, which is based on published text editions, there is orthographic variation. Some of this is an unavoidable consequence of working with historical data, from a period prior to standardisation. Additionally, the texts in POMIC were edited by various editors, following different editorial practices: some editions are more diplomatic, more or less directly reflecting the manuscript, while others attempt to restore a reconstructed "original" text by undoing modernisations or errors of later scribes.

One type of variation that can be controlled relatively easily at an early stage is the spelling of long vowels, which in POMIC are indicated either with macrons (ā, ē, ī, ō, ū) or with an acute accent (á, é, í, ó, ú). The two spelling practices are both used in editions of early Irish texts to denote long vowels, the former when a long vowel is not marked in a manuscript, the latter for when it is indicated with a diacritic. For the purpose of training a tagger on a small training corpus,[3] it is preferable to have just one spelling for each long vowel in the language as it reduces the number of unique tokens. Thus, for the moment at least, we automatically replace the spellings with macrons with those with acute accents. However, as the corpus develops and the accuracy of the tagger improves, we will be able to reintroduce spelling variation, reducing the amount of normalisation required during preprocessing. In the first instance, we expect this to reduce the accuracy of the tagger, but, with enough tokens in the corpus, it should be possible to retain a reasonable level of accuracy with a greater degree of orthographic variation.

3.2. Splitting and Combining Tokens

In the POMIC annotation scheme, an entire verbal complex (a prosodic element that can consist of preverbs, infixed or suffixed pronouns, aspectual particles, and the finite verb) is treated as a single token. In order to be able to use the POMIC texts for coreference resolution, these must be split into individual tokens. Consider:

[1]Regarding early Irish specifically, note the reference to it as an "under-resourced language" by Dereza (2019).

[2]For some historical languages, this situation has recently improved with the release of the Classical Language Toolkit (Johnson et al., 2021), but historical Irish is not presently covered by this toolkit.

[3]On the problems of orthographical variation in NLP, and the benefits and difficulties of "canonicalisation" as a way to address this issue, see Piotrowski (2012, ch. 3, 6).

(1) *do-* *s-* *raithminestar*
PV PRO-3PL call.ASP-VBD-3SG
'has called them to mind'

POMIC tags this as `(PV+X+VBD-RO)`, treating the entire verbal complex as a single token. Given that the infixed pronoun *-s-* can participate in coreference relations with other noun phrases in the text, subsuming it into a single token with the verb is undesirable. Moreover, such long tags with many variable components make it more difficult to automate the POS-tagging process with machine learning. We have to break up composite tags such as this into their constituent parts, the break point being denoted with the symbol `#`, resulting in this example being tagged as:

(2)
```
(PV do#)
(NP-OBJ (PROI-3PL s#))
(ASP-VBD-3SG raithminestar)
```

This allows us to enrich the annotation of the texts further downstream in the workflow, and should accelerate annotation of new texts.

Similarly, for a number of combinations, POMIC treats the sequence of preposition and possessive pronoun, which can form a single prosodic word in Irish, as a single token:

(3) *atá* *ocom chungid*
be-3SG at-my seeking-D
'she is seeking me'

POMIC tags *ocom* here as `(P+PRO$)`. We instead separate the possessive pronoun from the preposition, yielding:

(4)
```
(BEPI-3SG atá)
(PP (P oco#)
(PRO-G-1SG m)
(NP (VBN-D chungid)))
```

This means that only conjugated prepositions, which are not easily reducible to their constituent elements, are treated as single tokens (analogous to inflected verbs), while other combinations of preposition and personal pronoun are separated into discrete tokens.

There are also instances in which it is useful to combine tokens treated by POMIC as separate. This is particularly the case in stereotyped adverbial phrases, such as:

(5) *iar* *na* *bárach*
after POSSESSIVE morrow/milking.time
'the next day, tomorrow'

A particular problem presented by this collocation is that it is difficult to determine the gender of the possessive pronoun *a* (here nasalised as *na*), which anyway does not have an antecedent. In POMIC, this is treated as a prepositional phrase:

(6)
```
(PP (P ar)
(NAS n)
(NP (PRO$ a)
(N-D bárach)))
```

Given that this phrase functions as an adverb from an early stage of the language, we instead combine the tokens and tag as follows:

(7)
```
(ADV ar!na!bárach)
```

3.3. Refining the POS tagset

As well as using compound verbal tags, POMIC follows the Penn annotation scheme in including a number of compound nominal tags. These too are simplified; thus, `(ADJ+NS-G óc-ban)` 'young woman' is reduced to `(NS-G óc-ban)`. We also combine POMIC's mutation tokens with the following token, in order to avoid the corpus containing surplus tokens that might be susceptible to confusion with others that are more salient for our research questions. Representation of mutations in early Irish sources is a difficult topic in its own right, and indeed it is sometimes unclear whether a mutation should be considered a feature of the mutating or the mutated word. In our corpus, we attempt to achieve a reasonable degree of uniformity in their representation, while maintaining an awareness that this might not always be possible. Thus, in the revised corpus, (8) becomes (9).

(8)
```
(CP-ADV (C co)
(NAS m)
(IP-SUB (BED buí)))
```

(9)
```
(CP-ADV (C co)
(IP-SUB (BED-3SG mbuí)))
```

As the above examples make clear, we also enrich the POMIC tagset with person–number (and, where relevant, gender) information. This applies to verbs, pronouns, and conjugated prepositions. These alterations bring the revised corpus into alignment with the Welsh PARSHCWL corpus, and provide additional information useful for our research questions. Overall, we reduce the overall number of distinct tags to around 340, while also enriching the information contained in the individual tags.

3.4. Training a POS Tagger

POMIC gives us 30*k* tokens (including punctuation) that can be used to start training a POS tagger. This is too little material to train any off-the-shelf neural-network-based tagger, but it is enough to start incrementally training a Memory-Based Tagger such as the TiMBL MBT (Daelemans et al., 2003). Even though this is not a recently developed tool, it is one of the most effective methods for developing a POS tagger from scratch, since it can learn from such specific features as initial and final characters as well as the context, yielding high rates of accuracy even for extremely small data sets (Meelen et al., 2021). To train the POS tagger, we deleted all null elements, since they will not be present in the new texts planned for the future corpus. Initial results are given below with parameter settings that are manually optimised for this specific corpus. The Memory-Based Tagger (MBT) allows for optimisation of parameters for both preceding and following context, but also for up to the first three and last three characters of the word, which is useful for morphologically rich languages with various inflectional suffixes like Old Irish; for a full list of parameter options, see Daelemans et al. (2003) .

(10) Parameters:
```
-p dwdwfWaw
-P psssdwdwdwFawaw
-M 1100 -n 5 -% 8 -O+vS
-FColumns -G
K: -a0 -k1
U: -a0 -mM -k17 -dIL
```

We do a 10-fold cross-validation to evaluate the results, measuring the global accuracy, which averages the harmonic means of all 340 unique POS tags for seen and unseen (i.e. known and unknown) tokens. For the 10-fold cross-validation, we separate a 10% test set from 90% training data to make sure we do not evaluate on training data. In order to control for variation and repetition at any point in our training data, we repeat this test-training division 10 times and evaluate the results of each round, using precision, recall and f-scores to calculate the final global accuracy:

(11) Global Accuracy: 0.751
Global Accuracy seen words: 0.829
Global Accuracy unseen words: 0.580

These preliminary results are not optimal, but they form a first step to providing new Old Irish texts with highly detailed morphosyntactic tags. Once new texts are tagged and manually corrected, they will be added to the training corpus, which will at this stage – where we have only a $30k$-token Gold Standard, but over 340 unique POS tags – improve the results significantly. In addition, when more texts are preprocessed and added to the corpus, we can create word embeddings which will allow us to test neural-network based taggers like TARGER (Chernodub et al., 2019). Improving POS tagging results is important when new texts are added to our treebank, but we leave this for future research since these results are sufficient for our main Coreference Resolution trials at hand.

4. Coreference Resolution

We use the Cesax coreference resolution algorithm (Komen, 2013) as a starting point for our Old Irish Coreference Resolution (Komen, 2019). This software was originally designed for use on historical English data, but has since been extended to include support for several other languages, including Dutch, Chechen, and Welsh. Although Irish is not yet one of the languages supported by the software in its unmodified state, some relatively simple adjustments can be made to the software's settings in order to accommodate historical Irish data. Cesax is particularly appropriate for our corpus due to the fact that it can import Penn-style treebank files for IS annotation, which can then be exported back to PSD (phrase-structure description) format, as well as to a variety of other formats, such as Folia XML.

4.1. Semi-Supervised Method

The Cesax coreference-resolution algorithm uses a set of hierarchically ordered constraints to evaluate possible solutions. It evaluates every noun phrase in the input text individually, trying to find connections and ultimately the best antecedent based on the following information:

- NP type
- grammatical role (function)
- person, gender and number

NP types include pronouns, definite/indefinite NPs, demonstratives, proper nouns, etc. Grammatical roles include subject and object (of verbs and/or prepositions) as well as possessive/genitive. Pronominal elements manifest person, gender and number in Old Irish. Non-pronominal NPs are all considered to be third-person.

In order to process and annotate Irish texts in Cesax, we have to carry out a series of tasks:

1. Define the nodes that can be involved in coreference in Irish. By default, Cesax only targets NPs, nominal *wh*-phrases, pronouns and proper nouns. This works for historical English, but misses some nodes that we want to target for coreference in Irish, meaning that the resulting coreference chains would be incomplete. We therefore edited the settings of Cesax to add conjugated prepositions and finite verbs to the possible targets for coreference. Targeting finite verbs is particularly important, since this allows us to capture null subjects in coreference chains.

2. Replace the historical English pronouns in the Cesax settings with those for Irish. At this stage, we must try to avoid including homophonous pronouns in more than one category. For example, the emphatic pronoun *som*, which can refer either to a third-person singular masculine or neuter referent, or to a third-person plural one, has to be treated as generically third-person.

3. Import texts into Cesax. Cesax converts Penn-style .psd files into XML documents, which are then saved as .psdx files. At this stage, we can also check for any pronominals or demonstratives that fall outside our existing lists of such forms (Tools > Features > Renew features of… > NP – all noun-phrase features), and add any new forms, shown in the "Errors" tab, to the relevant categories.

4. Perform a manual check for conflicts by opening the .psdx file in an XML editor. Due to the use of wildcards to capture all of the possible forms of pronouns in our texts, some forms are assigned more than one classification. For example, the 1sg. emphatic pronoun *sa* is sometimes misclassified as "unknown" by the software. This is due to the presence of the string "s?" in the category "Pers", used to capture the Class A infixed pronoun *-s-* (tokenised in our corpus as `PROI-3SGF s#` or `PROI-3PL s#`). Performing a check for "unknown;" or any other conflicts in the person–gender–number (PGN) features of the NPs in the XML document, and correcting them there, avoids problems when running semi-automatic coreference resolution.

5. Run semi-automatic coreference resolution on the text. Cesax looks for likely coreference targets by assessing the text against a series of constraints, in order to suggest what the most likely coreference for a given NP might be.

4.2. Targets

Several part-of-speech types can act as target for coreference in our Irish texts. These include:

- pronouns
- NPs
- inflected verbs and prepositions
- emphasising particles (*notae augentes*)

Some of these are not automatically targeted by Cesax. Cesax supports targeting pronouns and NPs, as these are also potential targets for coreference in English. Emphasising particles (*notae augentes* in some scholarship) are tagged as pronouns in our text files, hence can be easily targeted for coreference. Inflected verbs and prepositions must be added manually to the categories to be targeted, however. This is done by adding the terms P-*, VB*-[1234]*, COP*-[1234]*, and BE*-[1234]* to the tab "Phrase Types" in the Cesax settings.

4.3. Constraints

The coreference-resolution algorithm in Cesax tests NPs (and, with our modifications, inflected verbs and prepositions) against various constraints in order to establish the most likely coreferent for a given NP. For now, these constraints are being retained, but will be refined if it is found that any of them do not apply to Irish as well as they do to historical English. The algorithm assigns each possible coreferent a score based on how many of the constraints it violates; the higher the score, the less likely a candidate is considered as a target for coreference. For example, the further a coreference source is from its potential target (for example, the further a pronoun is from an NP it might refer to), the less likely it is deemed to be that there should be a direct coreferential link between the two, and the algorithm will instead attempt to identify a target nearer to the source. The constraints are tested in a given order, which the Cesax manual itself notes is designed for Modern British English. It may therefore require additional adjustment and refinement for Irish, but it nevertheless provides a good starting point.

5. Case Studies

In the following case studies, we demonstrate how Cesax can be used to conduct coreference resolution on Irish texts, and how the result can subsequently be exported to other formats for future analysis. At present, the accuracy rate of the semi-automatic coreference resolution is low: on a test passage of four sentences, the algorithm selected the correct antecedent in just under 14% of cases. This is initially a disappointing result, but there are some positive trends that can be identified in the links that the algorithm makes correctly. The results become more accurate the further into a passage of text the algorithm is allowed to run. This is to be expected, given that the first section of any given passage of text is likely to include very few coreferential links, whereas later sections of the text are likely to contain pronouns (or finite verbs) that refer to NPs introduced in the earlier sections. Furthermore, the algorithm regularly correctly identifies the link between a finite verb with null subject and its nominal antecedent in a previous clause. Since this is a type of coreference target we added specifically for early Irish, this is an encouraging result. We are continuing to work to improve the results of the semi-automatic process through refining our settings.

5.1. NP

Fig. 1 shows a coreference chain for the proper noun (personal name) *Laisrén*. This coreference chain was generated semi-automatically using Cesax's coreference algorithm, and corrected manually. The chain for *Laisrén* includes the proper noun *Laisrén* itself; the finite verbs *áin* '(he) fasted', *cúala* '(he) heard' (twice), *glúais* '(he) moves', *to-ocaib* '(he) raises', *do-beir* '(he) bears, makes', and *con-aca* '(he) saw' etc.; the possessive pronoun *na* and *a* 'his' (three times); the infixed pronoun *-n-* 'him' and the conjugated prepositions *fair* 'over him' and *fris* 'to him'. It also crosses other coreference chains, such as that between *in guth* 'the voice' and *sodain* 'at that [voice]'. Cesax makes an error when processing this semi-automatically: due to *clúana* 'of Clúain' in the first line being a third-person singular NP, the algorithm automatically assumes that it is coreferent with *Laisrén*. This is corrected manually by deleting the coreference link.

5.2. Emphasising Particles Case Study

Language-specific adaptations of the Cesax algorithm are likely to improve its performance. One area that seems like a plausible area for improvement concerns the emphasising particles (*notae augentes*). Subject pronouns are obligatorily null with Old Irish finite verbs. However, in some contexts, verbs appear with emphasising particles. These particles have sometimes been analysed as pronouns, and this is how they are tagged in the corpus. It has also been suggested that there is an interaction between use of these elements and the marking of topics (Griffith, 2008; Griffith, 2011).

Correct coreference relations for an example containing multiple emphasising particles are shown in Fig. 2 (second person singular) and 3 (first person singular). It seems that use of the particles indicates repeated alternation between first and second person as the discourse topic. In this case, the existing Cesax algorithm produced the correct coreference resolution, since the two coreference chains clearly differ in person. Where they do not, the coreference-resolution algorithm could perhaps be improved by the addition of a resolution rule to disfavour an immediately preceding element as the antecedent for an emphasising particle.

6. Postprocessing

Once coreference resolution has been determined and corrected, the result is re-exported to PSD format, as well as other formats such as Folia XML, through Cesax. In PSD format, the coreference annotation is expressed as features added to the node of the original token. The following example demonstrates a second-person singular emphasising particle *su*, annotated as representing a subject grammatical function with information-structure marked as identical to a preceding element in the coreference chain.

(12)
```
(NP-SBJ (FS-IPdist 0)
(FS-RefType Identity)
(FS-NdDist 1)
(FS-GrRole Subject)
(FS-PGN 2s)
(FS-NPtype Pro)
(PRO-2SG (FS-IPdist 0)
(FS-RefType Identity)
(FS-NdDist 2)
(FS-GrRole unknown)
(FS-PGN 2s)
(FS-NPtype Pro)
(LEX su)))
```

7. Conclusion

In this article, we have considered the ways in which it is necessary to adapt existing resources to develop a historical parsed Irish treebank with rich mark-up information structure and coreference. To fully utilise the POMIC corpus for our needs, preprocessing was necessary, notably separation of compound tags into individual tokens, making those tokens accessible to the coreference-resolution algorithm in Cesax. For early Irish, it was necessary to adapt the Cesax algorithm so that finite verbs and conjugated prepositions can be incorporated into coreference chains. Further refinement of the process of semi-automatic coreference resolution may be motivated by other specific aspects of early Irish grammar such as the emphasising particles. Other such refinements, both to the POS-tagging and coreference-resolution algorithm, may be required as more texts are added to the corpus.

8. Acknowledgements

We gratefully acknowledge the support of the Arts and Humanities Research Council via the award of AHRC–DFG UK–German collaborative research project in the humanities, AHRC Research Grant AH/V00347X/1 for the project 'The history of pronominal subjects in the languages of northern Europe'.

9. Bibliographical References

Daelemans, W., Zavrel, J., van den Bosch, A., and Van der Sloot, K. (2003). MBT: Memory-based tagger. *Reference Guide: ILK Technical Report-ILK*, pages 3–13.

Dereza, O. (2016). Building a dictionary-based lemmatizer for Old Irish. In *Actes de la conférence conjointe JEP-TALN-RECITAL*, volume 6, pages 12–17.

Dereza, O. (2018). Lemmatization for ancient languages: Rules or neural networks? In Dmitry Ustalov, et al., editors, *Artificial Intelligence and Natural Language*, pages 35–47. Springer.

Dereza, O. (2019). Lemmatisation for under-resourced languages with sequence-to-sequence learning: A case of early Irish. In *Proceedings of Third Workshop "Computational linguistics and language science"*, volume 4, pages 113–124.

Fransen, T. (2019). *Past, present and future: Computational approaches to mapping historical Irish cognate verb forms*. PhD, School of Linguistic, Speech and Communication Sciences, Trinity College Dublin.

Fransen, T. (2020a). Automatic morphological analysis and interlinking of historical Irish cognate verb forms. In Elliott Lash, et al., editors, *Morphosyntactic Variation in Medieval Celtic Languages: Corpus-based approaches*, pages 49–84. De Gruyter Mouton.

Fransen, T. (2020b). Automatic morphological parsing of Old Irish verbs using finite-state transducers. *LanguageLeeds Working Papers*, 1:15–28.

Griffith, A. (2008). The animacy hierarchy and the distribution of the *notae augentes* in Old Irish. *Ériu*, 58:55–75.

Griffith, A. (2011). Old Irish pronouns: Agreement affixes vs. clitic arguments. In Andrew Carnie, editor, *Formal approaches to Celtic linguistics*, pages 65–94. Cambridge Scholars Publishing, Newcastle upon Tyne.

Johnson, K. P., Burns, P. J., Stewart, J., Cook, T., Besnier, C., and Mattingly, W. J. B. (2021). The Classical Language Toolkit: An NLP framework for pre-modern languages. In *Proceedings of the 59th Annual Meeting of the Association for Computational Linguistics and the 11th International Joint Conference on Natural Language Processing: System Demonstrations*, pages 20–29, Online, August. Association for Computational Linguistics.

Komen, E. R. (2013). Predicting referential states using enriched texts. In *The Third Workshop on Annotation of Corpora for Research in the Humanities (ACRH-3)*, page 49.

Lynn, T. (2012). Medieval Irish and computational linguistics. *Australian Celtic Journal*, 10:13–28.

McCone, K. (1996). *Towards a Relative Chronology of Ancient and Medieval Celtic Sound Change. Maynooth.* The Cardinal Press.

Meelen, M. and Willis, D. (2021). Towards a historical treebank of Middle and Early Modern Welsh, part I: Workflow and POS tagging. *Journal of Celtic Linguistics*, 22:125–154.

Meelen, M. and Willis, D. (2022). Towards a historical treebank of Middle and Modern Welsh: Syntactic parsing. *Journal of Historical Syntax*, forthcoming.

Meelen, M., Roux, E., and Hill, N. (2021). Optimisation of the largest annotated Tibetan corpus combining rule-based, memory-based & deep-learning methods. *Transactions on Asian and Low-Resource Language Information Processing*.

Piotrowski, M. (2012). Natural language processing for historical texts. *Synthesis lectures on human language technologies*, 5(2):1–157.

Santorini, B. (2022). Annotation manual for the Penn Parsed Corpora of Historical English and the Parsed Corpus of Early English Correspondence.

Sapena, E., Padró, L., and Turmo, J. (2013). A constraint-based hypergraph partitioning approach to coreference resolution. *Computational Linguistics*, 39(4):847–884.

Siewierska, A. (1999). From anaphoric pronoun to agreement marker: Why objects don't make it. *Folia Linguistica*, 33:225–251.

Uí Dhonnchadha, E. and Van Genabith, J. (2006). A part-of-speech tagger for Irish using finite-state morphology and constraint grammar disambiguation. In *Proceedings of the Fifth International Conference on Language Resources and Evaluation (LREC'06)*, pages 2241–2244, Genoa, Italy, May. European Language Resources Association (ELRA).

Uí Dhonnchadha, E., Pháidín, C. N., and Genabith, J. V. (2003). Design, implementation and evaluation of an inflectional morphology finite state transducer for Irish. *Machine Translation*, 18(3):173–193.

Uí Dhonnchadha, E. (2002). A two-level morphological analyser and generator for Irish using finite-state transducers. In *LREC*.

Van Gelderen, E. (2011). *The linguistic cycle: Language change and the language faculty*. Oxford University Press, Oxford.

Willis, D. and Mittendorf, I. (2004b). Ein historisches Korpus der kymrischen Sprache. In Erich Poppe, editor, *Keltologie heute: Themen und Fragestellungen*, pages 135–42. Nodus, Münster.

10. Language Resource References

[Royal Irish Academy]. (no date). *Historical Irish Corpus 1600–1926*. Royal Irish Academy.

Andersen, Erik. (no date). *Universal Dependencies treebank of Middle Irish*.

Bernhard Bauer and Rijcklof Hofman and Pádraic Moran. (2017). *St Gall Priscian Glosses*.

Chernodub, A., Oliynyk, O., Heidenreich, P., Bondarenko, A., Hagen, M., Biemann, C., and Panchenko, A. (2019). TARGER: Neural argument mining at your fingertips. In *Proceedings of the 57th Annual Meeting of the Association for Computational Linguistics: System Demonstrations*, pages 195–200.

Doyle, Adrian. (no date). *Universal Dependencies treebank for the Old Irish glosses of St. Gall*.

Kelly, Patricia, Brady, Niall and Fogarty, Hugh. (2006). *Thesaurus Linguae Hibernicae*. School of Irish, Celtic Studies, Irish Folklore & Linguistics, University College Dublin.

Komen, Erwin. (2019). *CESAX: Coreference Editor for Syntactically Annotated XML corpora*. Radboud University Nijmegen.

Lash, Elliott. (2014). *POMIC: The parsed Old and Middle Irish corpus. Version 0.1.* Dublin Institute for Advanced Studies.

Stifter, David, Bauer, Bernhard, Qiu, Fangzhe, Lash, Elliott, White, Nora, Nguyen, Truc Ha, Felici, Francesco, Osarobo, Godstime, Ji, Tianbo, Ganly, Ellen, Nooij, Lars, and Bulatovas, Romanas. (2020). *Corpus Palaeohibernicum*.

Willis, David and Mittendorf, Ingo. (2004a). *Historical Corpus of the Welsh Language 1500–1850*. University of Cambridge.

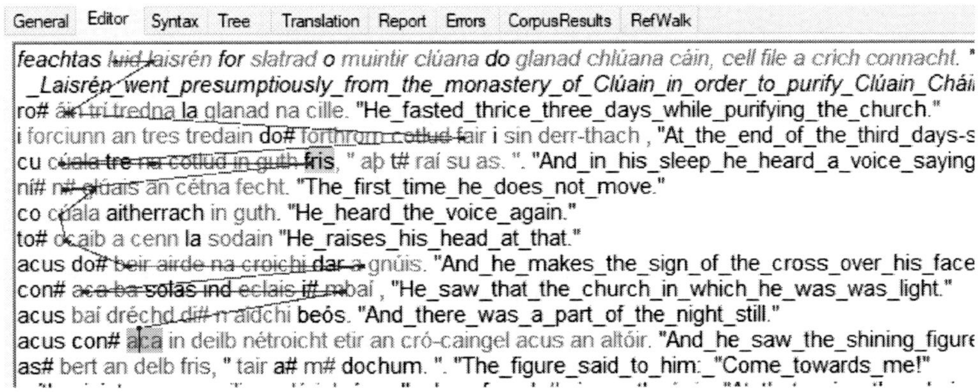

Figure 1: Coreference chain for *Laisrén*

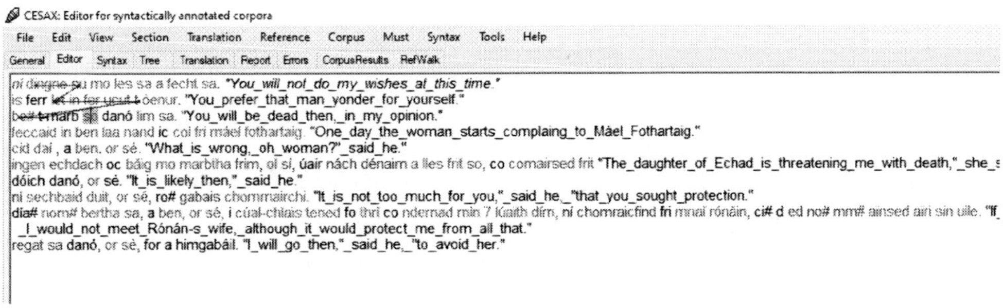

Figure 2: Coreference chain for 2sg *nota augens*

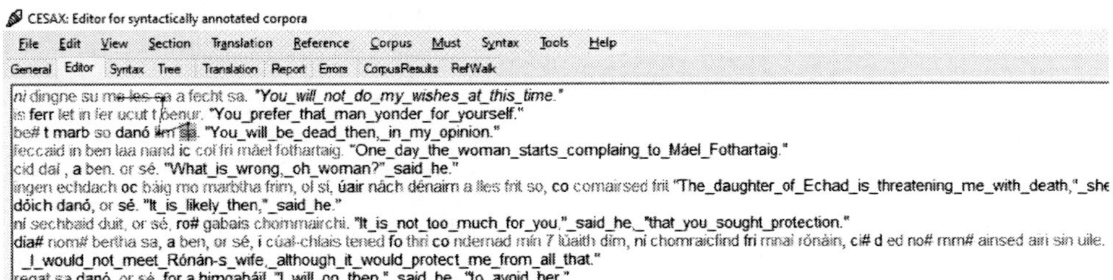

Figure 3: Coreference chain for 1sg *nota augens*

Proceedings of the CLTW 4 @ LREC2022 , pages 94–98
Marseille, 20-25 June 2022

Use of Transformer-Based Models for Word-Level Transliteration of the Book of the Dean of Lismore

Edward Gow-Smith[1], Mark McConville[2], William Gillies[3], Jade Scott[2], Roibeard Ó Maolalaigh[2]
[1]University of Sheffield, [2]University of Glasgow, [3]University of Edinburgh
egow-smith1@sheffield.ac.uk, Mark.McConville@glasgow.ac.uk

Abstract

The Book of the Dean of Lismore (BDL) is a 16th-century Scottish Gaelic manuscript written in a non-standard orthography. In this work, we outline the problem of transliterating the text of the BDL into a standardised orthography, and perform exploratory experiments using Transformer-based models for this task. In particular, we focus on the task of word-level transliteration, and achieve a character-level BLEU score of 54.15 with our best model, a BART architecture pre-trained on the text of Scottish Gaelic Wikipedia and then fine-tuned on around 2,000 word-level parallel examples. Our initial experiments give promising results, but we highlight the shortcomings of our model, and discuss directions for future work.

Keywords: Low-Resource Neural Machine Translation, Transformer-Based Models, Scottish Gaelic, Historical Manuscript

1. Introduction

As a material object, the Book of the Dean of Lismore (henceforth BDL) is a manuscript consisting of 159 paper folios, thought to have been assembled between 1512 and 1526 in eastern Perthshire, primarily by James MacGregor (c.1480–1551), the vicar of Fortingall and titular Dean of St. Moluag's Cathedral on Lismore (Thomson, 1993, 59–60). It is believed to have been acquired by James MacPherson, the Ossian 'translator', from a Portree blacksmith around 1760, and was handed over to the Highland Society of Scotland in 1803. It is now located in the National Library of Scotland (Adv.MS.72.1.37).

As an information object, the BDL is primarily an eclectic collection of traditional Gaelic poetry, including bardic, heroic and informal verse, by diverse authors, both professional and amateur, Scottish and Irish. Perhaps the most notable feature of the manuscript is that the Gaelic verse was not written in the traditional, morphophonemic Gaelic system of orthography but rather in a heterodox, semi-phonemic system based on the one used for writing Scots at that time. Consider, for example, the following two versions of the first line of p.128:

- Ne wlli in teak mir a hest a zramm a der a weit trane
- Ní bhfuil an t-éag mar a theist, a dhream adeir a bhith tréan

The first version is essentially the one that appears in BDL itself, and the second is a reconstruction of how this would have been written in the traditional Gaelic orthography of the time. Note the seventh word *hest:theist*. The initial consonant in this word would have been pronounced as the voiceless glottal fricative [h] and this is clearly reflected in the Scots-based orthography. However, the reconstructed Gaelic *th* includes a representation of the underlying morphophoneme T which is associated with (at least) two different phonemes – the fortis /t/ (written as *t*) and the lenis /h/ (written as *th*). The vowel in the final word *trane:tréan* is another example – the vowel here is the front mid [e:], represented in Scots orthography using the discontinuous digraph *a_e* and in Gaelic as the (non-discontinuous) digraph *éa*.

Over the last 100 years, attempts have been made to **transcribe** some of the poems in BDL (i.e. decode the handwriting) and then to **transliterate** these into some version of traditional Gaelic orthography, e.g. (Quiggin, 1937; Ross, 1939; Gillies, 1977; Meek, 1982). However, until recently an internally consistent transcription and transliteration of the full manuscript had not been attempted. Since BDL is an indispensable part of the textual foundation for the *Faclair na Gàidhlig* project, which aims to create a comprehensive dictionary of Scottish Gaelic on historical principles, this has now become a priority. This paper reports on the first two phases of this work: (a) the production of a consistent transcription of the full BDL; and (b) initial experiments in constructing an automatic transliterator from the Scots-based orthography into traditional Gaelic orthography using a small amount of parallel training data.

2. Data

The work on creating a consistent digital transcription of the whole of BDL was undertaken by the third and fourth listed authors. The first phase of this project involved digitally re-transcribing the manuscript transcription of BDL produced by Rev. Walter McLeod in 1893, when the BDL folios were in better physical condition than they are nowadays (NLS MS.72.3.12). Once this had been completed, a second iteration involved comparing this digital transcription with the handwriting in the BDL itself, in order to identify and correct any apparent errors in McLeod's manuscript. (We are grateful to NLS for providing us with high-resolution digital images of both manuscripts.) In creating the digital transcription, a standard set of Unicode character points was used to encode non-ASCII glyphs in the BDL. In general, scribal contractions were not expanded. Some light markup was included for scribal insertions and deletions, and page and line numbers.

In order to provide some training data for our automatic transliterator, the third listed author provided reconstructed 'Dean's Text' transliterations for twelve of the poems in the BDL. Due to the small amount of data available, we decided to run experiments on word-level transliteration. Thus, the original transcriptions and reconstructed transliterations were aligned, where possible, at the word level. The majority of the data is word-to-word transliterated, but there are some cases where one word in the BDL is transliterated into multiple words in Scottish Gaelic, and vice versa, making up 7.4% of the data. A discussion of the shortcomings of this approach is given in Section 5.1. In total there were 1,962 examples, and 50 examples were randomly selected to give eval and test sets.

3. Experiments

We are interested in transliterating from the BDL to Scottish Gaelic (henceforth referred to as bdl-gd) and vice versa (likewise referred to as gd-bdl), although the first direction is of greater practical importance. Character-level BLEU score (Papineni et al., 2002) is used as an evaluation metric. We ran experiments on this task using Transformer-based models, implemented in Fairseq (Ott et al., 2019)[1]. For all experiments, tokenisation was performed at the character-level. The maximum sequence length was set at 20, to cover all of the available data whilst keeping computational requirements low. We also set the batch size at 1 due to the limited size of the training data, and the known problem of poor generalisation with large batch sizes (Keskar et al., 2016). For all of our models, the best performing model (by epoch) on the eval set was taken and evaluated on the test set. Full results are shown in Table 1, and in the rest of this section we discuss the various models and approaches used.

3.1. Parallel Data Only

Our first experiments were using just the available parallel data. We trained a Transformer (Vaswani et al., 2017) architecture with 2 layers and 2 attention heads for the encoder and decoder, and an embed dimension of 64, referred to as Transformer (tiny). We experimented with larger architectures, but found they were unable to learn from the available data. Our model was trained for 100,000 updates (~52 epochs), with a linear warm-up of the learning rate for 4,000 updates to 5e-4, then a linear decay to zero. We used the Adam optimizer (Kingma and Ba, 2014) with $\epsilon =$1e-6, $\beta = (0.9, 0.98)$. On bdl-gd, this model achieved BLEU scores of 35.32 on the eval set and 41.16 on the test set. On gd-bdl, this model achieved BLEU scores of 30.17 on the eval set and 46.26 on the test set (Table 1).

3.2. Monolingual Pre-Training

The next approach was to utilise monolingual Scottish Gaelic data for the task, so that the model would hopefully learn something of Scottish Gaelic orthography. For this, we used the text of Scottish Gaelic Wikipedia[2], split to the word level, giving ~600,000 words. We then pretrained BART (Lewis et al., 2019) architectures with the denoising task on this data. We first implemented a model with 2 layers, 2 attention heads, and embed dimension of 64 (referred to as BART (tiny) in reference to the Transformer model). We trained this model for 100,000 updates (~43 epochs). This model was then fine-tuned on the parallel training data, with the same hyperparameters as for Transformer (tiny). On bdl-gd, this model achieved BLEU score of 44.93 on the eval set, performing better than Transformer (tiny), and 38.64 on the test set, performing worse than Transformer (tiny). On gd-bdl, this model achieved BLEU scores of 21.04 on the eval set and 22.18 on the test set (Table 1), performing significantly worse than Transformer (tiny). It is expected that pre-training on monolingual Scottish Gaelic data will not be of help in this direction, but the significantly worse performance is surprising (see Section 4).

We next tried the default BART (base) architecture, consisting of 6 layers, 12 attention heads, and an embed dimension of 768. On bdl-gd, this model achieved BLEU scores of 58.68 on the eval set and 53.32 on the test set, significantly outperforming Transformer (tiny). On gd-bdl, this model achieved BLEU scores of 36.17 on the eval set and 30.15 on the test set. We also ran the same model with additional pretraining, up to 400,000 updates (~172 epochs), which has been shown to be of benefit to other Transformer-based models (Liu et al., 2019). On bdl-gd, this model achieved BLEU scores of 62.47 on the eval set and 53.75 on the test set, showing an increase in performance on both. On gd-bdl, this model achieved BLEU scores of 36.77 on the eval set and 38.88 on the test set, also showing an increase in performance on both (Table 1). We also experimented with finetuning for longer (also 400,000 updates compared to 100,000), but this was found to lead to a general decrease in performance in both directions, although it did improve the performance on the eval set for gd-bdl (Table 1).

3.3. Data Augmentation

Next, approaches were taken at augmenting the available training data, a common approach in low-resource

[1]We release our data and scripts for running our experiments at `https://github.com/edwardgowsmith/transliteration-book-of-the-dean-of-lismore`.

[2]`https://gd.wikipedia.org/`

Model	bdl-gd		gd-bdl	
	eval	test	eval	test
Transformer (tiny)	35.32	41.16	30.17	**46.26**
BART (tiny)	44.93	38.64	21.04	22.18
BART (base)	58.68	53.32	36.17	30.15
BART (base) + p/t longer	**62.47**	53.75	36.77	38.88
BART (base) + p/t longer + f/t longer	59.46	52.09	**36.94**	34.68
BART (base) + p/t longer + homophones	59.60	**54.15**	34.75	31.77

Table 1: Character-level BLEU scores of the models on the eval and test splits. Best results are shown in bold.

neural machine translation (Haddow et al., 2021). Since we are interested in word-level transliteration, and thus a word may be transliterated into a homophone of the provided example with a different spelling (specifically, a heterograph), we took an approach to augment the training data with homophones. We used IPA information for Scottish Gaelic provided by English Wiktionary[3] - the data was parsed in order to find homophones for words it the training data. Unfortunately, IPA information was only available for a small number of items, which increased the training data from 1,862 to 1,938 examples (an increase of ~4%). With the addition of this augmented training data, the BLEU score of BART (base) on the eval set decreased (from 62.47 to 59.60), but the BLEU score on the test set increased (from 53.75 to 54.15), which makes sense as the introduction of heterographs should allow the model to generalise better (although we note that the increase in performance is small). Interestingly, this model performs significantly worse in the reverse direction, with BLEU scores of 34.75 and 31.77 on the eval and test sets, respectively (discussed in Section 4). It should be noted that this approach assumes that heterographs in modern Scottish Gaelic were also heterographs at the time of the BDL, which should be a valid assumption. An alternative approach to augmenting the data would be to use a rule-based approach, which we leave to future work.

4. Discussion

In this section we discuss our results. From Table 1 we can see that, in general, the performance on gd-bdl is significantly worse than that on bdl-gd. This is to be expected, since the models have access to a large amount of monolingual Scottish Gaelic (gd) data, but BDL (bdl) is effectively an unseen language, which previous work has shown results in poor performance (see e.g. Üstün et al. (2021)). What is perhaps unexpected, however, is that our best-performing model on bdl-gd, BART (base) + p/t longer + homophones, performs significantly worse than the best in the opposite direction (31.77 compared to 46.26 on the test set). In fact, our best-performing model on gd-bdl, Transformer (tiny), does not use any monolingual Scottish Gaelic data. It seems likely that our models are overfitting on the train and eval sets, as a result of their small sizes. Attempts to avoid this could be made, including using multi-fold cross-validation. Additionally, it is hoped that we will have access to more parallel data in the future which will alleviate this problem, as well as the variance of performance across the eval and test splits.

4.1. Error Analysis

In this section, we perform an error analysis by taking our best-performing model and investigating which examples in the test set this model performed worse on (by character-level BLEU score). These are shown in Table 2. We note that these examples are relatively long; for shorter examples, our model generally performs better, which is typically expected but likely exaggerated in this case due to the increasing ambiguity of a word in the BDL as length increases. We note that our model struggles with spaces: no space is added when transliterating "eflay", and a space is erroneously added when transliterating "waiwill" (although the space is correctly removed when transliterating "dwgis i"). Since examples containing spaces on either the source or target side only make up a small amount of the parallel data, and the pretraining data contains no spaces, this is an expected area of difficulty, which we discuss further in Section 5.2. We also note that, out of the seven examples here, our model appears to output only three true Scottish Gaelic words ("mha fhàil" meaning "if found", "chuaiseach" meaning "cavities", and "mhíos" meaning "month"). This is not necessarily a problem, since we want our model to be able to output unseen words, for example old-fashioned spellings and proper nouns. However, contextual information may help to determine the validity of a given transliteration, though the limited data available may prove to limit the efficacy of such an approach. Interestingly, the model transliterates "di" as the "[UNK]" token, which is problematic.

4.2. Learning of Scottish Gaelic Spelling Rules

We note that all of the outputs from our best model are *plausible* words, in that they obey the spelling rules of Scottish Gaelic. This is not the case for the Transformer (tiny) model trained only on the parallel data — as an example "dwgis" is transliterated by this

[3]https://en.wiktionary.org/

model into "duigas", which is not an acceptable Scottish Gaelic word, since a medial consonant must be surrounded by vowels of the same type (Gillies, 2009). This suggests that the training on monolingual data has allowed our model to learn the rules of Scottish Gaelic spelling, which has in turn improved performance on the transliteration task.

Input	Output	Reference
eflay	e'léamh	a' phláigh
dwgis i	duise	dtugas-sa
chotly^{t}sy^{t}	chuaiseach	chodlas-sa
wawaill	mha fháil	bhfaghbha'il
deinar̄	díonar	d'éinfhear
feanē	fén	phéin
zonicht	dhuanancht	dhona
di	[UNK]	do
gawe	gáimh	gabh
weiß^{t}	mhíos	bhíos

Table 2: The ten examples that our best performing model performed worse on for the test split (from bdl-gd).

5. Future Directions

Our preliminary experiments have shown promise in the task of transliterating the BDL, however there are many areas for improvement that we hope to address in future work.

5.1. Whole Sequence Transliteration

Since our work here is on word-level transliteration, it is unclear how this will extend to longer sequences, especially in the case of many-to-one transliteration. We take an example of transliterating a whole sequence with our model, shown in Table 3.

Input	A wēni^{t} za dwgis i grawġ
Output	a bhean dhá duis a' grádh
Reference	A bhean dhá dtugas-sa grádh

Table 3: Transliterating a whole sequence with our model.

In order to transliterate this whole sequence, we split it on whitespace and then pass each word individually to the model. Since, in this case, "dwgis i" is transliterated into a single word, our model cannot capture this (although note that this model fails to correctly transliterate these two words anyway (see Table 2)). An alternative approach to transliterating multi-word sequences may therefore be needed. Currently, due to our models being set at a max sequence length of 20, longer sequences cannot be directly given to the model.

5.2. Handling of Spaces

A related problem is the tendency of the models to struggle with handling spaces, both in the case of one-to-many and many-to-one transliteration. In order to help with this problem, it is likely we will need to include examples containing spaces during pre-training, or perform oversampling on the available training data to balance the number of examples with spaces and those without.

5.3. Data for Pre-Training

As stated in Section 3.2, we used data from Scottish Gaelic Wikipedia for pretraining, which is written in standardised modern Scottish Gaelic. For the purposes of our task, we are interested in generating transliterations which are faithful to the pronunciation at the time of the BDL. Hence, other data sources may provide more relevance for pre-training, such as Corpas na Gàidhlig[4] which contains transcribed texts dating back to the 17th century, and this is a direction of future work.

6. Related Work

There is no previous work, to the best of our knowledge, that uses Transformer-based models for tasks involving Scottish Gaelic. However, such approaches have been applied to other languages in the Celtic family: multilingual BERT (Devlin et al., 2019) contains Irish, Welsh and Breton in its training data, and there is a monolingual BERT for Irish (Barry et al., 2021) which was shown to outperform multilingual BERT on a dependency parsing test. There have been previous approaches at applying Transformer-based models to the task of word-level transliteration. Wu et al. (2021) applied the vanilla Transformer to the NEWS 2015 shared task (Zhang et al., 2015), outperforming previous models. Singh and Bansal (2021) also applied various sizes of Transformer architectures to the task of transliterating Hindi and Punjabi to English.

7. Conclusion

In this paper we discuss approaches to training Transformer-based models on the task of transliterating the Book of the Dean of Lismore (BDL) from its idiosyncratic orthography into a standardised Scottish Gaelic orthography. In particular, we outline our preliminary experiments training these models for word-level transliteration using both parallel word-level transliteration data for finetuning and monolingual Scottish Gaelic data for pretraining. Our best performing model was able to achieve a character-level BLEU score of 54.15 on the test set, showing significant promise, although there are many directions for improvement and future work, including extending this work to sequence-level (multi-word) transliteration.

8. Acknowledgements

This work was supported by *Faclair na Gàidhlig* and the Centre for Doctoral Training in Speech and Language Technologies (SLT) and their Applications funded by UK Research and Innovation [grant number EP/S023062/1].

[4]`https://dasg.ac.uk/corpus`

9. Bibliographical References

Barry, J., Wagner, J., Cassidy, L., Cowap, A., Lynn, T., Walsh, A., Meachair, M. J. Ó., and Foster, J. (2021). gabert–an irish language model. *arXiv preprint arXiv:2107.12930.*

Devlin, J., Chang, M.-W., Lee, K., and Toutanova, K. (2019). BERT: Pre-training of deep bidirectional transformers for language understanding. In *Proceedings of the 2019 Conference of the North American Chapter of the Association for Computational Linguistics: Human Language Technologies, Volume 1 (Long and Short Papers)*, pages 4171–4186, Minneapolis, Minnesota, June. Association for Computational Linguistics.

Gillies, W. (1977). Courtly and satiric poems in the Book of the Dean of Lismore. *Scottish Studies 21.*

Gillies, W. (2009). Scottish Gaelic. In *The Celtic Languages*, pages 244–318. Routledge.

Haddow, B., Bawden, R., Barone, A. V. M., Helcl, J., and Birch, A. (2021). Survey of low-resource machine translation. *arXiv preprint arXiv:2109.00486.*

Keskar, N. S., Mudigere, D., Nocedal, J., Smelyanskiy, M., and Tang, P. T. P. (2016). On large-batch training for deep learning: Generalization gap and sharp minima. *arXiv preprint arXiv:1609.04836.*

Kingma, D. P. and Ba, J. (2014). Adam: A method for stochastic optimization. *arXiv preprint arXiv:1412.6980.*

Lewis, M., Liu, Y., Goyal, N., Ghazvininejad, M., Mohamed, A., Levy, O., Stoyanov, V., and Zettlemoyer, L. (2019). Bart: Denoising sequence-to-sequence pre-training for natural language generation, translation, and comprehension. *arXiv preprint arXiv:1910.13461.*

Liu, Y., Ott, M., Goyal, N., Du, J., Joshi, M., Chen, D., Levy, O., Lewis, M., Zettlemoyer, L., and Stoyanov, V. (2019). Roberta: A robustly optimized bert pretraining approach. *arXiv preprint arXiv:1907.11692.*

Meek, D. (1982). *The Corpus of Heroic Verse in the Book of the Dean of Lismore*. Ph.D. thesis.

Ott, M., Edunov, S., Baevski, A., Fan, A., Gross, S., Ng, N., Grangier, D., and Auli, M. (2019). fairseq: A fast, extensible toolkit for sequence modeling. In *Proceedings of the 2019 Conference of the North American Chapter of the Association for Computational Linguistics (Demonstrations)*, pages 48–53, Minneapolis, Minnesota, June. Association for Computational Linguistics.

Papineni, K., Roukos, S., Ward, T., and Zhu, W.-J. (2002). Bleu: a method for automatic evaluation of machine translation. In *Proceedings of the 40th annual meeting of the Association for Computational Linguistics*, pages 311–318.

E.C. Quiggin, editor. (1937). *Poems from the Book of the Dean of Lismore*. Cambridge.

Neil Ross, editor. (1939). *Heroic Poetry from the Book of the Dean of Lismore*. Scottish Gaelic Texts Society.

Singh, A. and Bansal, J. (2021). Neural machine transliteration of indian languages. In *2021 4th International Conference on Computing and Communications Technologies (ICCCT)*, pages 91–96. IEEE.

Derick S. Thomson, editor. (1993). *The Companion to Gaelic Scotland*. Blackwell.

Üstün, A., Berard, A., Besacier, L., and Gallé, M. (2021). Multilingual unsupervised neural machine translation with denoising adapters. In *Proceedings of the 2021 Conference on Empirical Methods in Natural Language Processing*, pages 6650–6662, Online and Punta Cana, Dominican Republic, November. Association for Computational Linguistics.

Vaswani, A., Shazeer, N., Parmar, N., Uszkoreit, J., Jones, L., Gomez, A. N., Kaiser, Ł., and Polosukhin, I. (2017). Attention is all you need. *Advances in neural information processing systems*, 30.

Wu, S., Cotterell, R., and Hulden, M. (2021). Applying the transformer to character-level transduction. In *Proceedings of the 16th Conference of the European Chapter of the Association for Computational Linguistics: Main Volume*, pages 1901–1907, Online, April. Association for Computational Linguistics.

Zhang, M., Li, H., Banchs, R. E., and Kumaran, A. (2015). Whitepaper of NEWS 2015 shared task on machine transliteration. In *Proceedings of the Fifth Named Entity Workshop*, pages 1–9, Beijing, China, July. Association for Computational Linguistics.

Proceedings of the CLTW 4 @ LREC2022, pages 99–103
Marseille, 20-25 June 2022

Introducing the National Corpus of Irish Project

Mícheál J. Ó Meachair, Úna Bhreathnach, Gearóid Ó Cleircín
Dublin City University
Dublin, Ireland
{micheal.omeachair, una.bhreathnach, gearoid.ocleircin}@dcu.ie

Abstract

Abstract This paper introduces the National Corpus of Irish, an initiative to develop a large national corpus of written and spoken contemporary Irish as well as related specialised corpora. The newly-compiled corpora will be hosted at `corpas.ie`, in what will become a hub for corpus-based research on the Irish language. Users will be able to search the corpora and download data generated during the project from the `corpas.ie` website and appropriate third-party repositories. Corpus 1 will be a balanced general-purpose corpus containing c. 155m words. Corpus 2 will be a written corpus consisting of c. 100m words. Corpus 3 will be a spoken corpus containing 6.5m words. Corpus 4 will be a monitor corpus with a target size of 1m words per year from 2000 onwards. Token, lemma, and *n*-gram frequency lists will be published at regular intervals on the project website, and language models will be published there and on other appropriate platforms during the course of the project. This paper focuses on the background and crucial scoping stage of the project, and examines user needs as identified in a survey of potential users.

Keywords: corpora, Irish, resource evaluation

1. Introduction

This paper introduces the National Corpus of Irish project, an initiative to develop a large national corpus of written and spoken contemporary Irish as well as related specialised corpora. The project is being undertaken by the Gaois research group, Fiontar & Scoil na Gaeilge, DCU, with funding for the period 2022–24 from the Department of Tourism, Culture, Arts, Gaeltacht, Sport and Media, with support from the National Lottery.

The corpora will be hosted at `corpas.ie`, in what will become a hub for corpus-based research on the Irish language. The contents of the corpora will be presented in a way that facilitates use by both researchers and non-experts through the provision of simple and more complex searches. Users will be able to search the corpora and download data generated during the project from the `corpas.ie` website and appropriate third-party repositories. Comprehensive documentation pertaining to the data will also be available on the project website.

The following are the projected sizes of the corpora:

- Corpus 1: the National Corpus of Irish (CNG): c. 155 million words;
- Corpus 2: the Corpus of Written Irish: c. 100 million words;
- Corpus 3: the Corpus of Spoken Irish: c.6.5 million words;
- Corpus 4: the Monitor Corpus of Irish: one million words per annum from the year 2000 onwards

Corpus 1 will be a balanced general-purpose corpus that contains a wide and representative sample of Irish from the year 2000 to 2024. Corpus 2 will be a corpus that is focused on a higher register and will likely be of use to translators and terminologists, among other researchers. Corpus 3 will contain spoken data that will be of interest to phoneticians and researchers in the speech sciences, among others. Corpus 4 will include samples of similar sizes from the same domains for each of the included years, and is expected to be suitable for tests on language change as well as having limited general-purpose applications.

Token, lemma, and *n*-gram frequency lists will be published at regular intervals on the project website, and language models will be published there and on other appropriate platforms during the course of the project.

This project has 2 FTE staff, as well as benefiting from the technical and editorial expertise of the Gaois research group; who also developed the National Terminology Database for Irish, the Corpus of Contemporary Irish and the Corpus of Irish for Lexicography among other projects. Experts in software development (Kevin Scannell, Saint Louis University) and spoken corpora (Elaine Uí Dhonnchadha, TCD) are acting as consultants to the project. An Advisory Committee made up from a group of subject experts, drawn mainly from across the university sector, has been appointed to advise on both best practice and emerging research needs from the fields. These include, in alphabetical order, the fields of Computer-assisted Language Learning (CALL), Corpus Linguistics, Irish-language studies and analysis, Language Learning and Education, Lexicography, Linguistics, Natural Language Processing, and Terminology. Members of this committee are credited on the project website.

2. Background

Large corpora are one of the core digital resources needed for language technologies the world over. Corpora provide both linguistic knowledge and examples for researchers seeking to create dictionaries, term databases, and other knowledge bases. They are also essential in the creation of language tools, whether these are created using machine-learning techniques or from rules and conventions that have been extracted from said corpora.

The first large and publicly-available corpus of contemporary Irish was compiled in a one-year project in 2006 (Kilgarriff et al., 2006). It is known as *Nua-Chorpas na hÉireann*[1], comprising 30 million words, as well as both document- and word-level annotation. The corpus has not been maintained or supplemented since 2006 and is therefore out of date and unsuitable for research into contemporary language use (Ó Meachair, 2020).

The Gaois research group had hoped to secure funding for a larger corpus project for some time. The groundwork for this began in 2016 with the publication of *Corpas na Gaeilge Comhaimseartha* [2] (CGC). When first published CGC contained 5.3 million words; it now contains over 36 million words. CGC can be searched by members of the public without subscription or registration; 159,000 searches of CGC were recorded in 2021. The compilation of this corpus has been ongoing, but it will likely be subsumed into the National Corpus of Irish project with Corpus 2 taking its place.

The Gaois research group has also published a parallel corpus of Irish-English legal texts that the public can search without subscription or registration[3]. This parallel corpus currently contains 58.5 million words, 28.5 million in Irish and 30 in English. The compilation of this corpus is ongoing and it remains to be seen whether or not the entire corpus will be subsumed into the National Corpus of Irish project.

Subsequent to these projects another corpus compilation project called *Corpas Foclóireachta na Gaeilge*[4] (CFG), or the Corpus of Irish for Lexicography, was conducted by the Gaois research group with funding from Foras na Gaeilge in 2020–21. The aim of the CFG project was to compile a corpus of 100-million words from high-quality sources, tagged for part of speech and lemma, and to make this corpus searchable. It was not within the scope of the project to balance the corpus. Considerable metadata was developed to accompany the CFG corpus, however, this did not include all the metadata required in a national corpus. CFG includes all data from the CGC corpus and an additional 65 million words from a variety of other sources. It is a research corpus that is only available to members of the dictionary team at Foras na Gaeilge and researchers in the Gaois Research Group at present. A special agreement was made during the CFG project to facilitate the creation of by-products that could be used by Irish-language research groups namely, an ARPA language model, 1–5gram frequency lists, and an RNN language model suitable for Irish-language speech recognition. The CFG project's aims and objectives, as well as results from the first half of the project, are detailed in Ó Meachair et al. (2021).

The projects outlined above have contributed data, tools, practices, and experience that will benefit CNG from beginning to end. It is worth noting that numerous other Irish-language corpora have been compiled in the last ten years, but they were compiled for research purposes only and cannot be accessed by the public or registered users. These include (but are not limited to) Ní Ghloinn (2020), Ó Meachair (2020), Uí Dhonnchadha and Frenda (2013), and Scannell (2007).

3. Project planning

The CNG project began in January 2022 with a focused scoping and auditing step, to define all core deliverables, particularly workflow, technologies, and data sources.

A survey of future users was carried out as part of this step. This survey was publicised via social media and Gaois websites and was circulated to parties known to be interested. The survey, which received 27 responses, gave the respondents considerable scope to elaborate on their particular requirements. It served to test and elaborate on the research that had been conducted on use cases for Irish-language corpora during the application stage. The fields of research that had been anticipated at the application stage remained the same (e.g. linguistics, education, NLP, lexicography, terminology, and translation), but specific types of corpus searches came to light in survey responses. For example: it had been predicted that CQL searches were a requirement, as well as domain and publication-related metadata filtering. The way in which researchers intend to use the search functions for re-use in longer-term projects was also noted.

> "Deis ag gach úsáideoir fochorpais dá gcuid féin a chruthú, nó ar a laghad, na critéir chuardaigh i gcuardach casta a shábháil go mbeadh sé / sí in ann filleadh ar an 'bhfochorpas' sin go rialta. Bheadh sé seo tábhachtach dá mbeinn ag iarraidh a bheith ag obair i gcorpas iata. M.sh má tá obair ar siúl agam i 'bhfochorpas' thar thréimhse níor mhaith liom go dtarlódh sé go gcuirfí le hinneachar an mhórchorpais agus go gcuirfear le hinneachar m'fhochorpais gan choinnne—rud a chuirfeadh mo chuid staitisticí as riocht."

[1] `https://focloir.sketchengine.co.uk/run.cgi/index`

[2] `https://www.gaois.ie/ga/corpora/monolingual/`

[3] `https://www.gaois.ie/ga/corpora/parallel/`

[4] `https://www.gaois.ie/ga/corpora/lexicography/login/`

> [Translation: *An opportunity for users to create their own sub-corpus, or at least, to store the criteria of their advanced search so that he / she can return to their "sub-corpus" frequently. This would be important if I wanted to work in a closed corpus. For example: If I were to be working in a "sub-corpus" over an extended period of time I would not like for the contents of the large corpus to change, thus changing the contents of my sub-corpus and distorting my statistics.*]

The need to cater for specific research projects and their annotation needs was also raised, with the following respondent outlining a potential use for a customisable tagging tool:

> "Mura mbeadh sé clúdaithe faoin gclibeálaí séimeantaice, ba mhaith an rud uirlis anótála a bheith ar fáil go bhféadfadh úsáideoir torthaí a chuardaigh a anótáil (téarmaí / frásaí a aibhsiú; naisc idir téarmaí a léiriú), agus torthaí anótáilte a easportáil nó a chóipeáil agus a ghreamú go clár eile i.e. Word, PDF, Excel mar shampla."

> [Translation: *If it weren't to be covered by the semantic tagger, it would be good if a tagging tool were available to users so that they could tag the results of their searches (terminology / highlight phrases; display links between terms), and export these annotated results or have the ability to copy and paste them into another programme i.e. Word, PDF, Excel for example.*]

Another noteworthy point of feedback from the survey was the number of translators who reported using existing corpus searches as part of their verification process, and expressed a desire to continue this practice. A number of interested parties also expressed a desire for downloadable corpora or sub-corpora. It has subsequently come to light that sophisticated search functionalities on the project website would be more useful to these interested parties, rather than downloading the data only to use it in another corpus-querying tool. NLP practitioners will continue to want data to be available to them, because they have the computational skills and expertise required to manipulate the data for their specific needs, particularly larger datasets.

An Advisory Committee was assembled from as many of the fields related to the CNG project as possible. This includes experts from the fields of corpus linguistics and linguistics, education and language learning, phonetics, computer programming and natural language processing, lexicography and terminology. It is hoped that this committee will advise the research team throughout the project, advising on best practices and recent developments from their respective fields, as well as briefing the research team as to the specific corpus-based needs of linguists, lexicographers, or educators—for example.

4. Workflow and technologies

Workflow practices have largely been established during the previous corpus projects conducted by the Gaois research group. These practices include documentation of all computational processes, as well as the storage of both raw data and the corpus-ready versions of these data. A receipt system for data handovers was established, summarising the number of files being sent or the wordcount of the files sent, in order to ensure forks are avoided and data is not lost. This receipt system is inspired in some respects by the way GitHub[5] manages push requests. Database and file-storage specifications have also been audited to ensure the data is safe from a security point of view, and to ensure formats and encoding are maintained.

While the technology selection process is ongoing, it is clear that it will be more time- and cost-efficient to repurpose existing bona fide technologies than start developing our own technologies from scratch. Numerous examples of suitable existing technologies were gathered by the Gaois research group and presented to the appropriate experts from the committee in a number of meetings. During these meetings the pros and cons of each technology was discussed with a view to identifying which technologies work together best and which technologies, despite appearing suitable at first, were not suitable. For example: a considerable amount of pre-processing is done using Python, so the pros and cons of using Python in the project website as well were discussed. Ultimately, it was discovered that this was not necessary and was potentially limiting. For the purposes of the corpus project the technologies used to develop the website and its search functions simply needed the data to be processed appropriately and consistently, rather than those technologies needing to be integrated with the pre-processing and processing technologies.

The technologies that have been selected are still under development, or are still being adapted to the needs of the project, and may be subject to change. It is therefore too early in the project to provide specifications for them. It was agreed in the funding award that the Gaois research group would package a part-of-speech tagger, such that it would be usable for the present project and by others thereafter, and, if possible, a semantic tagger would also be packaged and made publicly available.

5. Data sources

Previously collected data were audited in order to identify gaps or imbalances in our corpora. This was done by calculating token counts for all definable subcorpora of the CFG project for year, genre (for example: news, literature, academic), and publisher. The

[5] `https://github.com/`

most useful results at this stage were found in the token counts for year and genre, with publisher counts being too variable to yield any concrete conclusions. Approximately 55 million of the 100 million words included in CFG were published after the beginning of the year 2000 and/or were not restricted by copyright agreements, therefore qualifying them for re-use in CNG; a practice that was successfully employed in the compilation of CFG (Ó Meachair et al., 2021) and CorCenCC (Knight et al., 2021b) to good effect.

The new potential sources were collated in an Excel spreadsheet along with information regarding the domain or mode of the language (sports, spoken, informative, educational, etc.), and the collection method (scraping of webpages, downloadable PDFs, request and/or collection required, etc). The focus here is on the collection of a wide variety of text types, and examples of language use in different contexts, as is desirable in modern corpora (Sinclair, 2003).

An additional consideration in prospecting for previously unfound Irish-language data was the collation of genres (news, governmental, literary, pop science, etc) and language modes (written, spoken, *e*-language / web data, etc) in order to ensure the corpus accords with best practices for national corpora, as much as is practicably possible in the minority-language context. 51 large corpora, most of which are national corpora, were surveyed for their size, balancing considerations, domains included, sampling methods, and the technologies used to deliver corpus searches—where possible. Notable among the findings were that the majority of the newest larger corpora sought to include as much data as possible (containing upwards of 500 million words). Rather than imposing prescribed balancing methodologies, users were expected to use search filters to create virtual sub-corpora, therefore tailoring their searches to their research aims (Davies, 2018; Kupietz et al., 2010).

The design of these very large corpora are of course different to each other in many ways, but empirical research can be conducted with them using very similar methodologies. Where this approach was not used, a significant number of the other corpora adopted an approach that was informed by BNC 1994 (Burnard, 1995), and then adapted it to fit their own language and/or research needs (Knight et al., 2021a; McEnery et al., 2006; Aksan and Aksan, 2009).

The exact design of Corpas Náisiúnta na Gaeilge will be informed by these approaches and influenced to some degree by the availability of texts. It is necessary in the minority-language context that a certain amount of collection be completed before the corpus design is finalised, because available texts are fewer overall than those written in languages that are more widely spoken and some domains are absent entirely (For example: biology and chemistry publications in Irish, instruction manuals).

6. Conclusion

The National Corpus of Irish project is only six months old, and is likely to evolve considerably before its conclusion at the end of 2024. This is an interdisciplinary project with many interdependent elements—newly-developed technologies, data from a variety of sources, legal agreements, and language expertise. Therefore, the planning and scoping stage described in this paper will be crucial to its success and timely completion.

7. Bibliographical References

Aksan, Y. and Aksan, M. (2009). Building a national corpus of Turkish: Design and implementation. *Working Papers in Corpus-based Linguistics and Language Education. Tokyo: TUFS*, (3):299–310.

Burnard, L. (1995). *Users Reference Guide for the British National Corpus. version 1.0.* Oxford University Computing Services.

Kilgarriff, A., Rundell, M., and Uí Dhonnchadha, E. (2006). Efficient corpus development for lexicography: building the New Corpus for Ireland. *Language resources and evaluation*, 40(2):127–152.

Knight, D., Morris, S., Fitzpatrick, T., Rayson, P., Spasić, I., and Thomas, E. M. (2020). The National Corpus of Contemporary Welsh: Project Report | Y Corpws Cenedlaethol Cymraeg Cyfoes: Adroddiad y Prosiect. October 2020. `https://arxiv.org/abs/2010.05542`.

Knight, D., Morris, S., Arman, L., Needs, J., and Rees, M. (2021a). *Building a National Corpus: A Welsh Language Case Study*. Palgrave Macmillan Cham.

Knight, D., Morris, S., and Fitzpatrick, T. (2021b). *Corpus design and construction in minoritised language contexts - Cynllunio a chreu corpws mewn cyd-destunau Ieithoedd lleiafrifoledig: The National Corpus of Contemporary Welsh - Corpws Cenedlaethol Cymraeg Cyfoes*. Palgrave Macmillan Cham.

Kupietz, M., Belica, C., Keibel, H., and Witt, A. (2010). The German reference corpus DeReKo: A primordial sample for linguistic research. In *Proceedings of the Seventh International Conference on Language Resources and Evaluation (LREC'10)*, Valletta, Malta, May. European Language Resources Association (ELRA).

McEnery, T., Xiao, R., and Tono, Y. (2006). *Corpus-Based Language Studies: An Advanced Resource Book*. Routledge.

Ní Ghloinn, A. (2020). Corpas Foghlaimeora TEG agus an Próifíliú Cumais sa Ghaeilge. In Eoghan Ó Raghallaigh, editor, *Léachtaí Cholm Cille L: Téamaí agus Tionscadail Taighde*, pages 119–156, Maigh Nuad. An Sagart.

Scannell, K. (2007). The Crúbadán Project: Corpus building for under-resourced languages. In *Building and Exploring Web Corpora: Proceedings of the 3rd Web as Corpus Workshop*, volume 5, pages 5–15.

Sinclair, J. M. (2003). Corpora for lexicography. In Piet van Sterkenburg, editor, *A Practical Guide to Lexicography*, pages 167–178. John Benjamins, Amsterdam.

Ó Meachair, M. J., Ó Raghallaigh, B., Bhreathnach, Ú., Ó Cleircín, G., and Scannell, K. (2021). Tiomsú Corpais don Taighde Foclóireachta: Corpas Foclóireachta na Gaeilge (CFG2020). *TEANGA, the Journal of the Irish Association for Applied Linguistics*, 28:278–305.

Ó Meachair, M. J. (2020). *Complexity Analysis of a Corpus of Educational Materials in Irish (EduGA)*. Ph.D. thesis, School of Linguistic, Speech and Communication Sciences, Trinity College, Dublin.

8. Language Resource References

Mark Davies. (2018). *iWeb: The Intelligent Web-based Corpus*. https://www.english-corpora.org/iweb/.

Uí Dhonnchadha, Elaine and Frenda, Alessio. (2013). *Comhrá: Corpas na Gaeilge Labhartha*. The Centre for Speech and Language Technology for Irish, Coláiste na Tríonóide, School of Linguistic, Speech and Communication Sciences, TCD. https://www.scss.tcd.ie/~uidhonne/comhra/index.utf8.html.

Proceedings of the CLTW 4 @ LREC2022 , pages 104–109
Marseille, 20-25 June 2022

BU-TTS: An Open-Source, Bilingual Welsh-English, Text-to-Speech Corpus

Stephen John Russell, Dewi Bryn Jones, Delyth Prys
Language Technologies Unit, School of Linguistics
Bangor University, Bangor, Wales, UK
{stephen.russell, d.b.jones, d.prys}@bangor.ac.uk

Abstract

This paper presents the design, collection and verification of a bilingual text-to-speech synthesis corpus for Welsh and English. The ever expanding voice collection currently contains almost 10 hours of recordings from a bilingual, phonetically balanced text corpus. The speakers consist of a professional voice actor and three amateur contributors, with male and female accents from north and south Wales. This corpus provides audio-text pairs for building and training high-quality bilingual Welsh-English neural based TTS systems. We describe the process by which we created a phonetically balanced prompt set and the challenges of attempting to collate such a dataset during the COVID-19 pandemic. Our initial findings in validating the corpus via the implementation of a state-of-the-art TTS models are presented. This corpus represents the first open-source Welsh language corpus large enough to capitalise on neural TTS architectures.

Keywords: text-to-speech, TTS, speech synthesis, speech corpus, open-source, bilingual, Welsh, English

1. Introduction

The prevalence of speech interfaces across modern society, often seen as "an essential component in many applications such as speech-enabled devices, navigation systems, and accessibility for the visually impaired" (Arık et al., 2017), poses an interesting challenge when developing text-to-speech solutions for bilingual communities. Tadmor (2009) noted that most languages contain loanwords from one or more other languages to some extent or another, however speakers in bilingual communities often take this further by alternating between languages mid sentence or word (Haspelmath and Tadmor, 2009). This linguistic trait, commonly referred to as "code switching" (Nilep, 2006), requires speakers to "include morphemes from two or more of the varieties of their linguistics repertoire" (Myers-Scotton, 2017). In order to ensure fair and unbiased access to technology in bilingual communities, and to help prevent against the threat of "Digital Language Extinction" (Rehm, 2014), it is essential that synthesised voices are equally proficient at articulating and disseminating the required information in both languages.

A member of the Celtic languages, Welsh has coexisted alongside English, in the United Kingdom, for hundreds of years (Cooper et al., 2019). Bilingual Welsh-English speakers often utilise code switching, by using English words mid sentence for named entities, convenience or to assist in communicating with learners. To address the phenomenon of code switching, previous works on bilingual Welsh-English text-to-speech synthesis have focused on statistical models, relying on "a bilingual pronunciation dictionary containing large numbers of words from both languages described phonetically with a series of phonemes" (Prys et al., 2021). Similar approaches can be seen for Mandarin and English (Chu et al., 2003; Zhiyong et al., 2009). More recent approaches to multilingual text-to-speech, exemplified by Casanova et al. (2021), have demonstrated how deep neural learning can be applied to multi-speaker datasets with impressive results. There are many benefits to a neural network based approach, synthesised voices demonstrate improved intelligibility and naturalness whilst also reducing the manual pre-processing and feature detection (Tan et al., 2021). However, "In comparison, deep neural models require substantially greater volumes of data than traditional TTS architectures" (Latorre et al., 2019), which can be prohibitive when working with lesser resourced languages.

In 2018, the Welsh Government released its Welsh Technology Action Plan, containing their plans for "technological developments to ensure that the Welsh language can be used in a wide variety of contexts, be that by using voice, keyboard or other means of human-computer interaction" Welsh Government (2018). Although previous works by Cooper et al. (2019) and Prys et al. (2021) have addressed many of the issues outlined, a comprehensive text-to-speech corpus, large enough to utilise advances in neural network architectures was not yet available.

In this paper, we present the first instalment of the Bangor University TTS Corpus,[1] a phonetically balanced, bilingual, Welsh-English corpus and prompt set, released under an open CC0 1.0 license.[2] The corpus contains 12,200 text prompts divided into

[1]https://git.techiaith.bangor.ac.uk/data-porth-technolegau-iaith/corpws-talentau-llais

[2]https://creativecommons.org/publicdomain/zero/1.0

9500 Welsh language prompts and 2700 in English along with voice recordings consisting of 2 male and 2 female native Welsh speakers, one of whom is a professional voice artist. Other lesser resourced languages have taken the approach of gathering source material from news reports or literature, such as the work done by Mussakhojayeva et al. (2022), and then post processing the recordings into shorter segments. We however, present the construction of a curated "phonetically balanced corpus" (Gibbon et al., 2012) and its purpose in providing a platform from which to build more specialised and domain specific voices.

Further to the prompt set and voice recordings, we also present our initial findings validating the corpus via a series of experimental implementations of a state-of-the-art TTS system, based on the VITS (Kim et al., 2021) architecture. The corpus presented is significantly smaller than intended and as such we detail the processes and adaptations implemented to deal with the disruptions and circumstance during the initial data collection phase. The synthesised voices were evaluated reading a selection of news articles in both Welsh and English to assess their intelligibility.

The organisation of this paper is as follows: Section 2 reviews a selection of Welsh language corpora. In Section 3, we describe the process of creating and compiling the data and give a statistical overview of the released corpus. A series of experiments and their architectures are set out in Section 4. Section 5 discusses the challenges faced implementing a bilingual Welsh-English text-to-speech solution and future research within this domain. This work is concluded in Section 6.

2. Related Work

Welsh is classified as a lesser resourced language, however "the availability of both text and speech corpora for Welsh has much improved in recent years" (Prys et al., 2022b). Cysill Ar-lein, the Bangor University free online spelling and grammar checker, has produced a corpus of over 400 million tokens by collecting user input, further reading can be found via Prys et al. (2022b). The CorCenCC corpus (Knight et al., 2021), contains in excess of 11 million tokens, annotated with parts of speech and semantic meaning. For the purposes of speech recognition, Mozilla's Common Voice is utilised extensively by over 1600 users, currently containing over 143 hours recordings. Open text-to-speech corpora, by comparison, are not so readily available, with the complete absence of an appropriately sized corpus for machine learning. The WISPR project (Prys et al., 2004) is one such corpus and contains 3 hours of speech recordings of a single speaker, with excerpts from the Bible and an undergraduate dissertation totalling 616 sentences of varying length. Off the back of this corpus one of the first Welsh text-to-speech voices was created, however it was restricted by the technology available, and as such produced only moderatly intelligible audio containing significant audio glitches. By 2016 this same dataset was utilised to create an open source voice, for the Welsh Digital Assistant Macsen (Jones, 2020), which by all accounts sounded much more natural, by utilising the MaryTTS framework (Schröder and Trouvain, 2003). The same technology is used for Lleisiwr, a project which sets out to create personal synthetic voices for users that may be at risk of losing their ability to speak. Prys et al. (2022b) provide further reading on the functionality of Lleisiwr.

Looking beyond the Welsh language, bilingual text-to-speech systems have been considered with a similar approach for the Manderin-English language pair (Chu et al., 2003; Zhiyong et al., 2009), also utilising bilingual pronunciation dictionaries to good effect. The presence of foreign words within a larger, machine learning ready corpus, has been considered by Mussakhojayeva et al. (2022) during the expansion and improvement of their KazakTTS corpus. The foreign words used here are limited to a subset of very important words imported from Russian which improves the ability to digitally communicate in Kazakh but falls short of a fully bilingual solution. Casanova et al. (2021) approaches a bilingual solution by utilising a combination of mono and multi speaker datasets such as Mozilla's Common Voice, LibriVox and LJSpeech to name but a few. The datasets are used to create pre-trained models that can be used to create one-shot voices via transfer learning mechanisms. This however produces a variety of voices from a single user due to the number of speakers used for training.

3. BU-TTS Corpus

This section details the creation of a phonetically balanced prompt set as well as the process undertaken to record it. We present both our intended methodology and the resulting processes that were required to complete the project.

3.1. Phonetically Balanced Text Corpus

The texts used to create our prompt set come from Mozilla's Common Voice, which in turn were curated from a variety of sources including self generated data from the Cysill Ar-lein corpus (Prys et al., 2016) and translations for under-represented categories such as recipes as well as open source or out of copyright external sources such as wikipedia, Twitter, Welsh language books and translations of selected English language books.

Due to the initial limitations of Common Voice, the sentences are limited in length to no more than 14 words. The process of segmenting and truncating longer texts into shorter sentences was undertaken by the terminologists and linguists within the team to ensure the quality and suitability of each sentence for open source distribution. Offensive or inappropriate language was removed with a focus instead placed on isolating interesting and easy to read sentences, appropriate for all ages. This process required a large amount of editing to segment longer text into sentences and remove any errors present in the text or to update old fashioned vocabulary, style or orthography. Further reading on the creation of this corpus will be available in the forthcoming Language and Technology in Wales: Volume II (Prys et al., 2022a).

From this master list a sub set of phonetically balanced prompts were compiled using the pre-built tools released in the MaryTTS toolset (Schröder and Trouvain, 2003), in conjunction with the Bangor University Pronunciation Dictionary (Prys and Jones, 2018). The pronunciation dictionary contains phonemes for both north and south Welsh accents, ensuring that the prompts chosen would represent a diverse range of dialect choices. Further to the phoneme coverage, the prompts were also checked to ensure values from the wordlists of the most common word-forms in Welsh, and the most common English words used in Welsh (Prys and Jones, 2019) were present in the final selections. The resulting 12,200 sentences form a series of 5 unique subsets, containing both Welsh and English prompts, each individually phonetically balanced to give an even distribution of phonemes.

3.2. Recording Process

Recording initially took place in the language laboratories at Bangor University. These laboratories are specially built to isolate recordings from outside sounds and, as such, provide an excellent low sound floor for recording as well as being fitted with a monitoring booth for supervising the recording process. In order to achieve an efficient and low noise recording process for amateur talents, iOS and Android apps, supporting the Sure MV88+ microphone, were developed for both the recording process and displaying prompts for the talents to read. In conjunction with the apps, an API web service and dashboard were constructed to collect the audio recordings and manage the users progress through the prompt set. Amateur talents were instructed to speak with a natural and relaxed tone whilst remembering to note punctuation and inflection as indicated in the sentences. Recordings were then reviewed via the dashboard and any non conforming recordings were discarded and re-introduced to the prompt set by the API service.

3.2.1. Remotely Recording Amateur Talents

We looked initially for amateur talents willing to donate their voices to the project and found many students at Bangor University eager to participate in the project. Having auditioned the voices we settled on 2 males voices with northern and southern accents and a female voice with a northern accent, whilst continuing to look for a 4th female voice with a southern accent. However due to the restrictions enforced by the COVID-19 pandemic, the laboratories were temporarily deemed unsuitable for data collection. Instead, we setup each of the voice talents with a mobile telephone and microphone to perform the recordings at home. Given the amateur status of the voice talents we quickly found that, without the direction of a supervisor, it was difficult to retain a consistent standard and rate of recording. At this point in the project, the potential benefits of such data to our voice cloning system Lleisiwr, where users are unlikely to have have professional recording equipment but are in great need of a voice, was highlighted. As such, we continued to gather as much data as was reasonable from the amateur talents, pursuing methods of audio cleaning and verification of the sparse and noisy recordings.

3.2.2. Professional Voice Talents

With an insufficient quantity of low quality data being produced by the amateur talents, we turned to a professional talent and recording company to complete the 4th voice. We provided them with the entire corpus of sentences, each tagged with an appropriate file name to be used for recordings. Once recorded the files were checked for accuracy and any silence was trimmed from the files. The professional talent was instructed to read the prompts in a neutral style, ensuring to emphasise where question marks and exclamation marks were present in the sentence. This process produced a plethora of high quality data in a relatively short time frame and forms the backbone of the BU-TTS corpus.

3.3. Corpus Overview

The format of the BU-TTS corpus is similar to that of the LJSpeech corpus (Ito and Johnson, 2017) where audio files are kept in a directory named "wavs", adjacent to a metadata CSV containing the file names of the wavs and the transcribed text. An illustration of the generic directory structure can be found in Figure 1. The recordings are released in 48 kHz 16-bit mono WAV files whilst the text is encoded with the UTF-8 format. All in, there are 9.8 hours of recordings from 4 contributors, the division of the speakers, and their number of recordings, can be found in Table 1 with the final language distribution of the prompt set outlined in Table 2.

4. Dataset Validation Experiments

To validate the potential of the corpus on neural network architectures, we made use of the Coqui-ai TTS repositories.[3] Coqui provide open-source frameworks

[3]https://github.com/coqui-ai/TTS

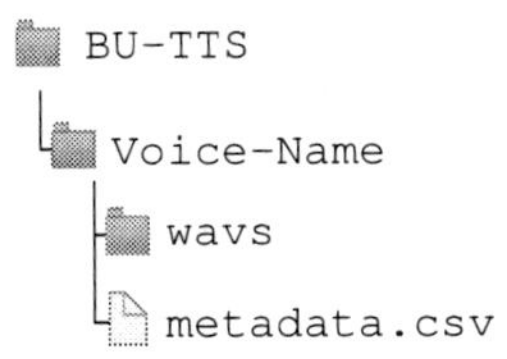

Figure 1: Generic Directory Structure.

Speaker	Batch	Recordings
F1	5	12,200
F2	2	3,653
M1	2	2,847
M2	2	2,630
Sum	N/A	21330

Table 1: Speaker Recording Distribution.

for both text-to-speech and speech-to-text that implement a variety of neural model architectures. Their libraries are intended for advanced text-to-speech generation and implement the latest research. Further to the codebase, Coqui-ai TTS is shipped with pre-trained text-to-speech models as well as tools for measuring dataset quality.

4.1. Experiment Architecture

Many text-to-speech models are based on a two stage architecture consisting of an initial aligner training phase and an independent vocoder training stage (Zeng et al., 2020; Ren et al., 2019). This can lead to long training sessions and requires the vocoder to be trained independently from the aligner. We instead chose to utilise the VITS (Kim et al., 2021) model architecture as it provides a simpler end-to-end process for speech synthesis. It was also decided to use exclusively graphemes to train the models due to multiple languages being used. This enabled us to focus on data curation and consolidation whilst also providing a benchmark standard from which to improve upon.

4.2. Single Speaker Experiments

Initial experiments were carried out using a single speaker VITS model with the southern accented female voice dataset, due to it being the only complete dataset and as such the only voice with a high enough volume of data for the neural architectures to be effective. This point was well illustrated when the largest dataset, with over 3000 recordings, from the amateur talents was utilised and only incomprehensible speech was produced. The successful model was trained using an NVIDIA RTX 3090 GPU for 3 days with the audio sampling kept at a full 44.1 KHz and 16 bit quality to attempt to retain the highest level of audio fidelity.

Lang	Batch	Prompts	Avg Words	Min Words	Max Words
cy	1	500	10	6	14
en	1	200	9	4	14
cy	2	1,500	10	4	14
en	2	625	9	4	14
cy	3	2,500	10	5	14
en	3	625	9	4	14
cy	4	2,500	10	5	14
en	4	625	10	6	14
cy	5	2,500	10	4	14
en	5	625	9	5	14
cy	All	9,500	10	4	14
en	All	2700	9	4	14

Table 2: Word - Sentence Distribution.

4.3. Transfer Learning & Multi-Speaker Experiments

Once a quality model had been achieved with a single speaker, attempts were made to use the lesser quantity and quality of data received from the amateur talents. Firstly we attempted using the pre-trained model for transfer learning and then subsequently via a multi-speaker implementation of the VITS model. During both experiments we utilised the cleaned and raw versions of the audio to get an understanding of any audio scrubbing requirements for future work.

4.4. Experiment Results

The trained text-to-speech models have only been informally tested, in house and at various live events, however initial reactions have been mostly positive and we can demonstrate an ability to code switch between Welsh and English within the same sentence. There are however still instances when words take the same form in both languages where errors will occur. Further to the ability to code switch, we have also demonstrated the ability to produce bilingual audio from large texts containing sequential Welsh and English content. Due to the way in which the training models utilise vectors in waveform prediction, the formatting of the input text has a significant effect on output quality. We found that when using the model as a screen reader for articles from Welsh language news sites, the models far outperformed the shorter sentences that tended to be written by individual testers. A further deterioration can be seen when the language supplied does not conform to standard sentence structures found in either language.

Our experiments with transfer and multi-speaker training to maximise the lesser represented speakers in the dataset gave mixed results with the trained models, verging closer and closer in terms of prosody to that of our largest speaker corpus. Although there are definite improvements that can be made to the training process, we have demonstrated the potential to train bilingual text-to-speech voices with the BU-TTS corpus and to more efficiently generate new voices with completing only a subset of the full prompt set.

5. Future Work

To further validate this corpus there is potential to train the dataset from phonemes which in many languages produces a higher quality voice. It would also be desirable to complete mean opinion score tests on all of the models generated to ensure a value approaching human speech can be achieved.

6. Conclusion

We presented BU-TTS, the initial instalment of the Bangor University text-to-speech corpus, an open-source Bilingual Welsh-English text-to-speech corpus. Four voices make up the corpus (two female, two male) with roughly 10 hours of recordings. Released under openly permissive CC0 1.0 international license.

7. Acknowledgements

We are grateful to the Welsh Government for funding this work as part of the Text, Speech and Translation Technologies for the Welsh Language project.

8. Bibliographical References

Arık, S. Ö., Chrzanowski, M., Coates, A., Diamos, G., Gibiansky, A., Kang, Y., Li, X., Miller, J., Ng, A., Raiman, J., et al. (2017). Deep voice: Real-time neural text-to-speech. In *International Conference on Machine Learning*, pages 195–204. PMLR.

Casanova, E., Weber, J., Shulby, C., Junior, A. C., Gölge, E., and Ponti, M. A. (2021). Yourtts: Towards zero-shot multi-speaker tts and zero-shot voice conversion for everyone. *arXiv preprint arXiv:2112.02418*.

Chu, M., Peng, H., Zhao, Y., Niu, Z., and Chang, E. (2003). Microsoft mulan-a bilingual tts system. In *2003 IEEE International Conference on Acoustics, Speech, and Signal Processing, 2003. Proceedings.(ICASSP'03).*, volume 1, pages I–I. IEEE.

Cooper, S., Jones, D. B., and Prys, D. (2019). Crowdsourcing the paldaruo speech corpus of welsh for speech technology. *Information*, 10(8):247.

Gibbon, D., Mertins, I., and Moore, R. K. (2012). *Handbook of multimodal and spoken dialogue systems: Resources, terminology and product evaluation*, volume 565. Springer Science & Business Media.

Haspelmath, M. and Tadmor, U. (2009). *Loanwords in the world's languages: a comparative handbook.* Walter de Gruyter.

Ito, K. and Johnson, L. (2017). The lj speech dataset. `https://keithito.com/LJ-Speech-Dataset/`.

Jones, D. (2020). Macsen: A voice assistant for speakers of a lesser resourced language. In *Proceedings of the 1st Joint Workshop on Spoken Language Technologies for Under-Resourced Languages (SLTU) and Collaboration and Computing for Under-Resourced Languages (CCURL)*, pages 194–201.

Kim, J., Kong, J., and Son, J. (2021). Conditional variational autoencoder with adversarial learning for end-to-end text-to-speech. In *International Conference on Machine Learning*, pages 5530–5540. PMLR.

Knight, D., Loizides, F., Neale, S., Anthony, L., and Spasić, I. (2021). Developing computational infrastructure for the corcencc corpus: The national corpus of contemporary welsh. *Language Resources and Evaluation*, 55(3):789–816.

Latorre, J., Lachowicz, J., Lorenzo-Trueba, J., Merritt, T., Drugman, T., Ronanki, S., and Klimkov, V. (2019). Effect of data reduction on sequence-to-sequence neural tts. In *ICASSP 2019-2019 IEEE International Conference on Acoustics, Speech and Signal Processing (ICASSP)*, pages 7075–7079. IEEE.

Mussakhojayeva, S., Khassanov, Y., and Varol, H. A. (2022). Kazakhtts2: Extending the open-source kazakh tts corpus with more data, speakers, and topics. *arXiv preprint arXiv:2201.05771*.

Myers-Scotton, C. (2017). Code-switching. *The handbook of sociolinguistics*, pages 217–237.

Nilep, C. (2006). "code switching" in sociocultural linguistics. *Colorado research in linguistics*.

Prys, D. and Jones, D. (2018). Gathering data for speech technology in the welsh language: A case study. In *LREC 2018*.

Prys, D. and Jones, D. B. (2019). Wordlists of the most common wordforms in welsh, and the most common english words used in welsh. Jan.

Prys, D., Williams, B., Hicks, B., Jones, D., Ní Chasaide, A., Gobl, C., Carson-Berndsen, J., Cummins, F., Ní Chiosáin, M., McKenna, J., et al. (2004). Wispr: Speech processing resources for welsh and irish. In *Proceedings of the SALTMIL Workshop: First Steps in Language Documentation for Minority Languages*, pages 68–71.

Prys, D., Prys, G., and Jones, D. B. (2016). Cysill ar-lein: A corpus of written contemporary welsh compiled from an on-line spelling and grammar checker. In *Proceedings of the Tenth International Conference on Language Resources and Evaluation (LREC'16)*, pages 3261–3264.

Prys, D., Jones, D., Prys, G., Watkins, G., Cooper, S., Roberts, J. C., Butcher, P., Farhat, L., Teahan, W., and Prys, M. (2021). Language and technology in wales: Volume i. 1.

Prys, D., Jones, D., and Prys, G. (2022a). Language and technology in wales: Volume ii. 2. forthcoming.

Prys, D., Watkins, G., and Ghazzali, S. (2022b). Ele d1.34 language report welsh.

Rehm, G. (2014). Digital language extinction as a challenge for the multilingual web. In *Multilingual Web Workshop 2014: New Horizons for the Multilingual Web*. META-NET Madrid.

Ren, Y., Ruan, Y., Tan, X., Qin, T., Zhao, S., Zhao, Z., and Liu, T.-Y. (2019). Fastspeech: Fast, robust and controllable text to speech. *Advances in Neural Information Processing Systems*, 32.

Schröder, M. and Trouvain, J. (2003). The german text-to-speech synthesis system mary: A tool for research, development and teaching. *International Journal of Speech Technology*, 6(4):365–377.

Tadmor, U. (2009). Loanwords in the world's languages: Findings and results. *Loanwords in the world's languages: A comparative handbook*, 55:75.

Tan, X., Qin, T., Soong, F., and Liu, T.-Y. (2021). A survey on neural speech synthesis. *arXiv preprint arXiv:2106.15561*.

Welsh Government. (2018). Welsh language technology action plan.

Zeng, Z., Wang, J., Cheng, N., Xia, T., and Xiao, J. (2020). Aligntts: Efficient feed-forward text-to-speech system without explicit alignment. In *ICASSP 2020-2020 IEEE international conference on acoustics, speech and signal processing (ICASSP)*, pages 6714–6718. IEEE.

Zhiyong, W., Guangqi, C., Meng, M. H., and Cai, L. (2009). A unified framework for multilingual text-to-speech synthesis with ssml specification as interface. *Tsinghua Science and Technology*, 14(5):623–630.

Proceedings of the CLTW 4 @ LREC2022, pages 110–120
Marseille, 20-25 June 2022

Developing Automatic Speech Recognition for Scottish Gaelic

Lucy Evans, William Lamb, Mark Sinclair, Beatrice Alex
University of Edinburgh, University of Edinburgh, Quorate Technology Ltd., University of Edinburgh
lucy.evans9@hotmail.com, w.lamb@ed.ac.uk, mark.s.sinclair@gmail.com, b.alex@ed.ac.uk

Abstract

This paper discusses our efforts to develop a full automatic speech recognition (ASR) system for Scottish Gaelic, starting from a point of limited resource. Building ASR technology is important for documenting and revitalising endangered languages; it enables existing resources to be enhanced with automatic subtitles and transcriptions, improves accessibility for users, and, in turn, encourages continued use of the language. In this paper, we explain the many difficulties faced when collecting minority language data for speech recognition. A novel cross-lingual approach to the alignment of training data is used to overcome one such difficulty, and in this way we demonstrate how majority language resources can bootstrap the development of lower-resourced language technology. We use the Kaldi speech recognition toolkit to develop several Gaelic ASR systems, and report a final WER of 26.30%. This is a 9.50% improvement on our original model.

Keywords: Scottish Gaelic, Automatic Speech Recognition, Low-Resource ASR, Alignment

1. Introduction

For a minority language with 57,100 speakers at the last census (National Records of Scotland, 2015), Scottish Gaelic has a surprising level of language technology provision. Over the past ten years, researchers have developed: a part-of-speech tagger (Lamb and Danso, 2014), a lemmatiser and word-embedding model (Lamb and Sinclair, 2016), a derivation of a categorical grammar (Batchelor, 2016; Batchelor, 2019), a syntactic parser (Boizou and Lamb, 2020), a Gaelic to Irish machine translation system (Murchú, 2019),[1] a wordnet (Bella et al., 2020) and a text-to-speech system.[2] Data sparsity is a major challenge for most minority languages attempting to gain entry to more advanced NLP tools and methodologies. In some ways, Gaelic is in a fortunate situation in this regard: the fieldwork efforts of the School of Scottish Studies (University of Edinburgh), along with a century's worth of Gaelic broadcasting by the BBC (Lamb, 1999, 143), have produced sizeable corpora of natural language data. At the same time, most are in the form of raw audio and paper-based text (typed and handwritten).[3] In order to move towards more involved NLP tasks and applications, we must first solve the issues of automatically and accurately recognising text and audio. The current paper focuses on the latter problem: automatic speech recognition (ASR).

ASR is already integrated into the lives of many majority language speakers. English speakers, for example, can take advantage of voice assistants like Alexa, Siri and Google Home, which recognize verbal commands and perform tasks in response. ASR is also used, of course, to enhance existing audio-visual resources by generating automatic transcriptions and subtitles. ASR methods are key to improving accessibility for certain users: many with dyslexia find it easier to dictate to a computer than to write, and those with physical challenges may find voice methods more accessible than touchscreens or keyboards. At a sociolinguistic level, building ASR systems for minority languages allows for their inclusion in new, technologically-mediated speech domains and encourages existing speakers to continue using them. Ultimately, this work has a key role in language revitalisation.

In this paper, we discuss efforts to develop a full ASR system for Scottish Gaelic, from a starting point of limited resource. We present a novel cross-lingual approach to creating acoustic model training examples, and describe several Gaelic NLP resources that were developed as secondary outcomes of the project.

2. The Low Resource Problem

The problem of low-resource ASR is widespread, as demonstrated by the small number of languages supported by speech assistant technologies. For example, Siri[4] and Google Home[5] each support only 12 languages out of the over 7,000 languages in the world. Their linguistic limitations are due, in part, to the strict requirements on the datasets and resources needed to build an ASR system. Of course, majority languages have much larger commercial potential, as well.

[1]Google added Scottish Gaelic to its Translate system in 2016.

[2]Developed by the University of Edinburgh spin-out, Cereproc: `https://www.cereproc.com`.

[3]A notable exception is Corpas na Gàidhlig – the 30M word corpus of historical and contemporary text based at the University of Glasgow (O Maolalaigh, 2016)

[4]Siri: Arabic, Cantonese, Dutch, English, Finnish, French, German, Hebrew, Italian, Malay, Mandarin Chinese, Spanish

[5]Google Home: Danish, Dutch, English, French, German, Hindi, Italian, Japanese, Korean, Norwegian, Spanish, Swedish

2.1. The Ideal Dataset

Constructing a conventional[6] ASR system requires 3 components: an acoustic model (AM), a language model (LM) and a pronunciation lexicon. The AM is trained on transcribed speech data, and learns to discriminate between the acoustic features of a target language's phonemes. The LM is trained on text data only, and learns typical sequences of words. Finally, a pronunciation lexicon is a list of words accompanied by phonetic transcriptions. Effectively, the lexicon is an intermediate between the two models at inference time. The AM uses the lexicon to map phonemes it recognizes to the words they form a part of, and the LM then estimates which combination of those words is most likely to have been spoken.

It is important that the transcriptions used to train the AM are verbatim, i.e., only containing the words that were spoken. This is because, in training, every frame of speech in the recording must be mapped to a component phone of a word in the transcription. The audio frame is then used as an example of how that phoneme is pronounced. If non-verbatim words are present in the transcript, some speech frames will be used as examples of phonemes that were never spoken. This leads to inaccuracy when recognising those phonemes. As a requirement for creating AM training examples, every transcribed utterance must also be time-aligned, i.e., assigned a start and end time within its corresponding recording. This would be laborious to perform manually, so it is usually done with an automatic aligner.

The text, both in terms of the transcriptions and the LM training data, has further requirements. Firstly, non-linguistic data, such as HTML tags or page numbers, must be removed. This is because they do not form part of a written sentence in the target language. Additionally, it must be possible to retrieve any word in the text from the lexicon. This enables the AM to map that word to its component phonemes to learn, and later recognize, the acoustic features of those phonemes. It follows that the pronunciation lexicon should contain at least one entry[7] for each distinct word in the training data. To avoid duplication of pronunciations in the lexicon, punctuation, capitalisation and digits in the text must be normalised. For example, if the tokens '9' and *naoi* ('nine') both occurred in a text, it would lead to ambiguity in the system; they would be mapped to the same pronunciation.

2.2. Low-Resource ASR

Modern approaches to ASR use deep neural network (DNN) models, which generally require hundreds of hours of transcribed audio and millions of tokens of text as training data. For this reason, data sparsity is a common hindrance in ASR modelling, especially with minority languages. Therefore, data augmentation techniques (Tüske et al., 2014; Renduchintala et al., 2018; Yılmaz et al., 2018) have become popular in low-resource ASR. These techniques strive to increase the quality and quantity of speech data by synthetically modifying existing data with noise, speed perturbation and other forms of variability. Other experimental methods, such as combining training data from multiple languages, are discussed further in section 3.

The collection and transcription of speech data is a significant challenge for most languages. As noted, most gathered text data requires cleaning and normalisation. For many majority languages, a wealth of NLP resources are available to facilitate this. English, for example, benefits from **num2words** (Dupras, 2022), a tool for verbalising digits in text, and **NLTK** (Bird et al., 2009), a natural language toolkit with modules for text cleaning and normalisation. Unfortunately, these kinds of tools rarely exist for minority and lower-resourced languages. Consequently, it takes more effort to acquire and prepare appropriate training data in 'low-resource ASR' contexts.

Typically, the pronunciation lexicon is even more difficult to obtain than the ASR training data. This is because the lexicon must be manually constructed by a language expert. Considering the number of tokens in a single language, this is an extensive and time-consuming task. As a result, comprehensive pronunciation lexicons do not exist for most minority languages.

3. Background

Popular approaches to tackling speech data sparsity in ASR involve using data from greater-resourced languages to bootstrap the low-resource system. One such approach applies the idea of multi-task learning (Caruana, 1997). This is where a single model simultaneously learns to perform multiple related tasks. For example, an AM learns to discriminate between phonemes from multiple different languages. Huang et al. (2013), for example, used a shared-hidden-layer multilingual DNN, in which the hidden layers of the model are trained on data from multiple languages. In this case, only the top, classifying layer is language-specific. Klejch et al. (2021) trained a similar multilingual acoustic model with language-specific output layers, and then fine-tuned the full model on monolingual data from each of its target, low-resource languages. This type of approach enables the feature extraction layers of the model to benefit from learning *global* discriminative speech features, while the output layer specialises in the target language.

Fully multilingual acoustic models have also been explored. Grézl et al. (2014) trained an acoustic model on multiple non-target languages, with the output layer

[6] Some modern ASR construction techniques, such as end-to-end and CTC, do not require a lexicon, or even a language model. They do, however, require quantities of data that far exceed the resources available for most minority languages.

[7] Multiple entries are used to recognise alternative pronunciations.

corresponding to all phonemes present in all of the training languages. The model was then adapted to its target low-resource language, reducing the number of outputs and shifting the model's weights towards the acoustic space of that language. Even before adaptation, the multilingual system was shown to outperform a monolingual target language system. This is a consistent finding in ASR research (Huang et al., 2013; Liu et al., 2018), and is likely due to an improvement in the model's ability to generalize to unseen speech data (Chen and Mak, 2015). From these results, we can conclude that non-target language materials are key to facilitating low-resource speech recognition.

Despite the aforementioned advances, previous work on Gaelic ASR is limited. Rasipuram et al. (2013) tackled the absence of a well-developed Gaelic pronunciation lexicon by exploring the use of grapheme-based ASR. The approach uses the Kullback-Leibler Hidden Markov Model (KL-HMM), in which graphemes are used instead of phonemes as the sub-word unit of the acoustic model. This exploited the fairly regular relationship between Gaelic graphemes and phonemes, and was shown as an effective approach to the problem. However, in years since, a substantial phoneme-based pronunciation lexicon has, in fact, been developed. Am Faclair Beag (Bauer and MacDhonnchaidh, 2022)[8] contains over 35,000 Gaelic words with IPA-style pronunciations, and is regularly maintained and updated. The existence of a large Gaelic lexicon enables a more traditional ASR approach to be undertaken, since numerous standard word-to-phoneme mappings have become available. In the sections that follow, we describe the development of such a system and demonstrate how non-target language resources can help prepare speech training data.

4. Resources

4.1. Collection of Resources

To train our AM, we collected transcribed speech data from the following sources:

- Clilstore,[9] an open-source repository of teaching videos,
- transcriptions made by Tobar an Dualchais (TaD),[10] from recordings of traditional narrative held by the School of Scottish Studies Archives (University of Edinburgh: UoE),
- output transcriptions from the Scottish Gaelic Automatic Handwriting Recognition Project, which utilised manuscripts of Gaelic traditional narrative at the School of Scottish Studies Archives (UoE),
- recordings of multi-speaker Zoom calls,
- audio books,
- and finally roughly 1000 short videos from LearnGaelic,[11] a language teaching resource created by MG Alba, the Gaelic media service.

Most of the data collected was from non-scripted interviews, with the exception of the pre-defined prompts, and as such can be classed as spontaneous speech. However, a sizeable proportion was also collected from oral narrative or lectures and so is less spontaneous. Written text data for training the language model (LM) was collected from all of the above transcriptions, as well as from: 1) An Crúbadán (Scannell, 2007), a web-scraped corpus of Gaelic text; and 2) short summaries of all of the Gaelic audio available on TaD. Finally, we used the aforementioned Gaelic pronunciation lexicon, Am Faclair Beag (Bauer and MacDhonnchaidh, 2022), as the starting point for the ASR system's lexicon.

4.2. Suitability of Resources

A substantial amount of Gaelic training data was collected, but it was by no means purpose-built for ASR. The text data included digits, page numbers, HTML tags, and notes, as well as punctuation and capitalisation. The transcriptions contained speaker labels and other non-verbatim text, and, most significantly, were not time-aligned to their audio recordings. To our knowledge, neither a text normalisation tool, nor an automatic aligner, existed for Gaelic. The data preparation stage, therefore, constituted a large proportion of the project time, and is described in the following sections.

In addition to the training data requiring cleaning, the lexicon was in need of modification. While the original lexicon included pronunciations for 35,000 words, this was for base-forms only; many morphological permutations were not present. The training data, however, contained over 150,000 distinct tokens. As we required an entry in the lexicon for every distinct token in the training data, we needed to augment the lexicon to accommodate out-of-vocabulary (OOV) tokens.

4.3. Solving the Suitability Problem

We removed capitalisation, punctuation, page numbers, speaker labels and other junk strings from texts using regular expressions implemented in Python. Our aim was to extirpate all non-verbatim or non-linguistic text, but any that did not match the specified patterns remained in place.

To tackle the presence of digits in the text, we developed a Gaelic digit verbaliser. One complexity of this task is that Gaelic uses both the decimal and vigesimal numbering systems. For many digits then, more than one verbalisation is possible. The token '80', for example, may verbalise to both *ceithir fichead* ('four twenties' - vigesimal system) and *ochdad* ('eighty' - deci-

[8] https://www.faclair.com

[9] https://clilstore.eu/clilstore/

[10] https://www.tobarandualchais.co.uk

[11] https://learngaelic.scot

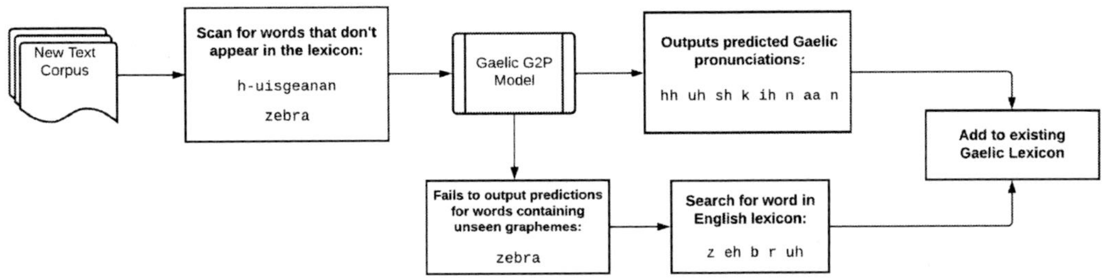

Figure 1: Diagram to show the grapheme-to-phoneme (G2P) process for adding words to the pronunciation lexicon.

mal system). It was important, therefore, that the verbaliser was compatible with both systems. The problem with verbalising transcribed digits with multiple verbalisation options is that, without listening to the audio, it is impossible to be certain which was actually spoken. Listening and manually transcribing each occurrence of a digit would be too time-consuming, so we required an automated solution. The numbering systems correlate with particular contexts, users and periods of times.[12] After examining each text type, and taking its age and context into account, we estimated its distribution of decimal to vigesimal verbalisations. Digits in the corpus were then verbalised at the estimated distribution.

For augmenting the number of pronunciation lexicon entries, a Grapheme-to-Phoneme (G2P) model was trained. This is a statistical model that learns the relationship between graphemes and phonemes in a given language. It is trained on pairs of words and pronunciations, and can be used to predict pronunciations for OOV words. We used the **Sequitur G2P** Python toolkit (Bisani and Ney, 2008) to train a G2P model on 90% of the original Gaelic lexicon entries. The model achieved a promising string error rate of 3.82% when tested on the remaining 10% of the words in the lexicon. We extracted the full list of words in the training data that did not appear in the lexicon (around 115,000 words), and used the G2P model to predict a pronunciation for each. With some words, the model failed to output a predicted pronunciation. This was often because the word contained graphemes, such as 'z', that are not in the Gaelic alphabet, and were hence unseen to the model during training. We deduced that most of these words were English. We looked them up in an English lexicon, provided by Quorate Technology Ltd., and their English pronunciations were added to the Gaelic ASR lexicon. The resulting lexicon was, therefore, bilingual. This does increase the risk of the ASR system substituting a Gaelic word for an English word in a transcription, however, this was not a noticeable consequence in our experiments. Figure 1 details the full lexicon augmentation process.

[12]For example, writers in more technical domains, and younger speakers at large, are more likely to use the decimal system, while older speakers tend to use the vigesimal one.

The final stage of data preparation was to align each transcription to its corresponding audio. Given the lack of a Gaelic automatic aligner model, this was our most challenging task.

5. Solving the Alignment Problem

5.1. What is Alignment?

Alignment is the process of assigning each word in the transcript a start and end time in its corresponding recording. An automatic aligner does this by mapping words in the transcription, via their component phonemes, to audio frames in the recording. Similar to an AM from speech recognition, the aligner learns the typical low-level acoustic features of each phoneme in the target language. At inference time, each word in the transcript is looked up in the pronunciation lexicon to generate a sequence of phonemes that are known to occur in the recording. The aligner then uses its learned acoustic knowledge to map each frame of speech to a phoneme in that sequence. This way, every word in the transcription is assigned a start and end time via its component phonemes.

5.2. Seed Model for Alignment

As an aligner is trained to recognize language-specific phonemes, it follows that a language-specific aligner is usually required. No Gaelic aligner model existed, and training our own would have required time-aligned training data. Manual alignment was a possible solution, but it would have been too laborious and expensive for the project. To mitigate this circular dependency, we experimented with a non-target language model to seed the alignment process.

Considering that the aligner is provided with a known sequence of words, which can be converted to phoneme sequences via the lexicon, its only task is to predict at which precise times those sequences occur. This is in contrast with speech recognition, where the model must also predict *which* phonemes, and consequent words, are spoken. As the aligner is not required to do this, it follows that cross-linguistic phonological variation (e.g. differences in phonemes versus allophones), may not be too problematic for the task. Take, for example, an aligner that has been trained on a language which does not distinguish between /k/ and its aspirated equivalent, /kʰ/. If that aligner is used for a language which *does* distinguish between the two, it will at some point be faced with a recording in which /kʰ/ occurs. In this case, the aligner would be able to pick up on the more global features of the /k/ phoneme to make a confident estimate at when its aspirated variant is pronounced. We hypothesised that using a non-target language aligner model would be a viable solution to the task of aligning the Gaelic data. This approach to the task is further described in the next sections.

5.3. Lexicon Phoneset Mapping

We used an English alignment model, provided by Quorate Technology Ltd., to seed the alignment process. The aligner uses a set of 29 English phonemes. The problem with this phoneset is that Gaelic has more phonemes than English. For example, where Gaelic distinguishes between /kʲ/, /kʰ/ and /kʲʰ/, English simply classes these as allophones of the phoneme /k/. The issue arises when the lexicon is used to map the words in the transcription to their known sequence of phonemes in the recording. Because the Gaelic pronunciation lexicon uses the additional Gaelic phonemes, these will be present in the resulting sequence of phonemes to be aligned. Upon encountering /kʲ/, /kʰ/ and /kʲʰ/ in that sequence, the aligner would fail, as these phonemes are not present in its phoneset. For this reason, it is important to match the phoneset used in the pronunciation lexicon to the phoneset that the aligner is able to recognize. We therefore created a mapping between the Gaelic and English phonesets to account for the additional phonemes in Gaelic.

The English aligner uses a computer-friendly English phoneset that is based on ARPABET (Klautau, 2001). Am Faclair Beag, on the other hand, uses a Gaelic adaptation of IPA. Both phonesets can be directly mapped back to Standard IPA (Brown, 2012), making it possible to convert between the two. The Gaelic IPA phonemes were first restored back to their Standard IPA equivalents, which can be found in the 'About' section of the lexicon's website (Bauer and MacDhonnchaidh, 2022). Then, a new mapping was created from the Standard IPA Gaelic phonemes to the subset of those phonemes available to our English aligner model. For phonemes that were shared between the two languages, this was trivial. For each of the Gaelic-exclusive phonemes, however, we decided on an English 'closest equivalent' phoneme. Taking the above example, the closest English phoneme for each of the 3 distinct Gaelic phonemes, /kʲ/, /kʰ/ and /kʲʰ/ was /k/. Each of these Gaelic phonemes was mapped, accordingly, to a single English phoneme. The full phoneset mapping is shown in Table 1. Once the phoneset

GD	IPA	EN	GD	IPA	EN
b	p	p	dʲ	tʲ	tʃ
p	pʰ	p	tʲ	tʲʰ	tʃ
ɟ	ɟ	g	ð	ð	ð
ɣ	ɣ	g	rʲ	ɾʲ	ð
ç	ç	k	r	ɾ	ɾ
g	k	k	R	rˠ	ɹ
gʲ	kʲ	k	a	a	ɑ
k	kʰ	k	a:	a:	ɑ
kʲ	kʲʰ	k	ɛ	ɛ	ɛ
x	x	k	e	e	eɪ
t	t̪ʰ	t	e:	e:	eɪ
d	t̪	t	i	i	i
l	l̪	l	i:	i:	i
Lʲ	ʎ	l + j	ɪ	ɪ	ɪ
L	l̪ˠ	ɫ	j	j	j
m	m	m	o	o	oʊ
n	n	n	o:	o:	oʊ
ŋ	ŋ	ŋ	ɔ	ɔ	ɔ
ŋʲ	ŋʲ	ŋ	ɔ:	ɔ:	ɔ
Nʲ	ɲ	n + j	u	u	u
N	n̪ˠ	n̩	u:	u:	u
v	v	v	ɯ	ɯ	ʉ
f	f	f	ɯ:	ɯ:	ʉ
s	s̪	s	ɤ	ɤ	ʊ
h	h	h	ʊ:	ʊ:	ʊ
ʃ	ʃ	ʃ	ə	ə	ə

Table 1: Phoneset Mapping. GD = Gaelic Adaptation of IPA, IPA = Standard IPA, EN = English IPA, i.e. Standard IPA phonemes present in the English phoneset

mapping had been constructed, every Gaelic phoneme in the pronunciation lexicon was converted into its English equivalent. This meant that the phoneset used by the lexicon matched the phoneset used by the aligner. The *pseudo*-Gaelic phoneset, therefore, allowed us to use an English AM towards Gaelic alignment.

The phoneset mapping was carried out with the assistance of Gaelic language experts, but their expertise was not necessarily a requirement for the task. This is because IPA is a set of phonemes described by their various qualities, such as place and manner of articulation. This information enables those who may not be familiar with certain phonemes, for example, because they are not speakers of a language that uses them, to understand which other phonemes they are related to. In addition, IPA is a fairly global phoneset, making the task possible for a large number of languages.

5.4. Training Data Alignment

Once the lexicon phoneset had been adapted to the aligner's one, the alignment could begin. As the aligned data would be used to train the acoustic model, it was important that the data were aligned accurately. Aligners have two outputs: word-level timings and a word confidence score for each aligned word. Word confidence scores (see Kemp and Schaaf (1997); Gillick et al. (1997)) measure the probability that a certain word is actually spoken at its given start and end times. The scores can be used to evaluate the accuracy of the alignment – the higher the score, the more likely it is to be accurate. We, therefore, used average word confidence scores to filter the aligned utterances for our final training set.

While aiming for high alignment quality, it is also important to keep in mind that the DNN models used for speech recognition require a large *quantity* of training data. Data that aligns well tends to be less noisy, so including only the best-aligned data would prevent the model from adapting to noisy audio conditions. When filtering the data, therefore, it was necessary to find a balance between quality of alignment and quantity of retained data. We judged that any utterances with an average word confidence score of $< 70\%$ should be discarded. Initially, only a subset of the full training corpus (the Clilstore dataset) was aligned with the English model. The frequency of average word confidence scores for utterances in this initial dataset can be seen in Figure 2.

Given the selection criteria, the initial yield of data was substantial: from 27 hours of data, 21.2 hours, or 78.5%, were retained. This is an indicator of the overall quality of the alignment, which is promising, given the novel cross-lingual approach used. We trained a Gaelic AM using this initial aligned dataset, and, because an AM can also be used as an automatic aligner, we were then able to *re-align* the data using a Gaelic-specific model. We did this twice: first using the Gaelic model trained on the s5b dataset (see Table 2), and again using the model trained on the s5c dataset. As model performance improved from training on a larger dataset, so did the quality of the alignment. This resulted in a higher yield of aligned audio being collected with every re-alignment, as shown in Table 2.

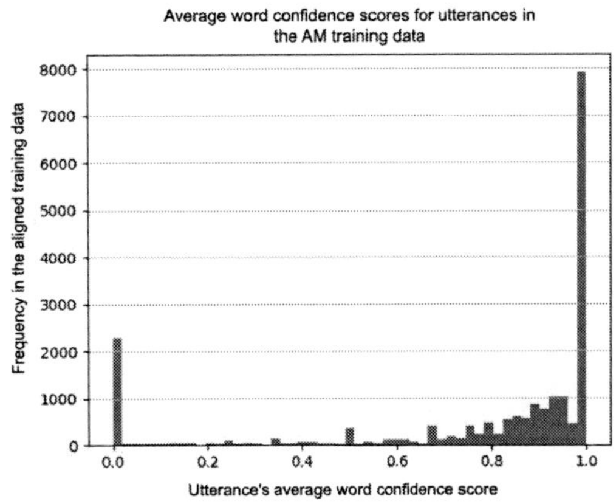

Figure 2: Histogram showing the frequency of average word confidence scores for aligned utterances in the AM training data. These statistics are used to filter well-aligned examples.

6. ASR Model Building

6.1. System Overview

We constructed a number of Gaelic ASR systems using the **Kaldi** speech recognition toolkit (Povey et al., 2011). Kaldi is an open-source toolkit that includes scripts, or 'recipes', that can be used to build and evaluate full ASR systems. Our ASR systems were constructed in an iterative manner. As explained, an initial speech dataset was first aligned with the English aligner. The resulting data was used to train our first Gaelic AM, which could then, itself, be used for alignment. After this point, every new speech corpus obtained was aligned with our latest and most accurate model. The yield from this filtered alignment was added to the AM training data, and used to retrain the AM. The full alignment and training cycle is shown in Figure 3. Additionally, the entire process of data preparation and Gaelic ASR system development is visualised in Figure 4 in Appendix A.

6.2. Acoustic Models

We used the Kaldi AMI recipe (Carletta, 2006) as a starting point for our AM architecture. The recipe, based on Swietojanski et al. (2013), constructs a 15-layer time-delay neural network (see Peddinti et al. (2015)), which increases the number of input context frames at every layer. The initial input to the model is one audio frame *t0* with six surrounding context frames, corresponding to *t-3* and *t+3*. The frames are input as high-dimensional MFCCs (80-dimensions) with 100-dimensional i-vectors. Training ran for 15 epochs. This setup was used for the s5, s5b and s5c models. After s5c, the full set of AM training data was finalised, and so we began experimenting with the model's architecture. This is further detailed in the results section.

6.3. Language Models

We trained various 4-gram language models using the KenLM language modelling toolkit (Heafield et al., 2013). Each model was trained on 90% of the full available text dataset, and evaluated for its perplexity score on the remaining 10%. Two models were used in our final experiments, their only difference being number of tokens of training data, shown in Table 3.

7. Evaluation

For the ASR evaluation dataset, we aimed to extract a set of utterances with a range of speakers, dialects, topics and acoustic environments. This is because our goal was to build a system that performed well on varied Gaelic speech. We extracted utterances from a larger

<table>
<tr><th></th><th colspan="4">Hours</th></tr>
<tr><th>Dataset</th><th>s5</th><th>s5b</th><th>s5c</th><th>s5d</th></tr>
<tr><td>Clilstore</td><td>21.2</td><td>21.2</td><td>22.7 (+1.5)</td><td>23.5 (+0.8)</td></tr>
<tr><td>TaD</td><td></td><td>17.9</td><td>22.2 (+4.3)</td><td rowspan="2">29.6 (+2.9)</td></tr>
<tr><td>TaD dump 2</td><td></td><td></td><td>4.5</td></tr>
<tr><td>Handwriting</td><td></td><td></td><td>13.7</td><td>17.6 (+3.9)</td></tr>
<tr><td>Zoom Calls</td><td></td><td></td><td>0.2</td><td>0.5 (+0.3)</td></tr>
<tr><td>Audiobooks</td><td></td><td></td><td></td><td>0.9</td></tr>
<tr><td>MG Alba</td><td></td><td></td><td></td><td>31.4</td></tr>
<tr><td>Total</td><td>21.2</td><td>39.1</td><td>63.3 (+5.8)</td><td>103.5 (+7.9)</td></tr>
</table>

Table 2: Yield of aligned data from each re-alignment. Model training occurred for each new dataset, and re-alignment occurred for dataset s5c and s5d. Bold is the additional hours of data gained from re-alignment.

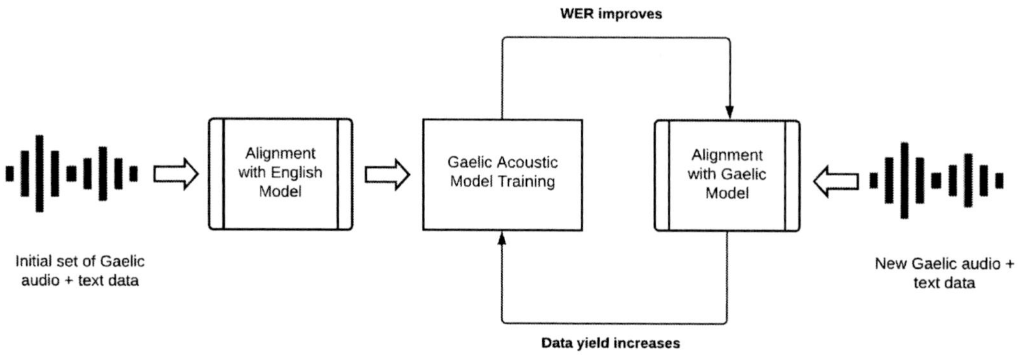

Figure 3: The alignment and training process carried out to iteratively train new models

Model	Tokens in training data	Perplexity
H	7,378,450	90.1
I	8,593,567	81.3

Table 3: Language Model Perplexity Results

number of short sessions to ensure that the final set had wide variability. We extracted an hour of speech data from the initial dataset that had been aligned with the English model. Of course, this was non-overlapping with the training data. Because the evaluation set is used to assess the performance of the final ASR system, we aimed for a dataset with greater alignment quality than our training data. To facilitate this, the word confidence score filtering threshold was increased from the original 70% to 95%. Once the aligned utterances had been extracted, a Gaelic expert manually corrected the automatic alignments to ensure 100% alignment accuracy. The final evaluation set amounted to 56 minutes of speech data with high quality reference transcripts. We used this evaluation set to generate a word error rate (WER) of each new ASR system, measuring its performance. WER is the standard evaluation metric for ASR, and measures how much the transcription output by the ASR system differs from a reference transcription (Jurafsky and Martin, 2021). WER can be considered similar to $1 - accuracy$.

8. Results

As shown in Table 4, our first Gaelic ASR system achieved a WER of 35.8%. Considering this model was trained on only 21.2 hours of speech data that had been aligned with an English model, this result was promising. As noted previously, the model architecture and training conditions were maintained for models s5, s5b and s5c. In ASR research, increases in training data tend to correlate with improved performance. We report the same: our system's WER improved by 7.6% by simply increasing our training set quantity from 21.2 to 63.3 hours (see model s5c, Table 4).

After training the s5c model, we received new speech data from MG Alba. This increased our AM training set to over 100 hours. It also increased our LM training data by over 1 million tokens. As this would be our final training set, we retrained the LM and began experimenting with the AM architecture. We first decided to reduce the number of training epochs from 15 to 4 as the training logs suggested many of the later epochs were redundant. Having too many training epochs also risks over-fitting to the training data. Combined with the new LM, we expected a fairly substantial WER reduction (WERR) from the s5c model to the s5d model. However, the WER only decreased by 0.8%. This led us to believe that the size and capacity of the model itself may have been a cause of over-fitting. The model was, therefore, retrained using 11, as opposed to 15 layers, again for 4 epochs. The dimensionality of the MFCCs was also reduced from 80 to 40, as we suspected that the extra input resolution likely did not add much value. This model, shown as s5d-small in Table 4, attained a more substantial WERR from the s5c model: 1.9%. The resulting WERR from our initial to final ASR systems is 9.5%, which is a significant relative improvement of 26.54%.

Model	AM data (hrs)	LM	WER(%)
s5	21.2	H	35.8
s5b	39.1	H	31.0
s5c	63.3	H	28.2
s5d	103.5	I	27.4
s5d-small	103.5	I	26.3

Table 4: ASR Results

9. Discussion

The performance improvements achieved for the Gaelic ASR system are very promising. WER is still high when compared to majority language ASR systems, however, and would not be classed as suitable for production-level ASR. That said, fully automatic transcription tasks have a much more demanding WER threshold than other related tasks. For example, the WER that we achieved is within the threshold required for machine-assisted transcription. Thus, the system could be used, for example, to align a transcription to a video and create subtitles. This would give much added-value to existing Gaelic language resources, and some of the project collaborators have already used the system to do just that. See, for example, the Island Voices videos on Youtube (Wells, 2012), which have been augmented with Gaelic subtitles using the Gaelic aligner model.

In addition to improving the quality of existing resources, the creation of new time-aligned Gaelic transcriptions also creates the opportunity for a feedback loop. This is where the Gaelic system is used to assist in transcribing and aligning new data that can be added to the training dataset. Thus, as the quantity of training data is increased, the performance of the ASR system improves. As shown in our re-alignment process, improvements in the ASR performance also increase the yield of data that can be extracted for training.

Regarding future work, we suggest that a multilingual approach, similar to those described in Section 3, is implemented for the AM. In particular, it could be beneficial to exploit the resources available for Irish. With 1,761,420 speakers in the 2016 census (Central Statistics Office, 2020), Irish is better resourced than Gaelic. It also benefits from dedicated Irish speech and language technology research centres at Trinity College Dublin (Trinity College Dublin, 2019) and Dublin City University. Not only would the incorporation of Irish increase the quantity of data available for training, it would also enable the use of a number of useful language tools that have been built for Irish. Finally, given that the language is closely related to Gaelic, we believe the addition of Irish to the training data would be beneficial: the similarity between the languages would facilitate the recognition of Gaelic phonemes specifically, whilst their differences would improve generalisability to unseen data.

10. Acknowledgements

We gratefully acknowledge funding from the Soillse Research Fund and DDI/SFC's BEACON Build Back Better Open Call: COVID-19 Response and Accelerating Economic and Social Recovery in Edinburgh & South East Scotland. We are also indebted to the following groups and individuals, who provided valuable language data and other support: Am Faclair Beag, Ceòlas Uibhist Ltd, European Ethnological Research Centre, Grace Note Publications, Guthan nan Eilean / Island Voices, LearnGaelic (MG Alba), National Folklore Collection (University College Dublin), Ruairidh MacIlleathain, Sabhal Mòr Ostaig, The National Library of Scotland, The School of Scottish Studies Archives, Tobar an Dualchais / Kist o Riches, University of the Highlands and Islands and Prof Wilson McLeod.

This work has made use of the resources provided by the Edinburgh Compute and Data Facility (ECDF). [13]

11. Bibliographical References

Batchelor, C. (2016). Automatic derivation of categorial grammar from a part-of-speech-tagged corpus in scottish gaelic. *PARIS Inalco du 4 au 8 juillet 2016*, page 1.

Batchelor, C. (2019). Universal dependencies for scottish gaelic: syntax. In *Proceedings of the Celtic Language Technology Workshop*, pages 7–15.

Bauer, M. and MacDhonnchaidh, U. (2022). Am faclair beag. `https://www.faclair.com/index.aspx?Language=en`. [Online; accessed 19-February-2022].

Bella, G., McNeill, F., Gorman, R., O Donnaile, C., MacDonald, K., Chandrashekar, Y., Freihat, A. A., and Giunchiglia, F. (2020). A major Wordnet for

[13] `http://www.ecdf.ed.ac.uk/`

a minority language: Scottish Gaelic. In *Proceedings of the 12th Language Resources and Evaluation Conference*, pages 2812–2818, Marseille, France, May. European Language Resources Association.

Bird, S., Klein, E., and Loper, E. (2009). *Natural language processing with Python: analyzing text with the natural language toolkit*. O'Reilly Media, Inc.

Bisani, M. and Ney, H. (2008). Joint-sequence models for grapheme-to-phoneme conversion. *Speech communication*, 50(5):434–451.

Boizou, L. and Lamb, W. (2020). An online linguistic analyser for scottish gaelic. In *Human Language Technologies–The Baltic Perspective: Proceedings of the Ninth International Conference Baltic HLT 2020*, volume 328, pages 119–122. IOS Press.

Brown, A. (2012). International phonetic alphabet.

Carletta, J. (2006). Announcing the ami meeting corpus. *The ELRA Newsletter*, 11(1):3–5.

Caruana, R. (1997). Multitask learning. *Machine learning*, 28(1):41–75.

Central Statistics Office. (2020). Irish language and the gaeltacht. `https://www.cso.ie/en/releasesandpublications/ep/p-cp10esil/p10esil/ilg`.

Chen, D. and Mak, B. K.-W. (2015). Multitask learning of deep neural networks for low-resource speech recognition. *IEEE/ACM Transactions on Audio, Speech, and Language Processing*, 23(7):1172–1183. DOI: `10.1109/TASLP.2015.2422573`.

Dupras, V. (2022). num2words. `https://github.com/savoirfairelinux/num2words`. [Online; accessed 14-April-2022].

Gillick, L., Ito, Y., and Young, J. (1997). A probabilistic approach to confidence estimation and evaluation. In *1997 IEEE International Conference on Acoustics, Speech, and Signal Processing*, volume 2, pages 879–882. IEEE.

Grézl, F., Karafiát, M., and Veselý, K. (2014). Adaptation of multilingual stacked bottle-neck neural network structure for new language. In *2014 IEEE International Conference on Acoustics, Speech and Signal Processing (ICASSP)*, pages 7654–7658. DOI: `10.1109/ICASSP.2014.6855089`.

Heafield, K., Pouzyrevsky, I., Clark, J. H., and Koehn, P. (2013). Scalable modified kneser-ney language model estimation. In *Proceedings of the 51st Annual Meeting of the Association for Computational Linguistics (Volume 2: Short Papers)*, pages 690–696.

Huang, J.-T., Li, J., Yu, D., Deng, L., and Gong, Y. (2013). Cross-language knowledge transfer using multilingual deep neural network with shared hidden layers. In *2013 IEEE International Conference on Acoustics, Speech and Signal Processing*, pages 7304–7308. DOI: `10.1109/ICASSP.2013.6639081`.

Jurafsky, D. and Martin, J. H. (2021). Speech and language processing (3rd edition draft). `https://web.stanford.edu/~jurafsky/slp3/`. [Online; accessed 13-April-2022].

Kemp, T. and Schaaf, T. (1997). Estimating confidence using word lattices. In *Fifth European Conference on Speech Communication and Technology*. Citeseer.

Klautau, A. (2001). Arpabet and the timit alphabet. `https://web.archive.org/web/20160603180727/http://www.laps.ufpa.br/aldebaro/papers/ak_arpabet01.pdf`. [Online; accessed 14-April-2022].

Klejch, O., Wallington, E., and Bell, P. (2021). The CSTR System for Multilingual and Code-Switching ASR Challenges for Low Resource Indian Languages. In *Proc. Interspeech 2021*, pages 2881–2885. DOI: `10.21437/Interspeech.2021-1035`.

Lamb, W. and Danso, S. (2014). Developing an automatic part-of-speech tagger for Scottish Gaelic. In *Proceedings of the First Celtic Language Technology Workshop*, pages 1–5.

Lamb, W. and Sinclair, M. (2016). Developing word embedding models for Scottish Gaelic. In *Actes de la conférence conjointe JEP-TALN-RECITAL*, volume 6, pages 31–41.

Lamb, W. (1999). A diachronic account of Gaelic news-speak: The development and expansion of a register. *Scottish Gaelic Studies*, 19:141–171.

Liu, D., Wan, X., Xu, J., and Zhang, P. (2018). Multilingual speech recognition training and adaptation with language-specific gate units. In *2018 11th International Symposium on Chinese Spoken Language Processing (ISCSLP)*, pages 86–90. DOI: `10.1109/ISCSLP.2018.8706584`.

Murchú, E. P. Ó. (2019). Using intergaelic to pre-translate and subsequently post-edit a sci-fi novel from Scottish Gaelic to Irish. In *Proceedings of the Qualities of Literary Machine Translation*, pages 20–25.

National Records of Scotland. (2015). Scotland's census 2011: Gaelic report (part 1).

O Maolalaigh, R. (2016). DASG: Digital Archive of Scottish Gaelic/Dachaigh airson Stòras na Gàidhlig. *Scottish Gaelic Studies*, 30:242–262.

Peddinti, V., Povey, D., and Khudanpur, S. (2015). A time delay neural network architecture for efficient modeling of long temporal contexts. In *Sixteenth annual conference of the international speech communication association*, pages 3214–3218. DOI: `10.21437/Interspeech.2015-647`.

Povey, D., Ghoshal, A., Boulianne, G., Burget, L., Glembek, O., Goel, N., Hannemann, M., Motlicek, P., Qian, Y., Schwarz, P., Silovsky, J., Stemmer, G., and Vesely, K. (2011). The kaldi speech recognition toolkit. In *IEEE 2011 Workshop on Automatic Speech Recognition and Understanding*. IEEE Signal Processing Society, December. IEEE Catalog No.: CFP11SRW-USB.

Rasipuram, R., Bell, P., and Magimai.-Doss, M. (2013). Grapheme and multilingual posterior features for under-resourced speech recognition: A study on Scottish Gaelic. In *2013 IEEE International Conference on Acoustics, Speech and Signal Processing*, pages 7334–7338. DOI: 10.1109/ICASSP.2013.6639087.

Renduchintala, A., Ding, S., Wiesner, M., and Watanabe, S. (2018). Multi-modal data augmentation for end-to-end asr. *arXiv preprint arXiv:1803.10299*.

Scannell, K. P. (2007). The Crúbadán Project: Corpus building for under-resourced languages. *Cahiers du Cental*, 5:1.

Swietojanski, P., Ghoshal, A., and Renals, S. (2013). Hybrid acoustic models for distant and multichannel large vocabulary speech recognition. In *2013 IEEE workshop on automatic speech recognition and understanding*, pages 285–290. IEEE.

Trinity College Dublin. (2019). Irish speech and language technology research centre. https://www.tcd.ie/slscs/itut/. [Online; Accessed 13-April-2022].

Tüske, Z., Golik, P., Nolden, D., Schlüter, R., and Ney, H. (2014). Data augmentation, feature combination, and multilingual neural networks to improve asr and kws performance for low-resource languages. In *Fifteenth Annual Conference of the International Speech Communication Association*. Citeseer.

Wells, G. (2012). Series 1 (Gaelic) Island Voices playlist. https://www.youtube.com/playlist?list=PL2770777DF19FEFAF. [Online; accessed 13-Apil-2022].

Yılmaz, E., Heuvel, H. v. d., and van Leeuwen, D. A. (2018). Acoustic and textual data augmentation for improved asr of code-switching speech. *arXiv preprint arXiv:1807.10945*.

Appendix A: Gaelic ASR System Development Process

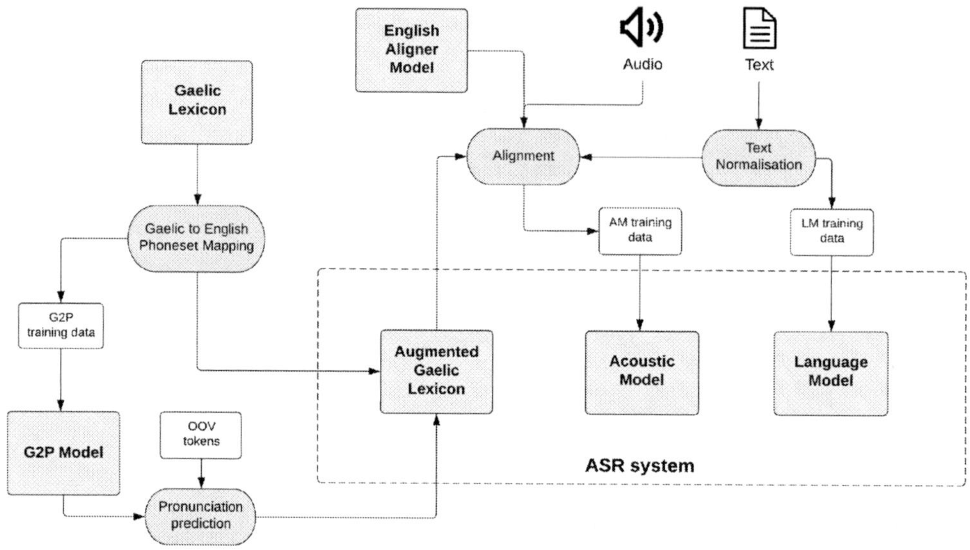

Figure 4: Diagram to show the full Gaelic ASR system development process. The lexicon is adapted (to use a different phoneset) and augmented (using G2P pronunciation prediction). Additionally, audio-to-text alignment creates acoustic model training examples, and text normalisation creates language model training examples. The full ASR system is composed of the augmented lexicon, the acoustic model, and the language model. OOV = Out of Vocabulary.

Proceedings of the CLTW 4 @ LREC2022, pages 121–126
Marseille, 20-25 June 2022

Handwritten Text Recognition (HTR) for Irish-Language Folklore

Brian Ó Raghallaigh, Andrea Palandri, Críostóir Mac Cárthaigh
Dublin City University, University College Dublin
Ireland
{brian.oraghallaigh, andrea.palandri}@dcu.ie, criostoir.maccarthaigh@ucd.ie

Abstract

In this paper we present our method for digitising a large collection of handwritten Irish-language texts as part of a project to mine information from a large corpus of Irish and Scottish Gaelic folktales. The handwritten texts form part of the Main Manuscript Collection of the National Folklore Collection of Ireland and contain handwritten transcriptions of oral folklore collected in Ireland in the 20th century. With the goal of creating a large text corpus of the Irish-language folktales contained within this collection, our method involves scanning the pages of the physical volumes and digitising the text on these pages using Transkribus, a platform for the recognition of historical documents. Given the nature of the collection, the approach we have taken involves the creation of individual text recognition models for multiple collectors' hands. Doing it this way was motivated by the fact that a relatively small number of collectors contributed the bulk of the material, while the differences between each collector in terms of style, layout and orthography were difficult to reconcile within a single handwriting model. We present our preliminary results along with a discussion on the viability of using crowdsourced correction to improve our HTR models.

Keywords: digital folkloristics, handwritten text recognition, Irish

1. Introduction

The research described here took place between Oct 2021 and Mar 2022 and was carried out as part of the AHRC/IRC-funded *Decoding Hidden Heritages in Gaelic Traditional Narrative with Text-Mining and Phylogenetics* project[1] being conducted jointly by researchers in the University of Edinburgh, Dublin City University, Durham University, University College Dublin and Indiana University. The overarching goal of the larger project is to collate and analyse a large number of the collected Gaelic folktales of Scotland and Ireland with a view to better understanding the joint cultural history of these two countries.

The Scottish component involves digitising material held in the School of Scottish Studies Archive in the University of Edinburgh and the Irish component involves digitising material held in the National Folklore Collection in University College Dublin. Once compiled, the Scottish and Irish corpora will be normalised and combined by the project team for analysis. While handwritten text recognition (HTR) for both the Scottish corpus and the Irish corpus is being carried out using Transkribus, a platform for recognising historical documents, this paper will focus only on the creation of the Irish corpus.

2. Irish-Language Folktale Corpus

The National Folklore Collection of Ireland is housed in University College Dublin and comprises several collections of material compiled by the Irish Folklore Commission and its successors during the 20th century (Almqvist 1977–9), for example the Schools' Collection and the Main Manuscript Collection (MMC). The *Dúchas* digitisation project,[2] which is running since 2012 (Ó Cleircín et al. 2014), has scanned and indexed the entire Schools' Collection (*c.*450k pages) and transcribed much of it via a crowdsourcing initiative. The Dúchas project has started digitising and indexing material from the MMC as well as the Audio Collection. The MMC is substantial and consists of 2,400 bound volumes comprising *c.*700k pages of material. The Decoding Hidden Heritages (DHH) project will supplement the work of the Dúchas project by scanning and converting 100 volumes (*c.*40k pages) of the MMC to text, focusing on volumes containing folktales in Irish.

Despite the success of the crowdsourcing initiative to transcribe the Schools' Collection on a number of levels (e.g. *c.*400k pages transcribed, active learning resource, positive user engagement, etc.), it was obvious given the advancement of AI-powered transcription tools that it would be incumbent upon us to use semi-automatic techniques to transcribe the MMC to create our Irish-language folktale corpus for the DHH project.

3. Transkribus

The software being used to automate transcription of texts from the MMC is Transkribus (Sánchez et al. 2014), 'a comprehensive platform for the digitisation, AI-powered text recognition, transcription and searching of historical documents - from any place, any time, and in any language.'[3] The program allows users to train unique AI-powered text-recognition models that can quickly reach relatively-low character error rates (CER) that yield automated transcriptions from handwritten manuscripts. Transkribus also offers the function to create a language model based on your transcription data which can further reduce the CER, and especially the word error rate (WER), of the automated transcription.

Transkribus offers a number of tools and functions that can be used to transform images of handwritten documents into text, which include: tools for the manual and automatic segmentation of a document image, called 'Layout Analysis'; a console for manual transcription adjoining the image of the document; a tool to train new models based on your transcription data; a function to run your model to automatically transcribe any number of pages; the option of creating a Language Model (LM) based on your training data or to upload one from elsewhere, enhancing the performance of the HTR model; a function to mark which user has corrected any number of pages; tools to compare

[1] https://www.gaois.ie/en/about/decoding-hidden-heritages
[2] https://www.duchas.ie/en
[3] https://readcoop.eu/transkribus/?sc=Transkribus

and evaluate the efficiency of any number of HTR models on a given text; tools to search your document once it has been transcribed. All data is stored on Transkribus' cloud service and users can create 'Collections' in which large numbers of documents can be managed simultaneously.

Training models in Transkribus that produce a CER of ~5% is a relatively rapid and straightforward process. We found that a first rough model, giving CERs of ~10%, could be trained with only 50 pages of transcription data from the MMC. After this the law of diminishing marginal returns applied, whereby any additional production in data resulted in progressively smaller increases in output. Generally speaking, once a CER of ~5% was reached, the additional production in data necessary to further reduce the CER in a meaningful way began to reach unworkable levels for our small team (one full-time postdoctoral researcher and one full-time postgraduate research assistant), and other strategies were discussed in order to further improve the models in the future. For example, our most recent model for Seosamh Ó Dálaigh (one of the MMC collectors) was trained on 558 pages of manuscript, 69,457 words, and produced a CER of 4.39% and a WER of 12.43%. The model prior to this had been trained on 396 pages of manuscript, 49,078 words, and had yielded a CER of 4.69% and a WER of 13.61%. Therefore, this labour-intensive 41.5% increase in the training data only resulted in a 0.3% reduction of the CER and a 1% decrease of the WER.

On the other hand, more promising progress was made with other models that used less transcription data and much was found to depend on the general legibility and orderliness of each individual scribe.

4. Handwritten Text Recognition on the Main Manuscript Collection

The MMC presents two main challenges to HTR technology:

4.1 Dialect Variation

Most collectors involved in creating the MMC placed particular emphasis on remaining as close as possible to their informants' speech in their transcriptions. This approach was exhibited by Séamus Ó Duilearga himself, who founded the Irish Folklore Comission in 1927, in *Leabhar Sheáin Í Chonaill* (1948) and is described in the introduction to that work.

> Ní raibh ionnam ach úirlis sgríte don tseanachaí: níor atharuíos siolla dá nduairt sé, ach gach aon ní a sgrí chô maith agus d'fhéadfainn é.[4]

Similarly, transcribers working for the Commission took great care to capture the dialects of their informants and in some cases we even find representations of pronunciation tendencies unique to individual speakers. For example, forms such as *do* replacing *go*, e.g. *dubhairt si do raibh sí do maith*, appear in Seosamh Ó Dálaigh's transcriptions of a number of informants from West Kerry,[5] spellings such as *cén chaoi a ngohat sí* for *cén chaoi a ngabhfadh sí* are used by Liam Mac Coisdealbha in Connemara,[6] and spellings such as *thenaic* for *tháinig* or *órc* for *amharc* are used by Liam Mac Meanman in transcribing speakers from West Donegal.[7]

While this feature of the MMC makes it a valuable resource for the study of twentieth century Irish dialects, this rich variation in linguistic forms makes the collection unsuitable to a general Irish Language Model (LM) that could assist the HTR. Indeed, an LM trained on the transcription data from the entire corpus would result in forms like *órc* or *ghohat sí* appearing in regions where those are not the pronunciations because of suggestions from the LM assisting the HTR. Similarly, given the uniqueness of spellings found throughout the MMC, the manuscripts' display of dialect variation would risk being lost to another Irish LM if this were to be uploaded from a dictionary or a corpus of printed texts.

Preliminary data compiled from Scottish Gaelic manuscripts and shared with us by researchers in the University of Edinburgh collaborating on the project showed that scribe-specific models that used an LM from the training data yielded the best results, i.e. produced the lowest CERs. For this reason and because of the linguistic nature of the MMC we decided to begin training a series of scribe-specific HTR and language models for the most prolific collectors involved in the gathering of *seanscéalta* 'folktales', the narrative form on which the project focuses, so that Tranksribus could yield more accurate transcriptions that required less correction time.

4.2 Code and Script Switching

Another challenge the MMC presents to HTR technology is the switching between Irish and English in most manuscripts of the collection, which is also usually reflected in a change in script, i.e. whereas Irish is usually written in a form of Gaelic script, English words are usually written in a form of cursive. This practise of using a different script to write non-Irish words is old in Gaelic tradition and can be found in Early Modern manuscripts as well, therefore this is a broader challenge that will face the application of HTR on Irish manuscripts more generally in the future.

Figure 1: An example of script switching in a seventeenth-century copy of Keating's Foras Feasa ar Éirinn written by Iollan Ua Maolchonaire (RIA MS 23 O 19, fol. 90): ní fíor an ní sin adeir Sanderus. 'That is not true according to Sanderus'.

In the case of the MMC specifically, preliminary data suggests a correlation between collectors with high frequency in script switching and models with high CER levels, i.e. low accuracy. Manuscripts written by Seán Ó Flannagáin, which contain a number of macaronic texts, are a case in point, for whom we have struggled to reduce CER levels to below 10%. In the following example, a comparison of the capital *d* in *d'fhiarthuigh* and *dad*, the *f* in *fhios* and *five*, the *s* in *sé* and *six*, the *r* in *dubhairt* and

[4] 'I was only a writing tool for the story teller: I didn't change a single syllable that he uttered, instead writing everything as accurately as I could.'

[5] MMC MS 242, p. 548.

[6] MMC MS 157, p. 29.

[7] MMC MS 168, p. 18.

or, the *g* in *geárr* and *night* and the *t* in *acht* and *night* gives some measure of what this scribe's HTR model is contending with.

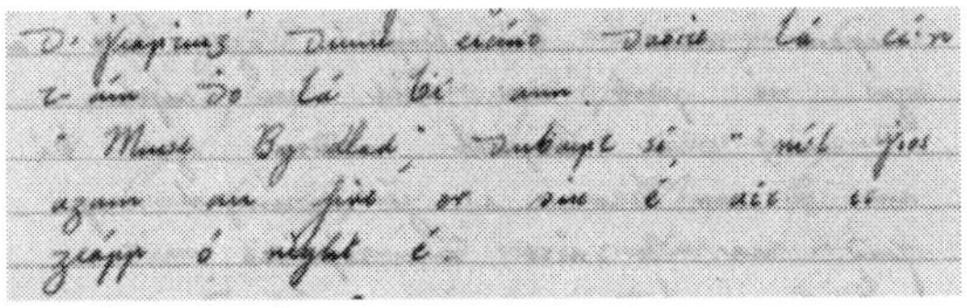

Figure 2: MMC MS 354, p. 207.

> D'fhiarthuigh duine eicínt daoithe lá cé'n
> t-ám dho lá bhí ann.
> 'Muise *By Dad*,' dubhairt sí, 'ní'l fhios
> agam an *five or six* é acht is
> geárr ó *night* é.[8]

One solution to this issue is to omit pages with large amounts of script switching, such as this one, from the training data in the hope of improving recognition of the Gaelic script. But in most cases script switching is confined to single words and is distributed so evenly throughout the pages of the MMC that large portions of data would end up being discarded only to filter out a handful of English words. This process would also produce a HTR model disproportionate to the language of the corpus, since many of these English words are integrated so seamlessly into the grammar of Irish that they form an integral part of its linguistic fabric, as shown by the following example from one of Tadhg Ó Murchadha's manuscripts where lenition (which occurs as a consonant mutation in Irish and is signified by a dot over a consonant letter in Gaelic script) is marked on the English word *practice* following the Irish word *aon*.

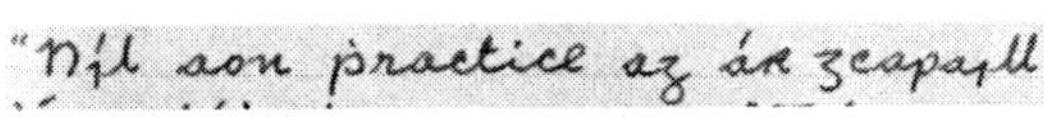

Figure 3: MMC MS 145, p. 14.

'Níl aon *phractice* ag ár gcapaill'

Keeping the English words in the training data remains the only option available for the moment and the hope is that the resulting AI-powered language and HTR models learn to cope with them. More often than not, however, these are mistranscribed, as shown by the following example from a Seosamh Ó Dálaigh manuscript containing the common Irish sentence *tá sé alright* 'it's alright', which was transcribed by a HTR model with a CER of 4.69% using a transcription-data LM as *tá sé aige*.

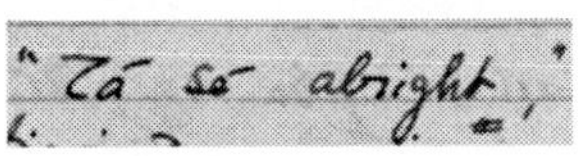

Figure 4: MMC MS 242, p. 548.

5. Method

5.1 Selecting Collectors

Since DHH is primarily concerned with the folktales in the MMC, the project also offers the Dúchas digitisation project a system for prioritising the transcription of material from the MMC, which consists of *c.* 700k pages.[9] In conjunction with the team in the National Folklore Collection in UCD, a list was drawn up of the most prolific field workers involved in the collection of *seanscéalta*, the narrative form that is to be the core focus of the DHH project.

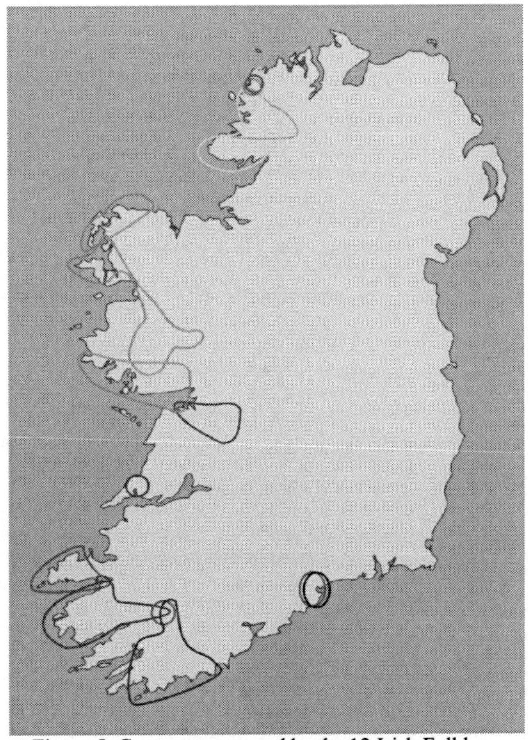

Figure 5: Core areas covered by the 12 Irish Folklore Commission field workers chosen by the project.

Aodh Ó Domhnaill	Liam Mac Coisdealbha
Aodh Ó Duibheannaigh	Seán Ó Flannagáin
Liam Mac Meanman	Seosamh Ó Dálaigh
Seán Ó hEochaidh	Tadhg Ó Murchadha
Pádraig Bairéad	Seán Ó Cróinín
Proinsias de Búrca	Nioclás Breatnach

In compiling this list special care was taken to ensure that as many areas of Ireland that were Gaelic speaking at the time the MMC was compiled were duly represented. The list was narrowed down to 12 full-time collectors who worked for the Irish Folklore Commission. These 12 collectors and their fieldwork areas are shown in Figure 5.

[8] Someone asked her what time of day it was. 'Well by dad,' she said 'I don't know whether it's five or six, but it won't be long till night.'

[9] https://www.duchas.ie/en/info/cbe.

5.2 Digitisation and Transcription

As was described in the introduction to this paper, the digitisation and indexing of documents from the MMC had already begun under the Dúchas project and all manuscripts used to train the HTR models for the collectors listed above had already been digitised by the time the DHH project started in Oct 2021. Therefore, since the project already had access to a large number of digitised manuscripts from the MMC, the next steps of the methodology were all implemented using Transkribus, as follows.

1. Importing Document images into Transkribus.
2. Running the 'Layout Analysis' (LA), i.e. automatic segmentation of the Document images:
    a. An automatic correction of the LA using the 'merge small text lines' widget was necessary in some cases.
3. Manual transcription of the Document, proofreading and marking of revised pages as 'Ground Truth' in the Document Manager.
4. Training a first model on *c.*50 transcribed pages, keeping 10 aside as a fixed validation set.
5. Evaluating the HTR model using the fixed validation set:
    a. Running the HTR model on the fixed validation set produced in step 4. At this stage you can choose to use a LM from the training data.
    b. Using the 'Compare' tool to produce accurate CERs and WERs.
6. Running the model on a set number of pages using the LM, about the same amount that was transcribed manually in Step 3.
7. Correction of the automated transcription produced in step 6, and marking of revised pages as Ground Truth in the Document Manager.
8. Training a new model on the increased data set.
9. Repetition of steps 5–8 until a model with satisfactory CERs and WERs is obtained.

6. Results

As of Mar 2022 eight scribe-specific HTR models have been trained using the method outlined above. The results of this work are presented in Table 1 which shows the size of the training data as a word count, beside the CERs and WERs of the latest model. A total of 234,693 words have been transcribed so far, the average CER produced by our models is 4.9% and the average WER is 12.5%.

Collector	#Words Transcribed	CER	WER
Seosamh Ó Dálaigh	69,457	4.39%	12.43%
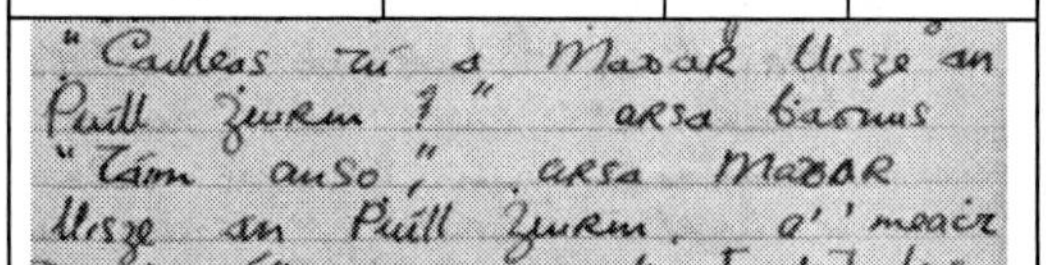 UCD CBÉ MS 242 p. 30			
Seán Ó hEochaidh	65,975	3.98%	6.1%
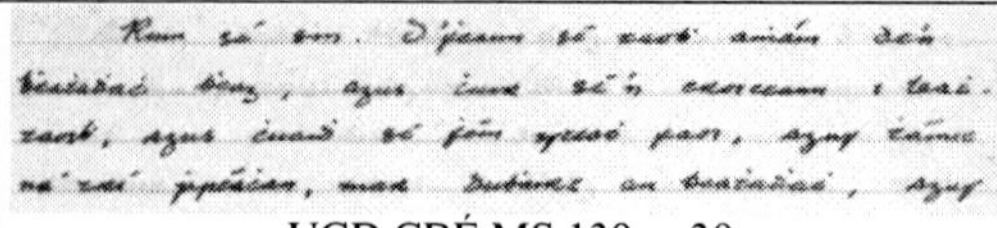 UCD CBÉ MS 139 p. 30			
Liam Mac Coisdealbha	34,758	**2.17%**	**2.66%**
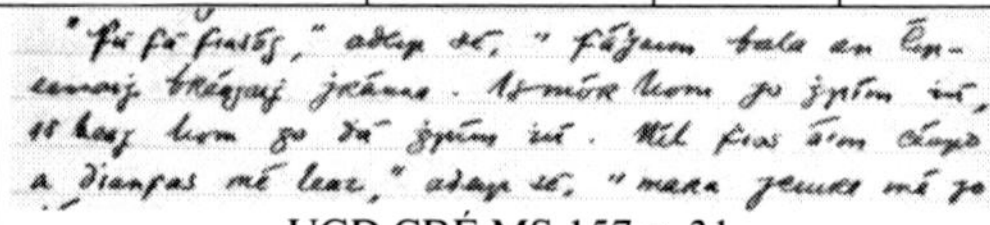 UCD CBÉ MS 157 p. 31			
Proinsias de Búrca	24,654	4.49%	13.74%
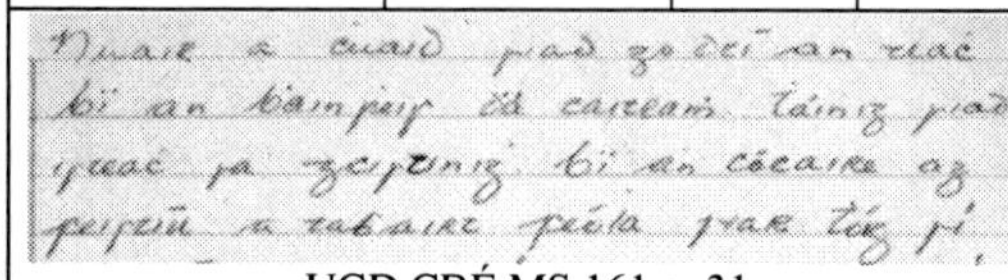 UCD CBÉ MS 161 p. 31			
Liam Mac Meanman	14,736	5.62%	17.97%
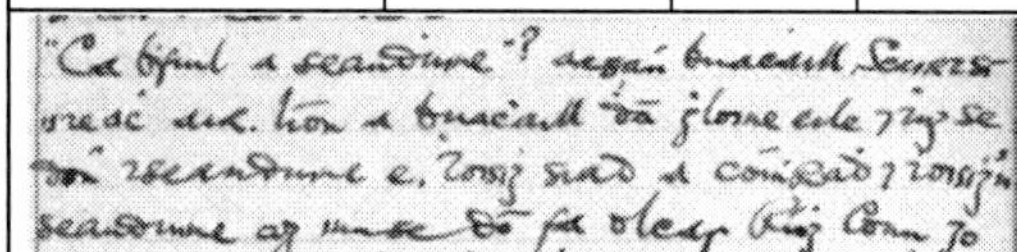 UCD CBÉ MS 168 p. 30			
Seán Ó Flannagáin	9,378	10.28%	26.26%
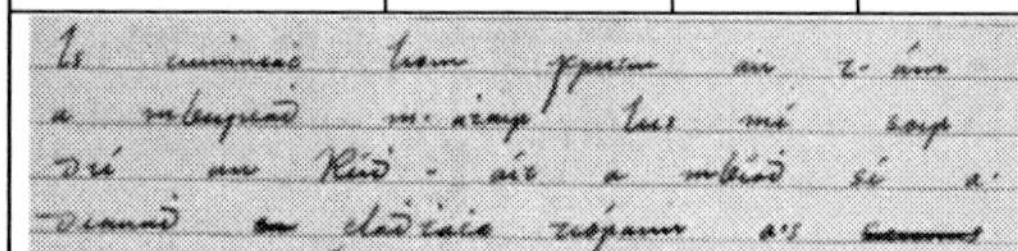 UCD CBÉ MS 354 p. 200			
Tadhg Ó Murchadha	8,102	3.59%	7.47%
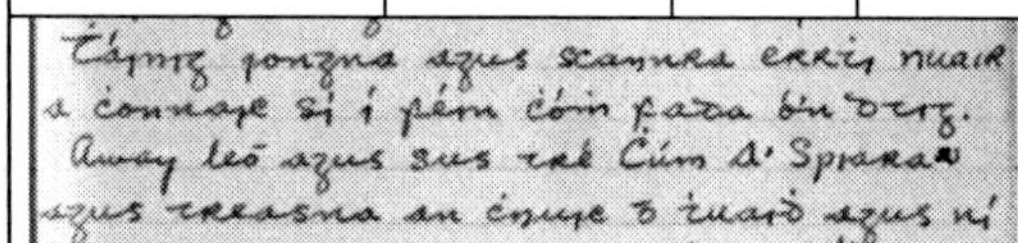 UCD CBÉ MS 145 p. 30			
Aodh Ó Duibheannaigh	7,633	4.28%	13.54%
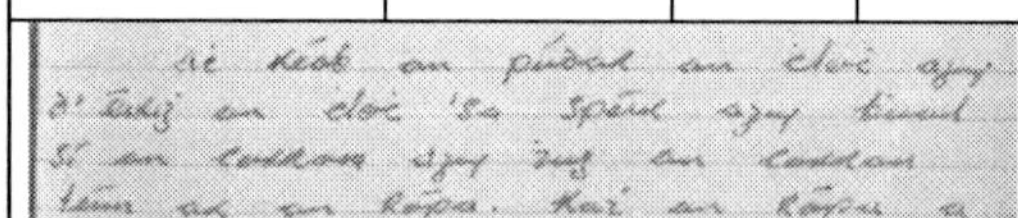 UCD CBÉ MS 370 p. 29			

Table 1: Results of the HTR models trained in Transkribus as of March 2022.

7. Discussion

Having successfully built models that give us a CER of <5% for 6 of our 12 collectors, we are satisfied that we will be able to do the same for the remaining 6. We are reasonably confident that we will be able to use the resulting textual representation of the manuscript writings to carry out digital folkloristic research on the folktales that occur in the dataset. We are satisfied that our approach of developing multiple HTR models (i.e. one for each collector's hand) was appropriate for obtaining a reasonably accurate transcription of a large quantity of data in multiple hands, within a short timeframe and with finite resources. In addition, as most subsequent processing can be automated, managing multiple HTR models will not be a burden. While a CER of <5% is satisfactory, a CER <2% is the ultimate goal, however, much of the errors we are seeing at *c.*5% are minor or are related to punctuation.

Other errors, such as the ones caused by the code and script switching described above, may continue to be a problem regardless. The law of diminishing returns means we are unlikely to reduce the CER much further with the resources and time we have, particularly for the more challenging handwriting styles. With this in mind, we are proposing to harness the resources of Meitheal Dúchas.ie,[10] a crowdsourcing initiative that was successfully utilised to transcribe the NFC Schools' Collection on Dúchas. We plan to carry out a pilot project where we will invite Meitheal members to correct MMC material which has been automatically transcribed using Transkribus. Researchers on the Transcribe Bentham project reported that volunteers were reluctant to switch from transcribing material from scratch to checking fellow volunteers' transcriptions (Causer et al. 2018). In our case, they will not be correcting human transcriptions, but we nonetheless expect less enthusiasm for correction over transcription. We want to test this hypothesis, and are also hopeful that enough volunteers will be sufficiently motivated to correct enough material to help us improve the HTR substantively. MMC material outside the scope of this project in both Irish and English will be made available to transcribe from scratch, so volunteers will have a choice.

Material being processed using Transkribus is stored on Transkribus Servers and is accessible via the Transkribus REST API. Dúchas material is stored on Dúchas Servers and is accessible via the Dúchas REST API. Dúchas images are stored in Azure Blog Storage in the Microsoft Cloud and are accessible via the Azure Blob service REST API. We plan to automate the steps below (if possible) with a Python script that will utilise the Transkribus REST API, the Dúchas REST API, and the Azure Blob service REST API, as well as other interfaces available to us as DHH and Dúchas administrators. API operations or endpoints are given in parentheses where possible. For each of up to 10 MMC volumes collected by each of the 12 collectors in Figure 5 (we have Transkribus credits available to us for HTR on *c.*40k pages and there are *c.*400 pages per volume) in which there is a substantial quantity of folktales, we will execute the following steps on each volume iteratively:

1. Create Document (/collection) in Transkribus within DHH Collection.
2. Upload (/uploads) volume pages (i.e. one image file per page) from Dúchas blob storage (Get Blob) to Transkribus Document.
3. Run Layout Analysis (/LA), Short Line Merge and HTR (/recognition) using scribe-specific model on Document.
4. Export Document to TXT format (i.e. one text file per page).
5. Import transcription text files into Dúchas and map to Dúchas metadata (which is being compiled by the DHH and Dúchas teams within the Dúchas system).
6. Make transcriptions available to the Meitheal Dúchas.ie crowd volunteers for correction.
7. Get corrected transcriptions from Dúchas (/api/{version}/cbe/?VolumeNumber={volume}) and import into Transkribus using TextToImage.
8. Retrain (/recognition) HTR model.

Given the full size of the dataset (12 collectors = 697 volumes, i.e. *c.*278,800 pages) and corresponding HTR cost implications, we plan to filter out volumes containing material other than folktales prior to recognition, and we will only process as many of the volumes containing folktales as is feasible within our timeframe and budget. We do not intend, however, to exclude individual pages within volumes from the recognition process. This is to simplify the administrative burden that partially transcribed volumes would create for the Dúchas team. This approach might be adapted should it become feasible to perform HTR on volume sections or even individual items (i.e. folktales) within volumes. Once the above steps are completed on 100–120 volumes, we will run An Caighdeánaitheoir[11] on the output and send the standardised texts along with associated metadata forward for text-mining and phylogenetic analysis.

8. Conclusion

In this paper we introduced the Decoding Hidden Heritages project which aims to carry out a deep analysis of the narrative traditions of Scotland and Ireland by analysing a large text corpus of Irish and Scottish Gaelic folktales using computational methodologies. This paper focused on the Irish component of the initial corpus creation phase of the project. We described how we are using the Transkribus software to carry out handwritten text recognition on a large number of scanned manuscript pages from the National Folklore Collection, and illustrated the difficulties we encountered in dealing with dialect variation, code switching and script switching that occur throughout the manuscript pages. We presented our methodology in which we are producing individual recognition models for each scribe. This was motivated by the significant interscribe variability in terms of style (e.g. letter size, angle), layout (e.g. spacing) and orthography (e.g. punctuation), but also by the fact that a manageable number of collectors (i.e. 12) would provide us with sufficient dialectal and folkloristic coverage for our study.

Our research so far indicates that Transkribus works extremely well at recognising historical documents, handwritten Irish-language texts in our case. A CER of <5% was achieved for six of eight different HTR models

[10] https://www.duchas.ie/en/meitheal/

[11] https://github.com/kscanne/caighdean

trained so far by manually transcribing or correcting an average of 30,000 words per model. These 8 models would allow us to transcribe up to 568 MMC volumes, the volumes handwritten by these 8 full-time folklore collectors whose handwriting we have so far modelled individually, should we wish to do so. This would give us fulltext access to *c.*227,200 pages of folklore material, thus enabling us to carry out the next stage of our research where we will investigate convergence and divergence in the narrative traditions of Scotland and Ireland using text-mining and phylogenetics. Moreover, this work will also feed back into the Dúchas project in its efforts to fully digitise the collections of the NFC. The Dúchas project already provides fulltext search of much of the Schools' Collection but is yet to provide the same for the MMC. This research will lay down the foundation for this to be achieved.

9. Acknowledgements

This work was supported by the Arts and Humanities Research Council (Grant no. AH/W001934/1) and the Irish Research Council (Grant no. IRC/W001934/1). The Dúchas project is funded by the Department of the Gaeltacht (Government of Ireland).

10. References

Almqvist, B. (1977–9). The Irish Folklore Commission: achievement and legacy. *Béaloideas 45–7*:6–26.

Causer, T., Grint, K., Sichani, A. M., and Terras, M. (2018). Making such bargain: Transcribe Bentham and the quality and cost-effectiveness of crowdsourced transcription. *Digital Scholarship in the Humanities, 33(3)*:467–87.

Ó Duilearga, S. (1948). *Leabhar Sheáin Í Chonaill*, p. xxiv. Dublin: The Educational Company of Ireland Ltd.

Ó Cleircín, G., Bale, A., and Ó Raghallaigh, B. (2014). Dúchas.ie: ré nua i stair Chnuasach Bhéaloideas Éireann. *Béaloideas, 82*:84–100.

Sánchez, J. A., Romero, V., Toselli, A. H., and Vidal, E. (2014). ICFHR2014 Competition on Handwritten Text Recognition on Transcriptorium Datasets (HTRtS). In *14th International Conference on Frontiers in Handwriting Recognition*, pages 785–790, Crete, Greece, Sep, doi: 10.1109/ICFHR.2014.137.

Proceedings of the CLTW 4 @ LREC2022 , pages 127–132
Marseille, 20-25 June 2022

AAC don Ghaeilge: the Prototype Development of Speech-Generating Assistive Technology for Irish

Emily Barnes, Oisín Morrin, Ailbhe Ní Chasaide, Julia Cummins, Harald Berthelsen, Andrew Murphy, Muireann Nic Corcráin, Claire O' Neill, Christer Gobl, Neasa Ní Chiaráin
Trinity College Dublin
The Phonetics and Speech Laboratory
ebarnes@tcd.ie, anichsid@tcd.ie, nichiarn@tcd.ie.

Abstract

This paper describes the prototype development of an Alternative and Augmentative Communication (AAC) system for the Irish language. This system allows users to communicate using the ABAIR synthetic voices, by selecting a series of words or images. Similar systems are widely available in English and are often used by autistic people, as well as by people with Cerebral Palsy, Alzheimer's and Parkinson's disease. A dual-pronged approach to development has been adopted: this involves (i) the initial short-term prototype development that targets the immediate needs of specific users, as well as considerations for (ii) the longer term development of a bilingual AAC system which will suit a broader range of users with varying linguistic backgrounds, age ranges and needs. This paper described the design considerations and the implementation steps in the current system. Given the substantial differences in linguistic structures in Irish and English, the development of a bilingual system raises many research questions and avenues for future development.

Keywords: AAC, assistive technology, speech synthesis

1. Introduction

The world we inhabit is largely designed to suit neurotypical and able-bodied people, often resulting in the disable-ing of those who think, learn or move differently. Opportunities – linguistic, educational, social and otherwise – of neurodivergent people are frequently curtailed. In the Irish educational context, it is not unusual to hear of professionals recommending that children speak only English at home, or that they not attend Irish immersion education. Such recommendations conflict with the concept of inclusion and are typically based on personal beliefs, rather than research and information pertaining to the person (Wight, 2015). Fortunately, attitudes towards bilingualism are changing, and neurodivergent people now make up a substantial proportion of those accessing Irish immersion education (Nic Aindriú, Ó Duibhir & Travers, 2020).

Without support, however, access does not equate to opportunity (Engstrom & Tinto, 2008). Support in education takes many forms; it includes the ethos of the school, the types of teaching strategies used as well as the practical concern of assistive technology. Assistive technology can be transformative in the lives of those who use it, removing barriers to communication and education. While there is plentiful provision of assistive technology for the English language, there is little available for the Irish language (though see Section 2). As a matter of equality of opportunity for those in Irish-medium education – and particularly for those who speak Irish in their communities as a first language – it is paramount that this discrepancy be addressed.

The present paper describes the prototype development of an Alternative and Augmentative Communication (AAC) system for the Irish language. AAC systems range from simple, paper-based ones to high tech speech-generating ones. The AAC system described in this paper falls into the latter category. It is a system – typically presented on a tablet – which allows the user to select a series of words/images to compose a sentence which is then read out by a synthetic voice. People use AAC systems for a variety of reasons; many autistic children and adults use AAC to communicate (Enderby et al, 2013), and people with Cerebral Palsy, Alzheimer's and Parkinson's Disease often use AAC to overcome communication challenges (Enderby et al, 2013).

Speech-generating AAC systems contain a large number of boards, one of which is illustrated in Figure 1. Each board comprises a number of buttons representing words or phrases which are typically linked semantically. Each button contains an image which symbolises the word, as well the orthographic form of the word. As the user selects the sequence of images/words, they appear in the bar at the top of the board. The individual words at this point do not carry the grammatical inflections, which are added when the sentence is synthesised.

The development of an Irish language facility within an AAC system requires expertise in a number of areas. An understanding of Irish semantics, syntax and morphology is necessary to identify issues and design solutions; knowledge and experience of AAC use and the practices of AAC users is paramount to ensure solutions are appropriate; technical expertise is necessary in order to implement the solutions. This interdisciplinarity is reflected in the number of authors who have contributed to this paper in some way or another.

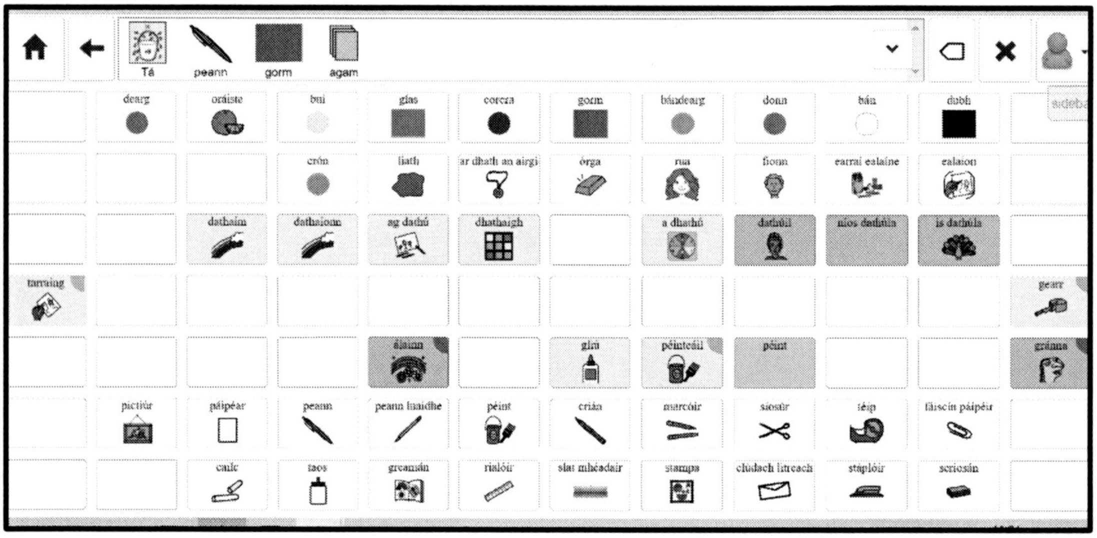

Figure 1. Image of a board in Coughdrop

This development is taking place as part of the ABAIR Initiative, described in Section 2. The linguistic structures of Irish give rise to some particular challenges in AAC development, discussed in Section 3. Subsequently, the design decisions made for the initial, short-term prototype development of the AAC system are described in Section 4. The next stage of the development is outlined in Section 5, including the research questions which will be addressed and the technical work which is outstanding.

2. The ABAIR Initiative and AAC

The design and development of the AAC system described in this paper is being undertaken under the umbrella of the ABAIR Initiative. ABAIR is a suite of projects which focus on the development of speech and language technologies for the Irish language (see Ní Chasaide et al, 2019 for an overview). All of the technologies developed as part of the ABAIR Project are underpinned by basic research and by linguistic resources developed by the team. The main core technologies of the ABAIR Initiative are the synthetic voices which have been developed for each of the main dialects of Irish; these voices are a key component of the AAC system described here. Automatic Speech Recognition (ASR) is currently under development, and the current Irish ASR prototype is presented in an accompanying paper.

Since the earliest days of the ABAIR initiative, the needs of the language community – and particularly of disabled members of the community – were a primary catalyst for developments. Thus, the present project expands on previous work undertaken as part of the ABAIR Initiative in the area of assistive technology and access. A plugin for the Nonvisual Desktop Access (NVDA) screenreader was developed for visually-impaired people – and involved a visually-impaired researcher working with the ABAIR group – in a collaboration with the National Council for the Blind in Ireland (NCBI) (McGuirk, 2015). In addition, basic research has been undertaken in the area of dyslexia assessments and literacy training (Barnes 2017, 2021), and literacy platforms are currently in development (Ní Chiaráin & Ní Chasaide, 2018; Ní Chasaide et al, 2019).

The development of an AAC system has been planned as part of the ABAIR Initiative for some time, based on requests from speech and language therapists who work with people with cerebral palsy, Alzheimer's and Parkinson's disease, as well as survivors of stroke. ABAIR has both the linguistic expertise as well as the speech technologies available to develop such a system for the Irish language.

An urgent request from a parent provided an immediate impetus which kickstarted the project. The parent who approached us needs an Irish AAC system for her children, Eoin and Máire[1]. Eoin and Máire who are based in Dublin, use an AAC system to communicate in English, however they do not have access to an Irish AAC system. Though English is their first language (L1), the lack of an Irish AAC system is an obstacle to them in communicating with their Irish-speaking family members (who are based in a Gaeltacht region; a region in which Irish is spoken as the language of the community), as well as in accessing the curriculum and engaging with friends and teachers in their Gaelscoil (Irish immersion school). Eoin and Máire are in primary school and are in the early stages of acquiring literacy.

As in the development of the screenreader, the design of the initial AAC system has critically involved the participation of this parent, her children and her large network of friends and acquaintances who are AAC users. This is affording us much insight into their requirements and also into the usability of various AAC platforms.

[1] Names have been changed to protect the children's identities.

Given the urgent need to develop an AAC system for Eoin and Máire, as well as the longer-term need to develop a bilingual AAC system for the broader population of AAC users in Ireland, a two-pronged approach has been taken to development. This involves:

I. The initial, short-term prototype development of an AAC system for the Irish language, motivated specifically by Eoin and Máire.
II. The longer-term proposed development of a bilingual AAC system for a broader group of users.

3. Challenges to AAC development in a Celtic Language

The linguistic structures of Irish pose a number of challenges to the development of an AAC system. Many of these will be relevant to AAC development in other Celtic languages, given their similarity.

Morphological complexity: Irish is an inflected language, with a number of cases for nouns and adjectives as well as inflected prepositions and verbs. This results in many more word forms than exist in the English language. However, including every form of a noun, adjective and verb on an AAC board would result in a more cluttered and clunky user experience. An additional issue is that many of the AAC users are likely to be young or in the initial stages of learning Irish and may not be well enough acquainted with reading or with the grammar to accurately select a word form for a given context.

Phrasal verbs: there are many frequently-used phrasal verbs in Irish. The meaning of these verbs with and without their accompanying preposition is often vastly different (see examples 1a and 2a compared to examples 1b and 2b).

(1a)	*ag éirí* 'rising'	(1b)	*ag éirí le* 'succeeding' ('rising' + 'with')
(2a)	*ag bualadh* 'hitting'	(2b)	*ag bualadh le* 'meeting' ('hitting' + 'with')

For these phrasal verbs, the verb and its accompanying pronouns (in this case *le* 'with') should ideally be placed in close proximity on boards. However, as prepositions are inflected for person in Irish (e.g. *le* 'with' + *mé* 'me' = *liom* 'with me'), these prepositional pronouns would also need to be included (entailing an additional six buttons). In addition, one of the principles of AAC system design is that there should not be multiple representations of the same word in different places, and many phrasal verbs use the same preposition/prepositional pronouns.

Bilingual mapping: given that Irish AAC users are highly likely to be bilingual, a system which would allow users to easily toggle between Irish and English is desirable. AAC users use motor sequences to select items and rely on visuo-spatial representations in memory to use AAC in a fluid way (Dukhovny & Gahl, 2014). This is similar to the motor plans we rely on when typing. This raises a question in relation to bilingual motor plans, and whether each language should have separate motor plans, as opposed to a common motor plan (insofar as possible).

Bilingual voices: a bilingual system would ideally be equipped with bilingual voices, which would allow the users to utilise the same voice across languages. This would also be very important given the prevalence of code-switching. Though this work is planned as part of the ABAIR Initiative, there are not yet bilingual voices available.

Code-switching and productive morphology: Novel words are often created in Irish by adding an Irish morpheme to a borrowed word from English. An example of this is the colloquial use of the verbal noun "ag zoomáil", which uses the Irish verbal noun structure with the English word 'zoom'. Ideally, it would be desirable to allow for the production of such words within the AAC system. Again, this relies on being able to easily toggle between the two language versions of the system.

4. Design features of initial prototype

This section describes the short-term, initial development of an AAC system for specific users. As mentioned, the involvement of the AAC community network, and particularly of the parent and children mentioned earlier is central to all design features adopted in this prototype. In addition to her involvement in the adaptation, this parent also tests features with her children and provides feedback which allows for the improvement of the AAC system.

The development of the AAC system to its current prototype stage has involved (i) collecting user requirements and developing user stories[2] (ii) selecting a platform for development (iii) adaptation of boards (words and phrases) to Irish (iv) the selection and adaptation of the ABAIR voices and (v) the technical development necessary to embed the ABAIR voices in the platform and to produce grammatically correct speech. The processes involved in each step are described in the sections that follow.

4.1 Collecting user requirements and creating user stories

Initially, a survey was conducted of AAC users to investigate how they used AAC and what features they considered important (Nic Corcráin, 2021). We also considered in detail the needs of Eoin and Máire, as well as the people who use the AAC system to communicate with them including their parents and their teachers. Based on this, we drew up user stories which illustrated the main needs of the prospective AAC stakeholders targeted in the present prototype (Eoin and Máire, teachers, parents).

We established that primary requirements for this iteration of the AAC system were to:

I. Have very good correspondence between the Irish and English versions of the system in terms of

[2] A set of illustrative stories explaining the specific needs of individual users.

layout. In practice, this means that the buttons for words in the Irish version are in the same place as the corresponding word in the English version, insofar as possible. As mentioned above, this is in order to preserve the motor plan that Eoin and Máire are already used to in English. This is particularly important given that Eoin and Máire are not yet proficient readers; they rely on visuo-spatial memory to access words, just as we do when typing. In the short-term, as Eoin and Máire are primary targeted users, maximising the portability between the two languages is a good strategy. Different cohorts may require different strategies in this regard, and this question will be further investigated, particularly with L1 Irish speakers.

II. Produce grammatically correct output, while avoiding cluttering the AAC system's layout with buttons for every possible form of a noun, verb, or adjective which exists in Irish. Including every possible permutation of a word would (i) result in cluttered boards which would be difficult for a child to navigate, (ii) preclude correspondence between the Irish and English motor plans and (iii) might be premature for users who have not yet mastered the grammar of Irish.

III. Be both available off-line and provide technical support to users. As AAC users typically rely on their devices to communicate, it is vital that it is accessible in all contexts and that technical issues that do arise can be quickly and expertly resolved.

IV. Include a range of voices which are appropriate to the user's age, gender and identity.

4.2 Platform selection

With the aforementioned user requirements in mind, we investigated a variety of platform options. Initially, designing an AAC system from scratch for Irish was considered. This option would allow the greatest amount of control in relation to the design and layout of the system. However, under the ABAIR Initiatives current remit, it would not be possible to provide the necessary technical support to users over a sustained period of time.

Instead, we researched existing platforms and enquired with representatives from these platforms in relation to adaptation for Irish. Following from discussion with platform representatives as well as users, the Coughdrop platform[3] was selected. Coughdrop is an open-source AAC platform which is available in a large number of languages. Technical support and training is provided within the platform, and it has offline functionality.

4.3 Initial adaptation of the AAC system boards

For this prototype iteration of the AAC system, the boards were created to mirror the layout of Eoin and Máire's AAC system in English. In the case of some words and phrases, there was a straightforward mapping from English to Irish. For many, however, there was not. For example, the verb 'to know' does not map neatly onto Irish, which contains a variety of verbs and phrases depending on whether the subject of the sentence is a person, a fact or an area of knowledge (*aithne, fios, ar eolas*, etc). This necessitated multiple buttons corresponding to a single button in English. Similarly, additional buttons were included to represent the counting systems in Irish, which differ depending on whether people or things are being counted.

As mentioned in Section 3, Irish contains many frequently-occurring phrasal verbs which require the use of prepositional pronouns. The challenge is to provide easy access to these prepositional pronouns while avoiding including them on multiple boards. The present solution to this is to include the prepositional pronouns in a sidebar which the user can open on any board; this feature will be tested to investigate its suitability.

An additional challenge pertains to producing grammatically correct word forms, given that the grammatical relationships within the phrase are primarily indicated through morphological inflection, rather than word order as in English. A technical solution was sought for this particular issue, which is described in Section 4.5. The present section describes just some of the challenges that arose in adaptation, and it is expected that more will emerge as the system is tested by AAC users.

4.4 Voice selection

The voice of the AAC system becomes the voice of the user, and this raises many questions of identity. This pertains in the first instance to the choice of dialect; ideally, a Conamara user will be able to use their own dialect. At present, the ABAIR Initiative has developed four synthetic adult voices (Ulster dialect – female; Connaught dialect – male; Munster dialect – male and female) and one other voice is currently under development (Connaught dialect – female). This affords a certain amount of choice to the user, but there are gaps; there is currently no Donegal male, and there are dialects for which no voice is yet available. Furthermore, even when we have a male and female representative for a given dialect, such as Conamara, there is an immediate issue of identity, when there are groups of more than one male or female user (e.g. in a classroom). A variety of voices are necessary in an AAC system, in order to allow for users to retain and express their individual identity and to avoid difficulties in communication arising from two identical voices conversing (e.g. Pullin et al, 2017).

There are currently no children's' voices available for the Irish dialects, and this will be a priority for the future. In the absence of children's synthetic voices, a temporary solution was sought to provide child-like voices for Eoin and Máire's AAC systems. An online system was developed in consultation with an expert on voice synthesis within the ABAIR Project; the system allows users to change the parameters of an existing synthetic voice in order to sound more child-like, more masculine or more feminine. Effectively, this would in principle allow users to create a bespoke voice for themselves, although the current results are only partially successful. Note that voice

[3] https://www.mycoughdrop.com/

adaptation, where we control and manipulate vocal parameters, is a complex field where parallel work is ongoing as part of ABAIR-RóbóGlór (Murphy et al, 2020). In the longer term, the goal would be to have robust ways of fine-tuning the parameters of the synthetic voice for the individual user.

Right now, in the current prototype we are using the female Donegal voice. It is planned to offer a fuller menu in the near future.

4.5 Technical architecture

The technical architecture for the AAC system is represented schematically in Figure 2.

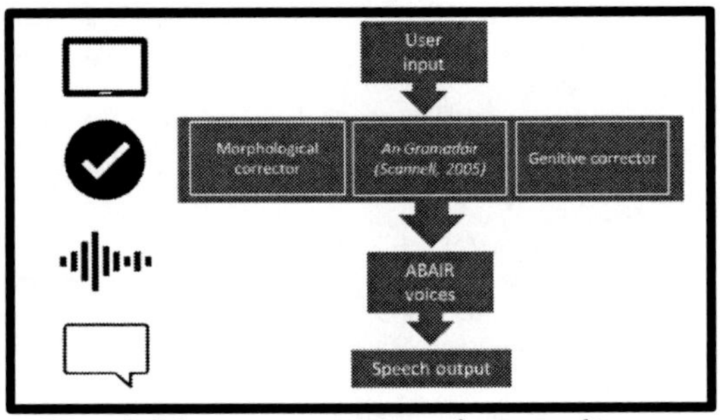

Figure 2: Schematic representation of system architecture

As explained in the Introduction, the user inputs a series of words/images by selecting a sequence of buttons. These appear in the bar at the top of the board, but do not carry the grammatical inflections. The sentence is sent to the ABAIR server, where three steps are carried out to generate the grammatically correct forms: (1) The sentence is passed through a morphological corrector, which provides a number of inflected forms, not catered for in an already existing grammar checker, An Gramadóir (Scannell, 2005). This initial processing step involved the hand coding of grammatical rules. In the second step (2) the output of 1 is fed to the grammar checker (Scannell, 2005). The final step (3) takes the output of the grammar checker and adds a further grammatical refinement in the form of a genitive case checker/corrector which has been developed within the ABAIR project.

An example of the original input is provided in 3 (a). In this case, the verb is not accurately conjugated, two initial mutations are omitted - one of which results in an inaccurate interpretation of possession – and the final noun is in the nominative rather than the genitive case. After being processed by the morphological corrector and An Gramadóir, these inaccuracies are resolved with the exception of the genitive case issue, as seen in 3(b). Finally, having been processed by the genitive case corrector, the input is grammatically accurate and can be send to the synthetic voices, as evident in 3 (c).

3 (a)	**Original input**	An gheobhadh siad a bronntanais ó fear an post? *'would they get their presents from the postman'*
3 (b)	**Morphological corrector & An Gramadóir output**	An bhfaighfidís a mbronntanais ó fhear an post?
3 (c)	**Genitive case corrector output**	An bhfaighfidís a mbronntanais ó fhear an phoist?

The corrected text is then synthesised and an ABAIR voice reads the output on the user's AAC system.

4.6 Current state of the system

At present, a prototype Coughdrop-based system is available online, and contains a single ABAIR voice. The grammatical accuracy of the system is very good in the small set of sentences on which it has been tested so far.

5. The next stage of development: a bilingual AAC system

Some of the design features of the current prototype AAC system were motivated by the urgent need of providing an Irish language facility that would suit Eoin and Máire's requirements. Future iterations will aim to encompass other potential users and contexts of use. This will include people from the Gaeltacht Irish language community, where requirements may differ from those of the current prototype in certain respects. We will also be catering to people of a range of ages and with a variety of needs.

Research questions. Important avenues of future research will be explored, including the following:

- the suitability of current solutions that focus on specific linguistic features of Irish (e.g. the sidebar for phrasal verbs) will be examined, and other possible solutions will be explored. These issues will resonate with the structurally-similar Celtic languages, and it is hoped that the present research could be broadened and strengthened by Pan-Celtic collaboration.
- the bilingual context of users (e.g. Gaeltacht native speakers and Irish speakers and learners outside the Gaeltacht) will be further explored, and the requirements of different cohorts investigated. This will include examining the needs and wants of users in relation to voice characteristics, including sociolinguistic, dialectal and voice quality factors.
- research is also needed on bilingual AAC systems in other languages where insights can be gleaned from the approaches adopted. Further research is intended in relation to motor plans, and whether they should be closely modelled on the language structure or should be harmonised to facilitate the early stages of acquisition, and indeed the code-switching that is a prominent feature of spoken Irish. In this regard, it is important to note that learning the layout of an AAC system typically requires a large time investment on the part of the user and often on the part of a parent or professional too.

- a related question involves ways to facilitate the productive derivational morphology whereby English words are borrowed but inflected to create new Irish forms (e.g. ag zoomáil).

User testing will be conducted with a broad group of users to examine their attitudes towards and opinions of the usability of the system, the quality and robustness of the synthetic voices and the grammatical accuracy of the system, among other things. The findings from this evaluation will feed back into the development of the system.

The development of an offline version is planned in order to allow for use in every context and environment. Early informal feedback from users indicates that this should be a priority.

Increasing morphological accuracy is also a priority. Though the morphological corrector is producing very good results at present, additional rules will be added to this system to increase the grammatical accuracy of speech output.

Children's synthetic voices are planned for the near future. This will involve the recording of corpora and subsequent development of children's voices, and will allow for more authentic child-like speech output.

Training courses for stakeholders will be developed. This is an essential accompaniment to the system which aims to support users, parents, guardians, teachers and other educational professionals in accessing and using the AAC system.

6. Acknowledgements

We gratefully acknowledge the support of An Chomhairle um Oideachas Gaeltachta agus Gaelscolaíochta (COGG). We also gratefully acknowledge An Roinn Turasóireachta, Cultúir, Ealaíon, Gaeltachta, Spóirt agus Meán. which support the ABAIR-RóbóGlór Project, as part of *Stráitéis 20 bliain don Ghaeilge, 2010-2030*.

7. Bibliographical References

Barnes, E. (2017) Dyslexia Assessment and Reading Interventions for Pupils in Irish- Medium Education: Insights into current practice and considerations for improvement, M.Phil. Dissertation, School of Linguistic, Speech and Communication Sciences, Trinity College Dublin, Ireland.

Barnes. (2021). Predicting dual-language literacy attainment in Irish-English bilinguals: language specific and language-universal contributions. PhD thesis, Trinity College Dublin.

Dukhovny, E., & Gahl, S. (2014). Manual motor-plan similarity affects lexical recall on a speech-generating device: Implications for AAC users. *Journal of communication disorders, 48*, 52-60.

Enderby, P., Judge, S., Creer, S., & John, A. (2013). Examining the need for, and provision of, AAC in the United Kingdom. Research Report. Communication Matters.

Engstrom, C., & Tinto, V. (2008). Access without support is not opportunity. *Change: The magazine of higher learning, 40*(1), 46-50.

McGuirk, R. (2015). Exploration of the Use of Irish Language Synthesis with a Screen Reader in the Teaching of Irish to Pupils with Vision Impairment, M.Phil. Dissertation, School of Linguistic, Speech and Communication Sciences, Trinity College Dublin, Ireland.

Murphy, A., Yanushevskaya, I., Chasaide, A. N., & Gobl, C. (2020). Testing the GlórCáil system in a speaker and affect voice transformation task. In *Speech Prosody 2020* (pp. 950-954).

Ní Chasaide, A., Ní Chiaráin, N., Berthelsen, H., Wendler, C., Murphy, A., Barnes, E., Gobl, C. (2019). Leveraging Phonetic and Speech Research for Language Revitalisation and Maintenance, Proceedings of ICPhS, Melbourne.

Ní Chiaráin, N. & Ní Chasaide, A. (2018). An Scéalaí: synthetic voices for autonomous learning. *Future-proof CALL: language learning as exploration and encounters–short papers from EUROCALL*, 230-235.

Nic Aindriú, S., Ó Duibhir, P., & Travers, J. (2020). The prevalence and types of special educational needs in Irish immersion primary schools in the Republic of Ireland. *European Journal of Special Needs Education, 35*(5), 603-619.

Nic Corcráin, M. (2021). 'AAC don Ghaeilge': A needs analysis survey for the development of Irish language augmentative communication devices for people with speech difficulties. Unpublished M.Phil. thesis, Trinity College Dublin.

Pullin, G., Treviranus, J., Patel, R., & Higginbotham, J. (2017). Designing interaction, voice, and inclusion in AAC research. *Augmentative and Alternative Communication, 33*(3), 139-148.

Wight, M. C. S. (2015). Students with learning disabilities in the foreign language learning environment and the practice of exemption. *Foreign Language Annals, 48*(1), 39-55.

8. Language Resource References

Scannell, K. (2005). An Gramadóir. Retrieved 7 April, 2022, from https://cadhan.com/gramadoir/

Author Index

Association for Computational Linguistics
209 N. Eighth Street
Stroudsburg, Pennsylvania 18360

ISBN 978-1-7138-6114-0

CURRAN ASSOCIATES INC.
proceedings.com